MW01519160

Indigenous Textual Cultures

Indigenous
Textual
Cultures
Reading
and Writing
in the Age
of Global
Empire

Duke University Press
Durham & London 2020

TONY
BALLANTYNE,
LACHY
PATERSON &
ANGELA
WANHALLA,
editors

© 2020 Duke University Press
All rights reserved
Printed in the United States of America on acid-free paper ∞
Designed by Aimee C. Harrison
Typeset in Minion Pro and Canela Text by Westchester
Publishing Services

Library of Congress Cataloging-in-Publication Data
Names: Ballantyne, Tony, [date] editor. | Paterson, Lachy,
[date] editor. | Wanhalla, Angela, editor.
Title: Indigenous textual cultures : reading and writing in the
age of global empire / Tony Ballantyne, Lachy Paterson
and Angela Wanhalla, editors.
Description: Durham : Duke University Press, 2020. |
Includes bibliographical references and index.
Identifiers: LCCN 2019054733 (print)
LCCN 2019054734 (ebook)
ISBN 9781478009764 (hardcover)
ISBN 9781478010814 (paperback)
ISBN 9781478012344 (ebook)
Subjects: LCSH: Literacy—Social aspects. | Indigenous
peoples—Education. | Indigenous peoples—
Communication. | Indigenous peoples—Books
and reading. | Indigenous peoples—Colonization. |
Colonization—Social aspects.
Classification: LCC LC3719 .I55 2020 (print) | LCC LC3719
(ebook) | DDC 371.829/97—dc23
LC record available at https://lccn.loc.gov/2019054733
LC ebook record available at https://lccn.loc.gov/2019054734

Cover art: Julie Gough, *Some words for change*, 2008
(detail). Site-specific outdoor installation: tea tree (*Melaleuca* spp.) and thirty-two book pages from *Black War* (Clive
Turnbull, 1948) dipped in wax. Ephemeral art exhibition,
Friendly Beaches, Tasmania. Photograph by Simon Cuthbert.

CONTENTS

PART IV
WRITERS

ACKNOWLEDGMENTS

This volume developed out of the symposium Indigenous Textual Cultures, organized by Tony Ballantyne and Lachy Paterson of the Centre for Research on Colonial Culture at the University of Otago on 30 June and 1 July 2014. The editors would like to thank the Hocken Collections and their staff, who provided the venue. We would also like to thank Sue Lang, the former administrator in the Department of History and Art History at Otago, for the invaluable support she provided in putting that event together. Sue has provided the administrative support for the center since its establishment in 2012, and we are deeply appreciative of her hard work and expertise.

The center is one of Otago's "flagship" research groupings and has been very well supported by the university's Research Committee, and the editors would like to acknowledge that funding and also the broader endorsement of the Research Committee.

The editors would also like to thank all the presenters at the symposium as well as the attendees who gave critical feedback. All but one of the presenters wrote chapters for this volume. We would like to acknowledge Alban Bensa and Adrian Muckle, Evelyn Ellerman, and Ivy Schweitzer, who subsequently brought their expertise to broaden the scope of the book. We would like to thank all the contributors to the volume for their engagement with and enthusiasm for a project that brings a diverse range of scholarly traditions into conversation.

A book such as this is a team effort. In particular, Lachy and Tony would like to express our appreciation to Angela Wanhalla, who joined as an editor for the book and spurred the project on to its conclusion.

We are also indebted to expert readers who gave valuable feedback on the manuscript, and to the staff of Duke University Press for bringing the collection to publication.

Indigenous Textual Cultures, the Politics of Difference, and the Dynamism of Practice

TONY BALLANTYNE
& LACHY PATERSON

INDIGENOUS TEXTUAL CULTURES offer crucial insights into the dynamics of communication, community formation, and political contestation within a modern world shaped by empire, mobility, and capitalism. Modernity was marked by the deepening and accelerating connectedness produced by aggressively expansive imperial orders, the encompassing reach of communication systems, and the integrative power of trade and markets that increasingly drew human communities into new forms of interdependence from 1492 onward. These connections were never total, nor uncontested. Even as the world became more connected through the early modern period, the networks that linked communities together developed irregularly in time and space, their reach was uneven in both geographic and social terms, and typically they were incomplete and in process, constantly being remade. Despite their globe-spanning aspirations, imperial rulers, advocates of evangelization, influential capitalists, and champions of new communications technologies in the nineteenth and twentieth centuries never produced the smooth and seamless global overlays that they often promised. Histories of connection were often fraught and violent and produced deeply unequal outcomes.[1]

The study of indigenous textual cultures illuminates the shifting cultural practices and social relations within native or indigenous communities that felt the pull of distant markets or directly faced the onslaught of colonialism. One of the promises of much work within indigenous studies is that it enables the reclamation of intellectual sovereignty and the reassertion of cultural autonomy. Key strands within that scholarly tradition have fundamentally transformed our understanding of indigenous histories and have been powerful forces challenging white domination and Eurocentrism in national and global politics.

At the same time, however, such projects are profoundly shaped by their engagement with and entanglement within these earlier histories of global connectedness, the very processes that disempowered traditional leaders, undermined local ways of knowing and organizing social life, and alienated labor, land, and economically useful resources.[2] Deeply and fundamentally, "native" and "indigenous" are relational social categories.[3] They are historically contingent, being produced out of the development of the often highly unequal outcomes of cross-cultural trade, evangelization, colonialism and colonization, and nation building. These identifications were and are produced as a consequence of cross-cultural debates, incorporation into imperial regimes, the experience of colonial power, and engagements with the developing authority of national sovereignties. Of course, at a fundamental level, they have depended on the ability to reference shared ties to places and territories, a common linguistic and cultural tradition, and an identification with a history and set of genealogical connections that predate the disruptions of cross-cultural meetings and the onrush of colonialism.[4] These are some of the key resources that might be mobilized in order to produce the key differentiations from other social groups and the identification with "indigeneity."[5]

Since World War II, the authority and reach of these identifications have also been enabled and supported by the interrelated development of global activist networks and the language of universal human rights.[6] As Ronald W. Niezen has demonstrated, the category of "indigenous peoples" gained purchase through the International Labour Organization in the 1950s and since then has been woven into a range of human rights initiatives and the platforms of a large number of international organizations. These global currents were crucial in enabling the development of increasingly expansive and dense connections among groups who identified as being indigenous. These identifications both were facilitated by and reinforced the recognition that their communities shared powerful commonalities, including the

Tony Ballantyne & Lachy Paterson

alienation of land, resources, and sovereignty; the undermining of treaties; the denial of full political and social citizenship; and the experience of cultural loss as a result of successive governments pursuing the goal of "assimilation" and the privileging of national identity. So while contemporary indigeneity typically is anchored in genealogical affiliation and territorial belonging, it is also underpinned by a simultaneous differentiation of the "indigenous" from dominant social groups produced out of colonialism and recognition of shared experiences with other indigenous groups who typically share a common commitment to the pursuit of greater autonomy.[7] More broadly still, as Niezen argues, the growing authority of the indigenous as a cultural identity reflects important shifts in the global political economy and public sentiment—including anxieties around the "uncertainties of a runaway world" produced by globalization—which have both helped legitimate indigeneity as a social and political category and invested it with a particular set of moral, political, and spiritual connotations.[8]

Writing and textual cultures were central to the processes of differentiation of "tribal" or "native" groups under colonial rule and the subsequent remaking of communities, in both (emergent) national and international contexts, as imperial regimes were dismantled or attenuated. Under modernity, writing has been a powerful instrument for cultural construction, playing a pivotal role in the "invention of tradition" (or its definition and reworking), in the production of "imagined communities," and in "writing" the nation into being. It not only has been a vital tool for intellectuals, activists, and anticolonial leaders but also was absolutely central to the operation of modern bureaucratic states and all those groups who interacted with these regimes, which were underpinned by the regularized circulation of paper, information, and opinion. Writing was a powerful tool in the struggles against colonialism and in subsequent efforts to cast off the legacies of empire and dispossession; it has never been the sole political instrument for those committed to overthrowing imperial regimes, but it has often been indispensable and effective.

Community formation and the struggle against colonial rule stand at the center of this volume, which explores the operation of indigenous textual cultures in a modern age of global empire. Bringing together a range of sites and scholarly traditions, it explores the various ways in which the written word was deployed by native or indigenous writers who sought to assert their intellectual power within the uneven cultural terrains created by colonial rule. Here it is important to note that the volume brings together work focused on Africa, the Pacific, Australasia, and North America. While Australasia, parts of the Pacific (especially Hawai'i), and the United States and Canada are prominent in recent work in indigenous studies, Africa and African peoples typically largely sit outside the dominant global understandings of the category "indigenous." For example, in 1992 the United Nations offered the following summation of indigeneity on a global scale: "The world's estimated 300 million indigenous people are spread across the world in more than 70 countries. Among them are the Indians of the Americas, the Inuit and Aleutians of the circumpolar region, the Saami of northern Europe, the Aborigines and Torres Strait Islanders of Australia and the Māori of New Zealand. More than 60 per cent of Bolivia's population is indigenous, and indigenous peoples make up roughly half the populations of Guatemala and Peru. China and India together have more than 150 million indigenous and tribal people. About 10 million indigenous people live in Myanmar."[9]

Some African communities—such as Nubians in Kenya and Basters in South Africa—do make claims to indigenous status, but their understandings of indigeneity have varied greatly and rarely aligned neatly with the developing global conventions. Of course, the particular depth of African history, as well as the complexities of mobility and trade over long distances within and beyond Africa, means that making claims to being the original occupants of a place or region—often a foundational element of indigeneity—is deeply problematic.[10] Nevertheless, certain understandings of what or who was indigenous played a key role in the operation of colonial power in parts of Africa, and as Mahmood Mamdani has argued, those understandings have played a role in shaping crucial elements of the postcolonial political economy in some African nations.[11] Mamdani has demonstrated that the idea of the native or indigenous was fundamental to the legally inscribed identifications that were central in the operation of colonial rule in much of Africa: the distinction between "natives," who were believed to possess ethnicities typically defined by tribal affiliations and who were bound by "customary law," and "nonnatives," those groups including Europeans, "Coloureds," Asians, and Arabs, who were seen to be distinct races and who were subject to civil law and, as such, able to exercise a range of rights that were beyond the reach of the "native" populations.[12] In light of this argument, there is real value in returning Africa to the fold of indigenous studies, especially given the centrality of the native as an organizing category in colonial thought in Africa, a powerful commonality with the Pacific, Australasia, and North America.[13] Reconnecting these histories might offer substantial intellectual rewards, as leading Pacific historian Damon I. Salesa has argued.[14]

One compelling way into the relationship between colonial rule and cultural difference is provided by the work of the Tasmanian indigenous artist Julie Gough. Gough's work is anchored in a set of conversations that weave together archival holdings, physical landscapes, and objects that carry traces of colonial pasts. Over the past two decades, she has produced a series of sophisticated meditations on indigenous experiences of empire building that rematerialize how language and knowledge were threaded through the dispossession and violence that were integral to the colonization of Van Diemen's Land. Some works primarily draw attention to the relation among knowledge, violence, and domination, while others function as a kind of counterarchive, sites where the experiences and even more fundamentally the names and connections of indigenous peoples and places can be recorded and recalled.[15] Both of these creative strategies foreground the "conflicting and subsumed histories" that are produced out of the entanglements of empire and the subordination of indigenous communities under colonial rule.[16] Language, found and repurposed objects, and media of various kinds are central to the assemblages that Gough constructs, drawing our attention to how regimes of colonial difference were created and to how things and words can carry the legacies of past inequalities into our present.

As scholar of Australian literature and visual culture Marita Bullock has observed, Gough's work not only picks at the silences and occlusions of official understandings of Tasmanian history but also draws critical attention to the divergence between those narratives and the understandings of the descendants of the indigenous populations who were displaced and dispossessed. Across an impressive set of works, Gough assembles a striking visual language that has been an important artistic intervention in the so-called History Wars in Australia, a set of fraught debates over the nature and consequences of colonialism.[17] That Gough's work focused on the experiences of Tasmania's Aboriginal populations and the violence of the colonial order that developed on that island was especially significant given that the evidentiary basis for revisionist academic histories that foregrounded both violence and Aboriginal resistance stood at the center of the History Wars.[18]

Gough's work is a rich departure point for this volume because it explores the entangled nature of colonialism, indigeneity, media, and knowledge production. In producing her work, she repurposes colonial images, fashions an alternative set of visual idioms that foreground questions

FIGURE I.1 Julie Gough, *Some words for change*, 2008 (detail). Site-specific outdoor installation: tea tree (*Melaleuca* spp.) and thirty-two book pages from *Black War* (Clive Turnbull, 1948) dipped in wax. Ephemeral art exhibition, Friendly Beaches, Tasmania. Photograph by Simon Cuthbert. Reproduced with the permission of the artist.

about indigenous experience, and explores the interplay between colonial domination and postcolonial reassertions of identity, rights, and cultural legitimacy. In her *Some words for change* (2008), for example, she presents a striking juxtaposition between the printed word and tea tree spears, markers of indigenous resistance. The leaves impaled by the weapons are from Clive Turnbull's *Black War: The Extermination of the Tasmanian Aborigines*, an influential 1948 study of the colonization of Tasmania. Turnbull's history emphasized the range and depth of the violence perpetrated by colonists in Van Diemen's Land at a point when many historians scripted Australian history within liberal progressive narratives that tended to occlude violence and dispossession. Simultaneously, however, such accounts denied the continued existence of indigenous communities in Tasmania, failing to recognize the capacity of indigenous peoples to remake themselves within radically different circumstances. Gough's work challenges this narrative in a potent way, mobilizing the spear as a reminder that colonial domination was never uncontested, viscerally questioning the authority of written history.

The questions about colonialism, power, knowledge, and belonging that stand at the heart of Gough's oeuvre are urgent sites of contestation in indigenous politics globally, but they carry a special freight within the context of Tasmanian history. The colonial history of Van Diemen's Land was structured by violence, both in the operation of its convict system and in the forcible dispossession, containment, and displacement of indigenous populations. Those populations were subject to extensive violence and faced the terrible consequences of disease and dispossession. Tasmanian Aboriginal communities have often been imagined as extinct by politicians, journalists, and historians, and recent scholarship has framed the island's history as an exemplary case of colonial genocide.[19] Although much recent work on settler colonialism follows Lorenzo Veracini and Patrick Wolfe to argue that such forms of politico-economic organization were propelled by an eliminationist sensibility, Gough's work simultaneously underscores the centrality of violence in colonialism's will to power and also challenges readings that imagine the complete erasure of Tasmania's indigenous populations, and their cultural presence, experiences, and memories, by colonial power.[20]

At the heart of this volume is a desire to recover the shifting configurations of indigenous communities and knowledge traditions, specifically through a close attention to ways in which important ideas and aspirations were articulated through textual cultures. When *Some words for change* was exhibited on heathland at Friendly Beaches on the Freycinet Peninsula in Tasmania in 2008, another installation of Gough's work with the same title drew attention to matters of language. A series of laminated pages recorded indigenous terms from nineteenth-century Tasmania for the innovations of the colonial order, listing words like *wetuppenner* (fence), *booooo* (cattle), *bar* (sheep), *linghene* (fire a gun), *lughtoy* (gunpowder), *licummy* (rum), and *nonegimerikeway* (white man). In her artist statement on this work, Gough described how this wordlist recorded the "clues in language and in print of Aboriginal efforts to understand and incorporate what had arrived" under colonial rule.[21] By foregrounding change, Gough stressed the adaptability and resilience of indigenous peoples, a crucial intervention given that many white Australians still frame Aboriginal communities in terms of tradition or unshifting racial difference or view them as essentially belonging to a primeval past.

Gough's work as an artist can be usefully read alongside Leonie Stevens's work on indigenous traditions of literacy in colonial Van Diemen's Land. Stevens's cultural history from below is anchored in a body of largely neglected sources: the writings of the indigenous exiles at Wybalenna, an "Aboriginal Settlement" established on Flinders Island to forward their "civilization" and "Christianization," in the 1830s and 1840s. Stevens deftly explores a rich body of primary source material, including letters written by indigenous people at Wybalenna between 1843 and 1847, records of school examinations, and a range of sermons delivered by the young men Walter George Arthur and Thomas Brune and the handwritten *The Flinders Island Weekly Chronicle* they produced in 1836–37. Drawing on these varied materials—which underscore the archival work that can still enrich our understandings of indigenous histories—Stevens keeps the indigenous actors at the center of the story, exposing the limits of readings that imagine these sources (or colonialism more generally) as the unfurling of an uncontested and complete form of hegemony. Against such readings, Stevens presents Wybalenna as a "vibrant, noisy, and often rebellious community" whose creativity and resourcefulness challenged colonial assumptions and created a body of texts that capture a set of crucially important indigenous aspirations, experiences, and arguments articulated in the face of the (literally) unsettling claims of colonial authority.[22]

LITERACY AND THE ELUCIDATION
OF DIFFERENCE

Questions of language and literacy were central to the operation of colonial authority. The extension of European commercial systems, territorial authority, and cultural aspirations into the "New World" of the Americas and the Caribbean during the early modern period produced a growing archive of reflections on language and cultural difference. Samuel Purchas, an influential English cleric and editor who produced important compilations of travel writing in the early seventeenth century, suggested that writing was the key measure of cultural capacity: "amongst Men, some are accounted Civill, and more both Sociable and Religious by the Use of letters and Writing, which others wanting are esteemed Brutish, Savage, Barbarous." Purchas stressed the particular significance of writing's power to communicate across time: "By speech we utter our minds once, at the present, to the present, as present occasions move (and perhaps unadvisedly transport) us: but by writing Man seemes immortall." Via literacy, an individual "consulteth with the Patriarkes, Prophets, Apostles, Fathers, Philosophers" and could communicate their ideas through time: "by his owne writings [he] surviveth himselfe, remaines (litera scripta manet) thorow all ages a Teacher and Counsellor to the last of men."[23] As Stephen Greenblatt has noted, there is a significant shift in the constitution of "barbarian" as a social category in Purchas's text. Where in the ancient Mediterranean world this term delineated the boundary between Greek speakers and those who spoke other languages, now the barbarian was marked by the absence of literacy.[24]

As modern empires took shape in the second half of the eighteenth century and in the early nineteenth century, language was particularly prominent in the articulation of imperial authority and the justification of colonial domination.[25] In the British case, philology was especially important in shaping understandings of cultural capacity and the path of human development. Language was, of course, both a key archive and an important grounds for the argument of leading Scottish Enlightenment thinkers who developed new "stadial" histories that traced the development of human communities from rudeness to "refinement": these arguments took shape in Thomas Blackwell's important treatment of Homer and were elaborated and refined by important later thinkers such as Adam Ferguson, William Robertson, and John Millar.[26] A later generation of Scottish thinkers drew on these arguments, as well as the pathbreaking work of Sir William Jones on Sanskrit and the deep linguistic affinities of what came be known as the Indo-European language family, to craft linguistically framed histories of the cultural development of Asian societies.[27] For the influential essayist and Sanskritist Alexander Hamilton philology was essential for historians of "Civilisation," as language was the "most imperishable guide" to the origin and progress of all human communities.[28]

As European imperial regimes extended their reach into the Pacific, language stood at the heart of European assessments of the sophistication of local peoples and was seen as indicative of their capacity to change.[29] During his first Pacific voyage in 1769, James Cook reflected on questions of language in the wake of a sojourn at the Endeavour River on the Cape York Peninsula, Australia. Cook observed that "the languages of the different tribes differ very much. This results from the continual state of war in which they live, as they have no communication the one with the other."[30] That Aboriginal peoples relied on the oral transmission of information and cultural knowledge was seen as a marker of a crude and unsophisticated culture. Indigenous communities in Australia were thus framed as "illiterate," "primitive," and "barbaric," reflecting the primacy of writing in European conceptions of civilization.

Indigenous knowledge orders that were anchored in orality were typically defined in negative terms, as *lacking* literacy. Such communities were variously understood as requiring special "protection," "uplift," or evangelization, or, in some cases, they were identified as a serious impediment to the project of colonial progress: they were consistently constituted as a "social problem."[31] In the Australian case, many influential churchmen and colonial politicians were convinced that because indigenous communities had little interest in cross-cultural trade and limited enthusiasm for literacy and books, they would not be able to be converted to Christianity and were incapable of cultural change more generally.[32] Joy Damousi has highlighted the importance of the oppositions between "oral and primitive" and "literate and civilised" in the operation of colonial power in Australia in the middle of the nineteenth century. These were not simply abstract questions as they troubled the actual functioning of the colonial state, most notably in the legal system. Damousi demonstrates the ways in which indigenous peoples were marginalized in colonial courts in the 1830s and 1840s because they were understood as incapable of rendering reliable oaths, a "problem" that occasioned much debate among colonial authorities and humanitarian reformers.[33]

Thus, at the level of both scholarly activity and colonial realpolitik, language was central in encoding difference. The presence of writing was especially crucial, not just in shaping European evaluations of the cultural sophistication of indigenous and colonized peoples, but also in structuring how colonial knowledge itself was produced and organized. Nonliterate societies were typically imagined as "traditional," ordering their life around tribal units, oral tradition, and the weight of custom. Understanding these communities was to be the domain of ethnology and, subsequently, anthropology.[34] Conversely, those communities that were literate were seen not only as more sophisticated but also as belonging to the domain of historical study, as they produced written sources and were capable of change. This opposition, which was forcefully articulated during Europe's "discovery" and conquest

Tony Ballantyne & Lachy Paterson

of the New World in the early modern period, was constantly reiterated and calcified during the aggressive extension of European imperial systems during the long nineteenth century. As Michel de Certeau has noted, this assessment of different forms of communication performed powerful cultural work, effectively "exiling orality outside of the areas which pertain to Western work . . . transforming speech into an exotic object."[35] Effectively, the native was seen as the embodiment of orality and the past, while the European colonizer was equated with writing and the ever-changing present of modernity.

STRUCTURING OPPOSITIONS

Questions relating to orality and literacy have been central to a range of work on the distinctiveness of native or indigenous epistemologies. Some foundational anthropological texts have been particularly influential in elaborating the literacy-orality opposition. In a number of his works, Claude Lévi-Strauss reflected on the impact of the introduction of literacy among the Nambikwara, a Brazilian indigenous community. Stressing the deleterious social effects that followed the Nambikwara's adoption of writing, Lévi-Strauss argued that writing undermined the authenticity and innocence of tribal communities whose social life was anchored in orality. Literacy centralized power, promoted and calcified social hierarchies, and underwrote the authority of the law: in his commentary on Lévi-Strauss, Jacques Derrida called these shifts the "violence of the letter."[36]

For Lévi-Strauss, the uptake of these new skills meant a shift away from tradition and a dilution of native status: literacy broke the bonds of community and attenuated long-standing links to the natural world. As an anthropologist he saw these changes as a kind of loss, an undermining of a tribal culture by corrosive external forces. Yet, as Derrida noted, the distinction between "historical societies and societies without history" hinged on Lévi-Strauss's concept of literacy. In particular, Derrida observed, the Nambikwara were not without a system of inscriptions—incised and engraved calabashes—and they also displayed a strong interest in writing when first provided with paper and pencils, something that Lévi-Strauss omitted from *Tristes Tropiques*.[37] Moreover, Lévi-Strauss's treatment of the Nambikwara's enthusiasm for the skills and technologies of literacy was dependent on the assertion that they had no word that was a direct equivalent of *write*; this was a narrow rendering of the linguistic possibilities that closed off any conception that preexisting indigenous graphic or representational systems facilitated the Nambikwara's interest in alphabetic literacy.[38]

Where literacy was a key concern in Lévi-Strauss's treatment of an imperiled "native" way of life, Walter Ong's work on orality and literacy focused on the impact of literacy on thought processes and ways of understanding the world. Ong argued that a substantial cognitive investment was required to master writing as a cultural technology. As a consequence, literacy effected a significant cognitive transformation, effectively restricting human thought as the world of signs and sight was privileged over the world of sound and listening. While Ong was interested in tribal communities and colonized groups, the key ground for his arguments was European culture itself. He suggested that a succession of deep cultural shifts—the Reformation, the Enlightenment, and the emergence of modern knowledge systems in the wake of industrialization—had cemented the centrality of writing and print literacy, as the key underpinnings of human consciousness under modernity. As Ong simply argued, "writing *restructures consciousness.*"[39] For Ong, these transformations were clearly evident in the European past, in which key medieval intellectual traditions of logic, rhetoric, and dialectics were transformed and subsumed with the growing ascendancy of print in the wake of the Reformation. But he was also aware that the arguments could be refracted beyond Europe's shores and that old oppositions between "Civilization" and the natural world of the "Primitive" had been rearticulated through the orality-literacy divide. In response, Ong highlighted the significance of the interaction between such modes, whether in "native communities" or within the high Western tradition itself (as seen in Tudor poetry, for example).[40] Thus, as Jane Hoogestraat has argued, Ong enabled a rereading of colonialism, making it "possible, and imperative, to imagine and to recognize the voices—absent, other and largely oral—that haunt the official languages that we still speak and write."[41]

Jack Goody's influential treatments of orality and literacy tended to occlude such dynamics, stressing the divergence between the worlds of literacy and nonliteracy. Across an arc of publications, Goody posited that writing renders the relationship between a written word and the thing it refers to as abstract and universal.[42] As a consequence, he suggested that literacy promoted ways of thinking that were abstract, structured, and formalized. For Goody, the emergence of literacy was central in the separation between history and mythology, the development of complex forms of bureaucratic governance, and the development of sophisticated forms of cultural expression. Even as he mobilized a wide range of case studies, Goody frequently dichotomized oral and literate forms of social communication, glossing over or blurring hybrid forms of practice, especially the ways in which orality might condition literate cultures. Moreover, he tended to identify literacy as both a driver of change and a marker of cultural distinctiveness, when assessments of the impact and meaning of reading and writing need to be embedded in the broader operation of social communication and cultural differentiation.

Goody's work embodies a tendency of anthropological scholarship to extrapolate from specific ethnographic case studies to generalize about the distinctive qualities of orality and literacy. In making this move from the local to the abstracted universal, these arguments undervalue the placedness of these practices. In emphasizing the thickness and coherence of "culture," these kinds of arguments tend to underplay the historical contingency of cultural formations. They also often flatten out what we might think of as the social texture of these practices: their distribution by age, gender, status, kin-group affiliation, occupation, and place.[43] As William H. Sewell Jr. has observed, Lévi-Strauss was the influential architect of a vision that imagined culture as "a realm of pure signification," emphasizing its "internal coherence and deep logic."[44]

The chapters collected here demonstrate the limits of such an abstracted reading of culture. The arguments of Lévi-Strauss, Ong, and Goody continue to have purchase in a range of fields, and particular readings of their work still enable indigenous communities to frequently function as grounds on which divergences between literacy and orality, civilization and nature, history and culture are articulated. This volume challenges and unsettles a number of these claims. Many of the contributions are deeply attentive to place; they are concerned with multiple and shifting forms of social differentiation that often complicate neat divisions between the indigenous and the colonial; and they highlight the centrality of literacy practices in the dynamic making and remaking of indigenous social life, cultural understanding, and political aspiration. In many ways, they demonstrate the enduring importance of Sylvia Scribner's insight that "literacy has neither a static nor a universal essence."[45] The skills and practices that we bundle into the tidy label "literacy" are contingent on time and place; they carry divergent meanings and variable cultural weight for various social groups; and their importance and influence are, in part, determined by their interrelationship with a whole host of other practices: from oratory to marriage practices, from child raising to economic relations.

Scribner and her collaborator Michael Cole clearly demonstrated this contingency and complexity in their ethnographic study of the literacies of the Vai people, a Manden ethnic group from Liberia. They explored the complex interaction among three distinct literacies within Vai society: a tradition in Arabic, closely associated with Islam and maintenance of correct religious thought and practice; the English literacy sponsored by the government of Liberia; and a vernacular form practiced through the Vai script—a locally invented syllabic script championed by Momolu Duwalu Bukele, probably from the 1820s. Scribner and Cole demonstrated how these quite distinct literacies coexisted and interacted, but they also underlined that none of these traditions had supplanted orality. Indeed, Scribner and Cole found that orality persisted in a multitude of practices and that a range of socially and economically significant activities and institutions functioned in the "traditional oral mode": for the Vai, there was little or no social cost for not embracing literacy.[46]

Similarly, the chapters in this volume move away from an abstract treatment of the qualities of writing, to focus on the practices that produced indigenous textual cultures as socially important and dynamic formations. If Scribner's insistence on the flexibility and multiplicity of literacies helps frame this volume, more broadly the chapters gathered here operate in the wake of a vital recent literature on the social history of African literacies. That scholarship is born out of a robust dialogue between a very strong African tradition of social history and histories of books and print, work that in the African context has been committed to casting off Eurocentric framings of the "nature of the book."[47] While this scholarship acknowledges the prominence of literacy and textual cultures in shoring up imperial power—what Karin Barber calls a "documentary form of domination"—African readers and writers stand at its center.[48] In exploring the literacy practices of "ordinary people—clerks, teachers, catechists, school pupils, local healers, entrepreneurs"—this work has recovered a striking array of nonelite textual cultures and begun to reconstruct the "explosion of writing of all kinds" that was characteristic of life in twentieth-century Africa.[49]

Recovering these "hidden histories" of literacy not only documents the great utility and flexibility of literacies as social tools for Africans but also challenges us to rethink cultural production in colonial spaces. It directs our attention to the history of hidden, forgotten, neglected, or marginalized cultural innovators who read, wrote, and used texts in endlessly creative ways: a theme that threads through several chapters in this volume.[50] The constructive nature of African reading practices has been vividly rendered by Isabel Hofmeyr's reconstruction of the transnational circulation of John Bunyan's

Pilgrim's Progress. White and African elite sponsors of missionary work, the expansive cultural networks of the Black Atlantic, and the explosive energy of African messianic traditions helped secure an influential position in the intellectual and cultural landscapes of Africa for that "portable text." But the reach of *Pilgrim's Progress* also reflected its embrace by a diverse array of local readers and the text's "lateral" mobility, as it was widely translated and moved between African linguistic communities.[51] Archie Dick's work has also directed our attention to the "hidden history" of reading in South Africa. He shows how diverse sets of readers—including slaves, Khoisan, "Free Blacks," Griquas, influential African Christian leaders, labor leaders, political prisoners, and exiled antiapartheid activists—sought out and engaged with texts and in the process imagined and reimagined social belonging and the possibilities of politics.[52] More broadly still, for many African individuals and communities, reading became a key instrument for "improvement" or "betterment," a trend that is partly explainable through reference to the cultural contests of the colonial order but that was part of a wider cultural shift under modernity in which *improvement* functioned as a global keyword and reading "good books" was widely identified as one of the most efficacious engines of improvement.[53]

Barber has drawn our attention to the particular importance in the African context of what she has termed "tin-trunk texts" or "tin-trunk literacy" and the "tin-trunk literati." These terms gesture toward individuals who were deeply committed to the value of literacy and textual production. Of course, the figure of the "tin-trunk" identifies the importance of a kind of vernacular archive, as many of these passionate readers and writers were committed to archiving their lives (through journal keeping, the keeping of correspondence, or a broader collecting of documents), recording the changing fortunes of their families, local institutions, and social networks. In some cases, these forms of practice were heavily shaped by preexisting modes of social communication and cultural memorialization that were steeped in orality: whether this was how the inscription of dates in Bibles echoed the memorializing strategies of long-standing oral genres or how letters might be shaped by traditions of oral praise poems or family histories. While these types of practice seem to be a common feature of anglophone colonial Africa, they were also inflected by the particular forms of "documentary domination" that underwrote colonial power in various locales. Tin-trunk literacies certainly were energized by a desire to remake the self and reimagine community, but they were also imprinted by engagements with colonial power, and often writing was particularly important to negotiating these relationships.[54]

In many cases, those relationships with colonial officialdom were also mediated through what Barber has termed "printing culture," or what we might think of as "printing cultures." As opposed to the large-scale and authoritative public texts of "print culture," printing cultures could often be small-scale and localized, serving the needs of particular families or individuals.[55] In some contexts, the small print shops—often financially precarious and reliant on job printing for much of their income—that were integral to these printing cultures might serve diverse and multilingual local communities but also produced textual artifacts that were part of larger-scale transnational circulations.[56] As Antoinette Burton and Hofmeyr have stressed, such outputs often had an improvised and homespun quality.[57] The dense print undergrowth of empire was full of half-formed arguments, partially recycled ideas, and contingent interventions in local debates that also had one eye on distant "world events." Such forms of production were responsive to the quickening circulations of empire and to the realities of colonial political struggles that were frequently global in nature.

The emphasis on everyday cultural innovation that is central in this African scholarship is mirrored in some important work on Native Americans, such as Philip Deloria's exploration of indigenous modernities ("Indians in unexpected places") and Ellen Cushman's cataloguing of the enduring cultural and political significance of Sequoyah's creation of the Cherokee syllabary.[58] But, more generally, work on Native Americans and First Nations literacies has focused on the ideological importance of indigenous textual cultures. That kind of work is making a key double move. First, in suggesting that Native American authors fashioned a rich and deep tradition of literary production, scholars such as Robert Warrior are challenging the rigidity of the orality-literacy divide, highlighting the strength of indigenous intellectual traditions.[59] Second, in some cases, these scholars have argued that the weight and significance of these works require a broader rethinking of literary studies and intellectual history in North America. Birgit Brander Rasmussen has, in particular, drawn attention to the complexity of indigenous forms of communication and the ways in which incoming Europeans misread these modes as they instantiated the dichotomies of "literacy" and "illiteracy," "civilization" and "savagery," that legitimated colonialism.[60]

The Osage scholar Robert Warrior's *The People and the Word: Reading Native Nonfiction* has been perhaps the key intervention in rethinking the importance of Native American writing in modern America. This work recovered a range of intellectual traditions expressed primarily through various forms of nonfiction writing: from the Pequot writer William Apess's *A*

Son of the Forest (1829), through a reading of the Osage Constitution (1881) as a work of literature, to N. Scott Momaday's influential essay "The Man Made of Words" (1970). While he does not discount the literary qualities of nonfiction, Warrior stresses the importance of its ideological motivation and weight, and its ability to mobilize the experience of being colonized and dispossessed for political ends. For Warrior, appreciating these traditions of production is fundamental to a project of recovering "intellectual sovereignty" as it is essential to recover the mediums, practices, and lines of argument through which Native American writers have understood themselves and their communities. His approach places indigenous ways of thinking and arguing at the center of a distinctive form of intellectual history but recognizes the multiplicity of ways in which such visions have been articulated in time and space.[61] A similar emphasis on the political utility of writing informs Jace Weaver's emphasis on the "communitism"—a lacing together of *community* and *activism*—in Native American writing traditions over the past four decades.[62]

Thus, North American work on indigenous textual traditions has been deeply concerned with Native American–produced texts as ideological interventions that have challenged colonialism, American nationalism, and white dominance. Similar approaches have considerable influence in the Pacific. Noenoe K. Silva's study of the politics of indigenous literacy in Hawai'i emphasizes the centrality of reading and writing in Hawaiian attempts to retain cultural and political autonomy. Silva demonstrates the misleading nature of the "persistent and pernicious" myth of indigenous passivity and acceptance of American rule by foregrounding the riches of political discourse in the Hawaiian newspapers.[63] In New Zealand a body of influential work on nineteenth-century Māori-language newspapers has emphasized the embeddedness of those print artifacts in colonial politics, highlighting the importance of government- and missionary-run newspapers in the cultural edifice of colonial rule and the ways in which later Māori-run newspapers challenged the inequalities of the colonial order.[64] Within that work, however, there is rich material that casts light on literacy practices, which can be read alongside more recent interventions that have recovered a broad range of indigenous uses for writing and reading.[65] Examining a range of texts produced by Māori women, Lachy Paterson and Angela Wanhalla's *He Reo Wāhine: Māori Women's Voices from the Nineteenth Century*, for example, not only highlights the links between gender and literacy but also indicates Māori women's diverse writing practices, as well as their deployment of literacy for a range of purposes, from the creative to the political.

Work that reconstructs the diversity of indigenous literacy practices not only is significant in its own right but also stands as a powerful corrective to an earlier body of scholarship on "cultural colonization" that imagined Māori as largely existing either as the *subject* of print culture or *outside* print culture altogether, an approach that valorizes a particularly narrow reading of orality and cultural authority.[66]

Kāi Tahu historian Michael Stevens has challenged framings of the indigenous past that unproblematically privilege orality and the persistence of tribal cultures on the grounds that they underplay the importance of mobility and engagements with various social collectives beyond the kin group.[67] Texts—both as the carriers of ideas across space and as material objects that were embedded in economic and social circulations—were powerful engines that created connections and entanglements of various kinds, including forms of social identification that operated at a variety of different scales. Stephanie Newell's work on newspaper readership in colonial West Africa underlines the limits of seeing the key cultural outcome of newspaper reading as the creation of national communities, a point that has also been made by Tony Ballantyne with regard to colonial cultures of newspaper reading in southern New Zealand.[68]

Newspapers could not only facilitate social identifications at levels below the nation—the locality or region—but also nurture more expansive affiliations that transected the boundaries of the colony or developing nation. The low cost and portability of newspapers, as well as the prevalence of cut-and-paste editorial practices, meant that they played a key role in enabling critiques of empire and colonialism and were central in the formation of anticolonial coalitions across space and time.[69] Modern communication networks shaped by steamers, the telegraph, news services, and a press system where copyright had variable purchase promoted the rapid and repeated circulation of "information," "intelligence," and "opinion." The routine use of quotations, cuttings, summaries, and abridgements was one key element of the "epic mobility of nineteenth-century imperialism," and these editorial techniques helped drive the "endless textual intersections" that were a crucial element of expansive imperial systems.[70] Within these dense and shifting patterns of long-distance circulation and the recycling of texts, indigenous editors and journalists used international conflicts and important historical events to articulate their own distinctive political positions within their own colonial situations.[71]

Recovering the mobility of texts and the ways in which they were used in particular local situations remains a key way forward for future work as it addresses a central problem in cultural history. Peter Mandler has identified this as assessing the "relative throw" of texts, an undertaking that requires the historian to evaluate the "breadth of circulation" of any text, the "imaginative work" it carries out, and the ways in which that text is itself reframed, deployed, and mobilized in various locations and social contexts.[72] Many of the chapters in this volume explore this problem, at least implicitly, as they seek to assess the transformative power of literacy and indigenous textual cultures.

The breadth of this volume is significant, spanning over two centuries, with chapters covering indigenous engagements with textual cultures in Africa, North America, Australasia, and the Pacific. This collection also highlights the range of text genres that indigenous peoples contributed to or produced, from letters, journals, and other manuscripts to newspapers, pamphlets, and books, demonstrating that they were more than merely passive consumers of colonial discourses. Taken as a whole, the collection brings together a strong interest in the interplay between the practices that produced textual cultures and the politics of such cultural formations. The volume's strong concern with literacy practices is not to discount the ideological significance of indigenous writing or the influence of particular texts. Rather, it reflects a commitment to understanding the contours of precolonial knowledge systems, idioms of communication, and the range of indigenous practices of knowledge production that developed in the face of imperial intrusion and colonization so that the range of political idioms that indigenous writers could mobilize, and the expectations of the publics (or counterpublics) they addressed, can be illuminated.

The first section of the volume examines material from three Pacific archives that house an abundance of indigenous written material but also questions why these repositories sit largely underutilized. Noelani Arista explores why historians investigating the Hawaiian past fail to consult the extensive archives of Hawaiian-language texts, preferring to reconstruct the Hawaiian native through English-language sources, sometimes including a meager selection of translated work, while completely ignoring the Hawaiian voice on offer. Not only was Hawaiian the language of the street, church, and early government in the nineteenth century, but kānaka maoli (Native Hawaiians), embracing the technologies of literacy, including nūpepa (newspapers), produced a vast textual output. Arista explains how the subsequent marginalization of the Hawaiian language and indigenous texts came about through colonization and demonstrates how its occlusions and priorities have persisted into academic research. Trained scholars, she argues, are needed, capable not just of reading ka ʻōlelo Hawaiʻi (the Hawaiian language) but also of listening to and hearing texts that often sprang from oral beginnings. Using *kanikau* (chants), she shows how these oral texts can shed light on Hawaiian history.

Similarly, in New Caledonia both academics and local Kanak generally bypass indigenous writings within the archive because they believe that authentic indigenous culture is essentially oral. Alban Bensa and Adrian Muckle seek to dispel this misconception with a case study on a local war in the north of Grande Terre, the main island of New Caledonia. As in many parts of the Pacific, evangelization and literacy grew in tandem, with many Kanak becoming literate in their own languages. Literacy in French was more problematic: on the one hand, it denoted civilization, but, on the other, the *indigénat* (colonial regime) also feared it as a unifying factor for culturally and linguistically diverse peoples, or a source of unsettling information and knowledge. Indeed, indigenous Kanak utilized French to collaborate with, critique, and resist colonialism; in 1917 this included not only letters from Kanak soldiers serving overseas but texts produced by chiefs communicating with the indigénat and by the insurgents fighting that colonial regime. Bensa and Muckle also explore another genre of Kanak literacy relating to the 1917 war. *Ténô*, epic poems in indigenous languages, were a feature of textual activity in the decades between the world wars that provides a more nuanced view of Kanak motivations and relationships. This chapter looks at two such poems that relate back to the period of revolt in terms of not just the political content but also the aesthetic qualities deriving from their ancient and oral roots.

As in Hawai'i, New Zealand's archives hold considerable textual material produced both for and by indigenous communities, in the form of letters, government documents, newspapers, and other printed items. With missionaries claiming a rapid spread of literacy across Māori society, academic debate has tended to revolve around literacy levels—how many Māori could read and write, and when they acquired these skills. D. F. McKenzie's *Oral Culture, Literacy and Print in Early New Zealand: The Treaty of Waitangi*, which argued against a high or deep uptake of literacy and asserted that Māori society remains inherently oral to this day, has been a particularly influential contribution to those debates. Lachy Paterson's chapter discusses these debates, but contends that the evidence is too fragmentary to definitively assess levels of reading or writing, and argues that more fruitful insights can be gained instead from investigating how texts and practices around literacy impacted Māori life. As colonization became embedded in New Zealand, Māori confronted an increasingly textual world that impacted on their existing oral culture. Illiteracy did not necessarily mean that individuals were excluded from textual practices, just as the knowledge of reading and writing did not provide immunity from the vicissitudes of the colonial rule. In many cases, new textual practices presented new opportunities for agency.

Using case studies of specific places and communities, the second section explores in depth the relationship between orality and textuality. Employing an ethnohistorical approach, Keith Thor Carlson looks beyond the more obvious connections between colonialism and literacy, offering a nuanced account of the latter's relationship with the Salish peoples of British Columbia. Carlson compares the communication systems and processes employed by both the indigenous and newcomers, arguing for a Salish time-based oral literacy inscribed within their landscapes as opposed to the European proliferation of textual materials across space. This chapter ranges widely, from the peregrinations of the explorer Simon Fraser, to a retrospective indigenous reclaiming of literacy, to Catholic uses of literacy to break down "superstition," to the government's use (and forgoing) of literacy as a means of securing Salish lands. Indigenous literacy proved threatening. Although missionaries considered it as a form of mimicry that indicated a transition to civilization, they nevertheless needed to define it as either appropriate or inappropriate. Similarly, as a means of asserting colonial control, the settler government sought to determine how indigenous peoples could utilize literacy.

Michael P. J. Reilly's chapter explores two versions of an oral tradition from Mangaia, in the Cook Islands. The first formed the basis of a sermon by Mamae, an indigenous minister, recorded by the resident English missionary in 1876 for Western consumption; in Mangaia, as in most of the Pacific, Christianity and literacy were significant features of modernity, but neither displaced the old oral world. In the tradition, a young woman leaves her abusive master to live with Te Maru-o-Rongo, a more exalted nobleman, which Mamae used in his sermon to explain aspects of Christianity. A century later, the Cook Islands government's Cultural Development Division facilitated an opportunity for elders to record the tradition again on tape, although only the transcription is now available. The government initiated the recording of traditions as part of a project to build a Cook Islands cultural identity but also to provide a resource for tourist guides. Reilly argues that Christianity did not supplant precontact knowledge, and neither did literacy replace the oral nature of that knowledge's transmission, with the transcription alluding to spiritual beings prevailed upon to restore harmony and order to both society and the environment. He compares the two renditions, composed for different reasons: one for religious purposes, the other harkening back to pre-Christian tradition and incorporating features more relevant to modern listeners.

Bruno Saura's chapter also demonstrates how orality informs textual culture in two areas of present-day French Polynesia. Saura explores indigenous manuscript books from Rurutu (Austral Islands) and Huahine, Borabora, and Ra'iātea (Society Islands) that contain genealogies and traditions relevant to political status and land rights, as well as narratives that rationalize the past to fit present-day social, religious, and political realities. Saura examines Goody's thesis that literacy imposes a logical progression on written texts, as well as skeptical thought in the mind of the reader, but demonstrates that these Polynesian texts are not fixed containers of systematic knowledge. The various customary oral traditions, rendered in text, are layered with adjustments and additions over time, not necessarily in dialogue with the existing stories, sometimes even contradicting them, with truth relative to the context of what is being discussed. Rather than being transformed by literacy, these indigenous societies adapted textual practices to fit their own cultural needs.

For missionaries or colonial officials, literacy and print were often seen as the means to govern or transform indigenous subjects, but indigenous peoples also sought to negotiate with these discourses and technologies, whether to moderate, influence, collaborate with, or even reject them. The chapters in the third section investigate three such negotiations. Emma Hunter explores two key Swahili-language newspapers of the interwar period: the Tanganyikan government's *Mambo Leo* and the Lutheran *Ufalme wa Mungu*, and their efforts to create reading publics in the East African region. Swahili was a pragmatic choice for both government and church: it was spoken by many Africans, albeit as a second language by most, and already possessed a literary tradition, albeit in Arabic script. Both newspapers proffered didactic discourses and sought to avoid contentious issues, but to create reading publics, they also needed to engage with readers and provide interesting content. Hunter reveals how Africans, at a time before indigenous-run newspapers had emerged in the region, wrote extensively to these colonial newspapers, providing letters, poetry, and local news, and offered suggestions on content, helping to shape not only the newspapers but the Swahili language itself.

For missionaries who operated in the Groote Eylandt archipelago in the Northern Territory of Australia in 1943, literacy in English was a boon that would enable the Anindilyakwa people to fully engage in the modern civilized world. Laura Rademaker argues that the Anindilyakwa chose alternative textual practices to those the missionaries advocated. Writing love letters constituted a punishable offense. Nor did missionaries appreciate critical letters and petitions, rejecting what they saw as an inappropriate engagement with modernity. They believed that Bible reading was crucial to Christian fellowship, but their textual practices were so enmeshed in their efforts to control Aboriginal peoples that many Anindilyakwa chose not to learn, rejecting literacy even when offered in their own language. Rademaker reveals a history of orality's adaptation through an excavation of textual archives, but at the center of her chapter are conversations with elders who remembered the mission and who experienced the advent of reading and writing in their community. They recount how they adapted these new skills to their own lifestyle needs, rather than following missionary mandates.

As the sun set on colonial rule in Papua New Guinea, relatively few indigenous people had been exposed to literacy and education, and in an effort to prepare the population for independence, missionaries sought to spread literacy more widely. For a largely undeveloped country with over eight hundred vernacular languages, mass illiteracy, and negative attitudes to reading, the path ahead might appear overwhelming. In the title of her chapter, "'Read It, Don't Smoke It!,'" Evelyn Ellerman alludes to the practical value New Guineans placed on newsprint, as opposed to the content of newspaper texts. Ellerman outlines the strategies and debates both Protestant and Catholic missions employed in an effort to create a functionally literate public, including literacy campaigns, the creation of reading material for the newly literate, writing classes and competitions, and publication of newspapers and journals. New Guineans, like the Anindilyakwa discussed by Rademaker, did not always follow the path laid out for them, embracing literacy for their own purposes in their own ways, causing some missionaries to completely rethink their strategies.

The final section of the volume centers on the projection of indigenous voices through writing. Isabel Hofmeyr argues that imperial copyright was designed to protect metropolitan authors and, far from being an imposition on indigenous writers, largely excluded or ignored their work. Focusing on southern Africa, Hofmeyr first investigates how customs officials applied copyright law at the turn of the twentieth century. She then explores W. B. Rubusana's book *Zemk'inkomo Magwalandini*, which he published in London in 1906. Rubusana, a South African clergyman and politician, was already an established author. But he sought to give the strongest copyright protection possible to his book, a collection of prose and Xhosa praise poems from various sources, much of which had already been printed in newspapers. Although Rubusana positioned himself as an imperial citizen,

Hofmeyr argues that his acquiring copyright was not about his personal property rights but, as with other African writers, about "constituting it as public property" and the creation of a "new repertoire of cultural power" in a world that privileged white men's textual output.

In the mid-1850s, Tāmihana Te Rauparaha wrote an account of his father, Te Rauparaha, the warrior chief whose Ngāti Toa and Ngāti Raukawa tribes migrated to and occupied the Cook Strait region of New Zealand in the 1820s. Unlike his father, Tāmihana Te Rauparaha was a Christian convert, literate and modern, who maintained a good working relationship with the new colonial regime. Arini Loader explains that in writing "kei wareware," Tāmihana was recording his father's life and times, "lest it be forgotten." Although successive authors utilized Tāmihana's account in biographies of Te Rauparaha, the writer and his text were often heavily edited and largely unacknowledged. Loader gives a genealogy of this borrowing, a "reading down," followed by a "reading up" in which she analyzes the text from an insider perspective. Tāmihana, Loader argues, wrote so that the memory of his father might not be lost in the future, but also so that his father would not be forgotten in the dominant colonial textual world of his own time.

The final essay explores the earliest texts covered in this volume. Samson Occom, a Mohegan of New England, sought out Eleazar Wheelock, an early missionary educationalist in the mid-eighteenth century, to gain an education. As Ivy Schweitzer explains, Occom became Wheelock's star pupil, and then a missionary and minister in his own right; he journeyed to Britain to raise funds for Indian education, until falling out with his mentor and establishing his own indigenous settlement of Brothertown. However, as a tribal counselor, Occom was also aware that his education was vital for the well-being of his people at a time when colonists wielded the English language and literacy to seize land from Native Americans. Schweitzer surveys the debates over orality and literacy but argues that when analyzing Occom's extensive writing, we need to "shift our frame of analysis to consider forms of literacy from a Native perspective"; what constituted literacy in the precontact Native American world was different from, and far wider in scope than, mere textual symbolic systems. In particular, she employs Lisa Brooks's concept of the common pot, in which "everyone and everything in communities is related and interdependent for survival and flourishing," including newcomers and their writing. Schweitzer has also brought this methodology to bear in establishing The Occom Circle, a digital archive of the writing of Occom and his peers. More than just a virtual shelf, this sort of approach to digital humanities seeks to re-create the common pot, demonstrating

Occom's rich and complex network of correspondents and the movement of texts over space and time.

What emerges in this volume is the dynamism and flexibility of indigenous textual cultures. In many parts of the world, reading and writing became not only increasingly important in the organization of indigenous life but also integral to the articulation of what it was to be indigenous within the fraught cultural terrains shaped by imperial intrusion and colonialism. In the face of the extended reach of global empires and the disparities of colonialism, reading and writing became effective tools for reorganizing economic and social life, for redefining and remaking communities, for recrafting and refining the self, and for reimagining the future.

NOTES

1. This reading of the global past draws from Ballantyne and Burton, *Empires and the Reach of the Global*; and Burton and Ballantyne, *World History from Below*.

2. The most influential statement of this perhaps remains Ania Loomba's *Colonialism/Postcolonialism*.

3. Niezen, *A World beyond Difference*; Klenke, "Whose *Adat* Is It?," 150–52; Merlan, "Indigeneity," 303–33; and Maybury-Lewis, *Indigenous Peoples, Ethnic Groups, and the State*, 54.

4. Identifying this repertoire of shared reference points is important if we are to recognize that even if "indigeneity" is relational, it does draw on substantive cultural elements and historical experiences.

5. Francesca Merlan notes that certain individuals and influential institutions, such as the United Nations and International Labour Organization, have offered definitions of indigeneity that are "criterial" rather than relational: in other words, they identify a fixed and finite set of attributes that enable such groups to be confidently identified. Such definitions are anchored in an understanding that indigeneity is a "large and self-evident category that has at last been appropriately recognized." Merlan, "Indigeneity," 305.

6. Of course, such networks have a long and deep history, as Jane Carey and Jane Lydon's edited volume *Indigenous Networks: Mobility, Connections and Exchange* makes clear; but what is qualitatively different after World War II is the ways in which these networks were increasingly mobilized around identification.

7. Niezen, *The Origins of Indigenism*.

8. Niezen, *A World beyond Difference*, 70–72.

9. United Nations, *The International Year for the World's Indigenous People*.

10. Nyamnjoh, "Ever-Diminishing Circles," 305–32. Also see Balaton-Chrimes, *Ethnicity, Democracy and Citizenship in Africa*.

11. Mamdani, "The Invention of the Indigène," 31–33; and Mamdani, "Beyond Settler and Native as Political Identities," 651–64.

12. Mamdani, "Beyond Settler and Native as Political Identities," 653–54.

13. Of course, the conceptualization and linguistic framing of the native was complex and shifting, overlapping in some ways like an array of other terms: Aborigines, Indians, or various more specific designations based on the tribal or kin-based identifications of local communities.

14. Salesa, "Opposite-Footers," 285–302.

15. Examples of the former category include her works *Some words for change,* comprising tea tree sticks and book pages from Clive Turnbull's book *Black War* (1948) dipped in wax (2008); *Incident Reports,* comprising a found Tasmanian oak bookshelf, tea tree sticks, and burnt-inscribed Tasmanian oak (2008); *The Missing,* comprising tea tree sticks and warrener shells (2008); and *A Half Hour Hidden History Reader,* comprising an altered book (*The Tasmanian History Readers 4,* Royal School Series, Education Department, Hobart): collage and handwriting on white paint over existing text (2007). Examples of the latter category include *Some words for Country Lowmyner, Marloielare, Tromemanner, Loirle, Melaythenner, Trounter,* comprising black crow (nerite) shells in cuttlefish bones on timber (2007); and *Some words for Tasmanian Aboriginal women ~ Armither, Luanee, Laggener, Lowanna, Neeanta, Nowaleah,* comprising black crow (nerite) shells in cuttlefish bones on timber (2007).

16. Julie Gough, "Artist Statement," accessed 2 April 2018, https://juliegough.net /artist-statement/.

17. Bullock, *Memory Fragments,* 25.

18. Ryan, "'Hard Evidence,'" 39–50.

19. Framings of colonial violence in Tasmania are explored in Curthoys, "Genocide in Tasmania," 229–52.

20. E.g., Wolfe, *Settler Colonialism and the Transformation of Anthropology;* Wolfe, "Settler Colonialism and the Elimination of the Native," 387–409; and Veracini, *Settler Colonialism.* For a passionate rejoinder to this approach, see Rowse, "Indigenous Heterogeneity," 297–310.

21. Gough, artist statement, *Some words for change,* 2008, copy provided by the artist. Also see this work on the artist's website at https://juliegough.net/artwork -about-unresolved-histories/.

22. L. Stevens, "'Me Write Myself,'" 240.

23. Purchas, *Hakluytus Posthumus, or Purchas His Pilgrimes,* 486.

24. Greenblatt, *Marvellous Possessions,* 10.

25. Cohn, *Colonialism and Its Forms of Knowledge.*

26. Blackwell, *An Enquiry into the Life and Writings of Homer;* and J. Turner, *Philology,* 71–73, 101–2, 141–43.

27. Rendall, "Scottish Orientalism," 43–69. A group of East India Company scholar-administrators, trained at the University of Edinburgh between 1784 and 1803, drew on their experience working in the "East" for the company in writing histories of Asian societies. Alexander Hamilton, James Mackintosh, and John Leyden all attended Edinburgh during Dugald Stewart's influential tutorship. Stewart suggested that language was the keystone to the history of civilization: it could

both reveal the sophistication of any given society and indicate the affinities among different nations.

28. Hamilton, "Wilkins's *Sanscrit Grammar*," 372.

29. Ballantyne, *Orientalism and Race*.

30. Cook, *Captain Cook's Journal during His First Voyage Round the World in H.M. Bark "Endeavour" 1768–71*, ch. 8.

31. Van Toorn, *Writing Never Arrives Naked*, 9, 184–86. On the emergence of "social problems," see Poovey, *Making a Social Body*, 1, 28, 58; and Poovey, *A History of the Modern Fact*, 1, 23, 29.

32. J. D. Bollen, "English Missionary Societies and the Australian Aborigine," 263–90; and A. Johnston, *The Paper War*.

33. Damousi, *Colonial Voices*, 7, 29–31.

34. "Ethnology is especially interested in what is not written." Lévi-Strauss, *Structural Anthropology*, 25.

35. De Certeau, *The Writing of History*, 212.

36. Lévi-Strauss, *Family and Social Life of the Nambikwara Indians*; and Derrida, *Of Grammatology*, 109–21.

37. Derrida, *Of Grammatology*, 129, 132–33.

38. Derrida, *Of Grammatology*, 133–34; for a variation of this argument in a very different context, see Gallagher, "'A Curious Document,'" 39–47.

39. Ong, *Orality and Literacy* (1982), 78–116, especially 78.

40. Peters, "Orality, Literacy and Print Revisited," 31–32.

41. Hoogestraat, "'Discoverers of Something New,'" 57.

42. For example, see Goody's *The Domestication of the Savage Mind*, *The Interface between the Written and the Oral*, and *The Power of the Written Tradition*.

43. The distinction made between thick and thin here draws on Sewell, *Logics of History*. Also see the arguments and discussion in Shankman, "The Thick and the Thin," 261–80. For a reading of the implications of this understanding of culture as thin for indigenous history, see M. Stevens, "'What's in a Name?,'" 333–47.

44. Sewell, "The Concept(s) of Culture," 44.

45. Scribner, "Literacy in Three Metaphors," 8.

46. Scribner, "Literacy in Three Metaphors," 15; and Scribner and Cole, *The Psychology of Literacy*.

47. R. Fraser, *Book History through Postcolonial Eyes*, 29; Ballantyne, "What Difference Does Colonialism Make?," especially 351; Hofmeyr and Kriel, "Book History in Southern Africa," 15; and C. Davis and Johnson, "Introduction," 1–17.

48. Barber, "Introduction," 6.

49. Barber, "Acknowledgements," ix; and Barber, "Audiences and the Book in Africa," 12.

50. Barber, "Introduction," 1–24; and Peterson and Macola, "Introduction," 1–30.

51. Hofmeyr, *The Portable Bunyan*, 26–27.

52. Dick, *The Hidden History of South Africa's Book and Reading Cultures*.

53. Barber, "Introduction," 3; on reading and improvement in another colonial context, see Ballantyne, "Placing Literary Culture," 82–104.

54. Barber, "Introduction," 6, 18.

55. Barber, "Audiences and the Book in Africa," 16–17.

56. Ballantyne, "Contesting the Empire of Paper," 232.

57. Burton and Hofmeyr, "Introduction," 13.

58. Deloria, *Indians in Unexpected Places*; and Cushman, *The Cherokee Syllabary*.

59. Warrior, *The People and the Word*.

60. Rasmussen, *Queequeg's Coffin*.

61. Warrior, *The People and the Word*, 182.

62. Weaver, *That the People Might Live*, xiii.

63. Silva, *Aloha Betrayed*.

64. J. Curnow, Hopa, and McRae, *Rere Atu, Taku Manu!*; Paterson, *Colonial Discourses*; and Paterson, "*Te Hokioi* and the Legitimization of the Māori Nation," 124–42.

65. For one such cluster of work, see M. Stevens, "Kāi Tahu Writing and Cross-Cultural Communication," 130–57; Ballantyne, "Paper, Pen, and Print," 232–60; and Potiki, "Me Ta Taua Mokopuna," 31–53.

66. The key statements on cultural colonization are Gibbons, "A Note on Writing, Identity, and Colonisation in Aotearoa," 32–38; and Gibbons, "Cultural Colonization and National Identity," 5–17. For a rereading of this issue, see Ballantyne, "Culture and Colonization," 1–22.

67. M. Stevens, "A 'Useful' Approach to Maori History," 54–77.

68. Newell, "Articulating Empire," 26–42; and Ballantyne, "Reading the Newspaper in Colonial Otago," 47–63.

69. Harper, "Globalism and the Pursuit of Authenticity," 263; Hofmeyr, *Gandhi's Printing Press*; and Ballantyne, "Contesting the Empire of Paper."

70. Hofmeyr, *Gandhi's Printing Press*, 8, 13, 16.

71. Paterson, "Kiri Ma, Kiri Mangu," 60–77; and Paterson, "Identity and Discourse," 444–62.

72. Mandler, "The Problem with Cultural History," 97, 103.

Part I
Archives &
Debates

CHAPTER ONE

Ka Waihona Palapala Mānaleo:
Research in a Time of Plenty.
Colonialism and the Hawaiian-
Language Archives

NOELANI ARISTA

THE HAWAIIAN PHRASE describing the archives is relatively functional: *ka waihona palapala kahiko,* or "repository for old manuscripts." A *waihona* is a place where materials are stored; however, our work in archives encompasses more than just "discovering" long-neglected sources and bringing them to light. The Hawaiian-language written and published corpus is the largest in any indigenous language in native North America and possibly the Polynesian Pacific, and yet it is still largely ignored. This "archive," and others of like magnitude (e.g., Māori, Lakota, Cherokee), dismantles commonplace assumptions that scholars writing native, colonial, or imperial history have to deal with source scarcity.[1] The handwritten materials and publications in Hawaiian comprise a detailed, almost daily accounting of colonial and imperial processes that span the period from colonial settlement to the overthrow of a native nation and its aftermath (1820–1948). Materials were produced by haole and Hawaiian writers documenting change and transformation from the nineteenth to the early twentieth century, with sources supplying innumerable firsthand accounts of native lives in transition.

The extent to which Hawaiians recorded previously orally preserved precontact histories, genealogies, chants, songs, and the like in writing and in print, which we can draw on to produce new performative materials in the present, is both astonishing and exciting. Difficulties arise for the scholar of Hawaiʻi in the world, not from source scarcity, but because of source abundance.[2] Given this situation, an important question to ask is, how does an "archive" of this magnitude get lost, hidden in plain sight? While I briefly historicize this disappearance, my work here is oriented toward describing what is in the Hawaiian-language archive, and how we might interpret and modify our approaches to native-language archives as sites of traditional *and* empirical knowledge. In addition, I suggest an archival praxis based on "ear witnessing" and orality, rather than "eye-witnessing"—in short, a methodological practice that is shaped by our interaction with the sources that were once oral and are now textual.[3] Just as Alban Bensa and Adrian Muckle seek to demonstrate that "'Kanak culture is not purely oral,'" so too this chapter makes the distinction of following the oral into the written as a way for scholars to dispose of the orality-literacy binary as insufficient for furthering knowledge of the Hawaiian past.[4]

The problem of the hidden Hawaiian-language archive is structural and attitudinal, a problem over a century in the making. Scholars working with Hawaiian-language materials are not faced with archival destruction, as happened in many Native American and other indigenous sites of colonial or imperial contest. Rather, these sources have been devalued by scholarly praxis, while colonial processes over time significantly decreased the population that could speak and write Hawaiian, resulting in the deskilling of an organic knowledge and scholarly labor force that might have continued to perform and produce scholarly discourse on Hawaiian history in the native language.

Language, history, life, and knowledge ways in many places were overwritten, erased, destroyed, hidden, or abandoned in the wake of colonial settlement or imperial domination. These cessations, or ruptures, were attended by violence—physical, intellectual, spiritual, and psychic wounds inflicted from the outside or self-directed. Rigorous accounts of the ongoing consequences of colonial and imperial violence are needed to explain the suppression of the archives and the way native languages were made "foreign" to our practice as scholars. In the Māori context, as Arini Loader notes in her chapter in this volume, studying "the ways in which Māori intellectual traditions have been presented back to Māori and the wider community" is important for understanding how "cultural colonization" also alienated Māori from their intellectual traditions and histories.

Historicizing the disappearance of the archives relieves communities of the burden of "not knowing," allowing people to suspend the weight of generational guilt, the personal responsibility many natives feel for not being organically literate or well-spoken individuals like our ancestors. Resultant sentiments of loss, grief, and grievance have begun to shape the field of native history and Hawaiian and indigenous studies, to the detriment of future historical understanding.

The Hawaiian-language archive has been devalued owing to a scholarly preference for working in English-language-only archives. Important anthropological works about Hawai'i and Hawaiians impose innovative methods that assume primary-source scarcity, an irony given the sheer size of the Hawaiian-language archive. Overreliance on English-language archives, along with a smattering of previously translated source materials, is widespread in writing on Hawai'i and Hawaiians, giving rise to what Puakea Nogelmeier has termed "A Discourse of Sufficiency."[5] This discourse has produced a historiography deaf to Hawaiian subjectivities, historical experiences, and modes of historical production.[6]

Few published scholarly essays and monographs use any portion of the untranslated archive, which constitutes probably 95 percent of the material housed in libraries and archives. Imagine the daunting problem of encountering a "new," vast, unread archive of materials, while engaging with over a century of historiography founded on few to none of these sources. The crisis currently facing scholars embarking on writing the history of Hawai'i, Hawaiian history, and Hawai'i in the world is nothing short of reassessing and rewriting accepted theses and narrativizations enshrined in books published over the past century. Once indigenous-language sources are mainstreamed through works written by scholars trained to fluency, a new future for the Hawaiian past can be charted. The historiography on nineteenth-century Hawai'i (and the United States) deserves particular attention since the historical conversation has too long been shaped and authorized by the primacy of *foreign*-language (English) sources to the exclusion of those produced in the Hawaiian language. If scholars want to know "how natives think," they might examine the words that *kānaka maoli* (Hawaiian people) spoke, composed, published, and wrote *ma ka 'ōlelo Hawai'i* (in the Hawaiian language).[7]

Understanding how the archives became hidden can be achieved by historicizing the late nineteenth-century forced assimilation of former Hawaiian citizens living in the Territory of Hawai'i, after an 1896 law functionally barred the Hawaiian language from education, requiring that "English language shall be the medium of instruction in all public and private schools" in the archipelago.[8] The law closed off all avenues of formal study and higher education in the Hawaiian language, leading to a sharp decline in native-language fluency. Or we might focus our attention earlier, in the 1840s and 1850s, when discussions raged in the *nūpepa* (newspapers) and within the kingdom's board of education over the place of the English and Hawaiian languages in the schools. These broadened to include the new role of English in "civilizing" Hawaiians and facilitating their upward movement in society, an important departure from the Protestant American Board's original mandate of disseminating the word of God through the vernacular of the people, *'ōlelo Hawai'i*.[9] One could even study the words of King Kamehameha IV, who was a strong advocate for transforming all Hawaiian-language schools into English-medium schools.[10] Interested researchers might also seek to conceptualize how deeply kānaka maoli considered language as constitutive of *'ōiwi* (indigeneity).[11]

The idea that language is inextricably entwined with identity is now commonplace among scholars, but there may be a problem with this assumption with regard to the work of researchers. Not only has much pressure been placed on language as a signifier of authentic identity in native communities, but there is also too much emphasis on reading texts anachronistically—out of context, as proofs of tradition and not empirical evidence. This ideological climate that privileges identity has also enabled claims to scholarly authority through indigeneity, in a strange inversion of racialized ideas of superiority once wielded only by haole settlers. The current fashion that dictates that "to be *is* to know" can be a corrosive standard, detrimental to kanaka maoli traditional modes of *'imi* (seeking after knowledge), since fostering Hawaiian *'ike* (knowledge) always came with years of disciplined study in formal schools where students were trained in listening, repetition, recitation, and memory.[12]

Language *and* practice that connect to a home place are arguably the core relationship that defines maoli. This is elucidated in expressions such as *'āina, one hānau, kulāiwi, kua 'āina, pua,* and *kupa,* all words that seal the intrinsic notion of people = land in a Hawaiian context.[13] In historicizing the absence of the Hawaiian language from everyday use, historians may be exposed to the myriad historical public debates over language and education, progress and civilization, that place Hawai'i and other sites of colonial settlement within a broader Pacific, and global, context. It is, however, possible to sketch these historical trajectories only if scholars are fluent enough to read the Hawaiian-language publications in which these debates raged. This is a methodological problem because what the archives need, what history needs, is adequately *trained* scholars.[14]

One of the most powerful outcomes of imperialism is that it makes the language native to a particular place, along with sources vital to the crafting of historical context, into a marginal and seemingly unnecessary part of writing the history of the constitution and reconstitution of nations—that of America in this case, or even that of the Hawaiian Kingdom and the chiefdoms that preceded the arrival of American settlers in the islands by nearly a thousand years.[15]

To read and understand Hawaiian-language sources, one need not be kanaka maoli. The archive and its sources have been divided into "native" and "scholarly" sections, often, curiously (or not), segregated by language. Further complicating matters are the disciplinary divides between "native" and "nonnative" history. Early twentieth-century ethnographers drew on the labor of native Hawaiian experts like Mary Kawena Pukui, who was directed to comb the archive for *momi* (pearls [of traditional knowledge]), to provide translations of these texts, or to gather information from native-language-speaking elders.[16] However, most academics have drawn on largely English-language sources as empirical evidence to provide authoritative renderings of the Hawaiian past. Neither method gave rise to extensive engagement with Hawaiian-language textual materials; instead, "traditional"—signifying knowledge that is oral, performative, experiential, and authentic—has slowly become the antithesis of "academic," which refers to written work that is viewed by many Hawaiians as inorganic or inauthentic labor requiring lengthy engagement, reading, and interpretation. Both, incidentally, are a product of colonial processes. Dismissive or rosy assumptions about the place of tradition in relation to scholarship occlude our ability to reevaluate and work with these sources in the fullest possible way. This kind of exotism of the archives does more violence, a complacency that threatens to keep us all from studying, knowing, and analyzing these genres of intellectual production.

As a way out of this obstructive dialectic, I offer a mode of archival praxis that merges an awareness of the pedagogical (formal and disciplined training of oral intellects), the performative (speaking, hearing, explicating), and the experiential (past and ongoing interpretation of experience) *along with* acts of reading and interpreting texted historical sources. I argue here, of course, that acquiring Hawaiian 'ike from *ka wā kahiko* (ancient times) to the present required *practice*: active learning and seeking: *'a'o, 'a'apo,* and *'imi* (learning, apprehending, and seeking). Additionally this practice of hearing textual archival sources (oral-to-text) is dialogic and mutually enriching.

Studying and understanding native genres of knowledge is essential (not optional) for work with the indigenous-language archives.[17] Just as

Māori historians Arini Loader, Aroha Harris, Melissa Matutina Williams, and Nēpia Mahuika "are engaged in writing Māori histories on Māori terms using methodologies, approaches and frames that enable us to tell histories that we (that is, Māori) recognize," so too this chapter suggests a similar orientation based on Hawaiian-language texts.[18] It is past time that the archives should inform native-language reclamation programs. For the title of this chapter, I have selected a different emphasis for the archive by changing the name to *ka waihona palapala mānaleo,* or the *repository of native-speaker manuscripts.* This adjustment allows kānaka maoli to engage people's desire to hear the voices of their *kūpuna,* their ancestors and elders. This simple recasting of the archive, as not a pile of written papers composed by anonymous contributors, but primarily the words of native-language speakers, allows me to suggest in part that archival research and labor with documents and published materials should be treated as part of the continuum that drives native-language reclamation projects. Such projects, for the most part, focus on reconstituting spoken-language communities through the training of fluent speakers, emphasizing the importance of speaking indigenous languages in the home and family.

It is now possible, certainly in Hawai'i, to spur research and writing that uses native-language textual sources to enhance and enlarge our knowledge of *'ōlelo* (speech). Engaging the archive as a way to improve our speech practices would occur through the study of rhetoric and linguistic structures. It would add hundreds if not thousands of new words to our current lexicon and aid us in identifying and examining word usage, genres, and hallmarks of performative speech, song, prayer, and chant. Scholars would even be able to utilize aggregating search features on digital databases to track how language changes over time.[19] The archive should allow us as a community to move away from fetishizing the leftovers (*momi*) to engaging the abundance within which the material is also framed: context, form, genre, and other ways of seeing that have yet to be discerned.

The loss of native-speaking elders each year is alarming, but how should communities measure the importance of reading what was written and published by those who composed orally what they published and wrote, especially if many of these writers spoke Hawaiian as their first (and perhaps only) language? Euro-American historical research methods *when combined with* Hawaiian methods and approaches to classifying and interpreting words and "texts" may allow kanaka maoli to delve deeper into that kupuna-wai spring of ancestral knowledge through the words that were in many cases spoken, or chanted, and then written down for future generations.

Suggesting that print and written materials are full of the hā (living breath), and the words and voices, of kūpuna may encourage people to feel more at ease and see themselves as engaged in the project of research in the archive. Indigenous communities thirsting for their mo'olelo (history, stories) to flourish may find that this recalibration and redefinition of what the native-language archive can offer facilitates better scholarship and healing for communities.[20] This shift in thinking about the native-language archive, from viewing it as a collection of "old" documents to seeing the archive as texts whose antiquity—through oral genres' ancestral reverberations—allows them to be revered or honored, restores an essential definitional core to the documents' existence as texts that were meant to be performed, heard, and passed on. Such recalibrations aid in deconstructing the unhelpful binary that pits the fetishization of orality against the fetishization of the written word, and dissolves our tendencies to narrate relationships between haole and maoli as marked only by misrecognition and animosity.

Merging speech "ear-witnessing" with print, encouraging the praxis of hearing the archives, is an important dialogic praxis, one that the enormity of the Hawaiian-language archive allows. A lot of what was written down or published in Hawaiian in the nineteenth century began as authoritative speech: words that had gained traction as previous utterances of import; words that when repeated in different contexts resonated with and projected the power (mana) of past performance, as the words of ali'i (chiefs) that had been preserved for generations. Consider that many oral "texts" were memorized and passed down before they were ever published. In order for these to be preserved faithfully, they were organized according to conventions governing particular genres of orature, or categorized as such. These genres included mo'olelo and ka'ao (terms sometimes used interchangeably to mean "history, story, legend, or myth"), mo'okū'auhau (genealogies), many genres of oli and pule (chants and prayer), 'ōlelo no'eau (proverbs or wise sayings), kapu and kānāwai (taboo and law), and the authoritative utterances of ali'i and kahuna (priests). Even those things that were composed after the introduction of the palapala (reading and writing)—new histories, stories, chants, and prayers—were still produced in relation to a set of normative ideas loosely governing Hawaiian intellectual and spiritual production, still had to sound to an orally "literate" community of readers like material that responded to the conventions present in particular genres.[21]

These sources allow scholars to pay particular attention to how the native communities of the past engaged in their own intellectual, cultural, and spiritual (re)production. The significance of this argument about identifying speech in print gives rise to recognition of another dialogic practice: Hawaiians were keepers of history even before the advent of literacy; Hawaiian history was kept orally, and much of it was eventually reproduced in written or published form. To write histories of the nineteenth and twentieth centuries, which necessarily concern the motivations of native actors and agents, historians need to become cognizant of Hawaiian narrativizations of the past in their own presents. Much of this scripted history is and shall remain untranslated, unprocessed primary-source material ma ka ʻōlelo Hawaiʻi. While this is true of the sources one might encounter in any archive, it turns out that native-language archives are especially rhetorically complex, presently requiring of scholars more analysis and intellectual engagement and a healthy vigilance against pressures to work from nostalgic romanticism. In addition, native-language archives still are at risk of being marginalized or ignored, as part of their fluctuating status in the long and multiperspectival histories of colonialism and imperialism. Our work as scholars needs to facilitate the movement of native-language sources off the homestead and reservation, out of the category of traditional knowledge and into the mainstream as "evidence." And historians must become used to utilizing these sources to write colonial, imperial, and national history. Obviously, this is a practice open to native and nonnative scholars alike.

AN INVITATION TO THE WORK

Kūnihi ka mauna, "steep stands the mountain," is a metaphor for the challenges that lie before a novice calling out for entrance or acceptance into a school of knowledge.[22] The *mele kāhea*, or entrance chant, is perhaps the most ubiquitous chant of its genre employed by *hula* students when asking to be let in to the *hālau* (school) prior to class. In its ubiquity are multiple messages: about what lies in plain sight, what remains hidden, and the knowledge that it takes to engage with and understand the information that is under study, and perhaps to enable it to be assimilated in a proper and disciplined fashion. Seeking entrance into a school is also seeking entrance into a world of plenty. The reiteration of *wai* (water) in different place-names—Waiʻaleʻale, Wailua, Kawaikini—points to this symbolic land beyond the threshold, which exists once students submit themselves to the discipline of learning from a *kumu* (teacher), kahuna, or other acknowledged expert.

According to Kaliʻi Reichel, a *Kumu Hula* (hula expert and teacher), "the student is looking in. It is dry and dusty where they are. They look beyond and want to enter into this place (hālau) that is rich and abundant with foundational knowledge."[23] Were scholars to delve into the history of the dissemination of this chant over time, and the changing venues of its performance and interpretation, they would also see that knowledge and the *waiwai* (richness) that is important always seek and find tributaries where they can flow. In a Hawaiian context—moving between past and present fluidly is more fitting for marking the passage of time—this movement is *relational* and predicated on maintaining continued communication with ancestors rather than being a unidirectional and forward movement. *Progress* is marked not by a unidirectional blind forward but through purposeful flow between past and present as a way to shape futures, like navigators fishing unseen islands up over horizons. If the Hawaiian saying, *I ka wā ma mua, ka wā ma hope*, "in the past the future," provides us a clue to Hawaiian historical practice, it also suggests a different orientation to time and progress, an understanding, a praxis that needs to operate as part of the interpretive toolbox historians utilize when thinking through and with Hawaiian sources.

This part of the chapter provides a general overview of the sources that make up the vast, unsounded depths of Hawaiian archival and print materials. In so doing it seeks to provide tantalizing flashes from those deeps that suggest moments of Hawaiian engagement with texts during the period of colonial settlement in the nineteenth century—and the ways in which aural/oral pedagogical standards of knowledge keeping and creation elided into print and written forms in order to further webs of dissemination, particularly through Hawaiian-language nūpepa. There are numerous stories that circulated about Hawaiians reading newspapers aloud, while listeners who had the facility would commit the material to memory and convey the printed material orally to a wider community. Print was utilized by already existing networks of formally disciplined and fluent Hawaiian-language speakers, and the spread of reading and writing did not reflexively extinguish aural/oral practices of knowledge keeping and dissemination. The unprecedented size of the Hawaiian archive offers scholars the ability to closely study conceptual frameworks, from which they can reconstruct methods and approaches for multiple schools of knowledge, including history, to a large extent from Hawaiian ontological and epistemological foundations of knowledge.[24]

This chapter offers an invitation to study, to reach the wai lands that can provide much intellectual sustenance beyond old attitudinal barriers and a beleaguered historiography. I ka wā ma mua, ka wā ma hope: while this chapter looks into the past, its final objective is to suggest the possibility of exciting future work. The Hawaiian source base challenges the idea of source scarcity. In many native territories settled and planted by colonists, language eradication was a by-product, if not an outright objective, of the actions of colonial administrators, ministers, missionaries, teachers, and settlers. Given these conditions, along with the commonplace mass deaths from diseases that were unleashed in the wake of settlement, learned people from many communities were lost, and entire histories, genealogies, songs, prayers, dances, and practices also disappeared with their passing.

Because of the relatively late Euro-American settlement of the Hawaiian Islands with the planting of the American mission in 1820, Hawai'i was spared what could potentially have been four or five centuries of colonization, as experienced by peoples on the edges of the Pacific and in North and South America. Though similarly devastating on many fronts, colonialism in Hawai'i did not yield the same level of totalizing disappearance of language and culture that it did in other cherished home places. In fact, Hawai'i's late emergence into the Euro-American world of colonial and imperial contest spared much of the people's knowledge and "traditions."

The thirst for literacy among Hawaiians was built on a long-established and strong intellectual tradition, coinciding with the end of formal public instruction in priestly schools of knowledge under kapu in 1819. The first generation of Hawaiian writers and historians was also the last trained as kahuna and as *kahu*, chiefly attendants who served ali'i under kapu in capacities related to governance, such as religious ceremonies and war. Because the ali'i sent their own trained intellectuals to learn the technology of the palapala, this allowed for some of the chiefly and priestly knowledge of genealogy, ceremony, and *mo'o 'ōlelo* (history) to pass into writing.[25] Still-robust Hawaiian oral intellectual traditions maintained among the general population also informed literary and print ambitions throughout the archipelago during the nineteenth and twentieth centuries, resulting in the richness of the Hawaiian-language archive that remains today.

The Congregational missionaries who settled in the Hawaiian archipelago in 1820 were from the Boston-based American Board of Commissioners for Foreign Missions, whose belief that people must be evangelized in the vernacular, ma ka 'ōlelo Hawai'i, meant that these missionaries were expected to become fluent in Hawaiian in order to fulfill their mission.[26] The Hawaiian language was not simply a node that was pressured in processes of cultural colonization, used to humiliate people who exclusively spoke a language that belied un-Christian and "backwards" ideas. Instead, the language became the very conveyer of the introduced colonial ideologies and belief systems, all the more powerful because enough missionaries gained deep proficiency in Hawaiian. The texts they wrote and translated thus communicated to kānaka on a deeper level by capitalizing on the resonances already prevalent in the mother tongue. Missionaries were not the only ones engaged in this work, since Hawaiian intellectuals who became early converts to Christianity along with their aliʻi also were earnestly engaged in the project to Christianize and civilize their own people.[27]

The Hawaiian language was the primary medium of educational instruction in the islands until 1894, while Hawaiian-language newspapers (there were over a hundred nūpepa titles) were published in the islands from 1834 to 1948. The longest-running Hawaiian-language nūpepa, *Ka Nupepa Kuokoa* (The independent newspaper), enjoyed a run of sixty-six years. This newspaper was patterned after American newspapers of the time: it was four pages long, double sided and frequently printed with six columns to a page; its large pages (almost 600 by 240 millimeters) meant that one issue was the equivalent of twelve standard pages of modern newspaper print.[28]

Information published in Hawaiian nūpepa ranged from government notices to advertisements, domestic and foreign news, the republication of speeches and new laws, notices of meetings, various church news and proselytizing, the arrival and departure of ships, general notices of probate, and notices about stray and found animals. Moʻolelo and kaʻao were written by learned and knowledgeable Hawaiians and serialized in the newspapers, along with *mele* (songs) and chants submitted by members of the public. People also wrote to the nūpepa to dispute traditional knowledge that was published in their pages, and debates flared about all manner of topics, from taxes, to farming and immigration policies, to the unjust actions of *konohiki* (land managers) and aliʻi. Public criticism arrived in the form of stinging prose, songs, and chants. In the nūpepa, all were made available for public consumption.

The nūpepa knitted together an archipelagic kānaka maoli world, introducing new modes of sociability, a sense of nationalism not necessarily predicated on maoli genealogies, and citizenship, which sat alongside older modes of *aloha aliʻi* (honoring the chiefs, and chiefly regard for people) and the mana of the aliʻi.[29] These attributes gained little purchase in nineteenth-century Euro-American constructions of power and politics, and therefore have been cast aside by scholars writing about governance and the Hawaiian Kingdom. Tracking back and forth between the Hawaiian- and English-language newspapers takes the labor of translating cognitive categories, where politics and law, ethics, and calling upon the past are dependent on the scholars' fluency in multiple languages, historical traditions, and thought worlds.

Along with nūpepa, books, and manuscripts, historians interested in writing about Hawaiʻi and its place in the world, Euro-American settlers in the islands, and the contestations of empires, along with the rise of American power in the Pacific, will have to contend with the many laws, treaties, and constitutions that were published by the Kingdom of Hawaiʻi (1840–93), as well as the voluminous records of the Hawaiian Courts, which were recorded in Hawaiian and English.[30] Though four Hawaiian Constitutions were promulgated in the nineteenth century, including the 1839 Declaration of Rights and the 1840 Constitution and Laws that inaugurated the Hawaiian Kingdom, not one book has been written to illuminate even one of these documents. There are also legislative records and minutes, the correspondence and records of all branches of government and their officials, and the records of special departments like the Department of Health, whose minutes and correspondence were kept in English and Hawaiian and also published in Hawaiian- and English-language newspapers of the time. Hawaiians also generated their own personal records in the form of letters, journals, handwritten books of genealogy, chants, songs, and history—papers that fill archives, libraries, and private family collections all across the archipelago.

The rest of this chapter will provide examples of ways of reading and thinking about Hawaiian history that necessitate the introduction of new methods and approaches, with source abundance assumed as a starting point. Some may categorize Hawaiʻi as a significant place (in the United States) that provides an exception to the "lack of sources." However, the Hawaiian-language source base (and others like it) can assist scholars in writing history because it provides materials that will contest normative assumptions about how to construct the category "native," what it means to govern a modern native state in a world of colonial and imperial contest, and how to do research in language archives with an emphasis on place and people in ways that have yet to be studied in depth.[31]

Many genres of Hawaiian oral literature were shared publicly through the Hawaiian-language nūpepa. The *mele kanikau*, Hawaiian grief chants, which gained significance over the course of the nineteenth century, comprise the largest genre of Hawaiian auto-representation to fill the nūpepa. The chants were traditionally chanted to honor the deceased and send the soul on its final journey to dwell with the ancestors. Certainly hundreds, if not a thousand or more of these chants, were published in nūpepa, composed by men and women of all different stations, ages, and backgrounds. Some were as brief as twelve lines while others were three hundred lines or more, composed by a single author. Sometimes chants were serialized owing to space restrictions and their extreme length. The kanikau present scholars with an important poetic form whose study will yield information on the

Hawaiian language and aesthetic practices, and supply important details of Hawaiian life, including biographical information about individuals, such as genealogies, shared relationships to homeland, and birth and death data, with insight into what was important to know and commemorate in the *world* of Hawaiian people.[32]

A kanikau was composed for the high chief and Kuhina Nui (Premier), Ka'ahumanu, the much-vaunted favorite wife of Kamehameha I, by one of her counselors, Davida Malo. "He Kanikau no Ka'ahumanu" first appeared in *Ka Lama Hawaii* on 8 August 1834. The chant was republished several times over the course of the nineteenth century for the beauty and complexity of its expression.[33] Subsequent composers may have reused some of the phrases and lines of Malo's chant, elevating their own compositions and perhaps poetic prowess through intertextual reference to Malo's "original" chant for Ka'ahumanu.[34] Or perhaps the stock phrases that scholars might attribute to Malo's chant actually belong to the class of chants composed strictly for ali'i.[35]

The kanikau begins with the movement of the chief's spirit departing the world:

> Mihalanaau i kuakahiki ka newa 'ana
> Ke kaha 'ana ka leina aku nei liuliu
> Liua paia aku nei kuanalia
> I analipo i analio
> Lilo aku ia i ka paiakuakane
> I ke ala muku ma'awe 'ula [a] Kanaloa
> Ke'ehi kūani akulā ka hele 'ana
> E malolokihakahakuleiohua
> Ke li'i kuluhi'olani 'aui newa aku nei
> I lele aku na i ke kōhi 'ana o ka pawa
> I ke anohia kohikohi 'ana o ka pō
> Ka lilo ane' ia;

> To pass out of sight on the path of the sun
> Coursing between the Tropic of Cancer northward
> And to the Tropic of Capricorn southward,
> The stance of the chief tramples like that of the sun,
> chief at the zenith (descending) from those since the time
>   of Hua
> (When she) ascends at the parting light of dawn,
> In the quiet time that parts night from day.
> When there (she) went beyond (our) sight.[36]

The formal language employed in many laments for ali'i belongs to sacred ritual, ceremonial rites performed after the death of a chief. The kanikau may be categorized as a form of traditional mele, and as literature, but they can also be used as evidence by historians about the construction of Hawaiian governing power. Scholars writing about the role of ali'i like Ka'ahumanu might not reflexively consider chants like kanikau as sources that relate information like this, largely because chants of this nature have not been traditionally viewed by historians as evidence. Privileging eyewitness prose accounts in English, historians have often left such literature for folklorists, language experts, and literary and religious scholars to examine. This kind of work focus requires training in *kaona* (metaphors, multiplicity of meanings) and Hawaiian poetry, a fluency that exceeds basic linguistic competency. Scholars can better interpret a source like the kanikau if they become familiar with the metaphors and oral formulaic language that dominate the genre.[37]

Finally, perhaps one of the most striking features of the kanikau is the extensive listing of place-names and wind and rain names, including famed places and those of fond remembrance that hold the memory of relationships that the living shared with the deceased and that were mourned.[38] The chant for Timoteo Ha'alilio, an ali'i and Hawaiian envoy who died on his return from a diplomatic journey in 1842, was published in *Ka Elele Hawai'i* on 10 May 1845. The kanikau provides a beautiful example of this kind of *helu* (listing) of Hawaiian place-names and wind and rain names that was a hallmark of this chant genre:

> Aloha ka limu kā kanaka o Mahamoku.
> Aloha ka lehua o Mokaulele.
> Aloha nā kō a ka 'A'alahina i ka pali.
> Aloha ka maile lau li'i 'o Ko'iahi.
> Aloha o Kanepūniu i ka wela a ka lā.
> Aloha ka uluhala o Kahuku i ka paia e ke onaona
> Aloha ka 'āhihi o Nu'uanu i ka welu hau.
> Aloha ka makani kūkalahale o Honolulu.
> Aloha o Pana'ewanui moku lehua . . .

> Farewell to the man striking limu of Mahamoku.
> Farewell to the lehua of Mokaulele.
> Farewell to the gusts that sweep the 'A'Alahina on the cliffs.
> Farewell to the dainty-leafed maile of Ko'iahi.
> Farewell Kānepūniu in the heat of the sun.
> Farewell to the hala groves of Kahuku, hedged in with fragrance.
> Farewell to the 'āhihi of Nu'uanu amid the draping hau.

Farewell to the Kūkalahale wind of Honolulu.

Farewell to great Panaʻewa, of the lehua groves . . .

Many of these places and the names attached to them have only recently been forgotten. The kanikau are a place repository, which when used in tandem with GIS technology, maps, and other archival materials can provide a way for Hawaiians to reacquaint themselves with their home places.[39] Kanikau serve as a memorial marking Hawaiian claims of relationship to ʻāina, evidence of the connection between the life of the land and its people.

Operationalizing the archives can be achieved through the application of this ear-witnessing technique in relation to archival sources. Nūpepa were sites where kānaka maoli writers, kupa (people born, descended from, and living in a place) of different communities on different islands, could present their views on important issues facing the kingdom. In 1873 an important question raised by haole plantation owners was whether or not the Kingdom of Hawaiʻi should enter into a treaty of reciprocity with the United States. Americans and naturalized descendants of Americans who were now citizens of the Hawaiian Kingdom sought a treaty in order to get sugar and other products into American markets free of duty. If one were to look only at the English-language source materials available on the subject, a very different picture emerges, one that is more focused on the gaining of reciprocity in exchange for the cession of Hawaiian territory, specifically of Puʻuloa (known more famously as Pearl Harbor).[40] Such a cession was also another way to deepen relations between the two nations in a way that would further emergent power imbalances in the United States' favor.

Many Hawaiians repudiated the idea of ceding Hawaiian territory to the United States. In numerous essays and articles Hawaiian writers from across the archipelago presented their arguments for and against reciprocity. This portion of the chapter focuses on some of the untranslated published materials written by those against the treaty because they perceived Puʻuloa— its oceanways, history, and lands—as something that should be inalienable from the *lāhui* (people, citizenry, nation) in perpetuity. One writer, Napoliana, wrote an earnest letter to the editor registering his surprise that his name had been published in a petition in favor of ceding Puʻuloa to the United States, "in order to get the Reciprocity treaty." The gentleman vehemently denied being in favor of the treaty:

Ke haʻi aku nei au i ka ʻoiaʻiʻo, ʻaʻole loa au i kākau inoa ma ia palapala, a ke haʻi aku nei au ʻaʻole loa au e ʻae e hāʻawi i kahi lihi o koʻu ʻāina hānau i mea e loaʻa mai ai ka pōmaikai no ka haole mahi kō, A ʻaʻole nō au e manaʻoʻiʻo

'ana e 'ae ana [i] kekahi kanaka Hawai'i e hā'awi i ke awa o 'Ewa i mea e
loa'a mai ai ka pōmaika'i no ka po'e 'u'uku me ke akaka nō iā ia 'a'ohe wā
e ho'iho'i hou 'ia mai ai iā ia, a i kana poe mamo mahope ona ua wahi lā.[41]

I speak the truth, that I absolutely did not sign my name on that document. And I firmly decree that I will not agree to give one slight piece
of the land of my birth as a means of acquiring profit for the haole sugar
planters, and I truly do not believe that any kanaka Hawai'i would assent
to giving the harbor of 'Ewa as a means to obtain benefits for so few
people, when it is clear to him that at no time will it be restored to him
and to his descendants after him.

Napoliana's letter is one of many that provided reasons for kānaka maoli to not
cede the bays of Pu'uloa to the United States, in an exchange that was viewed
as decidedly not reciprocal. As Americans of the time came to value freedom
and liberty so much that these values helped to fuel a civil war, so too Hawaiians had an aloha for the 'āina and 'āina hānau (birth land) that could not be
easily translated into Euro-American ideas of patriotism. But how can one historicize these important concepts when the source materials in Hawaiian have
not been engaged and interpreted, when scholars cannot discern the Hawaiian
oral rhetorical flourishes that stand apart from the printed page, or the dialogic
interplay between this and other Hawaiian performative textual materials?

Scholars who cannot read or interpret Hawaiian will not know that writers from all over the archipelago sent their critiques and protests about the
cession to be published in the nūpepa. Prior to nūpepa, people registered
particular concern for what was going on in their own home place; the chant
composed by D. A. Kekuakahili of Wahiawa, Kaua'i, "He Inoa no Kipe" (A
chant for bribery), is a great example of how mele were becoming a commonplace and effective means of promoting activism and mobilizing political action across the archipelago among kānaka maoli and foreigners who
were fluent speakers of Hawaiian in the kingdom. The chant begins coyly:

> 'Auhea wale 'oe ka 'ano'i lae-a
> Ka lei 'ilima a ke aloha lae-a
> He aloha e ka ua punohu lae-a
> Ko'iawe mai la i kanahele lae-a
> He lohe 'ōlelo mai ko'u lae-a
> Ka makani leo nui a ke kiu lae-a . . .

> Where are you / listen oh desire of my heart-lā 'eā
> The beloved ilima lei-lā 'eā

Cherished is the red mist rising on the sea-lā 'eā
The lightly showering rain in the forest-lā 'eā
I hear it speaking to me-lā 'eā
The loud blowing of the Kiu (spying) wind-lā'eā

The kaona embedded in words and figures like the 'ilima blossom in the chant are allusions to the beloved island of O'ahu. Later allusions are to the composer's home island of Kaua'i, and the voice (wind) of the people is expressed steadfastly in unity. The composer makes an aesthetically satisfying point that the reciprocity treaty will not benefit the common Hawaiian people while nourishing those who are elevated in society:

Ho'okahi waiwai a ke aloha lae-a
A ka mana'o e hana nei lae-a
Hana 'ole ka ua i ke pili lae-a
Ma'ū ka liko o ka lehua-lae-a
'Auhea 'oe e ka 'i'iwi-lae-a
E ke kahuli leo nahenahe-lae-a
Ho'i mai kāua e pili lae-a

There is only one prize bestowed by aloha-lā 'eā
of the ever-active mind lā 'eā
The rain does not fall on the pili grass lā 'eā[42]
but dampens/refreshes the buds of the lehua lā 'eā[43]
Where are you / heed me oh *'i'iwi* bird lā 'eā[44]
O sweet voiced kāhuli lā 'eā[45]
Let us become close again lā 'eā

The chant then takes a poignant turn when the composer imagines:

Ha'aheo ka ua i ke pili lae-a
Ke noe a'ela i ke kula lae-a
Hea mai ē ke ao Nāulu lae-a
"Ulu mai ke aloha a nui" lae-a
Kaumaha lu'ulu'u i ke kino lae-a . . .

The rain cherishes the pili (grass) lā 'eā
While it gently spreads over the country lā 'eā
The Nāulu (showering clouds) call out lā 'eā
Aloha is growing to its fullest extent lā 'eā
the body is bowed down with weight lā 'eā[46]

He communicates his contribution to the discussion about greed and the reciprocity treaty:

> Ua kuhi au ua holo pono lae-a
> Ka manaʻo paʻa e pua rose lae-a
> Ua komo hewa ʻia e ka uʻa lae-a
> Na rumi kapu o ia ʻona lae-a
> Aʻu i hoʻomalu ai e malu lae-a
> Ma ka ʻaha kōmike liʻiliʻi lae-a
> Haʻina ka inoa i lohe lae-a
> Kipe ka pua i ʻoi aʻe lae-a
>
> I have thought all had gone well-lā ʻeā
> full of certainty, oh my rosebud lā ʻeā
> futility improperly barged into lā ʻeā
> The off-limits chambers of that owner lā ʻeā
> where I sat in sole charge lā ʻeā
> of the small committee that I chaired lā ʻeā
> Tell the name that has been heard lā ʻeā
> Bribery, the finest of flowers lā ʻeā[47]

In Hawaiian discourse, chants played an important role in conveying critical ideas, which could, however, be hidden from those not fluent in the highly figurative language of kaona with which such chants were imbued. Whatever the threshold of literacy among Hawaiian readers, certainly the refrain of the chant "He Inoa no Kipe" was clear, driving home one important commentary on the entire negotiating process: those implicated in brokering the process and carrying it out were simply labeled by Mr. Kekuakahili as *lae-a*, or liars.

Samuel Manaiākalani Kamakau, a kanaka writer, historian, and cultural critic, relished healthy criticism.[48] By 1873 Kamakau had made quite a name for himself as a writer, a representative in the legislature, and a judge. A skilled Hawaiian rhetorician, he weighed in on the issue of reciprocity in a critical essay entitled "Huikau, Pohihihi ke Kuikahi Panai Like me Ka Uku Kaulele o Puuloa" (The haphazard, entangling treaty of reciprocity and the payment added of Puʻuloa). In Hawaiian the title builds momentum by engaging the aural/oral faculties of the reader.

In the title the words *Hui, hihihi, Kui,* and *Like* are attention grabbing because aesthetically they are pleasantly teasing when sounded on the ear, illustrating that the art of print persuasion still relied heavily on Hawaiian oratorical forms, more than fifty years after formal literacy was introduced by missionaries. The essay began by employing a helu calling to experts and posing a rhetorical question to the virtual gathering:

E ka poʻe kālai Papahulihonua, kālai Aupuni, Kālai ʻĀina, Kuhikuhi Puʻuone, a i ka poʻe Kilo-honua, a me ka poʻe Kilo-lani, e noʻonoʻo pū mai kākou i ke kālai i ka ʻōlelo e hāʻawi lilo loa i ke kūʻai ʻana i ke awa o Puʻuloa a me ka mokuʻāina o Ewa, e like me ka nune ʻōlelo a nā malihini a me ka poʻe ʻōpiopio o kēia mau la pokeʻo. He pōmaikaʻi ʻiʻo anei? He ʻawahia paha ka hope?[49]

Oh those who are knowledgeable in geology, government experts, politics, architects, and those seers of earth, and the people who navigate by stars, let us look at this expertise in words (sophistry) that proposes to once and for all sell off Pearl Harbor and the district of ʻEwa, as a result of the speculative discussions proposed by newcomers and the young people of these puerile times. Is this really to our benefit? Will the result not be bitter?

Kamakau went on to recount the many moments since 1791 when various aliʻi were faced with the "opportunity" to sell portions of the shoreline to foreigners seeking to buy parcels of land and the rights to the ocean depths fronting these areas. Producing similar moments from the Hawaiian past, Kamakau presented his argument in the nūpepa as a chiefly counselor might have presented *oral evidentiary arguments* before an ʻaha aliʻi (chiefly council).[50] Kamakau asked what the government's responsibility was in relation to the lands and bays of Puʻuloa, and he then laid out eight statements and questions culminating in this warning:

ʻAʻole i kūʻai aku ke au o nā Kamehameha i hala ʻā akula i ka make i kekahi lihi i kekahi ʻāpana ʻāina i ʻaʻahu lole ai kēia lāhui. Aia ma ka waha o ka mea hoʻokahi ke ola a me ka make o ka lāhui, a me ka make o ke aupuni, he hāmau ʻo ia i ka leo o kona lāhui ponoʻī.[51]

Not one edge, not one portion of land that clothed this nation was sold during the time of the Kamehamehas who have passed on in death. The life and death of the Hawaiian people and the kingdom are in the mouth of one, he is silencing the voice of his own people.

Kamakau recalled past history when he reminded readers that under the long rule of the Kamehameha aliʻi, lands were not sold. By evoking the *ʻōlelo noʻeau* (proverb) "i ka ʻōlelo nō ke ola, i ka ʻōlelo nō ka make" (In speech there is life, in speech death), he perhaps joined traditional ideas about the power of chiefly speech to grant life or death with more modern sensibilities about representative government. According to Kamakau, by not heeding the voice of the people, the king was perhaps directing the people and government toward destruction. Authoritative speech was a significant feature of Hawaiian government. Scholars hoping to write histories of Hawai'i need to be trained in multiple Hawaiian oral genres in order to be able to hear the archives as they read them, so that they can render an interpretation legible by applying Hawaiian methods and approaches.

———

I hope this chapter has not fallen on deaf ears, in making appreciable the continued importance of orality to kānaka maoli living and writing in the nineteenth-century Hawaiian Kingdom. Operationalizing special methodologies for texts based in orality and the pedagogies used to train Hawaiian aural/oral intellects will make it possible to historicize important historical kānaka maoli values and concepts like aloha 'āina, and help us come to terms with a robust sense of what maoli or indigeneity means through the sources left to us in the archive, rather than applying imprecise generic terms to native history in ways that are not contextually consistent with the Hawaiian oral and textual past.

What are the implications for the interpretive strategies I have proposed for engaging ka waihona palapala mānaleo? Crafting these interventions out of the sources and the contexts in which they were produced is necessary if better histories of colonial and imperial settlement are to be written, and the "progressive" rise of settler nations complicated. The writing of "native history" cannot be separated from the construction of histories of colonialism and the nation, and cannot be divorced from the way the materiality of the archive, its ink and print and paper, has over time disappeared. In the Pacific, languages that are given primacy and that have been normalized as "native," as the commonplace languages that history speaks in scholarly discourse, are and continue to be those of the colonizers: English, French, German, and Spanish.

The Hawaiian-language archive can also offer methods for research that might find application in other indigenous communities where archives may not be as voluminous but are nonetheless significant. Finally, there is a growing number of maoli and haole scholars working in Hawaiian-language archives whose work contributes to this future paradigm shift.[52]

This chapter has shown that oral formulaics were commonplace in print and written documents well into the late nineteenth century, and scholars must consider the challenge of writing native history as a methodological problem, not one of identity. The Hawaiian-language archive of print and written documents can assist scholars in developing new methods for interpreting and reading native-language sources, operationalizing the archive, and rewriting the history of settler-maoli encounters. While Hawai'i continues to labor under the introduced idea of "paradise," and therefore cannot be a serious source of cultural production on a global scale, it is well past time to engage the sources and recognize that Hawaiian-language materials can reflect, and have always reflected, a rich intellectual, literary, historical, and cultural production.

After students seeking entrance to the hālau have completed the chant "Kūnihi ka Mauna," they wait in anticipation of the voice of their kumu in response accepting them and inviting them to come in. The kumu chants:

> E hea i ke kanaka e komo ma loko
> E hānai ai a hewa ka waha
> Eia nō ka uku la o ka leo
> A he leo wale nō e.

> Call out to the person to enter
> Wherein to nourish until sated
> Here is the payment: the voice
> Merely the voice.

Voice has always played an important role in the transmission of Hawaiian knowledge. Oral forms infused in writing and print can be discerned by the trained scholar. The invitation to engage in the work of research in the Hawaiian-language archives is one that nourishes, until, *hewa ka waha*, the mouth has been so filled that it can take no more. What will it mean to do research in indigenous-language materials in a time of plenty? Only time spent working with the archives will tell.

NOTES

Mahalo to Dr. Adria Imada, Dr. Keola Donaghy, Matthew Uiagalelei, and Chad Hashimoto for assisting with editorial feedback and much-appreciated conversations about this piece. Thanks to the McNeil Center for Early American Studies, the Mellon-Sawyer Seminar on Race Across Space and Time, and the Woodrow Wilson National Fellowship for providing this work with support.

1. In referring to archives here, I make reference to all materials handwritten, published, or recorded in Hawaiian.

2. Several American historians have created innovative methods for writing native history where native-language sources were seen as scarce: Lepore, *In the Name of War*; Richter, *Facing East from Indian Country*; and Demos, *The Unredeemed Captive*.

3. A future essay might focus on how proof and evidence in Hawaiian arise from a different recognition of authority—while the historiography focusing on the written word privileges eyewitness accounts, Hawaiian intellectuals with trained faculties in listening, memorizing, and performance secured the veracity of an orally reproduced "text" through years of training, the teachers or experts who trained them, and those to whom they dispensed knowledge. In Hawaiian evidence of the "ear-witnessed" variety and genealogies of knowledge took precedence over what was "eye-witnessed." Misrecognizing this distinction may cause some scholars to dismiss Hawaiian-language material because they are not cognizant of how to secure the "truth" of any oral-to-text source and how to utilize such material as empirical evidence.

4. Emmanuel Kasarhérou, quoted in Bensa and Muckle, this volume.

5. Nogelmeier, *Mai Pa'a i ka Leo*, 1. "I [Nogelmeier] use the term discourse of sufficiency to describe this long-standing recognition and acceptance of a small selection of Hawaiian writings from the 19th century as being sufficient to embody nearly a hundred years of extensive Hawaiian auto-representation—Hawaiians writing for and about themselves." What Nogelmeier does not mention is that many haole writers also wrote in Hawaiian in the *nūpepa* (newspapers): they composed songs and wrote books, letters, and manuscripts, especially those individuals employed in government or the church. Hawaiian-language materials therefore are not simply a product or reflection of Hawaiian writers. It is possible to construct robust accounts of haole subjectivities through reports provided by Hawaiian writers in a reversal of normal scholarly practice: the "other" (haole) produced strictly through "foreign" (*kānaka*) accounts.

6. All the major and minor synthesis histories on Hawai'i, which are oft quoted, were written without the use of sources from the untranslated Hawaiian-language archive; see, for example, the works of Gavan Daws, A. Grove Day, Lawrence Fuchs, Arrell Morgan Gibson, Edward Joesting, Ralph Kuykendall, and, more recently, Stuart Banner, Sally Engle Merry, and Gary Y. Okihiro. Popular histories and works of literature also conform to this trend; see also the work of James L. Haley, James A. Michener, Susanna Moore, Julia Flynn Siler, and Sarah Vowell.

7. Marshall Sahlins's *How "Natives" Think: About Captain Cook, for Example*, Greg Dening's *History's Anthropology: The Death of William Gooch*, and Patrick Vinton Kirch's books *A Shark Going Inland Is My Chief: The Island Civilization of Ancient Hawaii* and *How Chiefs Became Kings: Divine Kingship and the Rise of Archaic States in Ancient Hawai'i*, provide quite recent yet fairly typical examples of scholars explaining Hawaiian governance after having consulted a few standard texts translated from Hawaiian, or drawing on those that were simply written in English.

8. I say "citizens" because Hawaiian people were not the only ones who spoke Hawaiian as a first language or were citizens of the Hawaiian Kingdom. *Laws of the*

Republic of Hawaii Passed by the Legislature at Its Session, 1896 (Honolulu: Hawaiian Gazette Company's Print, 1896), 191.

9. It should be noted that some writers assert that school superintendents and teachers who pursued a Hawaiian-language-first program of instruction were, by 1866, actively replaced by the king, Kamehameha V, who demanded that "English language should be taught, as best adapted to the future requirements of the people." Kamaaina, "Comments on Mr. Gulick's Lecture on the Sandwich Islands, by a Resident," *Hawaiian Gazette* (Honolulu), 24 March 1866, from the *New York Herald*, 9 January 1866.

10. "Haiolelo a ka Moi imua o ka Ahaolelo o 1862," *Ka Nupepa Kuokoa*, 3 May 1862, 2.

11. "Kapu ka Olelo Hawaii ma Lahainaluna," *Ka Nupepa Kuokoa*, 7 March 1868. Of course, this last observation can be made of any and all languages, that language serves as a transmitter of knowledge and as constitutive of reality.

12. John Charlot has written the most comprehensive work on the education of Hawaiians. See Charlot, *Classical Hawaiian Education*. See also Mary Kawena Pukui's large body of work on the subject.

13. *'Āina* means "land or that which feeds," *one hānau* means "birth sands," *kulāiwi* means "plain of bones, or homeland," *kua 'āina* means "backbone of the land, people dwelling in the country," *pua* means "flower, offspring," and kupa means "sprout, offspring, native of a particular place, citizen." This is just a short list of terms that equate people living or buried in a particular place with land. This cursory list could be greatly expanded. As I explain in this chapter, the concept of "first peoples" is nonsensical in Hawai'i simply because there are no texts that might be mobilized to fulfill the question of who landed first—this makes sense since the islands that kānaka maoli inhabit are in an archipelago. Unlike Māori, Hawaiians have not retained any *waka* (canoe) or *iwi* distinctions, if they ever had such categories. (*Iwi* "often refers to a large group of people descended from a common ancestor and associated with a distinct territory"; *Te Aka Māori-English, English-Māori Dictionary*, accessed 9 January 2020, https://maoridictionary.co.nz /.) *Koihonua*, chants of emergence and genealogy, which were necessarily ideological and "authorizing" texts that imparted mana to descendants of particular lineages, were not crafted in response to such a concern. Trying to determine who is "first" seems also to prepare "peoples" for discussions concerning ownership of lands, achieving a cognitive conversion of 'āina into property. Also, while there are many terms for the Hawaiian people in Hawaiian, the most generic and prevalent, *kānaka maoli*, has nothing to do with the English term *first people*. Clearly, language structures relations in important ways in different contexts. The appellation *first people* is a misapplication in the Hawaiian context and should not be used as a synonym for *native*.

14. Hawai'i has one of the largest and most successful language reclamation programs in the United States. Hawaiian language reclamation programs serve as a model for many indigenous language reclamation programs worldwide and has in the past twenty-five years secured an educational corridor of language immersion from

preschool and kindergarten through doctoral studies. Universities and colleges on every island offer courses with Hawaiian as the medium of instruction, which means that finding the funding to travel to the fiftieth state and enroll in coursework is the largest obstacle to obtaining fluency facing scholars today.

15. I highlight the nation here as a unit of study, since it is almost always the first mode and impetus behind why history is produced. The first historical synthesis and last comprehensive work on Hawaii's history in the nineteenth and twentieth centuries is Ralph Kuykendall's three-volume work *The Hawaiian Kingdom*. Kuykendall was hired by the Territory of Hawaiʻi to write a history that would provide a serviceable past for their presents and legitimatize the American extraterritorial presence. The limitations of the work were many: its assumption of "progress," the emphasis placed on "great" (white) men, and its dogged focus on political and economic developments mark it as a product of its time. For the purposes of this chapter, however, that Kuykendall could not read or speak Hawaiian meant that the Hawaiian archive was not available for his perusal, save those few sources translated into English. There is no historical synthesis *to date* that incorporates previously untranslated Hawaiian-language source materials in a consistent fashion in its construction.

16. Future scholarship should focus on the many works and research and translation projects by Hawaiian female scholars and trained experts like Leialoha Apo-Perkins, Frances Frazier, Rubellite Kawena Johnson, Edith Kawelohea McKinzie, Esther Moʻokini, Emma Nakuina, Patience Nāmaka-Bacon, and Mary Kawena Pukui.

17. More in-depth research can be conducted on the categories into which Hawaiian knowledges were divided. Rather than classifying Hawaiian texts into categories according to the territories identified by Euro-American academic disciplines or schools of knowledge—religion, politics, history, literature, and music, for example—Hawaiian textual materials should be understood as being shaped by the ontological and epistemological frameworks of those who composed, spoke, and produced these materials originally.

18. See Loader's chapter in this volume.

19. For digitized Hawaiian-language nūpepa and other resources in Hawaiian, see the Hawaiian Electronic Library, Ulukau, accessed 3 April 2018, www.ulukau .org; and Papakilo Database, accessed 3 April 2018, www.papakilodatabase.com.

20. In writing this, I am thinking specifically about language reclamation and revitalization projects in Wampanoag, Pequot, Ojibwe, Oneida, Cherokee, and Māori, which I have become familiar with either through the efforts of friends and colleagues or through institutions.

21. Hearing the archive is a practice that can be applied to the writings of missionaries in Hawaiʻi, who, like kānaka maoli, privileged the mana of the spoken word and the word of God. Scholars seeking to work in these sources need to be trained to fluency, however. I do not use the term *fluency* to refer to issues of grammar, vocabulary, or syntax but instead am concerned with making clear to historians that they also need to be attentive to the rules that govern Hawaiian authorita-

tive speech and oral genres, which will necessarily emerge if sought after *in print*. For works on the power of speech and ways of engaging the oral-to-text archive in U.S. history, see Kamensky, *Governing the Tongue*; and Gustafson, *Eloquence Is Power*.

22. For more on the chant Kūnihi Ka Mauna, its history in print, and the moʻolelo in which it is embedded, see Hoʻomanawanui, *Voices of Fire*.

23. In keeping with Hawaiian traditions of pointing out the source of a particular vein of oral interpretation, Reichel indicated that the scholar who shared this particular reading was Rubellite Kawena Johnson during one of her frequent presentations on poetry in the 1980s. Personal correspondence, June 2014.

24. In my book *The Kingdom and the Republic*, I present the way that historical methods of reading and interpreting sources can be crafted by studying the words and work of Hawaiian scholars trained before 1819 and the casting down of the *ʻai kapu* (to eat under tabu). Operating out of a kānaka maoli historical approach, I suggest that these techniques can and must be used when historicizing the encounter between settler colonial societies and indigenous peoples. Here I argue that maoli and non-maoli scholars' approaches need to arise from multiple ontologies—ways of framing information and being in the world. In this way the Euro-American methods and approaches that are legitimized and utilized in our disciplines and in scholarly publications are relativized. Why do the methods and approaches favored still segregate the bodies and institutions engaged in research? One need only look to the creation of the Native American and Indigenous Studies Association to see the situation facing indigenous scholars and systems of knowledge today. While doing the important work of supporting the scholarship of indigenous people and validating this knowledge, the institution also facilitates, along with national professional associations, the persistent divide between maoli and non-maoli scholars, between native and other. See the plenary remarks from the association's opening conference in 2007, especially those by Robert Warrior and Tsianina Lomowaima: Native American and Indigenous Studies Association, "Founding History," accessed 3 April 2018, https://www.naisa.org/about/founding -history/.

25. The very word used for "history" or "story," *moʻolelo*, an elision of *moʻo* and *ʻōlelo*, can be broken down to mean "succession, speech," pointing in some respects to the constructed nature of bringing together different oral texts that are memorized and passed down as a unit, or units of history or story, depending on the occasion in which they were performed.

26. American missionaries in Hawaiʻi have become so negatively identified as the agents of the overthrow of the Hawaiian Kingdom in 1893 that animosity toward them as a group distorts people's perception of history, even to the point that materials they produced are rejected outright. Many, for example, have come to believe that the missionary companies that arrived between 1820 and 1865 used English as a mode of instruction exclusively, and that it was the missionaries who compelled Hawaiians to stop speaking their language. In fact, it was the descendants of these first missionaries along with other foreigners who were largely

implicated in the overthrow. However, missionary descendants lived and operated in a late nineteenth-century world where Hawaiian was still used for correspondence, everyday interactions, and, to some extent, juridical proceedings and the business of government.

27. The case of Rev. William Richards provides an important illustration of how a missionary became proficient in the Hawaiian language. The female chief Keopuolani took Richards to live among her people in Lahaina in 1823 as a teacher and minister. He was taught Hawaiian by Davida Malo, one of the trained Hawaiian intelligentsia of the Kamehameha family, and I argue that it was Richards's subsequent skill in the language that recommended him to serve the ali'i and the Hawaiian Kingdom from the late 1830s through his death in 1846. Other missionaries were similarly fostered by ali'i and educated by the intellectuals and kahu on different islands. See Arista, *The Kingdom and the Republic*. Future studies might focus on the role that missionaries' language fluency played in facilitating the spread of Christianizing and civilizing projects among Hawaiians. It has been suggested by some scholars that deep fluency in the Hawaiian language was unavailable to foreigners because as colonizers they either were wholly uninterested in the language or remained outsiders to Hawaiian social circles—further study needs to establish whether or not these arguments reflect a presentist bias or can be supported through empirical research. The professional, legal, and political careers of many settlers, such as Richards, William Little Lee, Lorrin Andrews, and Lorrin Thurston, seem to suggest otherwise. See Silva, *Aloha Betrayed*; and Schutz, *Voices of Eden*.

28. For information on the history of nūpepa publication, their size, and their appearance, see Nogelmeier, *Mai Pa'a i ka Leo*, 63–67; and Chapin, *Shaping History*.

29. For an analysis on how print and newspapers contributed to a sense of indigenous nationalism during colonialism, see Paterson, "Print Culture and the Collective Māori Consciousness," 105–29.

30. Anyone familiar with the work of historians, translators, and legal experts in places like Aotearoa New Zealand can appreciate that much labor has been expended to illuminate Māori claims against the Crown. The work in Hawai'i through Hawaiian sources has scarcely even begun.

31. It is important to note that other scholars are drawing on oral, written, and print archives in other native languages. See Treur, *The Assassination of Hole in the Day*, as well as the work of linguist Jessie Little Doe Baird, Mashpee Wampanoag. In Aotearoa the list of scholars who are fluent in Māori is growing and distinguished. See, for example, the work of Jane McRae, Lachy Paterson, Aroha Harris, Arini Loader, Megan Pōtiki, Poia Rewi, and Te Raukura o Te Rangimārie Roa. Māori, Lakota, and Cherokee archives are also voluminous, and in the Pacific, Tahiti, Fiji, and Tonga also have more modest, yet important, native textual materials.

32. My work on mele kanikau was enabled only through my work as an assistant on the mele kanikau project under Kumu Rubellite Kawena Johnson and two other senior researchers, Kumu Hula Kimo Alama Keaulana and John Mahelona, for three years. As a graduate student in the late 1990s, I had the job of locating chants

in microfilm and copying and disseminating these to the three senior translators. After some time I was invited to participate in the actual work of translating and offering my thoughts on compositions. I continue to work as a junior to the more senior members of the project.

33. See Davida Malo, "He Kanikau no Kaahumanu," *Ka Lama Hawaii*, 8 August 1834; Davida Malo, "Kahi Mele: He Kanikau no Kaahumanu," *Ke Kumu Hawaii*, 28 October 1835; Davida Malo, "He Kanikau no Kaahumanu," *Ka Hae Hawaii*, 29 April 1857; and Curtis J. Lyons, "David Malo's Lament for Kaahumanu," *The Friend*, August 1895, 57–58.

34. A point of discussion here might be whether or not this kind of referencing in written form transferred to the published text the mana garnered through the genre's traditional mode of chanted performance. An important project would be to collect all of the kanikau published for ali'i, in order to compare the complexity of language and the poetic figures commonplace in the genre.

35. This appears to have occurred in Māori *mōteatea* (sung poetry/chants). See Roa, "Formulaic Discourse Patterning in Mōteatea."

36. Rubellite Kawena Johnson, trans., "Kanikau: Songs for the Soul," 2003, unpublished manuscript. See also the translation in Lyons, "David Malo's Lament for Kaahumanu."

37. By the mid-nineteenth century, kanikau were composed for prominent members of the settler community, such as missionary teachers and government officials, surely a sign of great regard. Hawaiians living abroad who lost a loved one would compose kanikau that were sent back to the islands to be published in the nūpepa, further illuminating the experience of diasporic kānaka maoli in the nineteenth century. Kanikau were also composed to grieve the closing of newspapers or schools and the loss of things like reason and even one's soul. When the everyday lives and loves of people connected to Hawai'i are studied in aggregate, a social history of communities and the *lāhui* (Hawaiian people, nation) emerges upon closer inspection.

38. See also Hauiti Hākopa's "The *Paepae*: Spatial Information Technologies and the Geography of Narratives," which posits a methodology by which people, places, and events as described in Māori mōteatea may be integrated with digitized mapping.

39. See Hākopa, "The *Paepae*."

40. Kuykendall has written of the first appearance of the discussion of reciprocity in print, which he noted was on 8 February 1873 in the *Pacific Commercial Advertiser*. Kuykendall was not aware that on this same day essays ran in the Hawaiian-language nūpepa *Ka Nupepa Kuokoa*, and then in *Ke Au Okoa* (The new age) on 13 February 1873. By November of that year, the nūpepa *Ko Hawaii Ponoi* (Hawai'i's own) had become a voice of opposition, with the 13 November issue practically filled with speeches, essays, and chants in opposition to the treaty and the cession of Pu'uloa. To date, no article or book has been written that studies these debates, or the divergent concerns that mobilized disparate populations: haole, maoli, and immigrant laborers.

41. Napoliana, letter to the editor, *Ka Nupepa Kuokoa*, 12 July 1873 (my translation).

42. *Maka'āinana* or commoners, "pili grass," do not benefit from this rain. Another level of translation for these lines: "The lover values one thing only, of the ever-active mind, the lover (*ua*) or we (*kaua*) cannot affect the pili (the person loved, or the connection)." *Pili* could refer to *ho'opili*, betting, or the agreement between the two governments.

43. People higher in status, like the buds of lehua growing on trees, would gain the benefit of rain first.

44. The 'i'iwi may be a symbol here of the ali'i.

45. *Kāhuli* are land shells, snails. The word taken as a phrase, *ka huli*, means "the turning or returning."

46. *Kaumaha* and *lu'ulu'u* are figures of sorrow that denote heaviness, like a person carrying a heavy burden, or the leaves of trees sodden with rain, causing branches to bow down.

47. D. A. Kekuakahili, "He Inoa No Kipe," *Ko Hawaii Ponoi*, 20 August 1873. I have kept the original spacing in the word *lae-a* from the newspaper in the Hawaiian text, while "translating" this refrain in the English version to reflect how it might have been chanted. Mahalo to Puakea Nogelmeier and Kapali Lyon for their input on the translation. Thanks also to Hawaiian studies master's student Anika Borden, whose work brought these chants and articles to our attention, and whose initial translation provided me with the foundation for my interpretation. While I am publishing this initial translation, it is clear that much more work needs to be done to place these chants in their historical context and to validate or contest this interpretation.

48. Kamakau's serialized works began to appear in *Ka Nupepa Kuokoa* and *Ke Au Okoa* from 1865 to 1871. In 1866, his popular series "Ka Moolelo o Kamehameha" was published in *Ka Nupepa Kuokoa* and would run under various titles through 1875. For more on Kamakau and his role as a writer and cultural critic, see Nogelmeier, *Mai Pa'a i ka Leo*, 105–58.

49. S. M. Kamakau, "Huikau, Pohihihi Ke Kuikahi Panai Like me Ka Uku Kaulele o Puuloa," *Ko Hawaii Ponoi*, 20 August 1873.

50. Kamakau "recited" the words of Kauikeaouli, Kamehameha III, in 1854 regarding the sale of the shoreline of Waikahalulu to the consul of Britain, Gen. William Miller, who offered to pay eighty thousand dollars for the land, before the readers of *Ko Hawaii Ponoi*: "'A'ole o'u makemake i ke kū'ai aku i kekahi wahi 'āpana iki o ko'u aupuni kū'oko'a 'ē aku, he mea ia e ho'opilikia mai ai i ko'u aupuni." (I do not wish to sell one small portion of my independent nation to another, it is an act that would bring distress to my kingdom.) In my book I detail two occasions when Davida Malo, a Hawaiian chiefly counselor, was called by the ali'i to provide evidence from the Hawaiian past, in order to facilitate decision-making in the present. I also detail an incident that made the Rev. William Richards a candidate for such an office when he presented testimony before the *'aha 'ōlelo* (Chiefly Council) in 1827 and proved himself to be quite fluent in Hawaiian formal

and diplomatic speech. Kamakau, it seems, carries on the tradition by addressing the leaders and readers using persuasive political arguments whose gravity was signaled through aural/oral conventions and aesthetics. Arista, *The Kingdom and the Republic.*

51. S. M. Kamakau, "Huikau, Pohihihi Ke Kuikahi Panai Like me Ka Uku Kaulele o Puuloa." Another translation of the second sentence would read: "The survival of the Hawaiian people and the Hawaiian Kingdom depends on the voice of a single person, and because of him his entire people are silenced."

52. See the work of Haʻiliopua Baker, Kaliko Baker, Leilani Basham, Kamana-maikalani Beamer, Marie Alohalani Brown, David Chang, John Charlot, Malcolm Chun, Kealani Cook, Kuʻualoha Hoʻomanawanui, Sydney Iaukea, Lilikalā Kameʻeleihiwa, Kekuhi Kanahele, Larry Kimura, Ralph Lalepa Koga, Kamaoli Kuwada, Charles Kale Langlas, Robert Keawe Lopes, Kapali Lyon, Kepā Maly, Keao NeSmith, Puakea Nogelmeier, Katrina-Ann R. Kapaʻanaokalakeola Nakoa Oliveira, Jon Kamakawiwoʻole Osorio, Hiapokeikikāne Perreira, Kalena Silva, Noenoe Silva, Ty Kawika Tengan, Noeʻau Warner, William Pila Wilson, Liana Wong, and Terry Kanalu Young.

CHAPTER TWO

Kanak Writings and Written Tradition in the Archive of New Caledonia's 1917 War

ALBAN BENSA
& ADRIAN MUCKLE

IN NEW CALEDONIA, as elsewhere in Oceania, the idea that the indigenous culture is essentially or primarily an oral culture has helped to obscure more than a century of Kanak writing and literary tradition despite its existence in plain sight. Foremost among the factors contributing to this neglect are the power relations that colonizing discourses entrenched, including those that linked literacy in French with the attainment of political rights, resulting therefore in an official blindness to the presence of this tradition. Critiques of the notoriously harsh colonial regime, which provided only limited access to schooling in French, and none in vernacular languages, also have helped to obscure the evidence of a literacy that spread informally and flourished in both vernacular and francophone forms. Further sustaining this blindness to Kanak textual culture are the divisions that have separated the practice of history and anthropology in New Caledonia. Generally lacking the linguistic training necessary to access vernacular texts, historians have tended to rely on the European written records while anthropologists have tended to privilege the oral culture and collection of oral texts. Finally, we might add as a factor the importance invested by Kanak themselves in recuperating and revalorizing Melanesian/Kanak identity and "tradition," including privileging oral over written sources, as part of a decolonizing project.

This chapter contributes to the demonstration that "Kanak culture is not purely oral."[1] It does so through an exploration of two discrete types of evidence of Kanak literacy in the archives of a small war that occurred in New Caledonia in 1917 in the midst of the Great War of 1914–18: the correspondence that Kanak conducted in French with the colonial administration, and the Kanak vernacular written traditions composed in the war's aftermath.[2] In our discussion of the former, we pay attention to the tensions that surrounded indigenous literacy in a settler colonial and wartime context as well as the textual middle ground that the administrative archive exposes. As compromised or attenuated as the Kanak writing under colonial domination may be, this archive cannot be overlooked, and the voices found there cannot be dismissed as inauthentic. In the second part of our discussion, we turn to the vernacular written tradition and locate the creative literary explosion that occurred following the war in the context of a distinct indigenous writing tradition that flourished in New Caledonia in the first half of the twentieth century.[3] Both parts of the discussion draw attention to the ways in which internal political dynamics and ideologies are expressed.

TRACING KANAK LITERACY IN THE
ADMINISTRATIVE ARCHIVE OF THE 1917 WAR

The 1917 war broke out in the center-north region of New Caledonia's Grande Terre (the main island), between Koné and Hienghène, in late April 1917 during French recruitment of Kanak for the Great War and lasted nearly a year, causing up to three hundred deaths. It occurred sixty-four years after French annexation in 1853, some thirty years after the beginning of European settlement in the Koné-Hienghène region, and at the end of the two decades in which Protestant and Catholic evangelization had intensified. During this time Kanak had come under a harsh colonial regime involving indirect rule through a hierarchy of administrative *petits chefs* (little chiefs) and *grands chefs* (high chiefs), confinement to reservations, the imposition of head taxation, and the native regulations known as the *indigénat* (1887–1946) that policed Kanak's everyday relations with colonial authorities and settlers.

By 1917 literacy among Kanak in the region was widespread, though not pervasive, and was almost certainly stronger in the vernacular languages (notably Cèmuhî and to a lesser extent Paicî and Fwai) than in French.[4] Evangelization provided a key vector for literacy's spread, under the Catholic mission from the 1860s and the Protestant mission from the late 1890s, but conversion was not complete until after 1917. There had been no mission monopoly on education owing to the early presence of settlers and the establishment of "native schools" under government-trained "monitors" from the 1880s onward, and it must be assumed too that literacy spread informally in advance of these frontiers. The French had also made some efforts to educate the sons of chiefs and to establish a cadre of interpreters who could assist the development of indirect rule, and there is evidence that at least the ability to communicate in French was a criterion for administrative positions in the eyes of both the colonial authorities and the communities that such chiefs represented.[5]

In colonial discourses surrounding Kanak literacy two competing sets of ideas can be discerned. Importantly, the idea that Kanak were linguistically divided *and* illiterate had served as one of the principal pretexts for the imposition of the indigénat and the denial of political rights that it entailed.[6] Its sponsor, Governor Nouët, wrote, "Only when the Canaque has learned to speak, read, and write French will I be prepared to facilitate his access to naturalization and to grant him more extensive rights."[7] Another of the arguments presented for the controls that the indigénat imposed was the fear that the emergence of French as a lingua franca would increase the likelihood of more unified resistance to French rule.[8] As a result, the maintenance of this regime until 1946 was in part predicated on a semiofficial blindness to the growing Kanak attainment of literacy in French.[9] (And, tellingly, when suffrage was gradually and begrudgingly extended to Kanak between 1946 and 1957, literacy was a key criterion that allowed certain Kanak access to the franchise.) Just as important, the 1917 war occurred in a settler colonial context in which indigenous literacy was perceived as a threat both on the grounds that it might facilitate rebellion and because of the longer-term political challenge that it represented for settler domination.

As the war drew to a close, therefore, it was the literacy of some "rebels" rather than their more widely decried "savagery" that caused critics of the administration's "native policy" the most consternation.[10] In December 1917 the president of the colony's General Council, Léon Vincent, called for a reform of the native policy and challenged the adequacy of the measures being proposed to prevent such events recurring. No one, he said, could deny the need to educate Kanak, but those involved in the rebellion were not just "brutes" but people capable of reading and writing French; education alone would not be sufficient.[11] For the Catholic mission as well, suggestions that expanding the secular state schools and building better roads might prevent future rebellions were misplaced and erroneous given that "some of the principal rebels knew how to read, write, and speak French."[12]

The preoccupation with rebel literacy was most closely associated with Pwädé Apégu (Poindet Apengou), one of the presumed Kanak leaders. As the Bulletin du Commerce saw it shortly after the war began, "This chief has in a way been raised on the stations, he knows how to read and write and speak French fairly well. He really has been taught a thing or two!"[13] As noted later in this volume by Keith Thor Carlson, those who too closely emulated the colonizers could be regarded with ambivalence and perceived as threatening. Protestant missionary Maurice Leenhardt privately lamented that the man that he had formerly catechized had been "led astray by the life of a pagan stockman."[14] That Pwädé had been able to read French was a key point in Koné settler Auguste Henriot's statement to the postwar judicial investigation. Several weeks before the war, Henriot related, he had encountered Pwädé "in front of the post office reading the cables. Poindet said to me: 'You see the French are done for.' I protested, but he replied: 'But yes, you see, they're retreating.' I asked him who had given him this idea, and he replied: 'Nobody, I can see things clearly, they're still being defeated, moreover they don't have any more men left.'"[15] Pwädé had been an enemy to be reckoned with in the settlers' eyes in large part because of his literacy.

While Leenhardt's private lament evoked the limits of mission influence in a settler colony, Henriot's statement echoed a long-standing settler suspicion of Kanak literacy—and especially the literacy associated with Protestant evangelization—as a potential threat to French and settler interests. Indigenous Protestant *nata* (teachers or pastors) and government-trained monitors had put their literacy to use as intermediaries in relations between Kanak and local settlers—often to the annoyance of the latter. In 1903 settler petitions had denounced the "furtive activities" of Protestant teachers from the Loyalty Islands and the "undesirable consequences" of their presence. As well as encouraging Kanak to defend their rights, including with regard to employment conditions, the teachers were believed to be spreading their own languages as lingua francas: "Soon the natives from all corners of the colony will be in a position, if they wish, to carry out an insurrection under the protection of an idiom that they will all know and a word of which we will not understand."[16] In the Koné region, a Protestant monitor who "forbade canaques from going to settlers without written permission and prohibited them from working for whites for less than two francs a day with rations" was denounced by the settler press, which called for his removal.[17]

In 1917 awareness of Kanak literacy also drove the censorship that was introduced following the outbreak of war. As the head of the Service of Native Affairs later explained, censorship had been introduced to prevent alarmist stories in the settler press (the *Bulletin du Commerce*) being read by Kanak for fear that they might aggravate the situation.[18] In December 1917 the administration had moved that the General Council's debate on native policy take place in a closed committee so as to prevent publicity being given to the ongoing events. The secretary-general informed the council, "It is a question of native policy. Censorship in New Caledonia was established for the natives: it is desirable that the natives not be kept informed of certain matters."[19]

Kanak had more compelling reasons for recourse to armed resistance than the destabilization created by the settler press, but there is evidence that exposure to the latter contributed to the mobilization of opposition by the so-called rebels. Europeans would single out the circulation of news of the war in Europe as one of the factors that had encouraged Kanak opposition. Gaston Bécu, a mobilized colonial clerk in charge of a military detachment at Hienghène during the war's first months, reported that local "canaquophiles" had sought to discourage recruitment: "Canaques in the Hyenghène region are supposed to have been shown terrifying images of the atrocities in the current war and of the quasi-invincible force of Germany." Nor could Kanak themselves, he noted, have been ignorant of discussions in the local press about the likelihood they might revolt.[20]

Indeed, two years earlier a former grand chef and political internee, Amane of Poyes, had written to the *Bulletin du Commerce* to reject rumors it had reported about his own intentions and the possibility he might revolt. Amane wrote to "show [his] loyalty toward France" and to explain that he had placed himself at the government's service hoping to serve as a soldier. Kanak voices seldom appeared directly in the local press, but Amane's was a notable exception. The letter conforms to a pattern (that shall emerge more clearly in the following) whereby Kanak who came under settler suspicion sought to publicly defend themselves by declaring their loyalty.[21]

The more direct contribution of Kanak literacy to the resistance to recruitment and the outbreak of war came through the letters sent by Kanak recruited as soldiers in 1916 and serving in Nouméa or overseas. These were especially evident in the east coast districts of Poindimié and Tiwaka—parts of the region with the longest exposure to literacy—where Catholic missionary Stéphane Berne reported the arrival of "distressing" letters in which the Kanak soldiers "complain bitterly about many things."[22] In their first letters from Nouméa in early 1916 the recruits had complained about their diet: "Us hungry. Little to eat."[23] Further letters followed from Sydney in July 1916 and eventually from France. In early 1917 Berne saw the news they brought as an impediment to further recruiting efforts: "As for the despatch of the tirailleurs [indigenous infantry], it's quite pointless given the unfortunate news sent back, for better or worse, by the tirailleurs. . . . I don't think that even a shot from a rifle would make them march."[24] He described a "deplorable scene" during a meeting in which the Bayes grand chef Bwëë Apwâ Pwëloaa (Appoint) "said that the tirailleurs who are in France have written that they are overwhelmed with work for five francs a day and soup that is only good for pigs."[25] In other instances, more positive letters were read out to encourage recruitment. Berne translated from Cèmuhî a "truly admirable letter" in which infantryman Noël Poindet wrote of his willingness to die for France.[26]

In a study of New Caledonia's participation in the Great War, Sylvette Boubin-Boyer notes that most Kanak recruits spoke French and that "those who had been evangelized generally knew how to read. A few, former students of the Catholic or Protestant missions, also knew how to write." Their letters, she observes, were "generally brief" and largely devoid of sentiment or description, in part for the reason given by Leenhardt in his deprecating commentary on the correspondence of the Kanak chaplain Acoma Nerhon, a former monitor: "'In his own tongue Acuma would write better: in French, a language learned by ear and never understood, he is obliged to make do with clichés.'"[27] Boubin-Boyer has noted the onomatopoeic quality of the extant letters, which reprise the punctuated rhythm of traditional chants and contain similar litanies of names. The Kanak soldiers were also eager readers; Nerhon requested 150–200 copies of the Protestant mission's newssheet, *Virherhi* (Onwards), to ensure that each of the hospitalized men might have his own copy to read.[28]

Various accounts of the 1917 war, including those composed by Kanak (as discussed in the following), draw attention to the ways in which the rebels mobilized tradition and modernity, notably in the adaptation of technology. That this was also true of the tools of communication has been less remarked upon. While Leenhardt made much of the traditional forms of communication and diplomacy involving packets of dried grasses and leaves arranged in configurations that were impenetrable to Europeans, the quotidian written correspondence carried out by Kanak on both sides (as well as by the Protestant nata) perhaps seemed less remarkable.[29] None of the writing that passed between the rebels has survived, and the writing material used may have been very fragile, but its existence can be gleaned from Pwädé Apégu's own testimony in 1918.[30] In the war's early months Pwädé had exchanged notes with other Kanak men concerning the actions of local settlers and a mine operator: "Léon Pobati wrote to me from Kopéto to tell me that Mr. Schmidt had told him that if Poindet and Bégui Apapa from Pouaouta should come to the mine he would shoot us up with his rifle.—This letter was read by the rebel Daniel Poindi who was killed at Nowáca and Boggan from Paola a rebel originally from Wagap who is currently in Nouméa."[31]

In passing, Pwädé also mentioned another, perhaps more intimate letter: "As for me I stayed at Gambo, but there I had a dispute with my wife over a letter that I had received from a mistress at Koné."[32] Before his own arrest, Pwädé told Julien Belet (the surveyor appointed to negotiate with the rebels), "I cannot surrender yet. I want you to send me a notebook in which to consign all my defense and when I have finished I will come back. I can assure you of that; trust me." Belet told Pwädé that he could have "everything needed to write" and that "you can also dictate to me what you have to say and come with me or if you wish at Poindimié you will have all the time to write your memoirs."[33] While any notebook that Pwädé might have begun to fill before his arrest did not make it into the administrative archive, Pwädé's declarations point to a potential archive of rebel missives that was never constituted and hint at what was clearly a widespread practice.

By contrast, the Kanak letters that entered the administrative archive are those that were addressed to the administration itself or, more rarely, those that the administration intercepted. Much like Amane's 1915 letter to the *Bulletin*, many of these took the form of protests of innocence and assurances of loyalty in the face of official or settler anxiety. In July 1917 the Néa (signing himself "X"), the petit chef of Nétéa, and Germain, the petit chef of Ouaté, wrote to the governor in broken French to deny reports in the local press that they had joined the rebels: "I affirm that I don't want to betray my conscience by telling you that no the rebels they are enemies whom I will publicly call savages [and] I don't want to be of the Germans whom I will treat also as men who were ignorant." They insisted that their own grand chef at Poya would confirm that all was calm in their districts.[34] Five days earlier Tia Houé Appi wrote to the same grand chef, Katchoué, asking him to tell the gendarmerie that he was Katchoué's subject and not a follower of those who had decided to revolt: "But I am not a servant of those who rebel the war but I am your servant."[35]

As is typical of many of the Kanak letters that can be found in the administrative archive from the previous decade, these notes betray clearly the uneven power relations and colonial hegemony, and the fine line that those who wished to maintain a degree of neutrality had to tread. In Australia, Laura Rademaker has described how Anindilyakwa petitioners positioned themselves within a moral order shared with missionaries in order to gain legitimacy for their claims; in the preceding examples, the moral order was that of deference to the administrative chiefs recognized by French authorities.[36] The chiefs of Ouaté and Nétéa also did not wish to "betray" their own consciences by publicly calling the rebels savages, nor did they themselves wish to be labeled as Germans, whom they also saw as misguided or ignorant; but they did want it to be known that they had not joined the rebels. A Protestant nata would later point out that the language of the French administration limited the ways in which the war could be discussed: "And to talk about it [the war] we only have the words of whites: rebels, savages, etc."[37]

Those Kanak who were directly threatened by the rebels wrote to the administration in more forthright terms. Like his settler neighbors, the Tiouandé petit chef Doui wanted rifles and a stronger military response following a rebel raid on his reservation. He requested supplies, "so that we can start over in our gardens without them we are going to die of hunger," and five rifles; "with that, by hiding ourselves in the rocks of Tiouandé we can easily kill these people when they come back to our village." Finally, he called on the administration to end the war: "Monsieur le Gouverneur we are calling on you so that you might send many soldiers to quickly finish the war that is making everyone unhappy."[38]

Insofar as they were sometimes penned by third parties, some letters from "1917" are testimony to a "middle ground" of Kanak-settler or Kanak-mission relations. They point to the networks of political, social, or familial relations that could be mobilized to advance or defend particular interests. In the month before the outbreak of war, as a cloud of suspicion settled around grand chef Téâ Antoine Katélia, his family called on local settler Jean Laurent to visit them, to set what they had to say down in writing, and then to deliver it to the local gendarme.[39] By his own later testimony, Laurent had also been twice asked by Katélia to write letters to the governor.[40] Nothing more is known about this relationship, but it points to a type of arrangement and understanding that was probably much more widespread. In other instances Catholic missionaries and Protestant nata served as the go-betweens or amanuenses, as did stockmen (such as the métis Emile Guillemard in an example mentioned later in this chapter).

With the war's end and the imprisonment of several hundred men and women for the duration of the judicial investigation, Kanak sought to intervene with authorities on behalf of prisoners and in some instances to denounce others. In January 1918 Poinda petit chef Oué Auguste Goroépata and his fellow tribesman Badzi wrote at length in French to a man from their reserve employed in Nouméa, asking him to assist a young man who had been arrested on suspicion of having used a stolen rifle to shoot at the governor and the officer in charge of the French forces during the war. The letter begins:

> To Mr. Poany Marova Léonard
>
> We send you the present letter to let you know that young Tiatéa Thy of Paouta has been arrested and will be sent to Nouméa on the return sailing of the St Pierre. In this case we ask that you wait for him when he arrives in Nouméa. So that you can help him as an interpreter and take him to Mr. Fourcade, the head of the Service of Native Affairs, to explain before him the reason for his arrest. Please take care to tell him that he has nothing to fear and that he must clearly explain how things happened beginning with the day that Poindé went to war. Which is as follows.[41]

Their letter to Poany sets out in fair but occasionally broken French—in a style and syntax that reflects an unmistakably Kanak voice—in some detail the task that Poany was being asked to undertake as an interpreter: what he should say on Tiatéa's behalf to the authorities, what Tiatéa should do with the money that was being forwarded to him, and what he should be told to do if prison authorities attempted to take it from him. Five days later Oué Auguste and his grand chef, Katélia, wrote directly to Fourcade setting out Tiatéa's case and asking that Poany be allowed to interpret for him.[42] More than any other documents, these two letters provide evidence of the everyday use of writing in French to mobilize family connections and loyalties and to facilitate dealings with the administration. As noted by Benoît Trépied, Oué Auguste held a key position as an interlocutor for Katélia. Here he appears as author and signatory, while elsewhere in the history of the 1917 war and its aftermath he appears as Katélia's interpreter and spokesperson in dealings with other Kanak groups and the administration.[43]

Another well-documented set of exchanges concerns the fate of the female prisoners who were left under the control of the chiefs who had allied with the administration. When this arrangement was called into question, the various allied chiefs wrote to the administration to defend their claims or to demand compensation. The Bayes grand chef, Apwâ, wrote, "With the goal of bringing about a moral metamorphosis of these subjects inclined toward bad ideas, I essentially intend to keep them close to me. By mixing with the personnel of my tribu, they will soon change their ideas and rapidly become good subjects."[44] Other chiefs wrote in a similar vein expressing similar sentiments.

Other Kanak penned letters of denunciation and sought to secure control of released prisoners and refugees. In January 1918 the Poyes chief, Titelet, wrote to Julien Belet calling for the removal of a petit chef (at Bopope) who had prevented refugees from escaping to Poyes: "I have asked you to remove this chief along with Augustin. These are the two who prevented the others from coming."[45] In May 1918 a Catholic missionary reported that Emile Guillemard, a métis stockman, had helped Titelet denounce the actions of another petit chef (Pelino), whom he accused "of abusing the rebels [a group of prisoners] by making them work a lot and not paying them."[46] Titelet was doing all that he could to secure control over groups displaced by the war. In a similar fashion, the Hienghène grand chef Doui Philippe Bouarate (the man who would later be denounced for instigating the war, but whose role was as yet unknown to the administration) twice wrote to the governor to explain what had happened when the fighting had spread to his own district and to distance himself from two chiefs who had been arrested: "I think that these two chiefs will be severely judged especially Goa!" However, he accepted responsibility for people who had been found innocent and urged that they be resettled under his authority and protection.[47]

While the authorship of such letters is not always clear, they betray distinctively Kanak voices and rationales that reflect Kanak political agendas, dynamics, and imperatives. Importantly, many of these letters point to the segmentary divisions that still structured Kanak society as well as the wider ambitions of the men commanding the chieftaincies recognized by the administration; chiefs wrote in not only to denounce, or distance themselves from, long-standing rivals but also to argue in the interests of their subjects and in the hope of increasing the population of their own districts.

1917 AND 1914–1918 IN KANAK WRITTEN TRADITION

The Kanak written sources relating to the 1917 war are not limited to the epistolary form or the administrative archive. In a series of notebooks—safeguarded for the most part among the records of Maurice Leenhardt—the memory of the war was set down in versified epics as early as 1919 while those arrested as presumed rebels still languished in prison awaiting trial, and as the surviving Kanak soldiers returned to New Caledonia from France. Their provenance suggests that they are in large part a product of the ethnographic method, described by James Clifford, whereby "Leenhardt encouraged a wide variety of people to record in school exercise books any traditional legends, ritual discourses, or songs that they knew well. When the *cahiers* were ready, the missionary discussed their contents with the authors, a long and arduous process, for the language was often archaic and the writing highly idiosyncratic."[48] Subsequently annotated and sometimes also partially translated (into Ajië or French) by Leenhardt or his students, the texts in these exercise books represent an important oeuvre with ethnographic, historical, and literary qualities. They are more than just a product of an ethnographic method, however; they belong to a distinct culture and writing tradition that flourished in New Caledonia from the early 1900s to the 1950s.[49]

In contrast to the texts written by, or at the behest of, administrative chiefs and others seeking to inform, disinform, or gain favor or protection, the versified epics in this collection recount the war's events, rituals, and tragedies from entirely Kanak perspectives unmediated by any need to be understood in French or to directly negotiate colonial relations of power. Two poems in the Paicî language—the language spoken by many of the so-called rebels—illustrate both the political dimensions and the literary qualities of the written tradition surrounding 1917. Both take the form of *ténô*, poems written in lines of eight syllables using highly symbolic language. One, entitled "The two of us lament for the country," is a *ténô* of 203 lines. The other, "Then comes the chill," runs to just short of 700.[50]

While there was no distinct caste of professional memorialists in Kanak society, the poets who composed these texts were generally not from the clans of chiefs or "masters of the soil"—the principal poles of Kanak society—but from the lineages that provided services on the ritual, military, or strategic level. Thus, while there is a strong probability that these and other works were written at Leenhardt's invitation, perhaps even while he conducted his own investigation into the war, it is also clear that their authors spoke for specific lineage groups or chieftaincies (even if they also carry the imprint of the mission's moral condemnation of the decision to take up arms). As shown here, each poem has its own particular lineage illustrating, in this instance, two distinct perspectives: that of a group of defeated rebels and that of the victorious "allies," as well as those of a particular descent group and chieftaincy.

The name Göröpwêjilèi identifies the presumed author of "The two of us lament for the country" as belonging to a lineage group that had been dispossessed of land in the interior of the Koné-Hienghène region (Pamalé) in 1903 and forced to seek refuge in another reservation (Näumêju), from which they were again dispersed during 1917. This lineage group had been involved in earlier struggles with colonial authorities and had committed fully to the war in 1917, whereas another branch of the same clan, associated with the aforementioned grand chef Katélia, took a more neutral position and perhaps even supported the administration. The little that we know about Bwëungä Cöpiu Göröpwêjilèi himself indicates that he had been directly involved in the events of 1917 and was among those who adhered to Protestantism in their wake.[51]

The poem unfolds as if the families involved, having abandoned all hope of returning to their country, have conferred on the poet the task of recording their disarray: "we lament the sacred places / because all that lived has been burnt."[52] At the poem's heart is the fate of the Göröpwêjilèi lineage. Their toponyms and the destruction of their ancestral hearths provide one of the poem's central threads: "all is burnt at Odro / everything incinerated at Pécigo."[53] Recounting their flight and determination to survive ("let's flee above to stay alive" and "save ourselves and regroup there / work to resist"), the poem relates the decisions that they and the other lineage groups accompanying them successively confronted: whether to keep fighting or accept defeat, where and with whom to seek refuge, whether to renounce the "clan spirits" and accept the tutelage of the missions.[54] In rebuffing a call for their surrender, those who decided to fight on sent a letter in which they rejected the proposal and called on the clan spirits for their support: "he replies down there in a letter / ... / rejected—forbidden to take it up / gather the clan spirits / get the spirits of the country moving."[55]

The hesitation that characterizes these and other decisions reflects the segmentary structure of Kanak society: each unit might at any moment decide to fight, negotiate, or withdraw; to accept or refuse a given authority; or to switch allegiance. Whereas Kanak writings in the administration's archive (the denunciations of rivals and claims to authority over discrete groups of refugees and prisoners) draw attention to status rivalry and the ambitions of the chieftaincies, this ténô foregrounds the war's more intricate and delicate diplomacy and the agency of the lineage descent groups.

The second and longer epic, "Then comes the chill," is attributed to two men from the Poindimié region, Dui Bwékua Poomä (d. 1925) and Félix Näpwé (d. 1933).[56] Dui Bwékua Poomä is remembered throughout the Paicî region for his exceptional capacities as a poet as well as for his abilities as a seer and healer. It is not known whether or not he could write; although he was known to carry a Bible, he had refused religious instruction. His presumed scribe, Félix Näpwé, was a former student of Leenhardt's mission school at Do Néva. He belonged to the lineage of the Bayes grand chef Bwëë Apwâ Pwëloaa, and the traces of this social and political identity—and the chieftaincy's centralizing ambitions—are very evident in the ténô that he and Poomä set down.

Whereas Göröpwêjilèi relates a rebel voice closely associated with a particular lineage group, Näpwé and Poomä represent the Näpwé chieftaincy associated in 1917 with Bwëé Apwâ Pwëloaa. Apwâ, as we have seen, had been critical of the conditions confronted by those Kanak who volunteered as soldiers, but he nevertheless lent his military and diplomatic support to the administration in attempting to bring the local war to an end. The poem exalts the alliances that expanded the Näpwé's influence as they entered both the war of 1914–18 and that of 1917 on the side of France and presents the recruitment of the auxiliaries as part and parcel of the recruitment for the war in Europe:

36. â pubu pa cöö kanô	gather the cannons in file together
37. â pëcé coda âgéré	the English soldiers fall into rank
38. â kââ tëua Paris	and Paris carries the bayonets
39. â pëcé kanô alemâ	the German cannons align themselves
40. âgö côwâ ti italia	repercussions for Italy
41. â èbé wâ sydney	and in all this Sydney takes its place
42. â pi-köpi wâ alemagn	and it blasts (spits) out in Germany
43. â uru wâ batavia	every man for himself in Batavia
44. â wékûû pa näpô pi-mêê	rumbling in the allied countries
45. ila pitiri cuwârî	they ask around them for help
46. â tûû nââ näpô mäinä	and the Grande Terre accepts
47. â pârî karitonia	New Caledonia can supply
48. â rë wécécé titaé	and they seek in doubt
49. â rë tamäki tawèè dö-ö	they jump up and question me
50. â ila pwëbwé pûînôâ	and ask for a protective wall
51. â dùwii au-nôwèi	on which to lean in hope
52. â atü pëi-ri cèikî	a rock on which to ground confidence
53. â o cimä cè pëdo u	a group of giant houp trees stands forth
54. â pa-cöö cè pwëbwé jëu	kauri ranged as a barrier
. . .	. . .
65. â rë o èdi kââ pëdo	they will carry the chieftaincy far

The poet underlines the importance of the decision to support France during a difficult period; the chieftaincy offers France "a rock on which to ground confidence." The grands chefs (the Houp trees) are joined by their petits chefs (the kauri trees). Also evoked are France's military needs, the military parades in Paris, and the conflict's global reach. The Näpwé, along with England and Australia, throws its weight in against Germany as well as against those whose transgressions, challenging the bounds of authority, had led to the war in New Caledonia.[57]

While most of the lines that follow are centered on the war in New Caledonia, the last seventy lines evoke the end of the two wars—"two crackling fires" that eventually consume themselves—and the mourning ceremonies for a soldier fallen in France. This final switch in focus from the war of 1917 to mourning for a victim of the Great War implicitly recenters the ténô on Näpwé's loyalist position yet also underscores the ways in which the two wars were bound together. More generally, the text abounds with metaphors evoking the political relations between chiefs (Houp trees, kauri, barracuda) and their subjects or men (clouds of fruit bats, swarms of crickets, anchors, or barges). The chieftaincies involved appear as autonomous political entities rather than as part of an administrative hierarchy or even as rebels or loyalists.

This written ténô also bears the traces of a third hand, the pastor Eleisha Näbai, who in recopying the text in 1948 added to it his own ending. Whereas the original version ends on an optimistic and triumphant note, recalling Näpwé's success with a certain pride ("thus was your history / you can take pride in it"), Näbai adopts a more negative and regretful tone: "pride has been appeased / with a breath the fire has been extinguished / oh how many regrets now that night has fallen / oh how disturbed is the land."[58] The entire country has been devastated, and an effort is still required to protect it even though Näpwé's adversaries have been defeated. In dwelling on the war's ravages Näbai's perspective is close to that of the rebels as presented by Göröpwêjilèi. Beneath the surface, in the space between these two texts, endings, and interpretations, we can read not only the tension between the so-called rebels and allies but also the tension between the segmentary order of the clan-based descent groups and the geopolitical order of the chieftaincies that was one of the conflict's principal fault lines within the Kanak world.

It would be a disservice to these texts, however, to read them only in terms of their political ideologies and functions or historical memory. They stand out also for their performative, literary, and imaginative qualities. Of especial note in this regard is the particular vehicle that the poets chose to contain their images and memories of the war: the ténô. Whereas the administrative archive shows Kanak taking up the epistolary form, here we see Kanak adapting an age-old oral form of their own.[59] Tightly composed in lines of eight syllables, ténô combine grammatical economy with the evocative power of words and names. The shortened form condenses numerous possible meanings and creates a poetic effect that is further enhanced by the rhythm of recital. Disjointed words, repetition, the drawing out of final syllables, and rising and falling pitches all come together to create a saturation of both sound and meaning that draws the performance toward song when the ténô is recited by two voices to the rhythmic beating of bamboo tubes on the ground.[60]

It is impossible, however, to say categorically whether the written ténô were dictated after being composed orally or whether they were composed with pen in hand. While it would be easy to assume the former scenario, analysis of their composition suggests that these works drew on the written word in intertwining patterns, and linking and repeating verses. And while many of the oral traditions recorded and collected between the 1960s and 2009 appear to be purely oral forms of expression with no known written versions, a good many others contain whole sections also found in the written texts. The following lines concerning the war's principal Kanak hero, Wâii, are among the most widely known passages of the ténô by Poomä and Näpwé and are frequently reprised orally and adapted at *pilou* (traditional dance ceremonies) throughout the Paicî region:

560. â wë co Wâii nä ètö	Wâii alone is invulnerable
561. jè a-pwëti tägo mäga	he has chewed the bitter herb
562. â doro upwârâ ibu	and the leaf of the stinging tree

All variations begin with these three lines and then either draw on others from the same ténô or invent and add new ones.

The ténô reveal a literary effort to rework an ancient Kanak poetic form and to rethink old tropes in light of new practices and developments. While some ténô relating to the 1917 war contain clear traces of earlier oral texts in that they reprise passages, images, and names relating to earlier events and wars, ténô such as "Then comes the chill" draw on new scenes and images linked with the war of 1914–18. In the same way that Guillaume Apollinaire integrated rockets, planes, and barbed wire into a far older poetic style owing much, as we know, to Paul Verlaine, the Kanak poets combined the traditional images of chieftainship (such as the houp and kauri trees), sacred spaces, and ritualized exchanges with the designation of tools and situations directly related to modern warfare (cannons and explosives). The poets drew on images etched in the memories of Kanak survivors at the end of a sojourn in France that was as barbaric as it was painful. In France, Kanak had experienced modern warfare: new weapons, planes, explosions, and battles of a relentless nature. Thus, while spears, clubs, and slingshots were used alongside guns in the fighting of 1917, and while the sporadic episodes of guerrilla warfare stood in stark contrast with the mass war of position in Europe, the traditional forms of Kanak combat were reconsidered in light of the events on the battlefields of France.

––––––––

From the early twentieth century to the present day, Kanak kept oral and written traces of their people's initiatives in the face of unprecedented change as well as in the face of settler hostility and suspicion. We cannot assume that the historical experiences of Kanak in the early twentieth century are contained only in oral tradition or that the written and spoken word are necessarily opposed.[61]

As Tony Ballantyne and Lachy Paterson observe in their introduction to this volume, both "community formation and the struggle against colonial rule" are central to the indigenous textual cultures explored in this collection. In New Caledonia the literary culture and the variety of Kanak writings exposed by the events of 1917—in letters, prose, poetry, songs, and memoirs—testify that the written word held a more important place within Kanak society than is commonly imagined, without of course replacing the immediate and daily predominance of oral communication. Not only did writing allow Kanak to communicate with each other and to negotiate with the colonial administration; it also allowed them to keep a new trace of the intellectual activity required in the complex world that colonization drove to new heights of narrative, memorial, and strategic innovation. The postwar literary project seen in the ténô involved the long-term recording of specific political and social contexts that had been subject to numerous transformations and upheavals but that nonetheless remained firmly attached to powerful points of reference: kinship, the organization of space, principles of hierarchy, and the memory of war and displacement.

The war of 1917 has been, and still is, a wellspring of memory on individual, familial, and regional scales. Though by no means the only expression of this memory, the written traditions testify to the immense labor undertaken in its preservation. In the months and years that followed the war, men who had been trained in the writing of French and of their own languages tasked themselves to compose in writing the memories of the tragic events that they thought should be passed on. Writing mainly in school exercise books, they set down poems that were carefully preserved and sometimes revised by a Kanak intelligentsia that had been won over to reading and writing since the end of the nineteenth century.

The Kanak writings that fall within the administrative archive illustrate the ways that the war of 1917 required Kanak to work within the constraints of French hegemony and the limits of the language of rebellion and alliance. In these texts we can occasionally see traces of a middle ground of Kanak-settler relations along with attempts to reconfigure relations between the administration and certain chieftaincies (sometimes at the expense of others).

The conjuncture of the Great War and the New Caledonian conflict in 1917 also led to the reconfiguration of links between metropolitan France and its Oceanic subjects by opening up a new referential space for thought and its expression. The ténô attributed to Bwëungä Cöpiu Göröpwêjilèi, Dui Bwékua Poomä, and Félix Näpwé show that the wars of 1914–18 and 1917 gave rise to a veritable creative explosion. Just as the 1920s in Europe were marked by great artistic production, these Melanesian works were literary responses to the postwar situation. Their content testifies to a desire to control events, to organize the world according to Kanak criteria and values, and also to consider the position of Kanak in the process of globalization in which the Great War played a decisive role. The Kanak poets did not hesitate to take possession of the events that had occurred and introduce them into creative texts of a far older style and narrative structure. This poetic expression also testifies to the relationship of Kanak with the globalized world. In renewing their creative productions, the colonized people took hold of the events of the time and brought them under literary and affective control. Nonetheless, while novel images and the names of hitherto-unmentioned people or places were introduced into oral and/or written poems, the rhythmic format remained the same, as did the general frame of reference: the Kanak world with its practices and its rules. These new borrowed elements and the permeation of the events taking place did not detract from a mode of expression firmly anchored in local experience and heritage.

NOTES

1. Kasarhérou, "Traces littéraires et poétiques," 19. Unless otherwise indicated, all translations from French are our own.

2. We set aside a third archive: the extensive vernacular prose correspondence among the various Protestant teachers living in the region affected by the war and the missionary Maurice Leenhardt. As yet only partially translated, these texts warrant a more serious treatment in their own right.

3. This chapter draws on and complements our research on the war of 1917: Bensa, "La tradition écrite kanak," 647–53; Bensa, Goromoedo, and Muckle, *Les Sanglots de l'aigle pêcheur*; and Muckle, *Specters of Violence in a Colonial Context*.

4. One indicator is that whereas the Cèmuhî language had been favored by the Catholic mission, which had published several Cèmuhî texts, including a dictionary by 1891, it was not until 1910–17 that any texts in Fwai or Paicî were published.

5. Examples abound of men with the ability to speak French being put forward to assume the administrative positions. A case in point is Téen of Pana, who was successively a pupil of the school established at the Gatope military post in the 1860s, a government-sponsored student in Nouméa in 1870, a designated monitor of the Koné native school in the 1880s, and, in the early 1900s, the petit chef of Pana, where he was known by the sobriquet "the schoolmaster."

6. There are twenty-eight Kanak languages, of which at least five are spoken in the region directly affected by the 1917 war: Cèmuhî, Paicî, Pije, Fwai, and the Voh-Koné dialects (notably Vamalé and Haeke).

7. Louis Hippolyte Nouët to Min. de la Marine et des Colonies, Nouméa, 15 November 1886, Série Géographique Nouvelle-Calédonie (hereafter NC) 45, Archives Nationales d'Outre-mer (hereafter ANOM), Aix-en-Provence.

8. Léon Gauharou to Directeur de l'Intérieur, Nouméa, 14 March 1887, NC 27, ANOM.

9. Marie Salaün suggests that levels of primary education among Kanak in the early twentieth century were similar to those among settlers and that relative to Algeria a higher proportion of New Caledonia's indigenous population had received basic education. Salaün, L'école indigène, 99–106.

10. Throughout this essay we use the term "rebel" to designate those Kanak who fought against the French authorities in 1917 and those who were at least the targets of the forces mustered by French authorities. As certain Kanak themselves observed, the term fails to adequately capture the complexity of Kanak motivations in 1917 and should at all times be treated as if within scare quotes.

11. General Council, 20th session, 22 December 1917, in La France Australe, 15 January 1918.

12. Claude-Marie Chanrion, "Simples remarques sur les chefs rebelles classés selon leur réligion" [ca. 1919], Archives de l'Archevêché de Nouméa, Oceania Marist Province Archives Microfilm (hereafter AAN) 39.6.

13. Le Bulletin du Commerce, "Les troubles canaques dans la région de Koné," 23 June 1917.

14. Maurice Leenhardt to Jeanne Leenhardt, 1 May 1917, 12J, Archives de la Nouvelle-Calédonie (hereafter ANC), Nouméa; and M. Leenhardt to J. Leenhardt, 19 September 1917, 12J, ANC.

15. Auguste Henriot, witness statement, 2 October 1918, AAN 21.7.

16. Nouvelle-Calédonie et Dépendances, Procès-Verbaux du Conseil Général, Session ordinaire de Mai 1903 (Nouméa: Imprimerie Calédonienne, 1903), 109–13.

17. Le Bulletin du Commerce, "Informations diverses," 14 March 1903.

18. Noumea Court of Assizes, 20th session, 9 August 1919, in Le Bulletin du Commerce, 15 August 1919.

19. General Council, 18th session, 21 December 1917, in La France Australe, 14 January 1918.

20. Gaston Bécu, "Notes sur Hyenghène" (October 1917–February 1918), AAN 39.6.

21. Letter dated 17 March 1915, in *Le Bulletin du Commerce*, 10 April 1915. Amane's desire to volunteer was first reported in *Le Bulletin du Commerce*, 13 March 1915.

22. Berne to Monseigneur, St Léonard, 16 April 1917, AAN 55.1.

23. Berne to Monseigneur, St Léonard, 11 February 1916, AAN 55.1; and Berne to Monseigneur, St Léonard, 27 March 1916, AAN 55.1; see also *La France Australe*, 26 February 1916. In February 1916 the editor of *La France Australe* urged that recruits in Nouméa be asked to write to their families to tell them how well they were being treated so as to encourage further volunteers.

24. Berne to Monseigneur, St Léonard, 14 March 1917, AAN 55.1.

25. Berne to Monseigneur, St Léonard, 8 January 1917, AAN 55.1.

26. Berne to Monseigneur, St Léonard, 10 June 1916, AAN 55.1.

27. Boubin-Boyer, *De la Première Guerre Mondiale en Océanie*, 439. Boubin-Boyer quotes a letter from Leenhardt to his wife dated 10 June 1916.

28. Boubin-Boyer, *De la Première Guerre Mondiale en Océanie*, 442–43.

29. M. Leenhardt to J. Leenhardt, Do Néva, 18 July 1917, 12J, ANC.

30. In 1913 Leenhardt reported receiving smuggled notes written on coconut leaves from a student serving a prison sentence, an example of the use of fragile writing materials. M. Leenhardt to his Parents, Do Néva, 5 December 1913, 12J, ANC.

31. Quoted by Julien Belet, undated notes, 1W1 (1071), ANC.

32. "Procès-verbal d'interrogatoire du nommé Poindet Apengou," 22 March 1918, AAN 21.4.

33. Belet, untitled report/diary, 3 October 1917, 1W1, ANC.

34. Néa, the chief of Nétéa, and Germain, the chief of Ouaté, to Gouverneur, Ouaté via Poya, 7 July 1917, 1W2 (1538), ANC.

35. Tia Houé Appi to My dear Katchoué, Koné, 2 July 1917, 1W2, ANC.

36. See chapter 8 in this volume.

37. Leenhardt, "Comptes-rendus des Conférences des Natas," Cahier 12: Conférence Oindo, 1918, 12J, ANC. Words attributed to nata Kaka.

38. Doui de Tiouandé to Gouverneur, Tiouandé, 18 July 1917, 1W2 (1007), ANC.

39. Nicolas Ratzel, "Cahiers de mes souvenirs," no. 8 (1944), 20J.1, ANC, citing a report by the gendarme Dubos dated 2 April 1917.

40. Nouméa Court of Assizes, 39th session, *Le Bulletin du Commerce*, 26 September 1919.

41. Auguste Oué and Badzi to Poany Marova Léonard, Poinda, 8 January 1918, 1W1, ANC.

42. Théin Gathélia and Auguste Oué to M. le Chef du Service, Poinda, 13 January. 1918, 1W1, ANC.

43. Trépied, "Langues et pouvoir en Nouvelle-Calédonie coloniale," 161–62.

44. B. Appoint to Gouverneur, Poindimié, 15 March 1918, in *Centenaire Maurice Leenhardt (1878–1954): Pasteur et ethnologue*, ed. Société d'Études historiques de la Nouvelle-Calédonie (1978; Nouméa: Société d'Études historiques de la Nouvelle-Calédonie, 1994), 87.

45. Titielet chief of Poyes to Belet, Poyes, 13 January 1918 1W1 (306), ANC.

46. Benoît Chalandon to Claude-Marie Chanrion, Touho, 28 May 1918, AAN 83.6.

47. Le Grand Chef de Hienghène Douÿ to Gouverneur, Hienghène, 27 February 1918, 1W1 (8), ANC; and Douÿ, "Rapport au Sujet des Chef Rebelles Goa, et Mindia," 9 April 1918, 1W1 (359), ANC.

48. Clifford, *Person and Myth*, 140.

49. This may be comparable in some respects with practices described elsewhere in this volume, notably by Bruno Saura.

50. The titles used are from the opening lines. The English translations and glosses used here and in following examples have been made from the French translation of the Paicî texts as published in Bensa, Goromoedo, and Muckle, *Les Sanglots de l'aigle pêcheur*, and should therefore be treated as indicative only.

51. Found in one of a set of five exercise books in Leenhardt's papers ("Cahiers rébellion 1917: Chants de guerre 1917," par Baunyan Copiou Goropoajelai, 12J92, ANC) with the Ajië title "Pe rhè ne cipà 1917" (Poem on the war of 1917), the poem "The two of us lament for the country" was transcribed and translated in 2009 by Alban Bensa and Yvon Goromoedo with Manon Capo and Jean-Claude Rivierre. Bwëungä Cöpiu Göröpwêjilèi is the presumed author (based on Leenhardt's notes), but it is possible that the scribe was someone else and that the name masks the contributions of other persons involved in its composition. The full Paicî text and French translation are in Bensa, Goromoedo, and Muckle, *Les Sanglots de l'aigle pêcheur*, 433–64.

52. Lines 3–4: bu wârî môtö-géé / baa töö diri âboro.

53. Lines 10–11: jè po töö wâ Pécigo / töö i wâ pëërë pô.

54. The parenthetical quotations are from lines 18 and 84–85: âgö dö mä pi-âgötùrù / . . . / po tü â po töri wêê / wakè cipa.

55. Lines 47 and 51–53: é pa côwâ géé nä tii / . . . / cibwaa pa të täjii / pitiri të nyûââ-rä-wâ / tä gù të nyûââ-rä-näpô.

56. A copy of the original Paicî text dating from 1918–19 was made in 1927 by nata Eleisha Näbai with a partial translation into Ajië. Näbai then made a second copy of the original in 1948. From this last copy, typed up by the linguist André-Georges Haudricourt in 1965, the linguist Jean-Claude Rivierre and Dui Novis Pöömô established a transcription with a word-for-word annotated translation in 1967.

57. Lines 24–25: baa gë tu-jai pinyî—and you're transgressing the sacred ties; â gë èa-jai nyä-kêê—you're violating his edict.

58. The original ending: jè pwiri jëkutä kä-wë / nä guwë pa-götù étö. Näbai's revised ending (lines 693–96): jè a cä-ba-puu étö / â u tëmwârâ udërù / â au wârîco baa nê / au baa bwia näpô.

59. This shift to the written form in itself perhaps reveals these writers' awareness of the literary value of their poetry. They may have compared them to biblical psalms, which they sometimes recall, and it should be noted that some authors also created *taperas*, religious Christian songs in Kanak languages.

60. See Ammann, *Kanak Dance and Music*, 127–29. Ammann explains that ténô "can be performed in either rhythmical recitation or in a song. When singing a *ténô* the lyric differs from the recitation form" (128).

61. "Colloque," 17–19.

CHAPTER THREE

Māori Literacy Practices
in Colonial New Zealand

LACHY PATERSON

VARIOUS NEW ZEALAND HISTORIANS writing on print culture or missionaries, or offering wider sweeps of the country's history, have discussed literacy, albeit rather briefly in many cases. How texts impacted on nineteenth-century Māori society is obviously an important part of a wider discussion on the effects of early European-Māori encounters and engagement, and subsequent British colonization. As Tony Ballantyne has pointed out, scholars have largely debated whether literacy acted "as a corrosive force" on Māori society that enabled European control, or "had limited impact on indigenous mentalities" owing to the inherent and enduring oral characteristics of Māori culture.[1] More recent work, to which this chapter contributes, allows Māori more agency. At times Māori were able to gain some control of texts for their own purposes, in order to conduct relationships with Pākehā (Europeans), to reinterpret religious truths, or to resist or mitigate the deleterious effects of colonialism.[2]

With some exceptions, much of the discussion on Māori and texts has focused on the period in which literacy was being introduced, and thus on the *acquisition* of literacy. Te Tiriti o Waitangi (also known as the Treaty of Waitangi) of 1840, perhaps the most contentious but influential of texts from

New Zealand's history, ushered in formal British colonization that exposed Māori to a far more intensive, extensive, and systematic textual world. Rather than debates on how literate Māori were, more work is needed on how Māori used the new skills within social, political, economic, and other contexts, and how this developed within an increasingly Pākehā-dominated nation-state. This chapter briefly surveys some of the existing literature, but its main argument is that literacy practices, the "cultural ways of utilising written language which people draw upon in their lives," have more relevance than the rate of individual literacy in the context of historical tribal societies, such as Māori of the nineteenth century, where social and political activity was of a more collective nature.[3]

Applying "a social theory of literacy" to historical settings is more productive for understanding the diffusion of cultural change over space or time than merely seeing literacy as marking a rupture between "before" and "after" states.[4] As David Barton and Mary Hamilton suggest, "Literacy is best understood as a set of social practices" mediated by, and embedded within, social institutions and cultural practice, which may vary from one situation to another, and change over time.[5] As cultural constructs, literacy (or literacies) are inevitably "historically situated."[6] Literacy practices should not be seen as the attainment of certain skills by individuals but are "more usefully understood as existing in the relations between people, within groups and communities."[7] In colonial settings, it was inevitable that the colonized would view and use literacy differently from the colonizers.[8] The dissimilarity existed not just because of the fundamental preexisting cultural differences, but also owing to the various social, political, and economic imperatives emerging from the asymmetric relationships generated by the colonial dynamic. As with other societies that had not yet achieved Western notions of modernity, literacy changed nineteenth-century Māori society but was also adapted to their own needs and understandings.

Twenty years after the Anglican mission to Māori was established in New Zealand, the Church Missionary Society missionary William Yate proclaimed in his 1835 book on mission activities in New Zealand that Māori were keen to learn to read and write, and to buy books and slates, even establishing their own schools to pass on the necessary skills to others. At the same time, slaves, freed by their newly converted masters, were returning to areas missionaries were yet to visit, bringing with them the knowledge they had acquired.[9] The missionaries, who arrived in the north of New Zealand in 1814, had initially struggled with writing *te reo Māori* (the Māori language), but the development of a workable orthography for te reo Māori from 1820 had facilitated the process, with the Māori desire for literacy and books from about 1830 coinciding with missionary success on the spiritual front. The books produced from the missionary presses were predominantly religious, and it is difficult to ascertain whether it was conversion that spurred enthusiasm for literacy or the other way around, but they were certainly concurrent phenomena.[10]

C. J. Parr's 1961 essay on early missionary printing and his 1963 essay on Māori literacy covering the period 1843 to 1867 utilized substantial missionary sources to assert a Māori eagerness for literacy and demand for books from the 1830s to the mid-1840s.[11] Historians generally accepted this. Parr's scholarship aligns with a nationalistic phase in New Zealand history at a time when the country's race-relations policy foresaw (and desired) "rapid racial integration, defined somewhat mystically as a combination but not a fusion of Maori and Pakeha elements in one nation."[12] Progressive Māori engagement with modernity in the past fit the prevailing intellectual mood. Parr went on to suggest that interest in literacy then faded and that although Māori interest in education waxed and waned in his research period, up to the passing of the Native Schools Act 1867, the enthusiasm of the 1830s never returned.

In 1985 D. F. McKenzie published the slim but influential *Oral Culture and Literacy and Print in Early New Zealand: The Treaty of Waitangi*, which critiqued the notion that Māori could have become functionally literate in such a short time. McKenzie judged the missionary evidence as "anecdotal," perhaps "wishful thinking," or based on a definition of literacy set "at a level far below that demanded by the social changes to which the Maori were being exposed."[13] The latter possibility has parallels with Jack Goody's theory of "restricted literacy," in which residual elements of orality inhibit the full transformative effects of literacy within certain societies, an argument that has been criticized for being ethnocentric, as it is based an ideal of post-Homeric Greece.[14] Indeed, as Brian V. Street has observed, "most societies would appear not to match up to Goody's ideal," including the ideal itself.[15]

Using the Treaty of Waitangi "as a test case for measuring the impact of literacy and the influence of print in the 1830s," McKenzie counted the signatures on the document among the over five hundred marks of various kinds, and concluded that at least 87 percent, that is, those who did not sign their names, were illiterate.[16] That the seventy-two signatures present were "so painfully and crudely written" indicates, he argued, that the signatories were not "fluent in the art" of writing.[17] McKenzie stated that Māori did not possess a culture of literacy when they encountered the treaty in 1840, and thus understood it through the lens of oral culture. Indeed, he also implied that there was no real Māori-language literacy and, more controversially, that Māori still continued to possess an essentially oral culture.

Several years later McKenzie's argument was in turn critiqued by Lyndsay Head and Buddy Mikaere in a short essay, "Was 19th Century Maori Society Literate?" Declaring themselves "moderately outraged," they argued that the treaty is not a suitable test case, having been signed by chiefs, who were less likely to have gained literacy skills: first, the acquisition of European knowledge, a source of mana (power/status), was more attractive to societal groups less well endowed with inherited mana than older chiefs whose status was in no doubt; second, given the scarcity of pens and paper, reading was a more widespread skill than writing; and, third, the treaty was presented as an oral event, and that is how the chiefs reacted to it, and their signing a document was part of the "theatre."[18] Head and Mikaere dismissed not only McKenzie's idea of little or no Māori literacy ever but also Parr's theory of early enthusiasm. Instead, they asserted that the 1830s was merely the infancy of Māori literacy and that "the great age of writing *only started* in the 1840s."[19]

While some scholars point to the continuing nature of orality practices within Māori society, most also accept the assimilation of written and printed texts into Māori intellectual culture and social life.[20] A few even accept McKenzie's notion that there was no Māori literacy before the mid-1840s. Swayed by McKenzie's argument, historian James Belich warns against accepting missionary claims and suggests that "Maori literacy in the 1830s has been exaggerated somewhat by writers overeager to praise the Maori for being like 'Us.'"[21] Similarly influenced, Danny Keenan, in his chapter in *Huia Histories of Māori: Ngā Tāhuhu Kōrero*, asserts that "Māori rates of literacy in 1840 were in fact very low" and that Māori did not fully understand the nature of the treaty.[22] However, noted historians such as Ranginui Walker, Claudia Orange, Judith Binney (in *The New Oxford History of New Zealand*), Peter Lineham, Binney again with Judith Bassett and Erik Olssen, Tony Ballantyne, and Raeburn Lange, among others, are more convinced by the historical sources than by McKenzie's critique.[23] At times the inclination is to go beyond a discourse of Māori merely being as good as Pākehā, instead describing them as having, in record time, surpassed Pākehā in the acquisition of literacy. For example, Pat Hohepa asserts that "by 1856 some 90% of the Maori population were able to read and write in their own language."[24] In his chapter in *Huia Histories of Māori*, Bradford Haami claims that by 1844 Māori were more literate than Pākehā.[25] *Te Ara*, the government's online encyclopedia, is perhaps the most bullish, stating that "by 1842 most Māori aged between 10 and 30 could read and write their own language, a higher literacy rate than in the non-Māori population."[26]

McKenzie's counting of signatures on the treaty gives a maximum Māori literacy level of no more than 13 percent in 1840. The methodology itself—based on the notion that schoolchildren were taught to read before learning to write—is open to question.[27] As Head and Mikaere and others have pointed out, the signatories represented a small, older group within Māori society less likely to have sought out literacy skills.[28] If we contrast the treaty with a "petition" signed at the Kohimarama Conference twenty years later (again, by men of chiefly rank), the same methods give a literacy rate of just under 50 percent.[29] Even if equating signatures with reading ability is an uncertain methodology, a shift from 12 percent to about half over twenty years within groups of a similar demographic makeup is a substantial rise that suggests significant societal change. However, other documents from the same decade merely confound any meaningful analysis of literacy rates based on signatures, other than indicating that not all individuals could sign their names. For example, 93 percent of signatories to an 1859 Waitōtara land deed signed with an X, but just 45 percent on the Waitara Block deed the following year; in 1863, 62 percent marked an X on a 1863 letter to the governor from Ōtaki Māori, as did nearly 80 percent of Tūranga Māori on an 1868 petition to Parliament.[30] As Ballantyne notes with regard to the South Island, "by around 1850, roughly 50 percent of high-ranking Kai Tahu men were able to sign their name on land deeds," although this varied from 36.8 percent to 66 percent across documents.[31]

While considerable primary evidence exists for the missionary period, it is qualitative and not reliable enough to point to definitive literacy rates. Besides, the missionaries were largely confined to the top half of the North Island until after the treaty was signed, with most of them north of Auckland. In her chapter in this volume, Noelani Arista notes the Hawaiian "thirst" for literacy; similarly, the writings of New Zealand missionaries confirm that the Māori they encountered were enthusiastic to learn to read and that there was a keen demand for books up to the mid-1840s (although we cannot necessarily equate book ownership with skill in reading). But notwithstanding the return of literate slaves, freed by their newly converted masters, what was happening on the east coast of the North Island, where missionaries arrived later and were fewer in number, was most likely very different from the situation in the Northland region with its much longer and more intense history of European contact.[32] We therefore cannot apply early missionary reckonings to the whole country.

McKenzie implies that a limited absorption of literacy skills meant that Māori were unable to cope in the new textualized world: that "for the non-literate, the document and its implications were meaningless; for the barely literate, the ability to sign one's name was a trap."[33] It is true that documents could sometimes ensnare Māori, particularly when they trusted Pākehā, or when literacy practices were divorced from *tikanga Māori* (Māori custom). In the 1830s Ngāti Toa chief Te Rauparaha signed a document giving Captain Blenkinsopp rights to timber and water at Cloudy Bay in exchange for a ship's gun. When the chief discovered that the written deed actually transferred ownership of the whole Wairau Plain, he tore his copy up.[34] Before formal colonization privileged paper and text, written documents possessed little value if they did not align with tribal imperatives. At that time Te Rauparaha possessed mana over the area, which trumped any doubtful authority that the deed may have had. But it was this scrap of paper, widely known to be fraudulent, that sparked the bloodshed at Wairau in 1843 between Ngāti Toa and Nelson settlers, when the latter tried to assert ownership on the basis of Blenkinsopp's deed.[35]

As noted in this volume's introduction, indigenous people became entangled within wider colonial processes. Similarly, Māori became increasingly at risk from legislative and judicial textual instruments and practices following the assertion of British sovereignty. The government established Native Land Courts from 1862 specifically to extinguish and convert native title, held by Māori under customary practice without recourse to paper records, into Crown titles, suitably documented and more easily understood by the English legal system. Once land and property rights were represented by paper, settlers could more easily acquire land through direct purchase, sometimes with dubious ethical standards. For example, Ārihi Te Nahu described how the wealthy Hawkes Bay runholder Henry Russell and his lawyer talked her into signing documents she could not read in the 1860s.[36] As late as 1901, newspapers discussed the case of a Pākehā and his lawyer tricking an illiterate Māori woman out of her land.[37] But there are also ample cases of fraud and duplicity relating to Māori who were literate, including in the English language, such as the wealthy and educated heiress Maata Mahupuku, who was embezzled by her lawyer in 1906.[38] Such cases would indicate that it was the praxis of colonialism in which literacy practices were embedded that threatened Māori rather than a perceived Māori lack of literacy.

McKenzie's assumption is that nineteenth-century Māori's lives were as atomized and individual as those of Pākehā, who could have been severely disadvantaged if illiterate.[39] Māori society evolved with the British annexation of New Zealand; the government's slow pursuit and consolidation of power through land purchase, war, legal chicanery, and assimilatory policies; and Māori exposure to, and even embrace of, aspects of the Pākehā culture, economy, and religion. But it never changed as much or as quickly as Pākehā missionaries and officials wanted. Māori society retained much of its communal and tribal nature and chiefly rule through the nineteenth century. As with much other imported cultural cargo, Māori attempted to fit literacy into their own societal practices, not the other way around.

McKenzie also suggests that the missionaries believed that the literacy that Māori of 1840 had incorporated into their culture in a relatively short time was somehow comparable to that of educated Europeans, supposedly having achieved "the reduction of speech to alphabetic forms, an ability to read and write them, a readiness to shift from memory to written word, to accept a signature as a sign of full comprehension and legal commitment, to surrender the relativities of time, place and person in an oral culture to the presumed fixities of the written or printed word."[40] Was this really the missionaries' "conviction"? As Head and Mikaere have posited, Māori literacy was in its infancy in 1840, a notion with which I am sure most missionaries would have concurred. However, McKenzie's argument conflates the skills of literacy (such as signing one's name) with other cultural practices. As he states, "a slate may prove that one can write, but not that one can write to any purpose," implying that, notwithstanding one's skills in reading and writing, one needs to be able to apply them to a particular set of cultural practices to be considered literate.[41] His discussion on the treaty betrays the same understanding, in which the Māori state of preliteracy is supposedly shown in their failure to understand the intent of the Crown, and their reliance on oral discussion at a public meeting. However, conferring the status of literacy based on how one applies the associated skills depends very much on where the bar is set. Do we deem a person who reads newspapers nonliterate if they cannot understand the fine print of a mortgage agreement? For McKenzie, being able to read and write, in essence a set of learned skills, had not yet sufficiently transformed Māori society.

Some scholars have argued that literacy possesses an agency or causative powers within societies that acquire it. For example, Head, who has been critical of McKenzie on several occasions, suggests that literacy undermined group consensus: this can be seen in "the large number of letters from individuals seeking to exclude others from a sale or . . . payment for land."[42] But was the *technology* of communication principally responsible for an erosion of tribal unity, or was it colonialism's various cultural *institutions* and *practices*, in which literacy was embedded? For example, individuals could also try to privilege their own land rights by oral means through private conversation with government purchasers, or testimony in the Native Land Court. Conversely, they could write letters asserting communal ownership of land.

It has also been argued that an individual's acquisition of literacy is instrumental in changing their cognitive processes, that is, how they might think. Walter J. Ong, in particular, asserts that writing "restructures thought"; that the thought and language of illiterates tend to repetition, redundancy, and formulae; and that "abstractly sequential, classificatory, explanatory examination of phenomena or of stated truths is impossible without writing and reading."[43] Literacy and abstraction therefore go together. Street, however, who described this linkage as the "autonomous model" of literacy, dismissed it in favor of an "ideological model" that defines literacy "in terms of concrete social practices" and "the ideologies in which different literacies are embedded."[44] In particular, sustained schooling and modern education, R. Scollon and S. W. Scollon's "Utilitarian discourse system," are far more significant than the ability to read and write for encouraging linear abstract thought.[45] This was substantially exhibited by Sylvia Scribner and Michael Cole's research among the Vai people of Liberia, where large numbers who have no formal education acquire literacy, in their own language and in an indigenous script, informally from friends or relatives, a situation not dissimilar to that of many Māori in the 1830s and 1840s.[46] They found that schooling improved aptitude in cognitive tests, but "there was no indication that the mere ability to use language in written form had any general impact."[47]

What does this mean for this discussion? McKenzie is right that Māori in 1840 did not exercise the same range of literacy practices as Pākehā, but this does not make their society nonliterate. As Scribner states with respect to the Vai literates who primarily use reading and writing for letter writing and domestic purposes, "literacy practices that arise in a given society are dependent on that society's history and structure."[48] Similarly, in their chapters in this volume, Michael P. J. Reilly and Bruno Saura show how some Polynesian societies fitted literacy into their own intellectual practices. Before 1840 Māori lived within tribal communities according to tikanga Māori, and for most day-to-day activities, people could easily speak to each other. Formal schooling was limited in quality, duration, and spread. Other than reading the printed material produced by missionaries—the only literature with the potential to reveal outside knowledge—and writing letters (perhaps as a novelty), literacy had few practical uses. However, after 1840 Māori were confronted with a nascent colonial administration, whose reach and power expanded over the course of the century. This possessed its own literacy practices—correspondence and official forms, instructions and threats, inquiries and demands, recorded statistics and data—to which Māori were initially encouraged, then increasingly expected or obliged, to respond, generally through reciprocal scribal practices.

Colonization also facilitated and helped diversify and expand literacy practices within and between Māori communities. Intertribal warfare became increasingly less prevalent in the first two decades, facilitating easier internal travel and the carrying of Māori letters between villages. A number of commentators described Māori enthusiasm for writing letters, some even scratched onto flax leaves.[49] Māori also used government mail services, some of which Māori contractors ran themselves.[50] In 1855 the government's Māori-language newspaper, *Te Karere Maori* (The Māori messenger), alerted Māori "to a number of letters lying in the Auckland Post Office," and especially called on those with friends in Sydney to inspect what was there.[51] Another newspaper, *Te Karere o Poneke* (The Port Nicholson messenger), in June 1858 published the names of Māori men who had mail waiting for them at the Wellington Post Office.[52] Māori experiences of colonization also led to inter- and pan-tribal cooperation, in political movements such as the Kīngitanga from the late 1850s and the Kotahitanga, which by the 1890s had developed its own Māori-run parliament. These initiatives all utilized their own literacy practices, including correspondence, petitions to the government, the publishing of newspapers, and, in the case of the Kotahitanga, printed debates from their parliament.[53] Māori published their own newspapers in which they discussed and debated their concerns: politics, land issues, the changing world, and *whakapapa* (genealogy).

During the nineteenth century other forms of literacy also emerged around Māori knowledge. This included the intellectual Te Rangikaheke, who collaborated with former governor Sir George Grey in the early 1850s, and the individuals paid by the page for tribal information by ethnographer John White, who went on to produce *The Ancient History of the Maori, His Mythology and Traditions*.[54] At the end of the century, some Māori were also writing to the *Journal of the Polynesian Society* to ensure that there was indigenous input into discussions of Māori custom.[55] Māori also collected genealogies and tribal histories for their own handwritten whakapapa books, some of which have been handed down to descendants.[56] In the face of these various modes of literacy, McKenzie's assertion that Māori society has never really been literate appears astounding. Parr's suggestion that Māori literacy after its initial flowering decayed during the second half of the nineteenth century also needs unpacking.

Parr's main argument for a declining literacy rate is based on fluctuating interest in missionary schooling, which he posits indicates a declining Māori interest in reading and writing.[57] It is difficult to get accurate numbers for Māori attending missionary schools that attempted to teach a bilingual curriculum, but it never appears high, numbering in the hundreds rather than the thousands. However, this does not necessarily equate to a low engagement with literacy skills, particularly for practical purposes. As the Anglican missionary Thomas Samuel Grace lamented in 1855, "as for reading, writing and arithmetic," there was "a nation of such scholars": a girl might be sent to a mission school to gain an education, but on her return "she finds there many who are able to read, write and figure as well as she, and, as for the fine accomplishments, they go for nothing."[58] A government report in 1858 described Māori students at Tūranga who wished to become teachers as having "had little or no previous education," thus requiring instruction in "almost everything, except reading and writing."[59] Many Māori may have lost their taste for missionary education over time, but it was the wars of the 1860s, through which the colonial state sought to demonstrate its coercive ability, that effectively killed off these schools: "By 1865 . . . only 22 Maori pupils in total . . . [were] attending any type of school in the colony."[60]

William Rolleston's report to the native minister in 1867 that the missionary schools had been largely ineffective in "breaking through the communism of the Maori pa" was the final nail in the coffin.[61] Parliament soon after passed the Native Schools Act 1867, giving the government the primary responsibility for Māori education, with a particular emphasis on primary schools (for children from five to about twelve years old) and the teaching of English.[62] Under the act, Māori communities were required to request a school, donate land, pay for half the building costs, and contribute to salaries, although these costs were ameliorated four years later.[63] Parr states that after a slow start "the number of Government day schools grew rapidly," implying a deep penetration into Māori society. There is no denying that the agenda was to assimilate Māori children into the mainstream Pākehā culture and to foist English on them as their working language, but the desire was not really matched by the results. Unlike Pākehā children, Māori children were not compelled to attend school under the Education Act 1877, and attendance could be patchy. For example, the Whakatāne Native School in December 1873 had seventy-six pupils on its books. However, when the inspector visited, only forty-three were present, and the rolls revealed an average daily attendance of thirty-three.[64] The 1878 national census gives a figure of 12,645 Māori children under fifteen years of age, quite possible an undercount.[65] If that figure is halved to discount infants and children over twelve, then the 1,920 pupils attending native schools in 1877 comprised about 30 percent of this demographic grouping.[66] The 1895/1896 census and school attendance data give a figure of about 37 percent, and by 1900/1901 it was 38 percent.[67] Although by the end of the century an unknown number of Māori students were attending schools intended for Pākehā, it would still seem that significant numbers of Māori received no schooling, or at best a patchy education, throughout the nineteenth century, and formal education influenced literacy practices less than we might suppose.

Formal education could and did have an impact. Individuals who were exposed to intensive schooling, such as the intellectuals Rēweti Kōhere and Sir Āpirana Ngata, who attended the premier Māori boys' school, Te Aute College, and subsequently studied at a university at the end of the century, wrote quite differently from earlier, less educated writers. Where previous Māori writers often tended to a more oral style, such as addressing the readers directly, incorporating *waiata* (sung poetry), or using rather terse descriptive prose, Kōhere's and Ngata's Māori-language writings are generally more expansive, often adhering to the structured essay style favored in formal education.[68] However, relatively few Māori received an education to this level.

While we might accept that overall Māori society had achieved a certain level of literacy, this did not mean that all individuals were literate. In research that Angela Wanhalla and I have undertaken on nineteenth-century Māori women's writings, we have found plenty of examples where documents were signed with an "X," or individuals stated that they could not read or write, even at the end of the century.[69] But does this mean that "the document and its implications were meaningless" to them, as McKenzie suggests?[70] Using the example of northern India, C. A. Bayly notes that although literacy rates were relatively low, people were nevertheless "literacy aware" and made use of individuals offering textual services "in complex and creative ways to reinforce oral culture and debate."[71] The communal nature of Māori society meant that illiterate people similarly had access to literacy, including generating letters. The use of scribes was not uncommon, particularly for chiefs. For example, in the mid-1840s J. C. Crawford recalled meeting the chief Hōri Pātene at Pipiriki, stating, "His chief scribe sat beside him writing a letter."[72] Māori might go to trusted Pākehā for help; for example, Ramarihi gave evidence in 1879 that she had asked Agnes Grace, a missionary wife and teacher, to write a letter for her.[73] The journals of Agnes's husband, Thomas Samuel Grace, tell of Māori women in the Bay of Plenty dictating messages to scribes, including singing waiata, for their husbands who had been taken to Auckland as prisoners of war in the conflicts of the 1860s.[74] Letters were often communal affairs, with many signatures, or purported to represent a wider grouping, such as a letter from Raihania Tamahērangi and Te Rēweti Te Hiakai to Governor George Grey, published in *Te Karere Maori*. The men signed the letter to the governor but added, "From all the people of Waipapa, Wāhikainga, and Kaikoura." However, the letter concluded with "Written by Kepa," indicating the use of a scribe, of an unknown status.[75]

One more example should suffice. In 1876 the government newspaper *Te Waka Maori o Niu Tirani* (The Māori canoe of New Zealand) published several letters defaming the runholder and politician Henry Russell.[76] One was from Ārihi Te Nahu and three men. Ārihi Te Nahu was a wealthy chiefly woman with extensive landholdings, and it is clear that she was the person initiating the document: her name is first, and most of the letter is in the first person singular concerning her experiences. She also sent a subsequent letter, signed just by her, to *Te Wananga* (The forum), a rival and hostile newspaper, in which she took all responsibility for the original correspondence. Yet, as a defense witness in the subsequent libel case against the newspaper, Ārihi declared, "I cannot read or write." She said:

> I know a newspaper called the *Waka Maori*. It is published in Wellington. I have sent a letter to that newspaper. I instructed Hamiora [her husband] to write it. I dictated the letter to him and was present when he wrote it. I told him to put my name to it. I told him to put the name of Nepia Te Hapuku to it. I told him to put the name of Hapuku te Nahu to it. I told him to put the name of Tipene to it. These natives were not present when the letter was written.
> Q.—*Had you their authority for putting their names to the letter[?].*
> A.—Yes; we talked over the matter beforehand and they agreed that I should publish it in the newspaper.[77]

Thus, we see that an inability to read and write did not inhibit Ārihi Te Nahu's access to literacy practices, in this case sending correspondence to Māori-language newspapers. But her engagement is mediated by the collective nature of Māori society at the time: her husband wrote it and added her relatives' names at her behest because she was confident that they supported her. Similarly, Māngai Uhuuhu, the author of another libelous letter, appended the name of his wife, Hemaima Whanako. Hemaima, who could read but not write, saw the letter in the newspaper after it was printed. She said, "I knew

Mangai was going to send such a letter. I gave my consent to my name being put to it after the letter appeared. I approved of the words of the letter."[78]

In her evidence Ārihi Te Nahu also discussed some correspondence from the lawyer and politician John Sheehan, regarding a meeting she was unable to attend that had relevance to the case. She said, "I have lost those letters. I have been searching for them. Some I found and some I have not found. There was a particular letter about the meeting. I have lost it. There are many natives who saw that letter."[79] That others saw the correspondence gave it validity within her own community, but for her, a woman unable to read or write, documents were not meaningless, nor their implications unknown. She was fully aware of their importance and lamented their loss.

Another feature of literacy practice, not unique to nineteenth-century Māori but certainly prevalent, was the interplay of oral and textual forms by the reading of documents out loud with subsequent group discussion. For example, Walter Brodie describes Māori chiefs coming to Auckland in the 1840s to pick up copies of *Te Karere o Nui Tireni* (The messenger of New Zealand), the government's first Māori-language newspaper: "One native of a party is generally selected to read the news aloud: when he takes his seat upon the ground, a circle is then formed, and after the reader has promulgated the contents, the different natives, according to their rank, stand up and argue the different points contained; which being done, they retire home, and answer the different letters by writing to the editor, who is the Protector of the Aborigines."[80] Texts, in the form of letters and newspapers, became inextricably linked to many Māori political meetings, as can be seen from the following examples concerning the Taranaki region in 1860. In that year the government precipitated a war against sections of the Te Āti Awa tribe in an attempt to enforce a disputed land sale; other Taranaki tribes, and the Kīngitanga, a pan-tribal movement espousing political independence, in turn assisted the tribe militarily. Many chiefs around the country were sympathetic to Wiremu Kīngi Te Rangitāke, the Te Āti Awa chief, while others were happy to side with the government. When Tāmihana Te Rauparaha of Ngāti Toa visited Māori settlements in support of the government's cause, he read out letters by Donald McLean, the native secretary, to those listening and encouraged them to send letters to McLean to express their loyalty.[81] Other chiefs gained information from the government's newspaper. In March 1860 Hākopa Te Waharoa wrote to *Te Karere Maori*, saying, "On the 6th we held a meeting on the subject of the Taranaki feud, about which we have read in this newspaper."[82] No doubt the newspaper's articles were read to the assembly. Similarly, when Waikato chiefs met at Waiuku in early 1860 to debate the direction of the Kīngitanga, and the deteriorating situation in Taranaki, letters from Te Rangitāke were read out asking for the movement to put pressure on the governor, along with an article from *Te Karere Maori* outlining the government's position on Taranaki. Given that neither Te Rangitāke nor the governor was present at the meeting, this public reading may perhaps be expected. However, when a general discussion ensued on the nature of mana and sovereignty, the faction that promoted political separation from the government chose to read out a paper to advance its arguments rather than rely solely on traditional oratorical techniques.[83]

This complementary nature of the textual and oral discourses within Māori politics can also be seen in a letter to Governor Grey signed by fourteen Taranaki chiefs that was subsequently printed in *Te Karere Maori*. The letter relates to a public debate at Kohanga in the Waikato in December 1861 between Grey and three Kīngitanga orators about the basis of the Kīngitanga's claim to represent all Māori. The Taranaki chiefs met to discuss the implications of this debate, which they had read about in the newspaper. The chiefs' letter itself has an oral style, as if they were themselves present at the original debate, with one of their number addressing both the Waikato orators and the governor. Their letter also discussed earlier correspondence they had received from the Kīngitanga, and a meeting they had attended at which a letter from Te Rangitāke had been read out. The chiefs concluded with "Let this be printed," indicating that they wanted their position to be broadcast to a wider audience, and possibly for further discussion.[84] Their letter shows not only to what extent they incorporated literacy practices into political discourse but also how that discourse could slide from oral to textual and back again. We cannot be sure how many of the fourteen chiefs were literate, but this was not really relevant. Textual information was shared and discussed publicly and responded to collectively. Individuals who could not read and write were not precluded from social and political engagement within the Māori world.

Much of New Zealand's historiography on historical Māori literacy has been concerned with the period when missionaries had their greatest influence and when Māori first gained the skills of reading and writing. However, there is little consensus on literacy acquisition. Some scholars accept missionary assertions of a widespread uptake, a position severely critiqued by D. F. McKenzie. However, he extrapolates from a single snapshot, the "signing" of the Treaty of Waitangi in 1840, and the fact that Māori literary practices did not adhere to modern Western norms, to suggest that Māori culture has been functionally nonliterate in nature to this day.

This argument, although influential, is far too simplistic and Eurocentric. While an individual's acquisition of literacy may be seen in "before" and "after" states, the application of the skills has been dynamic over time. Colonialism was mediated by paper and text, and literacy practices were embedded in, and mediated by, its wider cultural and societal institutions, systems, and processes. Given the structure and history of Māori society in 1840, it is unsurprising that what Māori *did* with reading and writing was rather limited at that time—they were not yet writing novels—but practices did develop and expand in the face of the demands and opportunities of the colonial period, as internal and external social, religious, political, and economic factors transformed society.

As a historian interested in culture, I feel that the study of literacy practices is more interesting and productive than just the acquisition of literacy, or literacy rates. A focus on literacy acquisition creates two binaries: preliterate and literate points in time, and illiterate and literate categories of people. As Ivy Schweitzer's discussion of literacy in colonial New England in this volume shows, these were conceptual divisions with a long colonial history. Māori literacy practices, like those of other indigenous peoples, were more inclusive and dynamic, evolving over time. There is also a large corpus of archival material that testifies to Māori engagement in literacy practices, providing a window not only on the social and cultural aspects of Māori communities in the nineteenth and early twentieth centuries but also on their intellectual lives. Inquiring into literacy practices can assist in understanding the many aspects of Māori life permeated by textual culture.

Māori engagement with literacy did change over time. The missionaries' primary aim was to enable Māori to read the scriptures. Some nineteenth-century Māori expanded their skills to become inveterate letter writers, writing to each other as well as to missionaries or government officials. Māori read newspapers in their own language, wrote letters to the editors, and then later in the century produced their own newspapers. Land dealings became increasingly textualized, through Native Land Court Minute Books, scrip and Crown grant certificates, and legal deeds. Education comprised mission schools and informal indigenous teaching, then later government-run village schools, but a significant proportion of nineteenth-century Māori remained illiterate. However, owing to the communal structure of Māori society, an inability to read and write did not preclude individuals from participating in a variety of literacy practices and modes of writing relevant to their lived experience.

1. Ballantyne, "Christianity, Colonialism and Cross-Cultural Communication," 29, 30.

2. On relationships with Pākehā, see Jones and Jenkins, *He Kōrero*. Although Alison Jones and Kuni Jenkins discuss how Māori engaged meaningfully with text prior to colonization, they adhere to a fatal impact thesis with regard to the colonial period, claiming that "the power of writing . . . had proved itself an illusion; it was not, after all, a tool to ensure tino rangatiratanga, authority and mana in Māori engagement with Pākehā" (202). On resistance to colonialism, see Ballantyne, "Christianity, Colonialism and Cross-Cultural Communication," 31, 55–57.

3. The definition of literacy practices is from Barton and Hamilton, "Literacy Practices," 7.

4. Barton and Hamilton, "Literacy Practices," 7.

5. Barton and Hamilton, "Literacy Practices," 9.

6. Barton and Hamilton, "Literacy Practices," 7–14, quote used on 2, 8, and 13.

7. Barton and Hamilton, "Literacy Practices," 8.

8. For example, Kulick and Stroud, "Conceptions and Uses of Literacy in a Papua New Guinean Village," 31–34; Peterson, *Creative Writing*, 5; and Van Toorn, *Writing Never Arrives Naked*, 226–27.

9. Yate, *An Account of New Zealand and of the Church Missionary Society's Mission in the Northern Island*, 239–41.

10. Within the Pacific this was not restricted to just Māori. Parsonson, *The Conversion of Polynesia*, 6–8. For a discussion of orthographic development and Māori-language print culture, see Binney, *The Legacy of Guilt*, 175–81; and McRae, "From Māori Oral Traditions to Print," 17–33.

11. Parr, "A Missionary Library," 429–50; and Parr, "Maori Literacy, 1843–1867," 211–34.

12. Biggs, "Maori Affairs and the Hunn Report," 361. See also Byrnes, "Introduction," 2–3.

13. McKenzie, *Oral Culture and Literacy and Print in Early New Zealand*, 15.

14. Goody, *Restricted Literacy in Northern Ghana*. See also Gee, "Orality and Literacy," 724. For criticism of Goody's view, see Messick, "Legal Documents and the Concept of 'Restricted Literacy' in a Traditional Society," 50.

15. Street, *Literacy in Theory and Practice*, 61, 62.

16. McKenzie, *Oral Culture, Literacy and Print in Early New Zealand*, 9.

17. McKenzie, "The Sociology of a Text: Oral Culture, Literacy and Print in Early New Zealand," 180.

18. Head and Mikaere, "Was 19th Century Maori Society Literate?," 18.

19. Head and Mikaere, "Was 19th Century Maori Society Literate?," 19.

20. On the continuing nature of orality practices, see, for example, Rewi, *Whaikōrero*, 23–27; and McRae, "Māori Oral Tradition Meets the Book," 2. On Māori assimilation of literacy, see, for example, Orbell, *Hawaiki*, preface; McRae, "Māori Oral Tradition Meets the Book," 1–16; and O'Regan, "The Fate of Custom-

ary Language," 299. McRae's "Māori Oral Tradition Meets the Book" is particularly instructive, as well as McRae's "From Māori Oral Traditions to Print." Other works that have looked at Māori engagement with literacy practices include Jones and Jenkins, *He Kōrero*; Haami, *Pūtea Whakairo*; Ballantyne, "Paper, Pen, and Print," 232–60; and Te Punga Somerville, "Living on New Zealand Street," 665–69.

21. Belich, *Making Peoples*, 167; see also p. 136.

22. Keenan, "'Separating Them from That Common Influence,'" 137.

23. Walker, *Ka Whawhai Tonu Matou*, 85; Orange, "The Māori People and the British Crown," 34; Binney, "History and Memory," 74, 78; Lineham, "Missions and Missionaries," page 5, "Māori Converts"; Binney, Bassett, and Olssen, *The People and the Land*, 37; Ballantyne, "Print, Politics and Protestantism in an Imperial Context," 154, 164; and Lange, "Indigenous Agents of Religious Change in New Zealand, 1830–1860," 283.

24. Hohepa, "Current Issues in Promoting Maori Language Use," 1.

25. Haami, "Tā Te Ao Māori," 172.

26. Derby, "Māori–Pākehā Relations," page 2, "Missions and Māori."

27. Kaestle, "The History of Literacy and the History of Readers," 20–21.

28. Head and Mikaere, "Was 19th Century Maori Society Literate?," 18.

29. *Te Karere Maori*, 15 August 1860, 9–10.

30. Appendices to the Journals of the House of Representatives (AJHR), 1860, E-02A, 3; 1862, E-03, 4; 1863, E-15, 1; 1868, A-16, 5. AJHRs can be accessed at *Papers Past: Parliamentary Papers*, National Library of New Zealand, accessed 17 December 2019, https://paperspast.natlib.govt.nz/parliamentary.

31. Ballantyne, "Paper, Pen, and Print," 244–45.

32. On the effect of the returning slaves, see Lange, "Indigenous Agents of Religious Change in New Zealand, 1830–1860," 281.

33. McKenzie, *Oral Culture and Literacy and Print in Early New Zealand*, 40.

34. Burns, *Te Rauparaha*, 185–86.

35. Burns, *Te Rauparaha*, 234, 239–42. See also Arini Loader's chapter in this volume.

36. "Evidence Taken at Napier before Commissioner George Edward Sainsbury, Esquire, Commissioner Appointed by the Supreme Court for the Purpose, Russell v. Grindell & Dinsbury Libel Case," MA/24 1/3, Archives New Zealand, Wellington.

37. *Auckland Star*, 9 December 1901, 5.

38. *Evening Post*, 22 December 1906, 5.

39. Miles Fairburn posited an influential, although heavily critiqued thesis of atomization within nineteenth-century Pākehā society. See Fairburn, *The Ideal Society and Its Enemies*.

40. McKenzie, *Oral Culture and Literacy and Print in Early New Zealand*, 10.

41. McKenzie, *Oral Culture and Literacy and Print in Early New Zealand*, 18.

42. Head, "Land, Authority and the Forgetting of Being in Early Colonial Maori History," 25.

43. Ong, *Orality and Literacy* (2002), 7–8, 8–9. For a discussion on the supposed nature of preliterate thinking, see pp. 36–49.

44. Street, *Critical Approaches to Literacy in Development, Ethnography and Education*, 13; and Street, *Literacy in Theory and Practice*, 96.

45. Scollon and Scollon, *Intercultural Communication*, 99, 104–5, 119–21.

46. Scribner and Cole, *The Psychology of Literacy*, 61–62; and Scribner, "The Practice of Literacy," 10.

47. Scribner, "The Practice of Literacy," 11.

48. Scribner, "The Practice of Literacy," 17.

49. For example, Wade, *A Journey in the Northern Island of New Zealand*, 182; Angas, *Savage Life and Scenes in Australia and New Zealand*, 56, 133; Lady Martin, *Our Maoris*, 72; and W. Brown, *New Zealand and Its Aborigines*, 98.

50. For example, Karehana Te Whena, a mailman in the Whanganui district. See *Te Karere o Poneke*, 24 December 1859, 3.

51. *Te Karere Maori*, 1 January 1855, 29.

52. *Te Karere o Poneke*, 26 June 1858, 2.

53. For example, *Paremata Maori o Niu Tireni i tu ki Te Waipatu, Hune 14, 1892*, New Zealand Electronic Text Centre, Victoria University of Wellington, accessed 6 January 2015, http://nzetc.victoria.ac.nz//tm/scholarly/tei-MaoPare.html.

54. J. Curnow, "Te Rangikaheke, Wiremu Maihi"; and Reilly, "White, John."

55. For example, Nahe, "Maori, Tangata Maori," 27–35.

56. Ballantyne, "Paper, Pen, and Print," 251.

57. Parr, "Maori Literacy, 1843–1867," 212–13.

58. Grace, *A Pioneer Missionary among the Maoris, 1850–1879*, 79–80.

59. AJHR, 1858, E-01, 7.

60. Openshaw, Lee, and Lee, *Challenging the Myths*, 36.

61. AJHR, 1867, A-03.

62. Simon and Smith, *A Civilising Mission?*, 8–9, 141–73; and Openshaw, Lee, and Lee, *Challenging the Myths*, 10, 40.

63. Simon and Smith, *A Civilising Mission?*, 9, 57.

64. AJHR, 1875, G-08, 5, 6.

65. AJHR, 1878, G-02, 10.

66. AJHR, 1877, G-04A, 1.

67. AJHR, 1896, E-02, 18; 1901, H-26B, 4; 1901, E-02, 24; 1901, H-26B, 4.

68. For examples of Māori writing that reflects an oral style, see McRae, "'E manu, tena koe!,'" 42–59; Tremewan, "Poetry in Te Waka Maori," 134–52; and Hogan, *Renata's Journey*, 75. On the structured essay, see Street, *Critical Approaches to Literacy in Development, Ethnography and Education*, 74. Both Ngata and Kōhere wrote prolifically in Māori, including editorial or opinion pieces for the newspaper *Te Pipiwharauroa* (The Shining Cuckoo) (1898–13). See also Kaa and Kaa, *Nga Korero a Reweti Kohere ma*; and Kaa and Kaa, *Apirana Turupa Ngata, Kt., M.A., LLB., D. LIT., M.P.*

69. For example, see Paterson and Wanhalla, *He Reo Wāhine*, 13–15.

70. McKenzie, *Oral Culture and Literacy and Print in Early New Zealand*, 40.

71. Bayly, *Empire and Information*, 39–40, 180.

72. Crawford, *Recollections of Travel in New Zealand and Australia*, 103.

73. AJHR, 1879, I-04, 27.

74. Grace, *A Pioneer Missionary among the Maoris, 1850–1879,* 176.

75. *Te Karere Maori,* 16 December 1862, 16.

76. I have written about this case in more detail in Paterson, "The *Te Waka Māori* Libel Case of 1877," 88–112.

77. "Evidence Taken at Napier."

78. "Evidence Taken at Napier," 24.

79. "Evidence Taken at Napier," 1.

80. Brodie, *Remarks on the Past and Present State of New Zealand,* 110.

81. *Te Karere Maori,* 15 December 1860, 6–9.

82. *Te Karere Maori,* 31 May 1860, 11.

83. *Te Karere Maori,* 15 March 1860, 7, 9.

84. *Te Karere Maori,* 1 May 1862, 13–15.

Part II
Orality &
Texts

CHAPTER FOUR

"Don't Destroy the Writing":
Time- and Space-Based
Communication and the
Colonial Strategy of Mimicry
in Nineteenth-Century
Salish-Missionary Relations
on Canada's Pacific Coast

KEITH THOR CARLSON

IN MAY 1895 a provocative article relating to the Indigenous use of Western-style literacy appeared in the pages of the *Kamloops Wawa*, a small monthly newspaper in Chinook Jargon shorthand edited and published by a Catholic priest in the interior of Canada's Pacific province.[1] The priest, Father Jean-Marie Le Jeune, had learned of a young Salish couple who had been caught composing "sinful" letters to one another. In the priest's eyes, this was an inappropriate use of literacy. But what bothered him even more was that the chief of the village where the young couple lived seemed to have associated their sin with literacy itself. Rather than punishing the young writers for the lustful content of their letters, as the priest would have preferred, the chief is recorded as having decided that literacy itself shared responsibility for the licentious behavior. According to Le Jeune, upon learning of the salacious letters, "the chief not only became angry with the couple, but also angry with the written word," and gathered up all of the writings in the village, including back issues of the *Kamloops Wawa*, and burned them.[2]

Regarded through a postcolonial lens, each of the historical actors was, in a fundamental way, seeking to decide who could use literacy and in what way. The youth were exercising personal agency, embracing a new technology and new communication media, and putting literacy to work to help them achieve a romantic and perhaps lustful relationship. The Salish chief (perhaps influenced by Christian ideas of morality or perhaps expressing an older Indigenous sense of propriety and chiefly control) might be interpreted as having been seeking to control literacy—an introduced form of communication associated with coercive colonial power and cultural change. The Catholic priest, for his part, also sought to discipline literacy, to ensure its deployment conformed with a strict moral code and reflected colonial hierarchies associated with control and surveillance.

To be sure, the Salish were learning to read and write (activities Europeans considered hallmarks of civilization), but in the eyes of the colonizers that did not make them civilized. Le Jeune's view, rather, was that the double misuse of literacy by the young writers and the chief together revealed the continuing uncivilized state of Salish society. For the priest, the misapplication of literacy therefore reinforced the ongoing need to sustain colonial control over Indigenous people's lives. In his *Kamloops Wawa* article, Le Jeune admonished, "This [account of the chief's burning of the newspapers] may be true, or maybe not. Maybe this is a rumour, but maybe not. And this is not good. . . . If a young man and a young woman are writing sinful things in shorthand, give a penance to this man and woman, but don't destroy the writing."[3] To justify his colonial authority, the priest not only identified those things toward which Indigenous people were expected to aspire (i.e., the proper use of literacy) but literally did so in a manner that defined such things in ways that Indigenous people, regardless of their efforts, would necessarily always fail to achieve.

Communication theorists continue to struggle to better understand the implications of the introduction of literacy for societies, and especially for colonized Indigenous communities. A central question in these discussions has been whether it is possible to reconcile literacy's alleged power to liberate (via the process of helping facilitate abstract thought) with the written word's role as a colonial tool used in subjugating Indigenous people and displacing them from their lands and resources. On the one side, communication theorists such as Walter J. Ong and Eric A. Havelock, along with anthropologists like Jack Goody, have argued that nonliterate people tended to aggregate knowledge, speak repetitively or redundantly, think conservatively and empathetically, and reason situationally. The nonliterate mind was separate

FIGURE 4.1 *Kamloops Wawa*, May 1895, 70. Original from Father J. M. R. Lejeune/Kamloops Wawa Collection, folder 75, Collection MG555, University of Saskatchewan Library, Special Collections. Image source: author's private collection.

and distinct from the literate one. But once people were introduced to the technology of writing, a cognitive shift occurred—one that could never be undone. According to Ong, once people were introduced to literacy, knowledge tended to be analyzed, thought became innovative, ideas were objectively distanced, and reason was approached abstractly. Literacy, according to this school of thought, enabled people to separate an idea from its speaker and the immediate context in which it was spoken, thereby rendering it less tied to an individual and more accessible and ultimately challengeable as an abstract notion. This distance, in turn facilitated the interiorization of thought, and where thought was interiorized, people were able to abstractly situate themselves within time. That is to say, they became historical beings. Additionally, drawing on the works of C. L. Becker, this approach to understanding communication also posited that one of the formal properties of the written word was that it allowed text to act as a repository for an idea—indeed, as an archive—thereby relieving people from having to remember what they could more conveniently write and retrieve later. In this way writing might be regarded as serving as a prosthesis of memory.[4]

On the other side of the equation, social scientists and humanists alike have responded that Ong's and Havelock's theorizing is based on a foundation of ethnocentric European evolutionary assumptions about the supposedly inherent superiority of literacy over orality. These more recent works have pointed out that abstract thinking, along with certain techniques of "archival" remembering, was indeed present in societies that did not meet the Western definition of literate (even if Europeans colonists could not, or would not, see it). More to the point, this second wave of communication-theory scholarship has argued that the ways that Indigenous people engaged with literacy did not result in the sorts of irreversible cognitive shifts that Ong assumed were inevitable when crossing the "great divide."[5]

What is now clear to those of us interested in assessing the implications of introducing European-style literacy into Indigenous societies within the context of settler colonialism is that textuality and orality are less oppositional than once assumed; that even at the moment of contact, they almost inevitably contain elements that scholars formerly regarded as oppositional. As such, their power to facilitate cultural change or to protect cultural continuity needs to be "read" subtly and with a focused eye to the dynamics within communities and not just between them. As Bruno Saura argues in chapter 6 of this volume, writing "does not immediately produce. . . . the emergence of a critical and synthetic thought." Rather, literacy's historical position is inherently ambiguous. It provided segments of Indigenous societies with new opportunities even as it was used by colonizers to exploit Indigenous people and alienate them from their lands. Literacy was never, as Laura Rademaker observes in the context of missionary literacies in Australia (chapter 8 of this volume), "a universal authority on the world."

Examined here are the nineteenth-century dynamics involving literacy as played out between the Salish Indigenous communities located along the Fraser and Thompson Rivers in British Columbia[6] and Catholic missionaries. My analysis is informed first by the classic scholarship of communication theorist Harold Innis, and especially his supposition that societies are characterized by the inherent biases of their predominant modes of communication. In *Empire and Communications*, Innis challenges us to recognize that media and societies can be divided into those that are primarily time based (including Indigenous societies) and those that are principally space based (epitomized by nation-states and empires): "The concepts of time and space reflect the significance of media to civilization. Media that emphasize time are those durable in character such as parchment, clay and stone. . . . Media that empha-size space are apt to be less durable and light in character such as papyrus and paper. The latter are suited to wide areas in administration and trade."[7]

Within this framework, Indigenous oral communities represented for Innis quintessential time-based societies. The centrality of intergeneration-ally transmitted ceremonies and ritual to their lives reflected the importance of "remembered things" and reinforced a sense of space that was anchored around "known places."[8] This did not mean that Indigenous societies could not or did not change (i.e., did not have a history), but it did mean that, seen through Innis's lens, Indigenous notions of temporality (their historical con-sciousness) were primarily characterized by repetition and cyclicality, rather than by change over time. This is why he and others were able to imagine the social structures of such societies as essentially timeless.

Empires (be they political or economic) were for Innis, by way of con-trast, the archetype of space-based societies. Their bias toward light, portable, inexpensive paper communication media ensured administrative acumen that in turn enabled supervision and control over people and resources spread across vast geographies. Indeed, in contrast to the time-based socie-ties, which preserved their cultures by means of oral traditions repeated in time, space-based societies spread their cultures by means of written media designed to carry their cultures efficiently across space. Space-based media, therefore, facilitated colonialism.

In this chapter I am less interested in Innis's question of determining how the tensions between time-based oral communication biases and space-based literate communication biases might account for the success or failure of empires throughout history.[9] Rather, I probe the issue of whether the abil-ity to balance time- and space-based media within a colonial relationship can help explain the political, social, and economic success or failure of Indige-nous peoples whose lands and resources were the targets of European settler colonialism. I am, in other words, curious to see what insights might emerge from using Innis's lens of media bias to evaluate Indigenous-colonial power relationships in the nineteenth century. However, I invert the trajectory of Innis's inquiry. Deploying an ethnohistorical methodology, I examine the effects of changing communication media for what they reveal about the way settler and Indigenous societies sought to negotiate the dynamic interplay of colonialism and modernity.

While it is important to situate colonial relationships within their imperial context, my principal interest is less in determining how Indigenous people fit into the history of colonialism than in interpreting the impact of colonialism and modernity within Indigenous society over time. Elsewhere I have explored certain dimensions of this issue by examining and historically situating those previously overlooked (by Western scholars) Salish legends and nineteenth-century prophecy narratives that describe an Indigenous literacy that supposedly predated the introduction of European literacy. Literacy within this context, I argue, was not merely something colonial authorities imposed on Indigenous people that then threatened their epistemology as well as their control over land and resources. Rather, it was something that, within the historical consciousness of Salish people as revealed through several legendary stories, was originally Indigenous but subsequently lost or stolen from their ancestors. Literacy is, in Salish historical consciousness, in need of repatriation.[10]

In addition to drawing on Innis, my analysis is informed by the work of postcolonial theorist Homi Bhabha, and in particular Bhabha's discussion of the discursive strategies that colonialism produces to justify and sustain power. In his essay "Of Mimicry and Men," Bhabha observes that historically Westerners have justified their colonization of other people and others' lands by defining the non-Europeans as uncivilized and therefore unqualified to control the resources of their territory.[11] This, in turn, enabled colonizers to argue that colonized people were in need of, even deserving of, colonization as a means to their improvement and happiness. The attitudes Bhabha identifies are perhaps most famously illustrated in Rudyard Kipling's 1899 poem "The White Man's Burden: The United States and the Philippine Islands," where Kipling argued that Western society had an obligation to colonize and civilize the world.[12] It was in this context that, soon after displacing the Spaniards from the island archipelago, Philippine governor (and future U.S. president) William Howard Taft "assured President McKinley that 'our little brown brothers' would need 'fifty or one hundred years' of close supervision 'to develop anything resembling Anglo-Saxon political principles and skills.'"[13]

Bhabha identifies a desire for a "mimic man" as a central strategy of colonial power—one in which colonial regimes seek for colonized people to become almost, but not quite, like their colonizers. He observes that such mimicry holds within it an ambivalence that makes it intrinsically threatening to the very colonial order that established it. For example, Bhabha notes that colonialism requires colonizers to identify markers or signifiers in order to indicate and demarcate the boundaries between what constitutes civilized and what constitutes uncivilized. For British colonizers in Salish territory in nineteenth-century British Columbia, such markers included, but were not limited to, Indigenous nudity, polygamy, slavery, cranial deformation, non-Christian spirituality, and systems of land use that did not meet the criteria set by John Locke's discussion of ownership being derived from the investment of labor into agricultural lands.[14]

Mimicry, in the sense that Bhabha uses the term, is a strategy of colonial power, and not a tactic of Indigenous agency. That is to say, it is "the desire [by colonialists] for a reformed recognizable Other."[15] Rhetorically, then, the Victorian-era British Empire was predicated on a nascent social Darwinism that justified the colonial control of others because it could be rationalized as something temporary—or at least humanitarians could rationalize it as temporary.[16] As such, the colonial rhetoric of mimicry was necessarily subversive to itself; it held within it the tools of its own demise. It was, Bhabha argues, "constructed around an ambivalence; in order to be effective [for the colonizer] mimicry must continually produce its slippage, its excesses, its difference."[17] To mitigate the danger, colonialism needed to constantly adjust the signifiers used to distinguish the civilized from the uncivilized so as to ensure that the colonial other was never more than "almost the same [as the colonizer], but not quite," "almost the same [as the colonizer], but not white."[18]

Overtly manipulative and oppressive for the colonized, the liminal state created through mimicry for the colonial subject inevitably proved vexingly ambivalent for the colonizer. For to the extent that such differences between colonizer and colonized can be regarded as "almost nothing but not quite," Bhabha points out that they are also inherently "almost total but not quite."[19] In this way mimicry transitions from an ambivalent replication to become a menace that the colonizer is compelled to try and neutralize lest it challenge colonial control. It is this concept of mimicry-turned-menace that sits at the core of the analysis in this chapter.

TIME- AND SPACE-BASED COMMUNICATION
ACROSS CULTURAL DIVIDES

When in 1808 Simon Fraser journeyed down the river that would eventually bear his name, he was no doubt cognizant that he was part of a colonizing process. He had been charged by his employer, the Montreal-based North

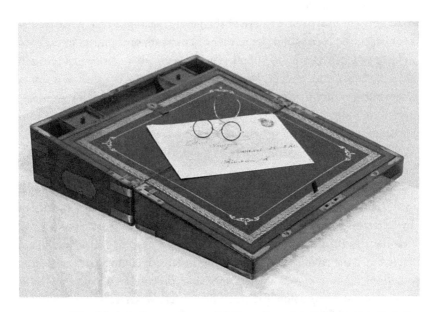

FIGURE 4.2 Travel desk similar to one carried by Simon Fraser into Salish territory in 1808. Image courtesy of the Harp Gallery, Appleton, Wisconsin.

West Company, with exploring the region downriver from Fort George (in what is now central British Columbia) to determine if what ultimately turned out to be the Fraser River might instead have been the upper waters of the Columbia. His movement by canoe and on foot was slow and adoptive of the technologies and strategies used by the Indigenous people he met along the way. But Fraser carried with him a most important portable desk. Inside it were paper, nibs, and ink. When rapids in the river required him to portage and therefore cache most of his provisions, the desk came with him. Fraser's visit may have been ephemeral, but copies and summaries of the written journal he composed during his sojourn traveled far and wide and as such had profound and lasting imperial implications.[20] It was a classic example of a communication medium used to facilitate the building and sustaining of administrative and economic empires in the late eighteenth and early nineteenth centuries. It captured and communicated descriptions of people and natural resources, and it also served as the basis for a map that the famed cartographer David Thompson subsequently made of the region, despite his never having visited the lower Fraser himself.

Meanwhile, the Salish Indigenous people whom Fraser met were oriented to time-based forms of communication media. Throughout their territory Salish people had alternately carved and painted symbolic petroglyphs and pictographs representing personal visions and familial histories that anchored them to a hereditary territory. Together, these constituted a form of literacy that, unlike Western text, neither separated words and concepts nor sought to communicate standardized meanings to others. After Fraser had descended through the river's main canyon (transitioning from the arid homeland of the Interior Salish into the rain forest of the Coast Salish), he observed and visited gigantic cedar longhouses—one of which was nearly half a kilometer long. The massive cedar posts that framed and supported these structures were themselves communication media, consisting as they did of carved depictions of ancestors and spirit helpers that explained who occupied the house and what the occupant's social position was within Salish society. But unlike Fraser's communication media, the stone pictographs and petroglyphs, and the monumental cedar carvings, were immovable. To be effective they required people to come to them and interpret them.

When the Indigenous people met Fraser, they situated him within their worldview, just as Fraser situated them within his. Oral histories collected in the nineteenth and twentieth centuries reveal that the Salish initially regarded Fraser as the returning legendary Transformer—the supernatural heroic figure of the myth age who had transformed a chaotic and dangerous world into the stable and predictable world of the present. This apotheosis, however, was short-lived—only a few days in duration.[21] By the time Fraser reached the sea, he had violated so many Salish cultural protocols that any suspicion that he might have been the Transformer had evaporated and his simple humanity was apparent to all.[22] Moreover, Salish people at the mouth of the river had already encountered European maritime traders and explorers over the previous twenty years—sporadic and fleeting though these encounters were. As such, the Salish literally chased Fraser back up the Fraser River, causing him to fear for his life. At one point, men under his command threatened to abandon him to fend for himself against the angry Salish. Despite the need to put as much distance between himself and the pursuing Salish warriors as possible, Fraser ordered his frustrated and seemingly mutinous men to beach their canoe on a sandbar so he could administer an oath of loyalty.[23] As an example of paper literacy's spatial power, Fraser's written account of the Salish people's hostility toward him subsequently reinforced in his eastern employer's eyes the savagery of western Indigenous populations, and this, in turn, shaped the way the Hudson's Bay Company (which had earlier absorbed the North West Company) and others would treat the West Coast people in the future.

Temporally oriented communication media, immovable in space, such as those the Salish deployed, were not limited to stone and cedar. Their oral and performative media traditions had been honed over generations through the forums of the giant potlatch gatherings, the sacred winter-season spirit dances (smílha, or, in Chinook Jargon, tamanawas), and the more intimate conversations that occurred around family cooking fires. Legendary traditions explained in detail how in the distant past the Transformer X̱á:ls had come into the world and changed it from a chaotic and dangerous place (where malevolent shamans regularly caused harm to others and where animals and humans casually shifted from one state to another) into the recognizable and predictable form that is present today. In making the world "right," as contemporary Salish knowledge keepers explain, X̱á:ls had turned certain people and animals into their present unchanging form and likewise summarily rewarded or punished others by turning them permanently into animals, plants, prominent stones, or mountaintops. Along with an even earlier generation of sky-born heroes, X̱á:ls had worked with the Salish to identify and create the people who would become the leaders of tribal collectives.[24]

In the Halqemeylem language of the lower Fraser River Salish people, the word used to describe this transformative process is x̱á:ytem—which contemporary knowledge keepers translate as referring to something/someone who has been "suddenly and miraculously transformed by X̱á:ls."[25] The word x̱á:ytem is in fact derived from X̱á:ls's name. The same proto-Salish root is also found in the Halqemeylem words for "petroglyph" and "pictograph." Unlike Western literacy, which ostensibly aspires to convey a standardized meaning to any reader, petroglyphs and pictographs are inherently esoteric. Their creators have an original meaning in mind, but subsequent observers are left, in part, to either try and interpret meaning on their own or deduce the meaning after learning the associated stories as they have been passed down across generations. These messages are literally inscribed on the landscape. Likewise, the supernaturally transformative works of X̱á:ls the Transformer are regarded as having been permanently marked and engraved into the landscape. The mountains and giant stones are there for all to see, but only those trained in the oral narratives are able to read the stories and interpret the messages embedded in them.

Within the Coast Salish historical consciousness, the transformative work of X̱á:ls thus stabilized the forms of both nature and humanity, creating meaningful boundaries where none had previously existed. Interestingly, this Salish production of forms resembles Western linguistic productions in that both processes bestow order and meaning on the world. X̱á:ls, therefore, can be seen as a producer of a form of Salish language that required orality as well as a certain kind of literacy to be sustained. The literacy here was not one that separated words from the things they signified (as in Western literacy) but rather one in which ancient transformations inscribed meanings on, or fixed them onto, things (i.e., certain rocks, animals, hereditary tribal leaders, and, importantly, the terrestrial and celestial landscapes of mountains, rivers, lakes, the moon, and stars). The extent and explicitness of the "collapse" between words and things resulted in a situation for the Salish where oral traditions were needed in order for the world to "be read." Rather than being opposed to one another (as the early communication theorists posited), orality and literacy in fact prove not only complementary but symbiotic—just as they are, for that matter, in Western literate languages, which also require both orality and literacy to be learned and passed on.[26] The difference is that in Indigenous cultures the oral is privileged, while in Western ones the literate is.

Insights into how Salish people made meaning from introduced items and ideas can be drawn from colonial encounters elsewhere. In examining the movement of European goods into Indigenous societies across the Pacific Ocean, ethnohistorian Nicholas Thomas argues that when people encounter new things, they seek to situate them within their existing understandings. Meanings ascribed to certain objects necessarily change as they cross the colonial divide. Copper pots, for example, designed in Europe to boil water for tea, were sometimes put to different ceremonial ends in Polynesia, and in so doing their meaning was transformed.[27]

Colonial encounters inevitably involve the negotiation of meaning. The words used to describe things provide insights into this process. In the Halqeméylem language, for example, the word xwe'ít'et means both "to draw a bowstring" and "to cock a gun." Guns are introduced objects, but their meaning was interpreted within the context of an existing technology and associated series of actions. The Halqeméylem word currently used by Elders to describe European writing (the sort of activity Salish children learn in British and Canadian schools) is xélá:ls.[28] This is also the word they use to describe the transformative actions taken by Xá:ls when he "made the world right." The Transformer, therefore, was literally marking and engraving the history of the Salish people onto the landscape. The accompanying stories that describe those actions give the world meaning and form the basis of what is perhaps best understood as Salish *oral literacy*, for within this "oral literacy" the operative separation is never between written words and the things they describe, but rather always between things inscribed with meaning and the oral tradition that must be brought to bear on those things in order to understand and communicate their meanings. Additionally, and importantly, in contrast to Western literacy, which involves a separation between the reader

FIGURE 4.3 Naxaxalhts'i (Albert "Sonny" McHalsie) sharing legendary stories of X̱á:ls while standing at the same location where his ancestors first shared one of these stories with the explorer Simon Fraser over two hundred years earlier. Photo by author.

and the writer, Salish oral literacy requires the presence of the "reader" or interpreter in order for the immovable things-as-texts to be deciphered.

As Simon Fraser descended the river, he met with Salish people who introduced him to temporally grounded Salish communication media (even if he was unable to appreciate the meaning of their message). When he arrived at a village near the present-day town of Yale, British Columbia, he was taken by local residents to a Transformer site and shown several lines that had been scratched into the rock. Fraser records that he was told a story, which he interpreted to mean that the scratch marks had been made by people like him who had visited the site before. The cartographer David Thompson subsequently understood the text in Fraser's journal to mean, "To this Place the White Men have come from the Sea"—a phrase he inserted onto the subsequent map he drew of the lower Fraser River.[29]

The Salish story of the scratch-mark site, however, was actually about a battle between X̱á:ls and a wicked local shaman. It continues to be a commonly shared story today. The story tells of X̱á:ls's victory and how, as a result, the region came to take its current physical form, and the local people their current tribal affiliation. Given the subsequently recorded oral histories explaining that the Salish initially interpreted Fraser as the returning Transformer X̲á:ls, the context of the sharing of the story was probably not merely to convey an important narrative to a stranger but to demonstrate to Fraser that they had remembered the stories of the Transformer's early exploits—that their time-based communication media had successfully and properly conveyed their message across generations.[30]

If this initial meeting of Salish people and Europeans had resulted in an exposure to one another's communication media, it would be another generation before the two sides started taking sincere notice of how the other communicated. It was then that representatives of colonial and Salish societies began strategic efforts to deploy communication media to advance their own agendas and to communicate across the cultural gulf.

The establishment of permanent fur-trading posts in Salish territory at Kamloops (1812) and Langley (1827) introduced the Salish to accounting books, ledgers, journals, and written correspondence. Rather than hosting large potlatch gatherings where families distributed wealth and where trained "speakers" publicly proclaimed debt accumulation and debt eradication, the European traders scribbled words and numbers onto paper to keep track of how much each Indian trader owed or was owed by the company. Signed paper contracts bound employees to the company for set periods of time, and annual reports and correspondence informed directors and boards of governors in distant lands of Aboriginal trading habits, Indigenous population statistics, and the "characteristics" of Native communities.[31] Salish people came to increasingly appreciate the power that literacy had to communicate over vast spaces when they themselves were hired by the traders to act as couriers delivering written correspondence between forts.

CHRISTIAN MISSIONARIES, LITERACY, AND
THE ANXIETY OF COLONIAL MIMICRY

Salish people developed a sometimes-frustrating and occasionally rewarding relationship with the Europeans who settled in their territories, and they acquired a similarly ambiguous relationship with literacy. One day in the late 1830s or early 1840s, a Salish man named St'a'saluk from the community of Shxw'ow'hamel, near present-day Hope, British Columbia, climbed a local mountain, where he fasted in the hopes of receiving a vision from the spirit world. Seers who acquired knowledge of occurrences in distant villages via spirit helpers were valued members of precontact and early-contact-era Salish communities. They informed people of the intentions of neighbors and guided warriors in terms of advising when to launch preemptive or retaliatory raids. Some seers probed the spirit world and received information about different times (both past and future).[32] According to oral traditions retained within the Kelly family and several others to this day, and first recorded by anthropologists in the 1940s, the vision St'a'saluk received was prophetic and foretold the arrival of European fur traders, Christian missionaries, and, ultimately, European settlers and the new technologies that would accompany them. However, what especially set St'a'saluk's prophetic message apart was his use of literacy in the form of pencil and paper to convey his predictions.

According to his great-great-great-great-granddaughter, Bertha Peters, St'a'saluk had acquired a special piece of paper from God himself during his vision quest. On it were "the fanciest capital letters," which "only the old man could read." In addition to messages about the coming of metal cross-cut saws, nuclear-family housing, glass windows, and domesticated fruit and vegetables, the paper also contained a moral code that forbade stealing and killing. Perhaps most remarkable, the scribbled words also consisted of a special creed aimed at cultivating positive relations between Salish people and the newcomers. According to Peters, the words on St'a'saluk's paper explained that the Europeans would be different and that they would have many new things that would benefit Aboriginal people. As it was explained to her, part of St'a'saluk vision included the message that the Salish people should treat the immigrants to their territory "like brothers." To hasten the "happy day" when the newcomers would arrive in numbers and the changes would commence, St'a'saluk led his followers in special ceremonies in which they "danced with their hands over their heads and looking up and begging God and the strange people to come. . . . They wanted these times to come."[33]

Elsewhere I have argued that a key significance behind Peters's recounting of this story rests in its power to link Indigenous literacy with the alienation of Salish lands by European settlers.[34] In the notes recorded by the anthropologist Marian Smith in 1945, Peters repeatedly states that the prophet's paper was "the reason these people here didn't fight for their country when the white people came." The paper had led them to believe that European settlement would be largely positive and beneficial, especially if the Salish treated the newcomers kindly. And yet settler society and settler literacy did not respond the way St'a'saluk had hoped. Instead of Salish people benefiting from the newcomers' technologies and products, settler society benefited by using these technologies to displace Salish people from their land and resources.

But there are additional meanings to be drawn from the relationship between the prophet St'a'saluk and Western literacy. St'a'saluk's deployment of an unsanctioned esoteric literacy that ostensibly did not derive from colonial sources proved troubling for Catholic missionaries who arrived in the wake of the 1858 gold rush. Priests regarded as dangerous what they considered to be Indigenous mimicry of European ways. According to Peters, when the first permanent missionaries arrived, they were brought to meet with St'a'saluk, who then showed them his wonderful paper with its accompanying God-given literacy. They did not like what they saw.

Like the Salish prophet, the Catholic priests also claimed to have special powers that had been bestowed on them by God. They could forgive people's sins, they could drive away evil spirits, and, most impressive of all, they could transubstantiate bread and wine into the body and blood of the son of the creator of the universe. Also like St'a'saluk, they pointed to written words on paper to legitimate their spiritual authority. St'a'saluk had taken special precautions to protect his sacred script. He had built a miniature house, not unlike a Roman Catholic tabernacle or the famed Jewish ark of the covenant, and also similar to a Salish cache house or mortuary box. St'a'saluk placed the little house high in the branches of a cedar tree (the most sacred of Coast Salish plants), and it was there that he stored his paper.

According to Peters, Father Paul Durieu arrived to meet with St'a'saluk and asked to see the paper.[35] St'a'saluk is remembered as having brought both the miniature house and the paper down from the tree and then told the priest the story of how he had acquired the prophetic text, and what it meant. For the prophet, the paper seems to have symbolized a reassuring sameness with the newcomers—a commonality that linked his Indigenous spirituality and epistemology to the newcomers' cosmology. It provided a reassuring version of the future to a people who had recently had their world shaken by the ravages of smallpox and the arrival of European traders, miners, and missionaries. Additionally, it suggested that Salish spirituality derived from the same holy source as European spirituality—that God had given the Salish people the same powerful tool of literacy that he had earlier shared with the Europeans.

Relatedly, in another context political scientist Alan Cairns has advanced the thesis that in acquiring all the rights of Canadian citizenship, First Nations have also retained their distinctive Aboriginal rights. This makes them, in Cairns's view, not just citizens but "citizens plus."[36] St'a'saluk, we might speculate, was proposing something similar to the Catholic priest in terms of spirituality, namely, that the prophetic literacy he had received rendered his Salish people "Christians plus."

For the priest, the paper and text represented not a synergetic form of prophetic knowledge to complement or enhance his own Bible but rather, to judge by the oral histories describing his reactions, a dangerous expression of undisciplined literacy carrying a subversive message from a potentially evil source. As a prophetic text, it appears to have represented for the priest a threat derived from what Bhabha calls the slippage inherent in colonial mimicry—it was almost the same as Christianity, but not quite; through its resemblance it constituted not a common ground but a threat. Indeed, it constituted a greater threat than other expressions of older Indigeneity (what the priest would have regarded as traditional shamanism), for it directly challenged the priest's own authority and the premise of his colonial power. For the priest, it seems, the only way to neutralize the threat was to destroy the paper. According to Peters, "The Bishop took the paper and burned it at Sk'welq. He was telling [St'a'saluk] it was the devil's work. As soon as he saw it, little house and all, he threw it in the fire. [My] mother saw him do it. She was 15 at the time."[37]

While St'a'saluk's prophetic writings were destroyed by the Catholic priest around 1864, another prophet emerged in the 1880s. His writings have been preserved in the Canadian Museum of History. As with Peters's descriptions of St'a'saluk's text before him, this later prophet's writings likewise contained "the fanciest capital letters," which "only the old man could read."[38]

The incident of the priest burning St'a'saluk's paper is not the only instance of a clash between colonists and Salish people that resulted from the slippage produced by the ambivalence of colonial mimicry. Nor is it the only example of colonial contestation over control of communication media in the battle to situate Western space-based communication in a position of authority over Indigenous temporal-based communication.

Shortly after Father Durieu burned St'a'saluk's prophetic paper, the Catholic priests established a residential school along the banks of the Fraser River. Much has been written about the goal of cultural genocide that informed the philosophy behind residential schools in Canada.[39] The work of Canada's national Truth and Reconciliation Commission has opened the door to allowing us to better appreciate the extent of the sexual, physical, and emotional abuse that occurred within the schools, as well as the lingering intergenerational legacies of that abuse.[40] The past thirty years of scholarship have demonstrated that the objective behind Canada's Indian residential schools was to remove children from their parents' influence, to emphasize the superiority of British/European culture over Aboriginal culture, and to prepare the students so they could be assimilated into mainstream Canadian society. As Duncan Campbell Scott, the superintendent of Indian affairs who oversaw the development of Canada's residential school system, stated, "Our objective is to continue until there is not a single Indian in Canada that has not been absorbed into the body politic."[41] As such, in addition to a curriculum that aimed to teach Salish children how to read and write in English and to do basic math, St. Mary's Catholic residential school also devised and implemented a pedagogy that saw priests directly challenge the foundations of Salish time-based communication through the displacement and appropriation of Salish space and spirituality.

Priests teaching youth at St. Mary's residential school apparently learned some of the legendary Transformer stories that the Salish understood to have been inscribed onto the landscape by X̱á:ls. Cedar trees, for example, were regarded as among the most sacred of all plants/beings in the Coast Salish world. Within the corpus of legendary narratives was an account explaining how in the past there had been an extremely generous man who was always giving of himself. Recognizing this trait, and wanting to reward it and preserve it, X̱á:ls transformed the man into the cedar tree. With the spirit of this man alive and active within the cedar tree, it continued to give generously. Salish people used its bark to make clothing and rope, its roots to weave baskets, its branches for snowshoes, its trunk for making canoes and house posts, giant planks from it for the walls and roofs of longhouses, and its withes for spiritual cleansing. Generous cedar trees literally covered the Coast Salish landscape. Likewise, another of the legendary stories described how X̱á:ls transformed a particularly evil man into a mountain that was located several miles away from the site of St. Mary's school. This man's spirit continued to inhabit the mountain, making it a dangerous place that Salish people fearfully avoided.

Knowing these and other Transformer stories, in 1863 the priests at St. Mary's orchestrated the first of what would become annual spring field trips where pupils were taken to dangerous taboo sites. There they would have their names written on paper by the priests and placed beneath the bark of living cedar trees. As Father R. P. Gendre explained in his report back to Oblate headquarters, "Before sending my dear children off on vacation, I had them go for a long walk on the mountain known as 'The Devil's.'[42] Tradition maintained that whosoever should challenge that fearsome mountain would pay for his foolhardiness with his life. All of the Savages sought to frighten me with ever more somber and dramatic tales. Thus, my students, who are as superstitious as their fathers, trembled in fear when I proposed we climb the mountain."[43]

This fearful field trip was not a spontaneous event. Rather, it was planned and announced to the children months in advance. According to the priest, this enabled the children to become accustomed to the idea. One can imagine that it would have also created a focal point of anxiety over a prolonged period. It also likely led to tensions between students as they wrestled with the idea of proving their individual bravery by respecting their Catholic teacher, while simultaneously rejecting the teachings of their parents. As Gendre explained:

> Nearly every day for three months, I attacked their ridiculous superstition and gradually, they grew accustomed to the idea of attempting this endeavor, which could not possibly present any danger, with me. I succeeded in conquering their hereditary superstition. Toward the evening of the 31st of May, we all set off in canoes, with the necessary provisions and we camped that night at the foot of the dreaded mountain on the shores of a magnificent lake. Early the following day, after prayers, we ascended the slope and towards noon we arrived, without a single mishap, at the summit, where none had ever stood before. There, we sang out our triumph and our victory. I was pleased to show these children to what extent their traditions were lies and that only the priest could speak the truth, which he receives from the Great Chief from above.[44]

Pulled between the alleged "lies" of their parents' traditions and the teachings of the Church, the children may well have understood the event as an example of the potency of one particular shaman's power (the priest's) over that of whichever Salish shaman had earlier identified the site as dangerous. More to the point, the children who participated in this allegedly transformative event were forever distinguished from their parents, and all others who had avoided the site, by the fact that the priest left lasting reminders of their identities on the mountain as proof of their separateness: "We amused ourselves and afterwards, I wrote a list of the names of all of the brave children who had climbed the Devil's Mountain. I placed the list beneath the bark of a cedar tree, where it will remain until next year when we return to this summit, which is now the 'Mountain of God.' On the eve of that very pleasant day, we returned to Sainte-Marie [school] singing the Litanies of the Most Holy Virgin."[45]

The missionaries did not limit their efforts at undermining the Salish ways and systems of knowing the natural environment to merely the opportunities that presented themselves in the school curriculum and student field trips. That is to say, they sought not only to discredit the stories that X̱á:ls had inscribed onto the land but also to discredit the Salish understanding of the history that gave those stories relevance and meaning. Salish culture inscribed historical significance onto the geography, creating a distinctive way of knowing and relating to their environment—an epistemology, in short. The mountains, the plants, the animals, and the people who lived in Salish territory were there, according to Salish traditions, because of the early transformative events of the great myth age. What Innis would have called the temporal bias in their communication systems worked to sustain their culture and articulated their title to the land and its resources. By way of contrast, the mid-nineteenth-century missionaries, both Catholic and Protestant, used the written stories in their printed Bibles and catechisms to deploy an alternate understanding of history that discredited the Salish Transformer stories. Their Christian version of history, most vividly illustrated on long rolls of parchment called "ladders" that priests and ministers carried with them when they visited Salish villages, presented a teleological narrative that situated the world's important historical events in far-off Europe and the Middle East.

Classic examples of space-based communication media, the missionaries' texts served to communicate a standardized history of the past and depiction of the future throughout a vast geography that was coming increasingly under the control of colonial authorities. Notably, the history conveyed on Catholic and Protestant ladders also provided a linear depiction of history that portrayed the future with as much certainty as the past and present. The only difference was that on the Catholic documents it was the Protestants who failed to be admitted into heaven after the apocalypse, whereas on the Protestants' it was the Catholics (led by the bishop of Rome, who fell headlong into the fires of hell). Salish people were challenged to embrace Christianity and with it a teleological narrative that served to undermine their sense of belonging in their traditional territories.

The contestation emerging from the deployment of different forms of communication media and epistemology as revealed through the missionaries' early encounters with Salish people was, of course, more complicated than it might appear. In seeking to control literacy and control Native lives, missionaries also sometimes acted as Indigenous people's advocates and allies—particularly on issues that missionaries regarded as complementary to Christianization. With the arrival of thousands of permanent settlers following the 1858 gold rush, Salish people found their lands being alienated through non-Native agricultural and urban developments. Initially the Indigenous populations sought verbal guarantees for the protection of their lands from government agents who were present on-site.[46] But it soon became apparent to them that the colonial government privileged written words over spoken promises. Paternalistically regarding the Salish people as charges who required protection from the more unsavory elements of colonial society, Catholic missionaries became active in the 1860s assisting Native leaders in

FIGURE 4.4 (LEFT) The Catholic ladder conceived by Father N. Blanchete in 1839 and used extensively among the Salish up until the 1860s, when it was replaced by a more colorful and interpretive version. Image courtesy of the Oregon Historical Society Archives, OrHi 89315.

FIGURE 4.5 (RIGHT) Protestant ladder composed by Presbyterian missionaries Henry and Eliza Spalding in 1845. Methodists are recorded as using this in their work among the Salish into the 1860s. Image courtesy of the Oregon Historical Society Archives, OrHi 87847.

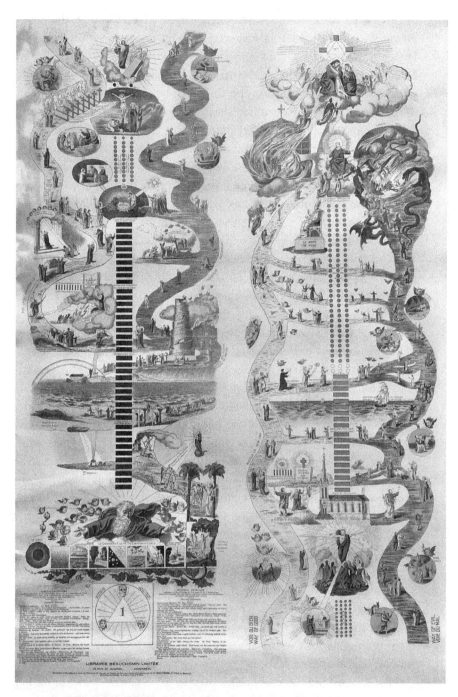

FIGURE 4.6 The Catholic ladder of Father Albert Lacombe was created in 1872 as an improvement on Blanchete's earlier work and as a rebuttal to the more colorful and provocative Protestant ladders. Lacombe's ladder more vividly emphasizes the "two roads to heaven" concept than earlier Catholic examples. From author's private collection.

seeking protection of reserve lands. On one illustrative occasion Father Léon Fouquet accompanied several Salish men to a meeting with Governor James Douglas and his chief commissioner of lands and works, Col. R. C. Moody. Douglas was known to be sympathetic to Indigenous interests, but Moody was notoriously opposed to supporting Indigenous people in the creation of their reserves, and indeed had several times already been chastised by the governor for failing to undertake surveys as Douglas had directed.[47] At the meeting Governor Douglas assured the Indigenous men that to expedite the protection of their proposed reserve lands, he was authorizing them to place white wooden stakes into the ground themselves. Formal surveys could follow when colonial budgets were more robust. The cedar posts were to be provided by the chief commissioner of works, who was instructed to have the word *reserve* carved onto the side of each stake.[48]

These posts were not entirely dissimilar to the much larger carved cedar house posts that Salish people used as mnemonic devices to recall and illustrate the Transformer stories and spirit visions that accounted for particular families' hereditary claims of title to tribal resources. Both were examples of geographically anchored temporal-based communication strategies, only unlike the earlier Salish house posts, whose authority was derived from verbally shared oral histories, the government stakes demarcating the boundaries of Indian reserves were designed to be merely referents to corresponding written documents in the colonial government's land title office. This latter fact, apparently, was not made known to the Salish people, who seem to have regarded the physical presence of the stakes alone as proof of the government's validation of their land claims. And thus it was with great frustration that they learned through their advocate Father Fouquet that Moody (now away from the governor's office and oversight) felt justified in not providing them with the stakes until the priest and Salish leaders first provided a host of additional information relating to such matters as the acreage claimed, the population of the community, and the names of the chiefs.[49] That is to say, Moody felt that he could forestall and ultimately sidestep the verbal promise made by the governor so long as he could justify the action through reference to the need to maintain written procedures for written records. Ultimately, Moody failed to provide the Salish communities with any of the promised stakes, and over the coming years settler incursions into Salish land accelerated.

For Moody and the many other colonial government agents of his ilk, the Salish people's association with the Catholic priests was creating an ambivalence that was producing a slippage in the colonizer-colonized binary.

This slippage, in turn, was undermining the rationale behind colonial authority. The more Salish people came to understand the systems of colonial control (that is, that the government issued stakes with a particular word carved into them to designate lands that settler colonists could not appropriate from Indigenous people), the more their participation in those systems signaled a threat to colonial control. As Bhabha argues in the context of colonialism generally, mimicry ultimately represents an ironic compromise between synchronic visions of control (and their associated demand for identity stasis) and the counterpressure of the diachronic imperative of history that requires change and, therefore, difference.[50]

This point becomes increasingly evident in the government's response to the series of written petitions that Salish people presented to colonial officials (typically with the assistance of Catholic priests, who in the early years of Salish literacy acted as scribes and translators). Space does not permit an elaboration of this history other than to note that throughout the 1860s, 1870s, and 1880s, Salish people delivered numerous petitions to British Columbian colonial officials on a host of issues.[51] Megan Harvey (an alumnus of the Stó:lō Ethnohistory Field School that my colleague John Lutz and I offer every second year in partnership with the Stó:lō community), has recently examined these petitions for what they reveal about the shifting discursive strategies employed by Salish people in the early colonial period.[52] She concludes that despite serious setbacks in their efforts to retain control of their traditional lands, the Coast Salish were able to "hold their ground in a narrative and relational sense, by aligning themselves with, or identifying and countering, the stories that had increasing power to shape their lives, by asserting stories of their own and pointing to the narrative infidelity of settler authorities."[53]

My research for this chapter confirms that the government strategy (if it can be considered to have been that coordinated) was to verbally acknowledge receipt of the petitions, and occasionally provide a verbal reply addressing the specific issue, but astutely avoid providing a written response.[54] In so behaving, the government was able to appear to appease Indigenous concerns without being bound by written text that would have created legal obligations—the breach of which might have provoked the ire of humanitarian organizations such as the influential Aborigines' Protection Society located in Britain.[55]

As settlement proceeded, the government and missionaries alike devised and implemented policies aimed directly at undermining Salish temporal-based communication while they likewise sought to mitigate the threat posed by the constitutive ambivalence of mimicry by regulating Salish efforts at space-based communication media. For example, Catholic and Protestant missionaries alike are described in still-circulating Salish oral histories as having collected the carved masks and other regalia of their converts and ritualistically burned these items in ceremonies on the shore of the Fraser River. And it was missionaries who likewise collaborated with the provincial and federal governments to make potlatch gatherings illegal and to outlaw tamanawas spirit dancing through an amendment to the Indian Act in 1884.[56] Without potlatch gatherings Salish people struggled to effectively communicate the intergenerational transfer of hereditary properties, rites, and rights, and without being able to gather as a community to participate in the winter dance Salish people were denied participation in a ritual that comprised the most common method of attracting and securing spirit helpers from the natural world. Likewise, the introduction of state funding for residential schools in 1892 caused the education system to expand, which increased the opportunity for Christian religious officials to closely supervise the introduction of literacy to Aboriginal people.

———————

Because literacy was so closely associated with nineteenth-century colonialism, examining its history in the context of Indigenous-newcomer relations reveals insights that might otherwise remain obscured into both the way colonial power was deployed and the way Indigenous agency was mobilized. As ambassadors of the Christian faith—a faith derived from gospel texts and written apostolic tradition—missionaries considered themselves to have a special relationship with the written word that made them explicitly interested in Indigenous people's association with literacy. Indeed, while secular colonial officials and corporate representatives of settler society were also interested in controlling Indigenous people's use of literacy, it was the missionaries who embraced the idea that it was their special prerogative to introduce and then shape the use of literacy in Salish people's lives.

Taken together, Innis's work examining the connections between empires and communication and Bhabha's musings on the colonial strategy of mimicry establish a foundation from which we can start to ask new questions aimed at better understanding the subtle ways in which colonialism was deployed and resisted within the British Empire. It is at the local level, where the historic interactions of individual Indigenous communities (such as the Salish) and distinct subsets of colonial actors (such as Catholic missionaries or government surveyors) played out, that we can come to a better understanding of the origins of the tensions that continue to plague contemporary Indigenous people living within the context of ongoing settler colonialism.

Bhabha identifies a desire for a mimic as a central strategy of colonial power—one in which colonial regimes seek for colonized people to become almost, but not quite, like their colonizers. What is most applicably insightful within Bhabha's theorizing is his observation that mimicry holds within it an ambivalence that makes it intrinsically threatening to the very colonial order that established it. Through Innis we can begin to appreciate the cultural significance of a shift within Indigenous societies toward new colonially introduced space-based communication technologies. The responses of Catholic priests to Salish deployments of both temporal- and spatial-based literacies reveal that when Indigenous people in British Columbia became regarded as too similar to their colonizers, the rationale for colonization itself became undermined. For this reason, the Oblate missionaries, despite their occasional advocacy for Indigenous rights and their alignment as Indigenous allies, were at the forefront of the settler colonial strategy of seeking new definitions of difference to sustain their power and privilege.

It was in this context, to follow Bhabha, that colonial authority alternated, as the situation demanded, between seeing the difference between colonizer and colonized, on the one hand, as "almost nothing but not quite," and seeing it, on the other hand, as "a difference that is almost total but not quite."[57] Both versions of difference are the effect of the ambivalence that infuses colonialism's demand for mimicry. And both, we might say, are just enough to serve as the legitimating grounds for perpetuating colonial rule.

In concrete terms, this meant that in the eyes of the missionaries, Indigenous literacy could never qualify the Salish for status as Christian colonial citizens. Instead, whether it was their Indigenous time-based literacy inscribed onto the mountains and landscape by Xá:ls the Transformer, the prophetic writings of a Salish prophet, or a space-based literacy in the form of sensual love letters between a young couple, Indigenous literacy always proved just different enough—just threatening enough—to compel the priests to adjust their definition of what constituted appropriate literacy so that there could be both improper and proper literacy. In so doing, they established a difference where previously the Salish had not regarded one as necessary, thus further legitimating their power, perpetuating colonial rule, and confirming the logic Bhabha describes.[58]

Examining Indigenous people's historical relationship with literacy reveals the hollowness of the discourse of humanitarianism as a counterbalance to colonial power and authority. It makes clear that the disputes associated with nineteenth-century Indigenous and Western literacy were at their core contestations over who within the system of settler colonialism had the authority to decide. Colonists wanted control not only over what got to be read and what got to be written but also (through literacy) over who got to decide what was sinful and what was not, who got to decide what was appropriate faith coupled with reason and what was superstition facilitated by the devil, who got to decide what was legitimate capital accumulation and distribution and what was illegitimate potlatch debt and redistribution, who got to decide what was appropriate land use (entitling one to a land base) and what was not. Of course, for the two youth who were caught and punished for exchanging love letters, for the Salish leaders who wanted survey stakes to demarcate their reserves, and for the children who were compelled to visit a taboo site and then have their names inscribed on paper and slipped beneath the bark of a sacred tree, such issues were no doubt beyond their immediate concern. But cumulatively such matters were the bricks and mortar of settler colonial strategies of control.

NOTES

I am indebted to Lachy Paterson, Tony Ballantyne, and Angela Wanhalla for their suggestions on an earlier draft of this paper. Likewise, to Mark Meyers, Scott Berthelette, James Handy, J. R. Miller, Michael Hayden, Lesley Biggs, and Ben Hoy for providing comments on a version I delivered at the University of Saskatchewan history department's Faculty Research Workshop. I am also grateful to the Coast Salish knowledge keepers (some of whom have now passed away) who have repeatedly kindled my interest in Indigenous orality and literacy and who have encouraged me in my investigations, especially Sonny McHalsie, Wesley Sam, Ralph George, Mike Kelly, Patricia Charlie, Nancy Philips, and Herb Joe.

1. Chinook Jargon was an intercultural trade language with a vocabulary of roughly eight hundred words. It emerged in the nineteenth century in response to Indigenous people's and European traders' need to communicate. It was eclipsed by English after the establishment of Indian residential and boarding schools. It consisted of words drawn from over half a dozen Indigenous languages as well as from French and English. Le Jeune sought to promote it as a lingua franca and adapted to the jargon a form of shorthand that he had learned in the seminary.

2. *Kamloops Wawa*, May 1895, No. 128. I am indebted to David Robertson for translating this text for me. For more information on Chinook shorthand, see Robertson, "Kamloops Chinúk Wawa, Chinuk Pipa, and the Vitality of Pidgins."

3. *Kamloops Wawa*, May 1895, No. 128.

4. Listed chronologically so one can appreciate the development of this field, key works include Becker, *Progress and Power*; McLuhan, *The Gutenberg Galaxy*; Havelock, *Preface to Plato*; Lévi-Strauss, *The Savage Mind*; Goody and Watt, "The Consequences of Literacy"; Luria, *Cognitive Development*; Goody, *The Domestication of the Savage Mind*; Ong, *Orality and Literacy*; and Havelock, *The Muse Learns to Write*.

5. Finnegan, *Oral Poetry*; Finnegan, *Literacy and Orality*; Niezen, "Hot Literacy in Cold Societies," 225–54; George, "Felling a Story with a New Ax," 3–24; and Street, *Cross-Cultural Approaches to Literacy*.

6. There are twenty-three mutually unintelligible Salish languages in the Pacific Northwest region of North America. In this chapter I am particularly interested in the Halkomelem-, Nlakapamux-, and Secwepmc-speaking communities located along the Fraser and Thompson River corridor. There are multiple tribal and overlapping familial communities within this region, including the twenty-seven Stó:lō First Nations of the lower Fraser River.

7. Innis, *Empire and Communications*, 7.

8. Innis, *Empire and Communications*, 11.

9. Interestingly, Innis thought that universities held the potential to counteract the spatial bias of modern nation-states by reinserting a sensitivity to time. Innis would, I suspect, be pleased with the current movement in Canada "to Indigenize universities," thereby bringing time-based priorities to the center of their academic and pedagogical missions.

10. Carlson, "Orality about Literacy," 43–69.

11. Bhabha, *The Location of Culture*, 85–92.

12. Kipling's poem was originally published in *McClure's Magazine* on 12 February 1899.

13. S. Miller, *Benevolent Assimilation*, 135. Elsewhere I have discussed in detail the struggles that occurred within the U.S. government over attempts to set a fixed date for Philippine independence. See Carlson, *The Twisted Road to Freedom*.

14. Locke, *Second Treatise of Government*.

15. Bhabha, *The Location of Culture*, 122.

16. For a well-balanced discussion of the waning role of humanitarianism in the mid-nineteenth-century British Colonial Office as related to New Zealand and what is now British Columbia, see Storey, "Anxiety, Humanitarianism, and the Press," especially ch. 6, "Colonial Humanitarians."

17. Bhabha, *The Location of Culture*, 122.

18. Bhabha, *The Location of Culture*, 122, 128.

19. Bhabha, *The Location of Culture*, 91.

20. See W. Kaye Lamb's discussion of Fraser's journals in the introduction to his edited work, S. Fraser, *Letters and Journals, 1806–1808*, 32–38.

21. For the Interior Salish, see Wickwire, "To See Ourselves as the Other's Other," 1–20. For the Coast Salish, see Carlson, "Reflections on Indigenous History and Memory," 46–68.

22. Fraser described in his journal numerous misunderstandings between his party and the Salish people they visited along the lower Fraser River—each inci-

dent eroding the goodwill on both sides. Ultimately, Fraser appropriated a leading Salish man's canoe despite protests. This seems to have been the breaking point in relations. Thereafter, the Salish became increasingly unwelcoming and hostile to the sojourning traders. See especially Fraser's journal entries for 1 July through 8 July 1808. S. Fraser, *Letters and Journals, 1806–1808*, 102–12.

23. S. Fraser, *Letters and Journals, 1806–1808*, 113.

24. See chapter 3, "Spiritual Forces of Historical Affiliation," and chapter 4, "From the Great Flood to Smallpox," in Carlson, *The Power of Place, the Problem of Time*.

25. Rosaleen George and Elizabeth Herrling, in conversation with the author, 16 May 1997.

26. I am indebted to Mark Meyers for this insight on this matter. He challenged me to consider, for example, how in Western society we *say* the alphabet and *recite* new vocabulary in order to learn how to read and write. In this light, mnemonics are just as required for Western children learning their ABCs as they are in Salish society when children learn to read the storied landscape.

27. Thomas, *Entangled Objects*.

28. Rosaleen George, Elder of Skwah First Nation, personal communication, 16 May 1997.

29. S. Fraser, *Letters and Journals, 1806–1808*, 100; and "A Map of America between the latitudes 40 and 70 North and Longitudes 80 and 150 west Exhibiting the Principal Trading Stations of the North West Company" (drawn by David Thompson but uncredited), 6763, National Archives of Canada, Ottawa, Ontario.

30. I am indebted to Naxaxalhts'i (aka Albert "Sonny" McHalsie) for the conversations we shared on this topic, and for the insights into Salish Transformer stories that he has provided me with over our more than twenty years of collaboration.

31. The Fort Langley journals have been made available in published form, whereas the Kamloops journals are available only as manuscripts. See MacLachlan, *The Fort Langley Journals, 1827–30*; and Fort Kamloops fonds, PR-1665, British Columbia Archives, Victoria.

32. See Duff, *The Upper Stalo Indians of the Fraser Valley, British Columbia*, 98–102.

33. Bertha Peters, quoted in the unpublished field notes of Marian Smith during fieldwork in the summer of 1945, MSS 268, box 3:4, no. 2 (unpaginated), Royal Anthropological Institute, London, UK.

34. Carlson, "Orality about Literacy," 54.

35. Fr. Paul Durieu was an Oblate priest who served as a missionary to the Coast Salish from 1855 to 1875, when the Pope appointed him bishop of British Columbia.

36. Cairns first floated the idea of "citizens plus" when working as a graduate research assistant for Henry Hawthorn in the 1950s and 1960s. More recently he refined the ideas behind the concept. These are found in his book *Citizens Plus: Aboriginal Peoples and the Canadian State*.

37. Bertha Peters, quoted in the unpublished field notes of Marian Smith during fieldwork in the summer of 1945, MSS 268, box 3:4, no. 2 (unpaginated), Royal Anthropological Institute, London, UK.

38. James A. Teit, "Dreambook of a Stalo Prophet," c. 1882, Canadian Museum of History, Ottawa, MS VII-G-19M.

39. For an overview of Canada's residential school history in terms of government policy, see Haig-Brown, *Resistance and Renewal*; J. R. Miller, *Shingwauk's Vision*; and Milloy, *A National Crime*.

40. Truth and Reconciliation Commission of Canada, TRC *Final Report*, December 2015, http://www.trc.ca.

41. Quoted in Leslie, *The Historical Development of the Indian Act*, 114.

42. I suspect that the mountain in question is Sumas Mountain. In 1858 the American surveyor and amateur ethnographer George Gibbs recorded a Salish legend about Sumas Mountain (located across the Fraser River from the site where St. Mary's residential school would be built four years later): "The Indians say there is a small lake, high up in the mountains. It is the habitation of demons resembling birds [likely thunderbirds] who have a house on a rock in its midst. They work at night, and all the rocks seem to be on fire. Everything is bad there. It is probable that there are pyrites in a state of combustion." George Gibbs, "Journal of an Expedition to Fraser River," WA-MSS S-1810, Beinecke Rare Book and Manuscript Library, Yale University, New Haven, CT.

43. Gendre, *Oblats de Marie Imaculée*, 302.

44. R. P. Gendre, OMI, *Missions*, 302.

45. R. P. Gendre, OMI, *Missions*, 302.

46. See, for example, James Douglas to the Right Hon. Lord Stanley, Victoria, 15 June 1858, C.O. 60/1 100684, 54–57, British Columbia Archives; Gov. Seymour to Earl of Carnarvon, New Westminster, 19 February 1867, C.O. 60/27, 227–40, British Columbia Archives; Brew, Chartres, to Joseph Trutch, Chief Commissioner of Lands and Works, 26 January 1866, GR 1372, file 943/13, British Columbia Archives; and "Williams McColl's Report," 16 May 1864, in *Papers Connected with the Indian Land Question, 1850–1875*, 43.

47. Elsewhere I have discussed both Douglas's and Moody's intentions and actions toward Indigenous people. See Carlson, *The Power of Place, the Problem of Time*, especially chs. 6–8.

48. See, for example, William Young to R. C. Moody, Colonial Secretary's Office, 9 June 1862, in *Papers Connected with the Indian Land Question, 1850–1875*, 24.

49. Col. Moody to Fr. Fouquet, OMI, 22 December 1862, BCA Lands and Works Correspondence Outward, vol. 4, 54, British Columbia Archives.

50. Bhabha, *The Location of Culture*, 122.

51. I have compiled and published a list of Salish petitions to the British Columbian colonial and Canadian governments. These can be found as an appendix in Carlson, *A Sto:lo-Coast Salish Historical Atlas*.

52. On the school, see Carlson, Lutz, Schaepe, and McHalsie, *Towards a New Ethnohistory*.

53. Harvey, "Story People," 79.

54. While I have not formally published these findings, I have meticulously documented them in several expert-witness reports that have been submitted to

the Canadian courts as part of litigation launched by Salish communities against the federal or provincial governments.

55. For example, during the 1858 gold rush the Aborigines' Protection Society lobbied the Colonial Office to ensure that Native rights and interests were protected from miners and developers. See F. W. Chessen, Secretary of the Aborigines' Protection Society, to the Right Honourable Sir Edward Bulwer Lytton, M.P., Her Majesty's Principal Secretary of State for the Colonies (enclosure in Sir Edward Lytton to Governor James Douglas), Despatch No. 12, 2 September 1858, in *Papers Connected with the Indian Land Question*, 12–13.

56. D. Cole and Chaikin, *An Iron Hand upon the People*.

57. Bhabha, *The Location of Culture*, 131.

58. In light of this analysis, while it has been beyond the scope of this particular study, one of the questions that now arises is whether similar menaces emerged in the eyes of the Indigenous people on the other side of the colonial divide. If mimicry was a strategy of colonial power that produced its own slippage through ambivalence, was a similar process at work in terms of Indigenous agency? Was there an anticolonial strategy of creating "resemblance" that, as with colonial mimicry, might hold the potential to become a threat to Indigenous identity? That is to say, did the struggle to resemble but still remain distinct hold within it the threat that the distinction might be subject to slippage so that the resemblance could become almost total, but not quite?

CHAPTER FIVE

Talking Traditions: Orality, Ecology, and Spirituality in Mangaia's Textual Culture

MICHAEL P. J. REILLY

THE ISLAND OF MANGAIA lies at the southern edge of tropical eastern Oceania, in a sea of islands once crisscrossed by voyagers on double-hulled ships.
The ancestors who founded Mangaian society deliberately brought with
them many things, including useful plants and animals. They also brought oral
traditions that were passed down the generations by experts called 'are kōrero.[1]
Over time these traditions have changed, being reworked in light of the changing interests and concerns of a newer generation. "Remembering," as the historian Jan Vansina points out, "is an activity, a re-creation of what once was."[2] The
content of traditions, especially those retold as stories, varies with each narration, even by the same expert. However, the core elements of these free-form
texts, such as key characters, actions, ancestral sayings, or set phrases, persist
through time, being retold by different experts with little variation.[3]

Since the nineteenth century Mangaia's oral traditions have been transmitted in a greater variety of ways. Following older practices, 'are kōrero pass on oral
traditions to others, perhaps someone in their community who wants to learn
about their place in the local world formed and lived in by their ancestors. Traditions are also presented at public gatherings through speeches or in song.

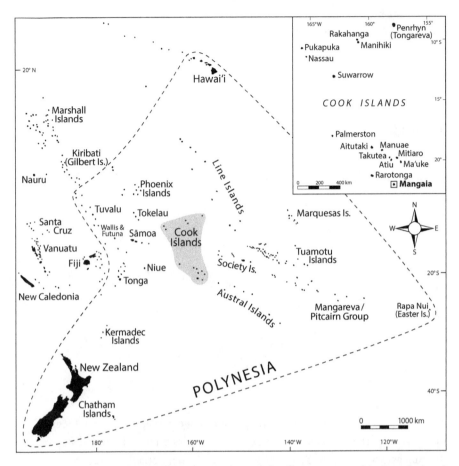

MAP 5.1 Mangaia in wider Polynesia. Map by Les O'Neill, Department of Anthropology and Archaeology, University of Otago. Courtesy of Les O'Neill.

Writing has also allowed 'are kōrero to record knowledge in family books, containing key ancestral stories and genealogies as well as the names of plantations and other food-producing places used by generations of the family.[4] These books have become cherished heirlooms in the care of senior family members.

This chapter explores an oral tradition first recorded as a sermon preached by a local minister, Mamae of Ngāti Vara, which the resident English missionary, William Wyatt Gill, wrote down and later published in 1876. Almost exactly a hundred years later, the tradition was told by the 'are kōrero Tere'ēvangeria Aratangi to an employee of the Cook Islands government's Cultural Development Division, who tape-recorded the story and typed up a transcript of it. The tradition concerns a chief, Kōtuku, whose

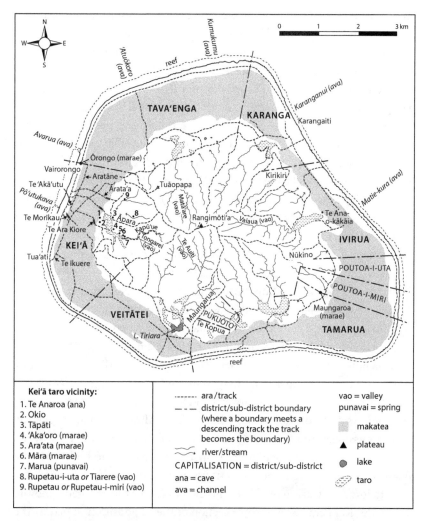

Kei'ā taro vicinity:

1. Te Anaroa (ana)
2. Okio
3. Tāpāti
4. 'Aka'oro (marae)
5. Ara'ata (marae)
6. Māra (marae)
7. Marua (punavai)
8. Rupetau-i-uta *or* Tiarere (vao)
9. Rupetau *or* Rupetau-i-miri (vao)

------- ara / track
— — — district/sub-district boundary
(where a boundary meets a
descending track the track
becomes the boundary)
~~~ river/stream
CAPITALISATION = district/sub-district
ana = cave
ava = channel

vao = valley
punavai = spring

▨ makatea

▲ plateau

⬤ lake

▧ taro

MAP 5.2 Place-names and geographic features in ancient Mangaia. Map by Les O'Neill, Department of Anthropology and Archaeology, University of Otago. Courtesy of Les O'Neill.

abusive behavior toward a young woman, Pata-ariri, results in an ecological crisis, and the consequential intervention of Te Maru-o-Rongo.

The microcosmic study of a single tradition highlights how 'are kōrero continue to draw deeply from the island's ancient wellspring of oral knowledge. Talking traditions is still how most locals get to hear about Mangaia's own knowledge world. Nonetheless, this is a world that has always been challenged and changed by new ideas, practices, things, and people from other places; as the New Zealand poet Allen Curnow writes, "Out of the sea comes change, comes danger."[5] The two versions of this tradition reveal how new media or technologies (paper, pen, printing press, tape recorder, typewriter) and skills (writing, reading, printing, typing) have recorded and disseminated the island's knowledge far beyond the range of any talk. The vitality of the old oral world is supported, even enhanced, by these new forms of communicating. Rather than replacing orality, these different communicative practices work together in various ways, allowing the island's experts to keep passing on to new generations the words and wisdom of their ancestors.[6] Without that knowledge Mangaians would all lose something vital to defining who they are as a distinctive and proud Oceanian people.

Christianity gained a first foothold in Mangaia in 1824 when the island's leaders allowed two Society Islanders from the London Missionary Society (LMS) to stay and evangelize in their communities. Teaching the Word was a key site of struggle between converts and those adhering to the indigenous spirit powers. Indeed, converts were known by a Tahitian term introduced by the first missionaries: *kai parau*, "book consumers," a reference to the instruction of converts in the teachings of Christianity's *parau*, the Bible.[7] But the Word was never enough: the missionaries and their supporters utilized violence to force conversion on those who did not follow the new god, Jehovah. In 1828 the Kai Parau beat a major section of their opposition in battle. The prisoners were taken to the Christian settlement and made "to learn their alphabet."[8] The ability to read and write was what set the Christians apart from their opponents, who adhered to the oral world of their ancestors.

The official language of the new religion at this time was the cognate language Tahitian, as missionaries from the Society Islands remained responsible for Mangaia.[9] In 1839 this oversight shifted to the Rarotonga LMS. When the first complete Bible in Rarotongan Māori was delivered in 1852, Mangaian readers received the volumes with "unbounded enthusiasm."[10] Also stepping ashore was Gill, arriving at his first mission posting. The island's leaders assigned him to the village of Tamarua, where Mamae had been serving since 1848. It is highly likely that among his other duties Mamae taught Gill the

Mangaian language.[11] Out of the bonds formed between teacher and pupil came a friendship that evolved into a scholarly collaboration to record what Mamae and his contemporaries knew of Mangaia's ancient knowledge world.

Mamae wrote numerous texts recording the stories, songs, and tribal genealogies he had been taught as a young child by his grandfather, a well-respected poet and chiefly titleholder. One of Mamae's major works was a family book of genealogies and narratives that subsequent generations continued to add to until it came into the possession of the 'are kōrero 'Akaiti Ponga.[12] In addition to recording what he knew of his ancestral past, Mamae regularly utilized this knowledge to explain Christian truths to his congregation by using local ideas and imagery. This was the origin of the sermon about Kōtuku.

Gill's collaborations with Mamae and other pastors, and his observation of their oratorical and intellectual powers as preachers, convinced him to put samples of their preaching before an English evangelical audience. Gill believed that such an audience would be impressed by the transformative effect of Christianity on the lives and minds of men like Mamae who had previously worshipped indigenous spirit powers.[13] The sermons preached by such men creatively utilized that ancient world's knowledge so as to explain the Christian message to their new convert communities. Clearly, such evidence also provided strong justification for the value of the work being done in foreign fields by the LMS and other missionary groups, who relied on the support of the English churches.

These changes to the world of Mangaians like Mamae were not at the expense of what had gone before. In his description of the local reception of these sermons, Gill himself drew attention to the continuing vitality of the oral transmission of knowledge and the value placed on retentive memories within these new Christian communities:

> No congregation in Europe or America could hang with more earnestness on the lips of the preacher. It is quite a common practice to take down the outline of the discourse on paper or slates, or even rudely to scratch it on the leaf of the banana or the cocoa-nut. The people converse on what they have heard in their homes; the usual course being for the husband first to call upon the wife for the text, and, if she fails to remember it, to appeal to the eldest son, and so on, proceeding in the same manner with the successive divisions of the discourse. I have known sermons to be well remembered even ten years after their delivery.[14]

The introduction of reading and writing was not accompanied by any diminution of the older skills associated with the oral world of pre-Christian

Mangaia. Instead, as in other indigenous societies, a "primacy of orality" was maintained alongside veneration for the Christian Bible.[15]

Mamae preached his sermon on a passage from Saint John's gospel: "If any man thirst, let him come unto me and drink" (John 7:37). He turned to the story of Kōtuku to highlight his key theme that only a commitment to Jesus Christ could provide people with lasting happiness, in place of the fleeting pleasures of this world.[16]

The "fierce chief" Kōtuku lived in "the sequestered and fertile valley of Kiriapi (on the south of Mangaia)." He ordered the young slave Pata-ariri to refill some empty calabashes at the neighboring spring. She went there but found it dry. She went to the next valley, but its water source was also dry. She ran to a third valley but found the stream that formerly irrigated the *māpura* (wild variety of taro) no longer flowing. She went on and on, carrying the calabashes under the hot sun, but could not find water anywhere. Tired, perplexed, she sat down to rest. When she looked up, she saw "a noble-looking man." He said his name was Te Maru-o-Rongo (The Shadow of Rongo). He asked her why she was so downhearted. She explained that she had looked all around the island for water but had found none. She feared Kōtuku would kill her if she did not return with some. Te Maru-o-Rongo said:

> "I am the lord of the fountains. It was I who dried up all the streamlets, in order that you might be driven to meet me. Follow me: I will give you water. But I give it on one condition—you shall be mine!"

He led her to "a copious fountain of purest water," from which she drank, before filling up her calabashes and returning to Kōtuku. Meanwhile, "her imperious master," thirsty and fed up with waiting, had decided to kill her. He concealed his club in his *maro* (loincloth). Pata-ariri gave him the largest calabash. She noticed his "ominous scowl," and as he raised his arms to drink, she spotted the concealed weapon. Stepping back outside of the door of the "fierce" chief's house, she said:

'Aitoa koe, e Kōtuku, kia inu i ta'u toto.	I defy you, Kōtuku, to drink my blood.
'A kai-rangi a Kōtuku!	Kōtuku, you are outwitted![17]

The astonished chief threw down his calabash and ran out of the house after Pata-ariri, but she had already escaped down a narrow path into a "dense forest" of hibiscus trees.[18] She kept on running until she had reached the distant residence of "the royal" Te Maru-o-Rongo. Foresee-ing her escape, he offered her protection. The angry Kōtuku hunted for her across half of the island, but he called it off on finding that she was living in Te Maru-o-Rongo's household. The slave became "the beloved wife of a king."

> "So runs [the] ancient story; but it has," said the preacher, "a higher and a nobler signification than our ancestors dreamed of. All the promises of real happiness which the world makes to us, one after the other, disappoint the soul. May we slake our soul-thirst at the fountain of the Divine truth! Let us gladly listen to the voice which says, 'If any man thirst, let him come unto Me, and drink.'"

This version of the Kōtuku story reveals several key themes. The most significant concerns the availability of potable water, and the hazards people faced when the island was afflicted by severe drought. This choice of story would doubtless have resonated for everyone listening to Mamae's sermon, as maintaining the supply of water has always been a major issue for Man-gaian society. One of the principal responsibilities of its leaders continues to be the effective management of the island's irrigation system, providing water for people and for their principal crops, notably the *māmio* (*Colocasia esculenta*, known elsewhere as taro). The story also stresses the value placed on the purity of the water that Te Maru-o-Rongo has access to. In a note Gill associates Te Maru-o-Rongo with Rongo, "the tutelary god of Mangaia," implying that the control of the people's water supply is under the author-ity of those with access to the land's spiritual powers.[19] In the text Te Maru-o-Rongo is identified as a "king": a missionary translation for *ariki*, which in Mangaia refers to the exceptionally sacred mediums of Rongo, who were selected from families tracing their descent directly to that spirit power.

The other significant theme concerns the abusive relationship that could arise between a person of mana and those under their power, such as a slave, who possessed no mana. Kōtuku is painted in highly negative colors, being "fierce," "pitiless," "imperious," "angry," and inclined to outbursts of violence toward subordinates who do not do as instructed. By contrast, Te Maru-o-Rongo is "kindly," generous, possessed of foresight, and protective. His highly sacred status explains why Kōtuku immediately abandoned his search for retribution against Pata-ariri when he realized that she was living with the king. To attack Te Maru-o-Rongo, with his connections to Mangaia's supreme spirit power, could have resulted in Kōtuku's own demise. The char-acters of the two men of rank allude to a classical Oceanic polarity between leaders who are peace-loving and look after their people and those who are violent, lack empathy, and abuse their followers.[20]

Pata-ariri, in spite of being a slave, is clearly attractive to someone of Te Maru-o-Rongo's rank. Besides beauty she has other personal attributes that make her stand out. In confronting Kōtuku she has the courage and presence of mind to compose a rejoinder to diminish his mana. When he seeks to kill her, she shows her athletic stamina in eluding his grasp and running the long distance to Te Maru-o-Rongo's house, which may have been located in the district of Kei'ā, on the other side of the island, where Rongo's sacred sites were located. The story suggests that someone of lower status can attain a higher social position, through marriage, by demonstrating outstanding personal abilities. It reveals the internal dynamism and flexibility of eastern Oceanic societies, where mana comes from one's own achievements just as much as through inheritance.[21] Leaders were also expected to show compassion, so that Te Maru-o-Rongo's response to Pata-ariri could also be seen as an expression of a leader's pastoral concern for their people. Te Maru-o-Rongo's name confirms his personality: in Mangaian society a leader enveloped someone within their protective mana by placing them in their *maru* (shadow).[22]

Gill introduces his foreign readers to the physical and cultural world of Mangaia. He identifies some place-names and explains the names of the key characters and of some relevant plants. He also alludes to the location of the people within the interior valleys, near planting lands and water supplies. However, he leaves out certain identifying names from his version in order not to present too many reading challenges for his English-speaking intended audience. Gill alludes to a major feature of Mangaian life, namely, the irrigation of the all-important plantations of māmio by the same water sources that provided the local pools utilized for drinking water. The disappearance of water risked the loss of this staple food, so that such a widespread drought would have been an economic and social catastrophe for Mangaian society. The errand of fetching water in calabashes was another familiar cultural detail, even in the nineteenth century, when young women and girls obediently undertook this daily activity at the request of their elders.[23]

The earlier oral tradition retains a ghostly presence in Gill's version, showing that Mamae's preaching retained a number of the performance aspects of the older oral arts. Gill hints at Mamae's abilities as a performer. He describes his presentations as "racy" (in the sense of exciting, spirited language) and possessed of "much wit," humor, and "true pathos."[24] The repetition in the story, as Pata-ariri made her way from one spring to another across three valleys, is most likely an echo of the original oral tradition. Repetitions are commonly used in such works as a device to build up dramatic tension.[25] The pieces of dialogue throughout the story are also found in other Mangaian traditions, where they lend a dramatic sense of immediacy that in the hands of a skilled performer must have enthralled an audience. Gill himself seems to have been moved by Mamae's presentation for he retained the powerful quotation in the original Mangaian language, when Pata-ariri boldly puts her master in his place. This may have been a critical passage in the tradition as well as a high point in Mamae's own sermon.

The sermon's presentation reveals its intended evangelical audience. This is particularly evident in the opening and closing episodes that locate the oral tradition in the new world order wrought by the conversion to Christianity. In a typical flourish, Gill allows "the preacher"—unnamed in this particular text—a chance to speak directly at the end, but only to testify to the transformational changes he and his fellow Mangaians had undergone, in contrast to their ancestors. At one point, in describing Pata-ariri's escape, Gill refers to her resolution "not to furnish her angry master with a meal," almost certainly Gill's own interpolation.[26] The eating of people as a part of a person's diet is a cultural distortion used, as here, to underscore the perceived depravity of the Mangaian ancestors, morally indifferent to the welfare of fellow human beings, in contrast (so Gill implies) to the more refined sensibilities of their converted descendants. To judge from Gill's version of the sermon, Mamae himself understood that like his congregation he had received a great gift that revealed a whole new world his own ancestors could never have imagined. While he remains connected to them through descent, he recognizes that Mangaia has been changed. The traditions retain their place but no longer simply as part of an ancestral knowledge world. Instead, the oral traditions have been dedicated to a new purpose: to help the congregation understand the beliefs and values of Mangaia's new religion.

During most of the nineteenth century, Mangaia's indigenous leaders continued to govern their own island with the advice of the LMS. Then in 1888 Mangaia became part of the formal British Protectorate of the Cook Islands. What had been a cluster of autonomous islands connected through visitations from Rarotonga-based supervising missionaries became a new political entity where individual indigenous governments, like Mangaia's, became increasingly subordinate to the rulings of a New Zealand colonial authority located in Rarotonga. In 1901 New Zealand annexed the Cook Islands, thereby extending the national boundaries of that country into the tropical zone of the South Pacific. The Cook Islands effectively regained its autonomy as a new nation-state in 1965. Mangaia, like all the other islands, remains an integral part of that postcolonial nation.[27]

The government of the charismatic first premier of the Cook Islands, Albert Henry, ruled the new nation from 1965 until 1978. Following the 1973 opening of the international airport in Rarotonga, the government took measures to promote a Cook Islands traditional culture both to attract mass tourism, with its potential economic benefits, and to create a distinctive national identity so as to counter any negative consequences of becoming more accessible to the wider world. To that end, in 1974 the Cultural Development Division was established within the Ministry of Social Services. Its primary function was to collect traditional knowledge from which the government could build this new sense of a unitary culture, particularly through the school curriculum. Students, educated in a Cook Islands culture, would entertain and instruct those tourists who flew in on the new wide-bodied jets. Various experts from the different islands were brought together at two conferences organized by the division: the first in August 1974 and a second one in March 1975. During the conferences Cultural Development Division officials recorded traditions told to them by the different experts from each island.[28]

A number of Mangaian 'are kōrero are credited with providing traditions for this project: Tere'ēvangeria Aratangi, Iviiti 'Aerepō, 'Akaiti Ponga, Ngātokorua (Ngā) Kaokao, Ma'arona 'Okirua, Ravengenge Rakauruaiti, Ave 'Ivaiti, Tangi'ānau Ūpoko, and Tīriamai Naeiti.[29] The vast bulk of the traditions recorded for the Cultural Development Division came from Aratangi and her brother, 'Aerepō.[30] Aratangi believed that all 'are kōrero should pass on their traditions to the younger generations, especially to schoolchildren, so that they would have the opportunity to learn their ancestors' knowledge.[31] The experts collaborated with younger Mangaians who worked for the government, such as Maki 'Area'i, then in his early twenties.[32] Thus, the experts seem to have been paired with younger officials off their home island. This ensured the recorders were familiar with the experts' language and recognized and understood aspects of local knowledge, such as the names of people and places. Doubtless the parties would have known each other through the myriad ties that connect people in small island communities. Their working relationship also imitated the way 'are kōrero customarily instructed selected youth in the knowledge of their ancestors. All these factors created a very positive recording environment, where the experts' traditions were allowed to flow without any noticeable hindrances, such as questioning by the recorder. The experts were in control of the recording situation.

The tape recordings were transcribed in 1975, with the typed texts subsequently ending up in the National Archives of the Cook Islands.[33] The whereabouts of the original Mangaian tapes are unknown. As the Cultural Development Division was closed down by the Sir Tom Davis–led government in 1980, it may be that individual recorders kept the tapes in their own personal collections, although at least some of the recordings for other islands appear to have been deposited in the archives.[34]

The identification of the source ʻare kōrero found at the end of each text yields some insights into the transmission of these traditions. Many stress the act of telling or recording, as if the account by that expert is just one version of a tradition.[35] Some texts confirm transmission between experts by identifying an unnamed collective of Mangaian experts as the ultimate authority of a tradition, which the source ʻare kōrero then recorded.[36] Sometimes this collective is identified as an older generation of experts, suggesting that the tradition had been passed down to the ʻare kōrero who recorded it.[37] In certain cases, the source ʻare kōrero apparently received their knowledge from another expert who was either about the same age or a little older.[38] Such stories were presumably passed around among a generation of ʻare kōrero, as each learned from another, more knowledgeable expert. There is no ultimate author of an oral tradition, but rather a series of authors, each performing a version of a tradition.[39] The authority of an ʻare kōrero arises not from themselves but from their place in a succession of experts recognized by their community as repositories of knowledge about the past.

The following summary in English follows Aratangi's story about Kōtuku, except for some minor rearrangements of the text and the deletion of repeated information. Noteworthy Mangaian phrases are quoted following their translations.

> Kōtuku lived in Tamarua village during the era of night's intense darkness ("te tuātau o te pō kerekere") in Aʻuaʻu ʻEnua. Kōtuku required his daughter, Pata-ariri, to undertake a sad task ("te mea tangi") whereby she had to walk to the district of Keiʻā in order to fetch him drinking water at any time of the day or night. Pata-ariri undertook this work, weeping and with high-pitched cries of fright ("auē ʻanga"). She belonged to the Te ʻAkatauira clan.
>
> Kōtuku did not drink from just any stream. He preferred water from a spring called Māra, in Keiʻā. He would know which location the water came from. If Pata-ariri brought it back from another source, he would break her calabashes and make her go and fetch the water again. Aratangi

explains that in the old days water was carried in an *ururua* container. Pata-ariri would carry four ururua containers tied up with sennit. She feared ("mataku") Kōtuku and longed to run away from him.

One day the land and all its streams became dry. The water no longer flowed in the streams around the island.

One night, Kōtuku woke up thirsty for water. He reached out for the bunch of ururua containers, but none contained any water. He called out to Pata-ariri, "Go quickly to the Kei'ā district and fill up the bunch of ururua containers with water." Pata-ariri took the ururua containers and ran away crying in that dark, moonless night.

When she reached Kei'ā, she was very surprised to discover that the stream was dry. There was no water. She went away looking about as she walked at the streams on A'ua'u 'Enua. There was no water. The land was all dry. As she returned to Tamarua, she really felt scared of Kōtuku. When he saw her, he called out to her to hurry up, as he was dying of thirst. She called out, "There is no water; the streams on the island are all dry." Kōtuku said to her that she must make haste to go and find some water for him to drink. If she did not get any, then he would kill her and drink her blood as water. Then she ran away to search for water in the caves and in the stone cavities. There was definitely no water. She arrived at the Taungakututu cave. There really was no water.

Pata-ariri wept and cried out in fear ("auē"). She saw a man there and was scared. The man called out, "Do not be afraid, Pata-ariri, I am the spirit being of the woman ('te atua o te va'ine'). I have made the streams dry in order to kill Kōtuku for his wrong courses of action ('nō tāna au ākono'anga kino')." Pata-ariri replied, "I will die. Kōtuku will drink my blood as his water, if I don't obtain water." Te Maru-o-Rongo said to her, "Come here, I will take you into the sanctuary ('te pā tīkoru') so that you may live ("ia ora koe')." Pata-ariri followed him into the sanctuary, and her life was saved. That is the nature of Kōtuku's story; he died of thirst.

In the opening of the story, Aratangi locates it in the pre-Christian era by using Mangaia's older name, A'ua'u 'Enua, and referring to its intense darkness. This image alludes to an important division of time in modern Mangaia that describes the era before Christianity as a world of darkness filled with violence, in contrast to the enlightened Christian world where peace and light reigned supreme.[40] Aratangi modifies the physical location of the story by shifting it from Kiriapi valley, probably in Tamarua district, to Tamarua village. This settlement was not founded until the early Christian era when the LMS concentrated populations near the coast for ease of interisland communication, rather than in the interior valleys where people's plantations and water supplies were. The 'are kōrero who transmitted this tradition after Mamae's time evidently changed the story's location to reflect the contemporary world of their own audiences.

Aratangi's text uses various devices that reveal its affiliations with the ancestral oral world. One of them is direct quotation. These quotations all occur in the critical episodes of the story, with the last three forming a piece of dialogue, as they follow on from one another. Clearly, the use of quotation signaled to the listener that they had arrived at the crisis of the story. The dialogue in the final part between Te Maru-o-Rongo and Pata-ariri, where he offers her an escape from certain death at Kōtuku's hands, is the most dramatic passage. Aratangi also uses repetition of phrases throughout the text, in order to carry the story forward from one part to another, to remind the audience of the important themes, and to develop a certain dramatic tension, so that the audience waits expectantly to learn what happens next.

With regard to its structure, Aratangi's text can be divided into two parts. In the first half she introduces a series of explanatory episodes: identifying characters, specifying the task, naming the water source; all told in the author's own words. At this stage, she introduces the key theme of drought into the story. This sets the scene for the crucial, final sections that follow, marked by their use of quotations. This part resembles a story within a story: a thirsty Kōtuku sends Pata-ariri off for water; she fruitlessly seeks some and in her despair encounters Te Maru-o-Rongo, who offers her sanctuary and a fresh start in life. Right at the end, as if it is an afterthought, Aratangi tersely explains the fate of Kōtuku. This abrupt ending contrasts with Gill's retelling of Mamae's sermon, which recollects a far longer, more complex tradition, involving a confrontation between Kōtuku and Pata-ariri, a defiant saying, and her successful escape and marriage to Te Maru-o-Rongo. These later episodes may have been selected out, and forgotten, during the subsequent transmission of the tradition down to Aratangi, or she may have chosen to tell a more abbreviated version at the 1974 gathering of 'are kōrero.[41] Despite these differences, the core themes of the tradition appear in both versions: the brutal demands of Kōtuku, Pata-ariri's fruitless search for water throughout a drought-affected island, her encounter with Te Maru-o-Rongo, his intervention against Kōtuku, and his protection of Pata-ariri.

Aratangi's story provides important local knowledge that Gill partially excluded when he recalled Mamae's original sermon. In the opening she explains that Kōtuku's daughter had to fetch water from Kei'ā district. This alludes to the division of Mangaia's landscape into six wedge-shaped *puna* (districts) controlled by leaders who had authority over the lands, waterways, and peoples. In the pre-Christian era, these puna primarily referred to the heavily populated valleys covered by a hydrological complex of irrigation streams, dams, ponds, and channels designed to feed water into the rectangular plots of māmio. Later on, Aratangi introduces further key elements of Mangaia's landscape when she refers to the caves and the stone cavities of the *makatea* region. The makatea is an extensive platform of limestone surrounding Mangaia's interior valleys like a wall. In the pre-Christian era, it formed a wilderness of sharp coral rock and impenetrable bush of benefit only to Mangaia's wildlife and to human refugees defeated in battle and forced to live there.[42] The wild nature of the makatea zone explains why Pata-ariri is frightened when she encounters Te Maru-o-Rongo there, since his presence would be unexpected and might suggest he was a potentially threatening escapee from the ordered valley world she was familiar with.

A major theme in this story, as in Gill's version, is the importance of maintaining year-round supplies of potable water. However, Aratangi goes further, explaining that ancestors like Kōtuku preferred their drinking water to come from particular pools. Other testimony indicates that the ancestors were able to tell which spring their supplies had been taken from by the particular taste of the water.[43] In Kōtuku's case he insisted on drinking from Māra, more commonly known as Marua, one of four major potable water sources in Kei'ā district; its water was proverbially sweet tasting.[44] Kei'ā lies on the far side of the island from Tamarua. In the pre-Christian era, travel between puna was by rough, single-file paths, so that Pata-ariri had to undertake a long and arduous expedition every day. She carried four ururua (large containers made from coconut shells), tied in twos on either end of a pole balanced on her shoulder.[45] The incident when Kōtuku smashed the containers may have arisen from occasions when Pata-ariri tried to shorten her daily journey by accessing springs nearer their home.

The abiding cruelty of Kōtuku throughout the story is one of Aratangi's most distinctive themes. The other is her identification of Pata-ariri as the daughter of Kōtuku, rather than his slave as in Gill and Mamae's version, and her depiction of the young woman's own emotional responses. Aratangi turns her version into a powerful story about domestic violence. The shift in Pata-ariri's identity, from slave to daughter, is another change made by experts after Mamae's time so as to reflect contemporary life, in which daughters had taken over menial roles following the end of slavery, an institution that disappeared with the acceptance of Christianity. Significantly, Pata-ariri is identified as a member of a prestigious descent group, Te 'Akatauira, one of the three groups constituting the *ivi* (tribe) of Ngāriki, the first people of the land and, as the tribal name suggests, the source for the island's sacred ariki. That only makes Kōtuku's cruelty toward his daughter even more appalling. Although girls commonly fetched water for their parents, Aratangi's narrative shows how Kōtuku enforces a far more severe regime that went well beyond any usual social norms. Aratangi's language graphically describes Pata-ariri's emotional reactions to her father's abuse. For Aratangi, subordinate women, such as daughters, may as well be slaves, for they are always vulnerable to an abuse of power within their own families.

The intervention by Te Maru-o-Rongo comes at a point when Pata-ariri is in fear of her life as she desperately searches for water even in the notoriously dry makatea region. His actions restore an appropriate social order to Mangaia. Significantly, in this version of the story, Te Maru-o-Rongo is not a human being but rather a spirit power with responsibility for women. Kōtuku's death from thirst results directly from his bad behavior ("ākono'anga kino"). *Ākono'anga* is a key word meaning "customs" or the "usual way of doing things."[46] Kōtuku's treatment of his daughter breaches the community's customary laws. Clearly, Mangaian parents were not expected to act like him. By extension, people were meant to treat each other with respect and without recourse to abuse or violence. Otherwise, they risked intervention by spirit powers who would punish the wrongdoer, save the victim, and restore the desired social harmony.

These story elements reveal how pre-Christian spiritual beliefs continue to exist in Mangaia. In this worldview, the human and spirit domains are intimately connected. As a consequence, a victim experiencing emotional or physical harm can call on a spirit power to help them by inflicting a punishment on the human perpetrator, such as illness, injury, or death. Spirit powers also intervene where customary laws are violated. Spiritual beings, like Te Maru-o-Rongo, are able to decide for themselves what kind of punishment to inflict on those who act violently toward others.[47] Kōtuku's death removes the lawbreaker and reestablishes the normal and desired social order.

Te Maru-o-Rongo offers Pata-ariri both protection and a life free from her violent father. In order to convey the idea of sanctuary, Aratangi utilizes the image of the *pā tīkoru*. In pre-Christian Mangaia, this referred to a screen of special white *tapa* cloth that covered spaces associated with the spirit powers, priests, or chiefs, such as the shrines within the homes of priestly mediums. A medium under threat of death might be offered shelter in such a sacred space, as no one would harm them there. Early Mangaian Christians continued to utilize this potent image in such phrases as *"te pā tīkoru o Jesu =* 'The curtained sanctuary of Christ.'"[48] Such ancient imagery remained available to the 'are kōrero who transmitted this tradition down to Aratangi's day, ensuring that these elements of the ancestral thought world continued to be known among a younger generation.

In this story about the divine punishment of Kōtuku's unacceptable behavior, the health of the land is just as much at risk as that of human society. His abuse over a long period precipitates the drying up of every single freshwater stream on the island. Not only might a person of mana like Kōtuku perish of thirst, but so might the plantations of māmio as well as other crops on which all of human life in Mangaia depended. According to this story, human society is a part of the surrounding natural world; they are mutually dependent. A serious disturbance in one of those domains will inevitably affect the other. Then only the spirit powers can make things right again. Te Maru-o-Rongo might well be described as a spirit power "of ecological and social balance," for his authority clearly extends over the people, the land, and the life-giving waters.[49] As Mangaian historian Papa Aratangi observes, "The prosperity of the land and the sea was believed to be the work of the gods and must be respected."[50] Te Maru-o-Rongo would presumably have ended the drought and restored the land to its former bountiful health.

This tradition carries a potent environmental and ethical message for Mangaia's leaders. All of their actions, even against those under their authority, had far-reaching consequences for the well-being of themselves and their world. If they and their communities were to prosper, then the leaders had to treat all the people, and the land, with respect. This was the burden imposed on leaders by their possession of the mana that came to them from the spirit powers who had brought the physical universe into being in the first place. Failure to act as the archetype of the ethical person resulted in intervention by the spirit powers and, as a consequence, the loss of mana and therefore of life.

The tradition about Kōtuku, the cruel chief; Pata-ariri, the abused subordinate woman; and Te Maru-o-Rongo, the protective priest or spirit power, is a morality tale intended to instruct people about the importance of adhering to core cultural values, by showing them what happens when someone acts outside customary laws. Despite a Christian repackaging, Mamae's sermon retains the same didactic purpose. For him, the story becomes an allegory of the Christian pilgrims who must turn away from the world of human imperfection and rededicate themselves to the ultimate truth provided by their new religion. Since Mamae himself was an adult convert, this message may have meant a lot to him personally. While Aratangi locates the tale in the violent world of pre-Christian Mangaia, she almost certainly retold this story to warn people of her own day about the consequences of domestic abuse. An individual's negative actions could bring destruction not only on themselves but on the wider community and the land itself. Despite the various adaptations made by Mamae, Gill, and Aratangi, all of them evidently found the oral tradition's underlying moral message a highly relevant one. The story may have changed to suit new generations, but it continues to be told because people still learn something from it about themselves and their relationship to the surrounding world.

The threads of continuity found in these two stories highlight the strength of the ties that bind Mangaia's oral world of ancestral knowledge with that of recent generations. This impression of a continuing connection between past and present appears at many levels. For example, the ancient pattern of plantations and their sophisticated hydrological system still provide people with their daily food; the old techniques of husbandry persist; the chiefs maintain their authority over the planting lands and determine people's customary land use rights; the Mangaian language continues to be the principal medium of day-to-day communication; people still encounter *aitu* (ghostly lights) when abroad in the pitch-black darkness of Mangaia's tropical nights; and *tūpāpaku* (spirit beings, ghosts) still take possession of human beings. The extent to which the new has been incorporated into much older cultural forms is arguably one of the most striking features of Mangaian society.[51] Even institutions brought to the island by foreigners, such as Christianity, seem in many ways to have been converted for use in the existing cultural order.

The retention of so many older practices may suggest that these remain the best-adapted and most effective in the contemporary social and economic environment. It may also reflect Mangaia's relative isolation from global systems, especially as Rarotonga increasingly became the dominant island, in terms of trade and political authority, during the protectorate and after annexation. Mangaia's more marginal location within that colonial world, it might be argued, gave its leaders the opportunity to establish a different kind of social, economic, and cultural order, one over which they had far more control. However, such a geopolitical interpretation only goes so far.

Indigenous agency is the key to understanding the formation of Mangaian society during the nineteenth century and beyond. The people of Mangaia worked actively to retain the old ways, inherited from their forebears, even in the face of outside pressure. While they welcomed foreign missionaries to service their new religion during the nineteenth century, many Mangaians went to great lengths to prevent other outsiders from settling in their island permanently, much to the chagrin of the colonial authorities.[52] When New Zealand's colonial administration sought to introduce the Land Court to Mangaia beginning in 1904, many locals, led by their chiefs, resisted the hearing of cases. Ultimately, the court was restricted to determining title on lands for public use, intended to benefit the whole community.[53] All this can be found in the archives, but I first heard about the absence of a land court from my hosts while on a visit to Mangaia. They were very proud of the actions of their ancestors who stopped this important engine of colonization in its tracks. Mangaia struck out on its own and retained many older practices, not because of its geographic isolation, but through the deliberate decisions and actions of the community and its leaders. They retain a commitment to the cultural world of their ancestors, as it has been passed down to them in the form of oral traditions.

The complexities of this world, and the ways it was communicated to others, are revealed in the works by Mamae, Gill, and Aratangi. Mamae was educated within the pre-Christian oral world of his ancestors but acquired literacy by embracing Christianity. With Gill's evident encouragement and support, Mamae converted his new skills to the writing down of the traditions he had acquired through oral transmission. Gill published some of this material, before ensuring his whole collection of Mangaian traditions was carefully preserved in the colonial archives that were emerging by the time of his death (he died in Sydney in 1896).[54] Mamae's family book remained on the island; its contents were continually added to with each passing generation by those who looked after it. Mamae applied techniques from the ancient oral performance arts to the church sermon, which became an ideal vehicle for their practice and preservation. By such means Christianity became an integral part of Mangaian society. From the early violence of the new, foreign religion emerged an indigenous institution, under local leadership, that maintained many ancestral arts, just as the early church buildings themselves were decorated by practitioners in carving and weaving.

The community maintained the older oral arts in the twentieth century. For example, a dramatic performance of the story of the cannibal ancestor Tangi'ia took place before a mass audience in Oneroa in 1973. While containing topical elements, the presentation strongly resembled older pre-Christian dramas recorded by Gill, including dance ensembles, songs, dialogues, and musical accompaniment.[55] The adaptations of such older art forms, along with the intergenerational transmission of traditions by 'are kōrero, show how dominant orality remains for recent generations such as Aratangi's. As an older woman she embraced new recording technology because she wanted to ensure that the children received their ancestral inheritance. The recordings and transcriptions were a means of reaching out to them through the publication and dissemination of traditions within the educational system.[56] By a process of reading, remembering, and retelling, the young would ensure that these ancestral traditions passed back out again into Mangaia's wider oral world, to the benefit of the whole community.

Since the nineteenth century the 'are kōrero have proven highly adaptable, embracing new communicative practices that helped them pass on oral traditions to their communities. Even the publications of traditions by outsiders, like Gill and the anthropologist Te Rangi Hiroa (Peter Buck), have been co-opted by some locals, whose talk about the past seamlessly weaves together references to such written knowledge with content from oral sources.[57] The ancient oral intellectual heritage of the Mangaian world continues to course strongly through the lives of people today. Paper records and the art of writing are like fresh streamlets that contribute to this existing flow of learning. Together, orality and literacy sustain the community's knowledge of important cultural ideas, values, and practices, forming, as Keith Thor Carlson observes in this volume, a complementary, even symbiotic relationship. So long as they do, Mangaian society will carry on into the future, a source of great pride to all those who can claim an affiliation with it, wherever they may live in the world.

NOTES

This chapter is dedicated to the memory of Tere'ēvangeria Aratangi. I had the good fortune to meet her in 1988 with the help of Īana Ta'ua'i. Her dynamic delivery of stories remains for me a vivid memory testifying to the art of the expert storyteller. Many thanks to George Paniani, National Archives of the Cook Islands, for allowing me access to the Mangaian Kōrero Series, and to Tere Atāriki, mayor of Mangaia, for permission to use one of the stories from this collection. Also thanks to Les O'Neill, Department of Anthropology and Archaeology, University of Otago, for drawing the maps.

1. Shibata, Mangaian-English Dictionary, 104; Buse, Cook Islands Maori Dictionary, 194; and Savage, A Dictionary of the Maori Language of Rarotonga, 116.

2. Vansina, Oral Tradition as History, 147. This chapter has also been influenced by the work of Judith Binney. See Binney, Stories without End, 70–85; and also chapters 13, 20, and 21.

3. For two examples of core sayings repeated in traditions recorded a century apart, see Reilly, Ancestral Voices from Mangaia, 211–15; Reilly, War and Succession in Mangaia from Mamae's Texts, 62; and Tere'ēvangeria Aratangi, "Tō tātou ora'anga i

teia tuātau nei e tā tātou 'anga'anga e rave nei," Ministry of Social Services, Cultural Development Division, Mangaian *Kōrero* Series, Rarotonga, National Archives of the Cook Islands (hereafter MKS).

4. This statement draws from my reading of Mamae's family book (see later in the chapter) and from conversations with the late Mr. Mataora Harry about his own family's book, in his possession.

5. A. Curnow, *Four Plays*, 54. The quotation is from a 1948 play, *The Axe*, composed about Mangaia (and, by reflection, its colonial master, New Zealand).

6. Ballantyne, *Orientalism and Race*, ch. 5; and Ballantyne, *Talking, Listening, Writing, Reading*.

7. Buck (Te Rangi Hiroa), *Mangaia and the Mission*, 19, 55n13; Savage, *A Dictionary of the Maori Language of Rarotonga*, 80; and Shibata, *Mangaian-English Dictionary*, 70–71, 202.

8. Reilly, *Ancestral Voices from Mangaia*, 274. The quote comes from a report written by the missionary George Platt: see "Remarks during a Voyage of Inspection to the Hervey Islands in 1829–1830," box 6, South Seas Journals, Reports and Letters from South Seas Missionaries to London Missionary Society 1796–1899, Council for World Mission Archives (microfilm series at Hocken Library, Dunedin).

9. The Austronesian languages Tahitian and Cook Islands Māori are both descended from Proto-Tahitic, as are New Zealand Māori and Moriori, but other Cook Islands languages like Rarotongan Māori are closer to Mangaian and therefore easier to follow for speakers of Mangaia's *tara* (language) than Tahitian is.

10. W. W. Gill, *From Darkness to Light in Polynesia*, 346.

11. W. W. Gill, *From Darkness to Light in Polynesia*, 337, 346; W. Gill, *Gems from the Coral Islands*, 95; and Reilly, *Ancestral Voices from Mangaia*, 20–21. William Gill was an LMS missionary primarily based in Rarotonga but who regularly visited Mangaia. He was not a relation of William Wyatt Gill, also an LMS missionary.

12. Te Rangi Hiroa transcribed one version of this family book in 1929–30; see "Genealogical Tables of Te 'Amama or Ngati-Vara Tribe," MS Case 5 Co 2, Bernice Pauahi Bishop Museum Library, Honolulu. A second version, with additional material, appears as "Genealogy Book of Akaiti Ponga," MS 171, Macmillan Brown Library, University of Canterbury, Christchurch. Both texts are typescripts derived from an original handwritten manuscript. A photocopy of this manuscript is located in the Donald Stanley Marshall Cook Island Research Papers, box 9.5, University of South Pacific, Cook Islands Campus, Avarua, Rarotonga. Access to this collection was kindly provided courtesy of the campus director, Rod Dixon.

13. See W. W. Gill, *Life in the Southern Isles*, 113, 116.

14. W. W. Gill, *Life in the Southern Isles*, 113–14.

15. The phrase is from Binney, *Stories without End*, 324; for the persistence or privileging of orality in other indigenous societies, see this volume's introduction and chapters 4 and 6.

16. W. W. Gill, *Life in the Southern Isles*, 141–43. The sermon is summarized in my own words. Passages in quotations marks are taken directly from Gill's version. His

own quotations of Mamae's words, either in translation or in Mangaian, appear as indented sections in this summary. This includes Pata-ariri's two-line rejoinder to Kōtuku.

17. Appropriate diacritics have been added to Gill's text, and I have modernized his translation. The saying might also be rendered: "Serves you right, o Kōtuku, for (trying) to drink my blood. / Kōtuku is outwitted!"

18. This was the 'au (lemon hibiscus or beach hibiscus; *Hibiscus tiliaceus*).

19. W. W. Gill, *Life in the Southern Isles*, 142n1. In Mangaia, Rongo was considered the dominant spirit power, closely associated with war, who defeated his elder brother, Tangaroa, and became the senior offspring of the foundational spirit powers, Avatea and Papa-ra'ira'i.

20. A classic example from Mangaia concerns the contrastive leadership pair of Mautara, who preferred peaceful alliance building, and Ngāuta, who resorted frequently to violence. See discussion in Reilly, "Leadership in Ancient Polynesia," 43–63; and Walter and Reilly, "A Prehistory of the Mangaian Chiefdom," 359–60, 362–65.

21. See, for example, Mead, *Tikanga Māori*, 51–52.

22. For the ideology of care and compassion for people by chiefs, see Reilly, "Leadership in Ancient Polynesia," 46–53.

23. See, for example, T. Aratangi, "Te Puna Kei'ā," MKS; and Lamont, *Wild Life among the Pacific Islanders*, 87.

24. W. W. Gill, *Life in the Southern Isles*, 115–16.

25. Vansina, *Oral Tradition as History*, 76.

26. W. W. Gill, *Life in the Southern Isles*, 142–43.

27. For useful histories of the colonial period in the Cook Islands, see Gilson, *The Cook Islands, 1820–1950*; and Scott, *Years of the Pooh-Bah*.

28. Sissons, *Nation and Destination*, 71–80.

29. Aratangi, 'Aerepō, Ponga, Kaokao, 'Okirua, and Rakauruaiti appear in MKS transcripts, the others in Shibata, *Mangaian-English Dictionary*, 104–5.

30. Papa Aratangi, personal communication, 21 March 1989.

31. T. Aratangi, "Tu'anga Rua: Tō tātou ora'anga i teia tuātau nei ē tā tātou 'anga'anga e rave nei," MKS.

32. George Paniani, national archivist, personal communication, 10 May 1988; and Mataora Harry, *kavana* (chief) of Kei'ā district, personal communication, 27 March 2015.

33. One transcript is date-stamped 18 June 1975, suggesting it was completed then; see T. Aratangi, "Te Tuatua ia Tavaitua," MKS.

34. George Paniani, personal communication, 10 May 1988; Sissons, *Nation and Destination*, 87; and Kauraka, *Manihikian Traditional Narratives in English and M[a]nihikian*, 4.

35. See T. Aratangi, "Te Tuatua ia Tavaitua," "Te Mana o te au Atua o tō tātou ui Tupuna," "Te Tua ia Vari Mango," "Te Tatau mataiti a tō mātou ui tupuna," "Te Tua i te Mate'anga o Uakoe," "'Ai," and "Tō tātou ora'anga i teia tuātau nei ē tā tātou 'anga'anga e rave nei," all in MKS.

36. See T. Aratangi, "Te Umu Tangata Mua i runga ia Aʻuaʻu ʻenua" and "ʻE Mire teia nō te Ara," MKS.

37. See T. Aratangi, "ʻE Tua teia nō te ʻānau tamaiti," MKS.

38. These and other similar examples occur in T. Aratangi, "ʻE Mire teia nō Miru," "Part II: ʻO Te Rua teia o te tuʻanga i te tua ia Panako," and "Te ʻĀanga taro a Te Vaki," MKS.

39. Vansina, *Oral Tradition as History*, 55.

40. See Reilly, *War and Succession in Mangaia from Mamae's Texts*, 14. This imagery also appears in P. Aratangi, "The Entry of Christianity into Mangaian Society in the 1820s," 81, 87, 92, 102. Papa Aratangi is Tereʻēvangeria's son. For similar divisions of time in the Society and Leeward Islands, see chapter 6.

41. On selection processes and forgetting, see Vansina, *Oral Tradition as History*, 118–19.

42. Marshall, *Geology of Mangaia*, 20–23.

43. Mataora Harry, kavana (chief) of Keiʻā, personal communication, 24 January 2003.

44. Shibata, *Mangaian-English Dictionary*, 88, 127, 131; Te Rangi Hiroa (Buck), *Mangaian Society*, 137–38; and personal communication, Mataora Harry, 24 January 2003.

45. Jeanne Van Loon Apeldoorn and Ngametua Kareroa, "The Last Peacemakers?," pt. 3, ch. 5, "Foreigners Visit Island," [1980?], unpublished book manuscript in author's possession; Gill, *Life in the Southern Isles*, 67, 132; Gill, *Myths and Songs from the South Pacific*, 325; and Shibata, *Mangaian-English Dictionary*, 87. Little information is available concerning the ururua, which seems to have been less common than the better-known *taʻa*, a container made from the *ue* (bottle gourd; *Lagenaria siceraria*). See T. Aratangi, "Te Puna Keiʻā," MKS.

46. For glosses see Buse, *Cook Islands Maori Dictionary*, 55; and Shibata, *Mangaian-English Dictionary*, 24.

47. Apeldoorn and Kareroa, "The Last Peacemakers?," pt. 1, ch. 4, "Perspective on Time, Life and Death"; and P. Aratangi, "The Transformation of the Mangaian Religion," esp. 51–52.

48. See W. W. Gill, *From Darkness to Light in Polynesia*, 71n1, for the Christian usage; on pā tīkoru, see Buck, *Mangaia and the Mission*, 14; Te Rangi Hiroa, *Mangaian Society*, 143, 173; and W. W. Gill, *From Darkness to Light in Polynesia*, 70–71, 153.

49. The wonderful phrase "of ecological and social balance" is from Levy, *Tahitians*, 182.

50. P. Aratangi, "The Transformation of the Mangaian Religion," 44.

51. Clerk, "The Animal World of the Mangaians," 166, 170, 172, 173; P. Aratangi, "The Transformation of the Mangaian Religion," 109–12; and McMath and Parima, "Winged Tangiʻia," 216n3, 217. Various Mangaians have told me about their own fearful encounters with aitu and tūpāpaku.

52. See the case of the trader H. W. Pearse, in Reilly, "Mangaia in the Colonial World," 8–17.

53. Crocombe, *Land Tenure in the Cook Islands*, 115; Allen, "The Development of Commercial Agriculture on Mangaia," 48; and Resident Commissioner to Secretary, Island Territories, Rarotonga, memorandum, 10 September 1952, Department of Island Territories, Cook Islands: Mangaia: General File, 1912–64, IT 90/20/17, Archives New Zealand, Wellington. Originally called the Cook and Other Islands Land Titles Court under an Order in Council in 1902, its name was changed to the Native Land Court under the Cook Islands Act 1915; see Crocombe, *Land Tenure in the Cook Islands*, 102, 105.

54. Significant parts of his papers went to the Auckland Public Library (now Auckland City Libraries) to form part of the Sir George Grey Manuscript Collection. S. Percy Smith obtained further manuscripts for the Polynesian Society, a number of which he published with translations in the *Journal of the Polynesian Society* from 1911. The manuscripts are now held in the Alexander Turnbull Library, National Library of New Zealand, Wellington.

55. McMath and Parima, "Winged Tangiʻia," 215–55.

56. See comments in Simiona, "ʻAkamāramaʻanga," vii. A number of published collections of traditions from different islands were based on the recordings and transcriptions made by the Cultural Development Division. See Kauraka, *Manihikian Traditional Narratives*; Te Are Korero o Aitutaki, *Te Korero o Aitutaki*. The anthropologist Kauraka Kauraka also recorded and published stories told by elders; see Kauraka, *Oral Traditions of Manihiki*.

57. A good example is my conversations in 1988 with the late Pōkino Aperahama, a *rangatira* (subchief) of Karanga district, about Mangaia's history and culture. However, other experts, like Tereʻēvangeria, who was about the same age as Aperahama, did not mention these written histories when talking about the past. Her knowledge came solely from what she had heard from other ʻare kōrero.

CHAPTER SIX

Polynesian Family Manuscripts
(*Puta Tupuna*) from the Society
and Austral Islands: Interior History,
Formal Logic, and Social Uses

BRUNO SAURA

CHRISTIAN CONVERSION AND LITERACY generated a diverse array of written texts in nineteenth-century Polynesia.[1] Many scholars working in Polynesia, including P. J. Epling, Anthony Hooper, Judith Huntsman, Anna-Leena and Jukka Siikala, and Michael P. J. Reilly, have researched and written on these historical indigenous manuscripts.[2] In the Society Islands these texts are known as *puta tupuna*—from the English *book* (adapted into Tahitian as *puta*) and the Tahitian *tupuna* (ancestors or ancestral)—and are still mainly preserved within the sphere of the family.[3] But some of them are now circulating out of their original places, having recently been published and at times translated.

This chapter deals with several such manuscripts from both the Tahitian area and Rurutu in the Austral Islands.[4] It first discusses the way these documents were created and the nature of their contents. It then analyzes the content, in terms of both meaning and purpose, with the help of Jack Goody's theories about literacy and the logic of writing. Goody's main thesis lies in the affirmation that the arrival and the development of literacy, where it happened, changed drastically what he calls "the technology of the intellect," that is, the implementation of thought, which in turn had consequences in the social and political organization of the societies concerned. But the cultures from which the puta tupuna emerged were, and are still, largely oral, and this chapter explores how literacy, rather than reshaping these societies to a more "rational" Western model, was in turn transformed to fit indigenous thinking and behavior.

THE VARIOUS PUTA TUPUNA OF RURUTU

The island of Rurutu (and more broadly the Austral Islands) is an important site of neo-Polynesian Protestant culture, becoming in the late nineteenth and twentieth centuries a prolific producer of puta tupuna. The authors of these manuscripts very often belonged to the most educated people of the island: all male, they included Protestant dignitaries such as pastors and deacons, as well as local chiefs and land judges, all specialists of customary law. Having gained an excellent knowledge of the Tahitian translation of the Bible, the first scriptural texts having been introduced to the island in the 1820s, they wrote in Tahitian when creating their own texts rather than in the cognate language of their own island.[5] Their motives were twofold: to record genealogies that asserted and legitimized their political rights and ownership of family lands but also to transmit the memory of those lands and sites, through myths and pre-Christian legends connected to them.[6]

The prolific output of puta tupuna in the Austral Islands, which is comparable to the situation in Mangaia, in the Cook Islands, as described in Michael P. J. Reilly's chapter, contrasts with that in neighboring island groups. The dominance of Catholicism in the Marquesas and Gambier Islands, for example, resulted in an inferior knowledge of the Bible and writing, and thus a less pronounced literacy culture.[7] This religious specificity may explain the rarity of Polynesian manuscripts in these island groups. Even though its population was mainly Protestant, the island of Tahiti also seems to have produced few puta tupuna. There could be material reasons for this situation (both external and internal movements of population perhaps resulted in the loss of family documents), but some cultural explanations might also pertain. The spread of the French language among the well-educated Tahitians (especially those called *Demis*, or individuals of mixed descent) might have curbed the emergence of writings in Tahitian, despite the absence at that time of a significant written production in French about local history and traditions.

Another explanation for the relative scarcity of Polynesian manuscripts in the Society Islands in comparison with the Austral Islands can be found in land tenure. France annexed the Austral Islands of Rurutu and Rimatara in 1900 and 1901. For this reason, they did not evolve under the same legislation as Tahiti and the Leeward Islands. In Rurutu and Rimatara, there was no official written registration of the lands as occurred in Tahiti through the *tomite* titles, a procedure that involved the declaration of landownership in front of a committee, which then registered titles with the Tahitian High Court.[8] In contrast, landownership in Rurutu and Rimatara was, and continues to be, disputed on the basis of oral traditions and genealogies. The transcription of this traditional knowledge therefore resulted out of necessity, held within families rather than recorded in official documents.

In Rurutu, in fact, the writing process with regard to puta tupuna never ended. Around 1960, the Protestant pastor Teriimana Poetai, a native of Rurutu, and other holders of oral traditions gave their manuscripts to an American resident of the island, Martin Brunor, who passed them on to the Peabody Museum of Salem, Massachusetts, for preservation.[9] Before their precious books left the island, their authors or last owners made handwritten copies of them, sometimes adding new elements and contemporary interpretations. I have previously written about some of these alterations and additions, such as the identification, in those manuscripts, of the ancestors of the Rurutu population with the "Red-skin people" or "Incas" from South America.[10] This notion most likely derives from the presence in Rurutu in the 1950s of Eric de Bisschop. One of the main proponents of the theory of pre-European contacts between Polynesians and South American indigenous peoples, this French navigator died in Rakahanga (Cook Islands) in 1958 after an attempt to reach central Polynesia from Peru, on a raft. He was buried in Rurutu, where he had lived for several years with a local woman. Through his influence, the local people most likely reinterpreted their own traditions of the glorious and chiefly red color, the Polynesian 'ura, associating it with "Red-skin people" of South America.

The logic of these additions undoubtedly stems from the internal characteristics and dynamism of oral tradition, as characterized by Goody in *The Domestication of the Savage Mind* and *The Interface between the Written and the Oral*. One of Goody's central ideas is that oral tradition is particularly subjected to the context of its emission, in contrast with literacy, which offers a more "decontextualized" knowledge, or a process of "decontextualization" of knowledge. In another text, *The Power of the Written Tradition*, Goody also noticed that "a written work necessarily has a beginning, a middle and an end. An oral composition may be added to at any time and by different people."[11] However, the latter occurs with the puta tupuna from Rurutu, which have been adjusted many times, by different persons, through writing and rewriting or recopying, with no stress or concern about the integrity of the global structure of the book.

Indigenous logics can also be seen in the story of the puta tupuna of Rurutu detailed in the text "Bibliography of the Polynesian Manuscripts at the Peabody Museum of Salem," in which Brunor explained that the very first manuscript of the island might have been written by its king, Paa Teuruarii, in the second part of the nineteenth century, providing the source of inspiration for most of the puta tupuna subsequently archived in Salem.[12] Brunor added that he never saw King Paa's original puta tupuna himself. Nor does any trace remain of this mythical manuscript in London, where, according to tradition, King Paa lived for three years. But it appears that the exigencies of traditional understanding may have shaped the narrative. There is no historical evidence confirming that King Paa ever went to London, including within any puta tupuna. However, it may be because his memory is so closely tied to the London missionaries that some people believe he did travel there and that he is the author of the first manuscript of the island. Brunor stated that nobody had ever seen the text, but the people of that time used to tell him that the book might have remained in London! Anyway, the logic dictates that Paa, as the king who embraced the literacy-bearing missionaries, would have written the first puta tupuna of his island, which was subsequently followed by many others that were inspired by it.

More recently, some puta tupuna of Rurutu have begun circulating more publicly and openly. In 1997 Daniel Terooatea, from Rurutu, edited and partially rewrote elements of a puta tupuna belonging to his family as a 191-page publication, *Te va'a ta'ata mātāmua i tapae i Rurutu* (which can be translated as "The first canoes arrived in Rurutu"). The title refers to, and the book incorporates, stories and traditions of the settlement of the island that are found at the beginning of some puta tupuna, such as the famous one by Puna Taputu, a great judge of the island at the beginning of the twentieth century, as discussed by Martin Brunor in his "Bibliography of Polynesian Manuscripts" referred to above.

In the first years of the twenty-first century, some elders of Rurutu who are the present holders of traditions and owners of puta tupuna (or their copies) have started to meet to work together on a project of writing down a history of the island, utilizing the various puta tupuna owned by each family. The idea or hope that all of these texts, which are often contradictory, could fuse together harmoniously to give birth to a single definitive version of history is for me illusory and in total contradiction with the idea, discussed later in this chapter, that oral tradition is rather like a series of speeches or viewpoints, and not a synthesis acceptable to everybody. If a "harmonious" version of the history of Rurutu were to appear, it would obviously be just a new version added to the others without replacing them. However, the ideal of producing a unique "Book" must be understood in the context of the island's local Protestant culture. It would be good, indeed perfect, if oral tradition (like God's words) was One: fundamentally unique. As the locals might say, it would be a *parau mau*, incorporating the double meaning of being true (*mau*) and fixed (*mau*), indeed true because it would be made permanent in written form.

TWO PUTA TUPUNA FROM THE LEEWARD ISLANDS

Similar to Daniel Terooatea's puta tupuna from Rurutu, two other indigenous manuscripts from the Leeward Islands have recently appeared in whose publication I participated. These latter volumes were published in Tahiti under the authority of the minister of culture of French Polynesia as part of a series of heritage publications, within a specific subseries intentionally entitled Puta tumu (meaning "original/source/foundation books")—rather than Puta tupuna (meaning "ancestral book"). The latter concept (puta tupuna) might have led some people to think that private or family knowledge was being inappropriately disclosed to the public. In practice, both concepts (puta tumu and puta tupuna) are very close, even quite interchangeable.

To my knowledge, the first of these texts is the oldest puta tupuna known in French Polynesia. Written in 1846 in the Leeward Islands, it was produced in 2000 as *Histoires et Traditions de Huahine et Pora Pora* (Borabora).[13] The second was published under the title *La lignée royale des Tamatoa de Ra'iātea (îles-sous-le-Vent): Puta 'ā'amu nō te 'ōpū hui ari'i Tama-toa nō Ra'iātea* in 2003.[14] In both cases, no titles existed on the original manuscripts, and they were therefore provided by the publisher.

The first manuscript, from Huahine and PoraPora, came to me in 1998 as a photocopy of the last copy made in 1963 from the original text of 1846. The thirty original pages of the manuscript became a critical edition of eighty-nine pages composed of an introduction; the written reproduction of the original text; the transcription of this text, including the orthographical addition of macrons and glottal stops; a translation into French; and notes. Written by an (unfortunately unknown) Polynesian person from the Leeward Islands, this text relates the story of the crucial period of both Huahine and

PoraPora, marked by the arrival of the first Western ships and the settlement of the English missionaries.

The events addressed by the manuscript's author extend from around 1770 to the early 1820s. He does not deal with the so-called antimissionary movement Mamaia of the late 1820s, nor with the French political intrusion in the area ten years after that. This small book mostly highlights the story of the main chiefs and the renowned warriors of these islands, including the battles that they led up until their conversion to Christianity. The author hails the relinquishment of the old religion (particularly its martial excesses) in favor of Christianity, represented as a peaceful religion. However, he does not portray the missionaries as heroes; on the contrary, he focuses on the *ari'i* (chiefs) and their genealogies, dwelling on their personal characteristics, both good and bad, such as their courage or their cruelty.

At times, the author's chronology of the events proves to be at variance with missionary correspondence describing the same events. His genealogical data also could provoke debates. Nonetheless, such "mistakes" do not really harm the value of this document; scholars can now precisely analyze this first handwritten Polynesian manuscript from a certain distance. For example, we can be amazed at the similarity between some extracts of this text and passages from *Ancient Tahiti*, written by Teuira Henry (first English edition published in 1928) based on traditions collected by her missionary grandfather John Orsmond in the 1820s, 1830s, and 1840s. It is not unreasonable to assume that the manuscript's author had learned the same recitations of oral history as Orsmond's informants.

The manuscript is not animated by any nostalgia for the pre-Christian past. The author of the text delivers a Manichean description of the damaging effects of the old religious rules, in contrast with the benefits of the new religion. He ends his text with a glorious "amen." His text is therefore a long way from the "vision of the vanquished," an expression made famous in Nathan Wachtel's 1971 work about the Andean societies of the sixteenth century.[15] In this puta tupuna, conversion is not a question of defeat before foreigners but a salutary and voluntary indigenous religious acculturation.

This old text is perhaps the best example of a puta tupuna that reveals "orality clues," a term used by Paul Zumthor to describe oral culture in medieval Europe. Defining the phenomenon as *manuscripture*, Zumthor, echoing Marshall McLuhan and Walter Ong, refers to the old European texts he studied as "overwhelmed by noises that characterize oral communication. . . . It often happens to us to perceive in the[se] text[s] the manifest or confused rumor of a speech talking through the voice that bears it."[16]

The second Leeward Islands manuscript, *The Tamatoa Dynasty of Ra'iātea*, extends into the contemporary period more than the former text does. It is an intimate history of the dynasty of the sacred Tamatoa chiefs of Ra'iātea, focusing on the nineteenth century, and appears to have been written successively by two members of the family. The first author of the text, writing around 1874, was possibly a son of a key figure of the manuscript, King Tahitoe. The second author, who wrote during the 1910s, is most probably King Tahitoe himself or another of his sons.

In this manuscript penned by two hands, the first part contains mainly genealogies, but the second is written in a narrative form, quite modern and not dissimilar to the novel form, giving an approximate version of history in terms of chronology and identification of the different kings of the Tamatoa family. Its main significance lies precisely in the fact that this indigenous or emic writing is partially a late reconstruction of the past to create a simplified history that meets the needs of the writer's own times. The manuscript gives sense to events and assigns functions to individuals that were not theirs at the time they lived, thus explaining or rationalizing, long after the event, the actions and behaviors of key historical figures.

The best example is the justification of the naming of one of the main characters of the 1870s, King Tahitoe. The author states that Tahitoe's grandfather, King Tamatoa III (Tamatoa the Great), chose this name with the following meaning: the one (*tahi*) who remains (*toe*). Tahitoe was thus destined to be the last sovereign of his island. Actually, this etymology is problematic, especially given that other members of the family before him had already been bestowed with this name, which casts doubt on the particular meaning provided by the author.

In this text King Tahitoe, who lived in the late part of the nineteenth century, acts as the last sacred chief or king (ari'i) of the island of Ra'iātea acclaimed on the *marae* (ancestral temple) Vaeāra'i. Indeed, Tahitoe appears to have had a double destiny. Not only was he the last king of the island, the one who would have to transfer his political power and authority on the island to the whites (which had been predicted, well before his birth, by his grandfather), but it also seems that he would, first, have had to accept the arrival of the new religion (Christianity), according to an omen delivered by the *tahu'a* (priest, oracle) of the God Ta'aroa. Here is the narration of these facts:[17]

> 'Aita e huru i te māuruuru ō te ari'i i tōna huira'atira i te fāri'i mai i tā na mau 'ohipa i fa'atupu i roto i taua 'ōro'a ra, fa'a'ite atu ra te ari'i i tāna parau, 'oia ho'i o Tamatoa III i mua i te aro ō te hui ari'i tā'ato'a, teie:

"Te fa'a'ite atu nei au ia 'outou, e te hui ari'i ō Ra'i-ātea-nui e Taha'a-nui i tō'u nei māuruuru rahi i tō'u 'itera'a e ua hapū te vahine ā tō'u tamaiti o Tamatoa IV. Te ma'iri nei au i te i'oa nō tā'u mo'otua ia Tahi-toe, 'oia ho'i te aura'a : e tahi ari'i e toe nei. Tō 'outou teie ari'i hōpe'a e maeva hia ai i ni'a i te marae i Vaeāra'i nei!"

Pārahi ihora Tama-toa III i raro, ti'a atu ra te tahu'a o Maeva-atua i ni'a, pāhono atu ra i te parau ā te ari'i o Tama-toa III, nā 'ō atu ra:

"Ua ti'a roa tā 'oe parau, e te ari'i o Tama-toa III, ua tano maita'i tā 'oe ma'irira'a i te i'oa i ni'a i te mo'otua ia Tahi-toe, 'oia ho'i e tahi ari'i e toe nei, te aura'a ia ō taua i'oa ra, o te ari'i hōpe'a ia i ni'a ia Ra'i-ātea-nui nei e Taha'a-nui; nāna e tāmarū i te Hau Ra'i-ātea, nāna e hōro'a nō te Pōpa'a."

Oti a'e ra tāna parau i mua i te aro ō te hui ari'i; i taua taime ra fā mai ra te atua o Ta'aroa, te 'ohu ra i roto i te ata.

'Ite atu ra te hui ari'i i tō rātou atua i te fāra'a mai, ha'amori atu ra rātou e mo'e atu ra te atua o Ta'aroa.

I te reira taime, fa'auru mai ra te atua o Ta'aroa i te hō'ē vārua parau mai roto mai i te tahu'a ia Maeva-atua nō te fa'a'ite i te mau 'ohipa e tupu i muri a'e, 'oia ho'i nō te tāmaura'a i te fa'aro'o ā te atua ō te Pōpa'a i Tū-fenua-poto, 'oia ho'i i 'Uturoa.

Nā teie tamaiti ari'i o Tahi-toe e fāri'i i te mau 'orometua pōpa'a tei hōpoi mai i te 'Evanelia ā Ietu-Metia i ni'a i te fenua Ra'i-ātea, nāna e fa'ati'a i te hō'ē fare nō te ha'amorira'a nō taua atua ra.

Fa'a'itehia mai taua parau ra e te tahu'a o Maeva-atua i mua i te aro ō te hui ari'i tā'ato'a.

Then, the king, who was extremely satisfied by his people, who had pleased him in organizing that ceremony, delivered a speech in the presence of all the noble members of the royal families assembled who were there:

"To you, noble people from Ra'i-ātea-nui (great Ra'iātea) and Taha'a-nui (great Taha'a), I announce with great joy that the spouse of my son Tama-toa IV is pregnant. Here is the name that I have chosen for my grandchild: Tahi-toe, which means the only one (tahi) who remains (toe). He will be your last king acclaimed on the *marae* (temple) Vaeāra'i!"

Tama-toa III sat down and the priest Maeva-atua stood up to answer his words in these terms:

"All you have said is right, O king Tama-toa III. Right also is the name that you have chosen for your future grandchild, Tahi-toe: the only king to remain/who will remain. It means that he will be the last king of Ra'iātea-nui and Taha'a-nui. He will transfer the authority over his kingdom to a Western power, to White people."

As he had just finished delivering his message in front of the noble people, the god Ta'aroa appeared, wheeling around in the sky. The members of the royal families saw him, said grace to him, and then he disappeared.

But immediately after, the god Ta'aroa took possession of the priest Maeva-atua, who delivered a prophecy regarding the event that was soon going to happen, the settlement of the religion of the Whites in Tū-fenua-poto, that is to say, in 'Uturoa.

It will be that child, Prince Tahi-toe, who will accept the White missionaries bringing with them the Gospel of Jesus Christ to the island of Ra'iātea; it will be he who will build them a house, for the adoration of that god.

These were the words of the priest Maeva-atua, delivered by him in front of all the aristocrats assembled there.

Such an anticipation of history reminds us of the famous prophecy of Vaitā, a great priest of the marae Taputapuātea, in Ra'iatea, who predicted the arrival of both the voyaging Europeans and the missionaries a little before 1767, the year the first European, Samuel Wallis, arrived in Tahiti. In the course of a meeting on the marae of Taputapuātea, a tornado tore off all the branches of a *tamanu* tree (reputed to be very strong), which caused Vaitā to prophesy:

"Te 'ite nei au e, tei mua ia'u nei te aura'a o teie nei peu maere rahi! Tena mai te fanau'a 'una'una na te Tumu, e haere mai e hi'o i teie uru ra'au i Taputapuatea nei. E tino 'ê to ratou, e tino 'ê to tatou, ho'e ana'e rà huru, no te tumu mai, e e riro teie nei fenua ia ratou. E mou teie ha'apaora'a tahito nei, e e tae mai ho'i te manu mo'a o te moana, i te fenua nei, e haere mai e ta'iha'a i ta teie ra'au i motu e ha'api'i nei."

"I see before me the meaning of this strange event! There are coming the glorious children of the Trunk (God) who will see these trees here, in Taputapuatea. In person, they differ from us, yet they are the same as we, from the Trunk, and they will possess this land. There will be an end to our present customs, and the sacred birds of the sea and land will come to mourn over what this tree that is severed teaches."[18]

This prophecy is not the only one to have been recorded in eastern Polynesia. In his excellent article, H. A. H. Driessen mentions different versions of a similar prediction made by Pa'ue in Ha'apape (Tahiti), later transmitted to, and recorded by, the missionaries John Orsmond and Robert Thomson, and compares Vaitā's prophecy as recorded by Orsmond with that of William Ellis.[19] The most interesting thing about Driessen's article is that it lists European shipwrecks and recent visits to Polynesia before Wallis's arrival in Tahiti in 1767. It highlights that some Polynesians had long known about canoes without outriggers, which may account for the existence of a tradition prophesizing first contacts. I do not intend here to analyze the mechanics of the prediction or to try and downplay its spectacular character with a discussion of what "really happened." Yet one can note two contrasting approaches to a historical event: one in which the prediction of an event planned by God is the primary element, with the arrival of the Westerners, the historical event, realizing the prophecy; and another that gives primacy to the historical event of the ships' visits, the prophecy being delivered after the fact as an ex post rationalization, without God's will operating as the cause or even a requisite for its realization.

The same logic can be seen in another famous event of the Tahiti and Ra'iātea area narrated by Henry in *Ancient Tahiti*: the "trance" of Ariipaea vahine, daughter of Tamatoa III of Ra'iātea, wife of King Pomare II of Tahiti, and queen of Huahine.[20] The incident is supposed to have taken place in Huahine, at the beginning of the nineteenth century, not long before the establishment of Christianity, at a time when people knew about the existence of a new religion but had not yet accepted it. Without any apparent reason, Ariipaea vahine experienced a long sleep lasting one month, during which her spirit traveled in the region. One day,

> she met a spirit lover who carried her in his bosom to his home—a beautiful place with a large house. . . . The two congenial spirits travelled over all the islands of the group, and on one occasion, at Ra'iatea, they went to a beautiful clear spring in a ravine, which the queen had never seen before, and there she enjoyed a bath, as in life. . . . Soon afterwards, the queen found herself surrounded by a higher class of spirits; they were the goddess To'imata (Axe-with-eyes), daughter of the god 'Oro, and her train, who told her she must return to her body and remain yet awhile in the flesh among her people. Upon knowing this, her lover told her that he would continue to visit her in her earthly body, provided she did not embrace the Christian religion as the people of Tahiti were doing, in which case he would not be permitted to visit her.[21]

In Huahine, while the high priest of marae Manunu was proceeding to a funeral ceremony for the queen, who had now been considered dead for four weeks and whose body was going to be led to an underground vault, her spirit finally returned to her body, brought back by the medium of a white 'otu'u (stork).

> The queen continued [to live] among her people in Huahine until in the fifties. She never lost the gangrene spots, which were like large black freckles upon her face and hands [footnote: I can testify to the truth of this statement, as when a child, I saw the queen—T. H.]. For a year or two after Ari'i-paea-vahine's recovery, she stated that she had frequent communion with her spirit lover, until she finally went to Mo'orea, where Christian Tahitians were learning to read and study the Scriptures, when she also became interested and joined the class of students. Then one day, when she was alone he came to her, and looking very sad he said: "Ei onei ra 'oe, e ta'u hoa vahine e, e 'ore taua e farerei fa'ahou" (Now farewell, my woman friend, we shall never meet again). And she, spellbound, watched him go away, until he disappeared in the distance never to return.[22]

Concerning the birth of King Tahitoe and his destiny, in the Ra'iātea manuscript, as for Vaitā's prophecy and the trance of Ariipaea vahine in the oral traditions of the Society Islands, I have suggested that these events be interpreted as "Total Historical Events," after Marcel Mauss's concept of the Total Social Fact, referring to "an activity that has implications throughout society, in the economic, legal, political, and religious spheres."[23] For their protagonists and for those who preserved and transmitted their memory, these historical events fulfill an essential function: to make acceptable the renunciation of contacts with the ancestral spirits and gods, which was going to happen with the conversions. In the case of the Ra'iātea manuscript, these episodes also allowed the acceptance of Tahitoe's foretold destiny, which means the equally necessary renunciation of indigenous sovereignty on his island. Like Vaitā and Ariipaea vahine, the main character of the Ra'iātea manuscript, King Tahitoe, is at the hinge, the turning point between two universes. He can be considered what I would call a "Total Historical Character."

In this manuscript each of the principal characters of the Tamatoa dynasty is assigned a function. Even if Tahitoe was supposed, at the time of his conception, to be the one who would accept both the new religion and the new political order, in fact the continuation of the manuscript tells a different story. There is no doubt that Tahitoe's grandfather, Tamatoa III, embodies the resistance to religious acculturation. But through the text it is Tahitoe's father, Tamatoa IV, who accepts the Christian religion and the new laws established in Ra'iātea. This adjustment, in contradiction with the initial prophecy, was needed because Christianity was established in Ra'iātea in the late 1810s, while formal colonization began in 1888; a single historical actor could not, in fact, pave the way for both changes. In reality, in this puta tupuna, Tahitoe's function is essentially political, that is to say, to promote acceptance of French colonization.

This simplified version of history obviously conflicts with European reports, mainly those of missionaries present at the time. Another interesting thing about this text is the precise way its author introduces a social order for Ra'iātea and Taha'a, in which one sacred chief dominates each island, a concept far removed from the structural reality of political power in the Society Islands, which was characterized by the existence of many chiefs living on the same territory or on the same island.[24]

The lack of certain elements that one can perceive in this Ra'iātea manuscript is also significant. For example, the author underplays the warlike dimension of these islands and reduces the activities of the ari'i to speeches and travels. Politically speaking, he also chooses to reduce the historical importance of the Tamatoa-Pomare line (of Tahiti) in order to allude to and promote the sole branch of the Tamatoa-Tahitoe (inhabitants of Ra'iātea), to which he seems to belong.

On the whole, in the case of Rurutu, as for the Leeward Islands, the indigenous manuscripts known as puta tupuna often constitute reconstructions or reinterpretations of traditional society, of a past not directly lived by their authors, at least for their pre-Christian part. The only one who could have lived during the pre-Christian era is the author of the Huahine and PoraPora manuscript (dated 1846), who perhaps learned to write in the 1820s and acquired enough writing skills to produce, twenty years later, the elaborated text that we know.

The Tamatoa family manuscript from Ra'iātea may be a reconstruction of the past that does not adhere strictly to historical "realities," but a reconstitution is worthy of consideration nevertheless. Indigenous historical characters created their accounts of the past in a context quite different from that of archive-based historians in the Western tradition. The preceding examples from puta tupuna confirm that there is no ontological gap or difference in nature between history and memory. Some Polynesian writers of the nineteenth and twentieth centuries, moved by a "historical consciousness," to quote the words used by Anthony Hooper, have tried to offer a vision of the past that could satisfy the needs of their contemporary fellows, providing them with time markers and useful meanings.[25] They have sometimes been able to provide a coherence in their ex post facto histories that the individuals and events may have actually lacked.

GOODY'S WORKS: LITERACY AND THE
ELABORATION OF THE "SKEPTIC MIND"

The last part of this chapter touches on some of Goody's ideas about literacy in the context of oral cultures and societies and applies them to the Polynesian puta tupuna. Far from the Saussurean concept that writing would be the mere representation of words or speeches, Goody developed the idea, in *The Domestication of the Savage Mind*, that the fact that some data or elements of knowledge became written, through lists, for instance, sometimes produced a real "linguistic codage" or reorganization of the information that impacted on society.[26]

This argument seems to me quite relevant in reference to some Polynesian manuscripts previously studied, and especially those from Rurutu that I have studied, such as the one by Daniel Terooatea. There, the royal (or chiefly) genealogies were not necessarily transcribed in the nineteenth century in the same form as when they had been orally recited. Indeed, it appears that an evolution occurred through the process of writing, leading to an emphasis on the patrilineal aspects of genealogies, which came to be presented as exclusively masculine lineages. That certainly took place at the beginning of the nineteenth century, in a context of Judeo-Christian acculturation and of political centralization in Polynesian islands where power was reorganized and influenced by the Salic law of the European monarchies.[27]

In the past the kinship systems in the islands of eastern Polynesia were relatively flexible, and descent was mainly undifferentiated or cognatic: a person is attached to a specific social group and to its titles, either from their father's side or their mother's side, hence the use of the term *ramage* rather than *lineage* by anthropologists to characterize those social groups with constant bifurcations. Although some of Rurutu's genealogies written in the nineteenth century describe real Polynesian ramages, others often present properly patrilineal lineages in which only the descent of male individuals, supposedly the firstborn, is detailed. Michel Panoff explains the difference between *'opu ta'ata* (more correctly as *'ōpū ta'ata*) and *tui ta'ata* in Rurutu as follows: "All the persons who belong to the *'opu ta'ata* X can go further back to a common ancestor X counting equally in their ancestries men and women. . . . On the contrary, the term *tui ta'ata* is less used nowadays. The word *tui* in the Tahitian language refers to the action of stringing or threading or enfilading [like flowers on/for a *lei*], and *tui i'a*, for instance, means a netting of fishes (on a string). In traditional texts and land matters, *tui ta'ata* is the enumeration of the male descendants of an ancestor, generally from eldest to eldest."[28]

Inside the genealogical manuscripts of Rurutu (puta tupuna), any mention of women often appears as additional to the succession of men: a list of wives' names was written, at a later time, to the right of the column of male chief names (tui ta'ata). This subsequent addition is easily perceptible through the discrepancies or disjunctions seen in different versions of the same genealogies in which the husbands' and the wives' names appear. Without doubt, the resetting, the sudden subtraction, the later addition, and other means, all utilized in oral tradition, were still available to those who recorded the genealogies on paper but are now more readily apparent to the reader with time to analyze the different written versions of these texts.

Goody also posits that literacy enables not only the accumulation of knowledge but also the development of critical and skeptical thought in the reader. The time that in a society of orality used to be devoted to the practice of memorization can now be invested in the criticism of textual sources and of their contradictions. It is against the authority of these initial texts, often religious or of some religious nature, that scientific thought, and critical and impersonal reasoning, can be built up.

Despite this affirmation, the puta tupuna of Rurutu and the rewriting of these texts until the end of the twentieth century show that the people of that island have not really adopted Western-based rational skeptical criticism, nor do they really practice an intertextual dialogue in their puta tupuna. They keep writing their books without any direct reference to previous authors, and without any formal and explicit criticism of other texts. Very often, they merely copy a text, and a few pages later they introduce another version of the same story, or even a version of the same genealogy that contradicts the first text or the previous pages of their book. We are here in the presence of a succession of points of view more than in front of a critical speech that would be synthetic and well argued. This is what Goody called a situation of socially and culturally "restricted literacy." He explains that "in the first place, early writing (and a significant part of later writing) was restricted in various ways: in terms of persons, either because of the nature of the script or because of hierarchical constraints, and in terms also of subjects, because of largely religious control of the uses of writing. . . . History in Greece begins with genealogies and chronicles, leads into the more narrative forms of Herodotus, and develops strict notions of evidence with Thucydides. Such a progression holds for written knowledge more generally."[29] The restrictions he noted and saw as cultural obstacles to the immediate emergence of skeptical thought make sense in a traditional Polynesian society, where different speeches, coming from different persons, each of them with a specific rank or status, often follow one another without necessarily engaging a real dialogue or leading to a real synthesis of all those sources.

What is true in literacy about Polynesian traditional topics or knowledge, in puta tupuna, can also be observed in some other Polynesian social activities, where literacy is never far from the logic of orality. This can be seen, for example, in the biblical culture of the inhabitants of the Austral Islands and the Tahitian cultural area, who hold conversational meetings, known as *tuaro'i*, regarding a scriptural verse. The meetings, which may also occur during mortuary nights (as part of funereal customs), enact a pivotal exercise in the Protestant parish life. During a tuaro'i, each person can stand up and speak in order to solve the enigma or the hidden message of the biblical verse proposed as the topic, *tumu parau*, of the exercise. This is certainly a modern manifestation of an old culture of *piri*, riddles or enigmas, which Polynesian people are traditionally fond of, riddles that possess an interior logic using many elements of formal thought, including syllogism.[30]

During the tuaro'i nights, it is expected that somebody will reveal a new possible meaning for the biblical verse, not the one immediately understood by everyone, and orators compete in delivering their interpretation of the verse—but never in a direct dialogue. Speakers follow a specific hierarchy: first, they let women and the youngest people express their ideas, and then the oldest men and the people most trained for this kind of exercise. I have underlined elsewhere that sometimes people's speeches seem to be farfetched or irrelevant to the topic; that is to say, they stay focused on the formal aspects of the verse.[31] In reality, a tuaro'i consists in finding an answer to a biblical question but not immediately, in order to make the (mortuary) night last, and as a result the best part, devoted to persons with a high position, is revealed only at the end of the night. This is why participants do not necessarily say what they have in mind, what they really think, or what they would like to say, but rather what they can "think about," not only in connection with what has already been said but also in anticipation of what later speakers will probably say. Hence, there is a strong tendency to take verse words literally, to use all the motives of the formal rhetoric, to launch into comparisons that are apparently incongruous but fill up time without being absurd. All opinions are valuable as they are all crucial for the evolution of the reflection through a process of elimination and refinement of successive meanings. But not all of the opinions are always serious. Some are aimed at relieving the atmosphere, marking a parenthesis, or taking a break in the process of thought.

The principal difference with the Western philosophical essay, such as the Jewish tradition of the interpretation of the text, lies in the collective and hierarchical aspects of the elaboration of the Polynesian biblical commentary during these meetings. Each speaker accepts developing just a single argument, which is not really his or her thought, nor a relevant argument to reach directly a crucial point of the topic, but a thought that enables the others to prepare themselves for intervening. This "social construction" and even "social necessity" that makes the interpretations last also obliges the line of orators to tackle all the possible tracks, enabling the most formal, the most symbolic, and the most stunning interpretations. It is a collective elaboration, but there is no direct dialogue, because it is not meant to happen. Each person says something, according to their position and social status, without directly quoting or contradicting another one, without referring directly to what has been said before, and looking instead for something different to say.

For me, this logic is very similar to that involved in the process of writing and rewriting manifested in some puta tupuna. It comes from an old oral and hierarchical culture. Indeed, the puta tupuna are composed through the layering of speeches from different sources, although an author never refers to previous texts explicitly or formally. Thought is not formally skeptical in a puta tupuna, even though we may consider that adding further text to an initial puta constitutes proof that the last writer was not satisfied with the original state of knowledge that it contained. But the first author of the book is never directly referred to, quoted, or contradicted.

In Rurutu the same cumulative and nondialogic use of speeches, of words, can be noticed during wedding ceremonies through long recitations of genealogies, and also in the annual so-called tradition of *tere*, or a trip around the island that happens during the first weeks of January. The tere, in which most of the population takes part, occurs three times over a space of three weeks. Each of the three main villages organizes its own tere, marked by historical speeches performed by the orator of the village on the high places of the island, such as marae and cliffs, the memory of which is celebrated. The tere also consists of physical challenges such as, in the village of Hauti, men lifting a 145-kilogram stone. Therefore, strength of body and strength of speech, both symbolizing the pillars of power in this society, go hand in hand in this ritual. Just as the strong trained men stretch their muscles before the challenge, the orator of the day does not miss the opportunity to immerse himself in his puta tupuna before going to the historical sites.

But just as stone carriers, unlike fighters practicing a martial art, do not exactly fight against each other, the orator performs alone without reference to others and is never contradicted publicly during his speech. People from the second or the third village will have to wait for their own orator to speak a week later, in order to tell another version of the same story during a new tere. At this moment, the villagers listen to their own orator's speech, whereas the people from the two other villages generally show a very limited interest, if not a general indifference.

At the beginning of the 1960s, in his wonderful study *Tahitians: Mind and Experience in the Society Islands*, the anthropologist and psychologist Robert Levy considered as a distinct characteristic of the inhabitants of the Tahitian cultural area their tendency to "relativize" ceaselessly concerning the veracity of one another's words. Interviewed about what may be considered to be true from their viewpoint, all of them answered that, except for the Bible, a thing proves to be true or false "in situation," in a precise context, depending on who is making the statement: in another context, or said by somebody else, the statement would no longer be true. There is no truth "in itself." Of course, for us, such a fact makes us feel worried in terms of education, about the possibility of the existence of a scientific thought or truth that would be accepted by all. Levy attributed this relativistic state of mind to the existence of a culture that inhibits people from directly contradicting one another but that allows them to make and receive statements within their own context and thus avoid direct debate with others.[32]

Levy's analysis, and the examples I have given of different Polynesian situations and materials, help us to understand that 150 years of literacy have not necessarily turned Tahitian or Austral Islands people into adepts of critical reflection as in the Western scientific approach. The existence of writing does not immediately produce, among all societies, the emergence of a critical and synthetic thought. This obviously shows the limits of the literacy theory, which Jacques Derrida and Brian V. Street reproached Goody for neglecting, even though he did his utmost to contradict these critics in arguing that he did not believe in the idea of "instant literacy."[33]

Where speeches are tied to the social status of individuals and to the identity of social groups, oral tradition is multiple, because powers are multiple. Declaimed or written, oral tradition remains an important element of power. This is why cumulative and alternative speeches or texts, which manifest this diversity of powers, are often preferred by Polynesian people to a definitive well-constructed or elaborated skeptical synthesis that could assert the supremacy of a writer, of an individual.

1. See Parsonson, "The Literate Revolution," 39–57.

2. Epling, "O le Gafa o Talo'olema'aga o Satalo," 164–75; and Hooper and Huntsman, *Matagi Tokelau*. See also Huntsman, "Just Marginally Possible," 138–54; J. Siikala, *'Akatokamanāva*; A. Siikala and J. Siikala, *Return to Culture*; Reilly, *War and Secession in Mangaia from Mamae's Texts*; and Reilly, *Ancestral Voices from Mangaia*.

3. The Society Islands comprise the Windward Islands, including Tahiti and Moorea, and the Leeward Islands, including Ra'iātea (also known as Ra'i-atea or Ra'iatea), Huahine, Borabora (Porapora or PoraPora), and Maupiti. The Māori equivalent of puta tupuna are similarly known as *pukapuka tīpuna*.

4. The Austral Islands are an island group that sits south of Tahiti and east of the southern Cook Islands.

5. On the Tahitian translation of the Bible, see Nicole, *Au pied de l'écriture*.

6. On the recording of genealogies, see Saura, "Les généalogies de Rurutu sont-elles vraies?," 32–52.

7. Saura, "Quand la voix devient la lettre," 293–309.

8. Arutangai and Crocombe, *Land Tenure in the Pacific*, 50.

9. Saura, "Quand la voix devient la lettre," 297.

10. Saura, "Des Incas en Polynésie?," 45–68.

11. Goody, *The Power of the Written Tradition*, 13.

12. Brunor, "Bibliography of the Polynesian Manuscripts at the Peabody Museum of Salem," Martin Brunor's Papers, E-12, James Duncan Phillips Library, Peabody Museum, Salem, Massachusetts.

13. Saura, Daubard, and Millaud, *Histoire et traditions de Huahine et Pora Pora*.

14. Saura and Millaud, *La dynastie des Tama-toa de Ra'iātea*.

15. Wachtel, *The Vision of the Vanquished*.

16. Zumthor, *La lettre et la voix*, 37. See also McLuhan, *The Gutenberg Galaxy: The Making of Typographic Man*; McLuhan, *War and Peace in the Global Village*; and Ong, *Orality and Literacy* (1982).

17. Saura, Daubard, and Millaud, *Histoire et traditions de Huahine et Pora Pora*, 106–7.

18. Henry, *Ancient Tahiti*, 4–5. The prophecy was recorded by the missionary John Orsmond and transcribed by his granddaughter Teuira Henry.

19. Driessen, "Outriggerless Canoes and Glorious Beings," 3–26.

20. The story was "recorded by the late high chiefesses, Ari'itaimai Salmon and Ninito Sumner (an adopted daughter of Queen Ari'i-paea-vahine), sisters to whom the queen always related the story consistently and in suppressed tones as if fearing the return of the spirit lover." Henry, *Ancient Tahiti*, 220n22.

21. Henry, *Ancient Tahiti*, 222–23.

22. Henry, *Ancient Tahiti*, 222–23.

23. Edgar, "Cultural Anthropology," 64. For more on my view of these events as "Total Historical Events," see Saura and Millaud, *La dynastie des Tama-toa de Ra'iātea*, 21–22.

24. See D. Oliver, *Ancient Tahitian Society*, vol. 3; and Baré, *Tahiti, les temps et les pouvoirs*.

25. Hooper, "Orality, Literacy, Tradition, History," 6.

26. Goody, *The Domestication of the Savage Mind*, 74–111; see also Ong, "Writing Is a Technology That Restructures Thought," 25–50.

27. Baré, *Tahiti, les temps et les pouvoirs*.

28. Panoff, *La terre et l'organisation sociale en Polynésie*, 69–70.

29. Goody, *The Power of the Written Tradition*, 25.

30. Saura, Daubard, and Millaud, *Histoire et traditions de Huahine et Pora Pora*.

31. Saura, "Est-ce que dire, c'est penser?," 150–60.

32. In a stimulating review, Hooper has himself "relativized" the "relativistic" state of mind of the Tahitians as perceived by Levy. He suggested that their tendency to avoid direct debate with others could be explained by the small size of these island communities, rather than by a specific psychocultural Tahitian personality. Hooper, review of *Tahitians*, by Levy, 374.

33. Derrida, *L'écriture et la différence*; Street, *Literacy in Theory and Practice*; and Goody, *The Power of the Written Tradition*, 25.

Part III
Readers

Print Media, the Swahili Language, and Textual Cultures in Twentieth-Century Tanzania, ca. 1923–1939

EMMA HUNTER

IN 1931 the journal *Africa* included in its pages a few notes on a Swahili-language periodical, *Ufalme wa Mungu* (The kingdom of God), which the Bethel Mission in Tanganyika, now mainland Tanzania, had recently begun to publish. After briefly describing its content, the journal noted, "It is read among a number of peoples in Tanganyika, Kenya, Congo, Zanzibar, Italian Somaliland, and even in Europe, and it greatly helps to strengthen the feeling of mutual attachment among the many people speaking the language."[1]

As Tony Ballantyne and Lachy Paterson remind us in their introduction to this volume, earlier generations of anthropologists who sought to understand the development of literacy practices in Africa did so in a way that tended to "undervalue the placedness of these practices" and "underplay the historical contingency of cultural formations." In contrast, more recent historical and anthropological accounts of literacy have instead shown the diverse ways in which the written word was employed in colonial settings to create new political, social, and intellectual worlds, building on the oral and literate cultures that had come before.

In this regard, it is worth pausing at that description of *Ufalme wa Mungu* and the feeling of "mutual attachment" it was said to be creating among Swahili speakers in eastern Africa. The Swahili language, a Bantu language with many Arabic loanwords, had long been the vernacular language of the coast of East Africa. But over the course of the nineteenth century, the language spread along the trade routes that linked the coast with the interior of East Africa. By the 1920s, when *Ufalme wa Mungu* was founded, in part thanks to colonial government policies, Swahili was understood as a second language by many people beyond the coastal populations for whom it was a mother tongue.

While in some ways it is therefore not surprising that the Bethel missionaries chose Swahili for *Ufalme wa Mungu*, their decision nevertheless fits awkwardly into wider patterns of the development of textual cultures in general and newspaper and periodical publication in particular in Africa in the first half of the twentieth century. A contrast is often drawn between West and East Africa that stresses the growth of anglophone or francophone textual cultures in West Africa and vernacular-language textual cultures in East Africa, a contrast that maps onto postcolonial debates around language, in which the Nigerian author Chinua Achebe's defense of the use of English as a language for postcolonial literature ran directly counter to the Kenyan author Ngũgĩ wa Thiong'o's argument for the vernacular.[2] For some historians of colonial language policy and the history of language in Africa, the contrast between pan-ethnic and pan-territorial textual publics that employed a colonial language such as English or French and vernacular-language textual publics amounts to one between outward-looking and connective publics in the former case and smaller-scale publics in the latter, publics that could and did think comparatively but that were primarily concerned with very local debates.[3]

In some cases, this closing down of connections was precisely the aim of colonial language policies. In German East Africa, the decision to use Swahili was influenced in part by a fear that teaching German would offer Africans the potential to read radical texts, which would threaten the stability of German rule.[4] In this regard, German colonial policy to use Swahili, continued by the British government, which took over German East Africa as the League of Nations mandate of Tanganyika after World War I, mirrored British policy toward language in Kenya and Uganda, promoting vernaculars such as Kikuyu, Luo, or Luganda rather than English. But Swahili does not fit straightforwardly in the vernacular side of the global versus vernacular language equation. In fact, like other regional languages or lingua francas of colonial Africa, it sits somewhere between pan-ethnic and pan-territorial languages such as English and French and vernacular languages such as Kikuyu and Luo.

This chapter explores the relationship between what I term here *colonial print media*, language, and new textual cultures in the colonial world in an East African context. More specifically, it explores the ways in which a specific form of print media—government and mission newspapers—served to create new publics that, though working in an African language, nevertheless transcended locality, building on existing textual cultures but remaking them in new ways. It does so through a case study of two Tanganyikan newspapers from the interwar period, the Protestant missionary periodical *Ufalme wa Mungu*, with which I started, and the government periodical *Mambo Leo* (Current affairs). While neither might fit conventional definitions of a newspaper, both were referred to as such and understood in these terms by their readers and editors.[5]

A focus on language and colonial print media serves here as a prism through which to understand some of the divergences in the making and remaking of textual cultures in the colonial world that this collection draws out, the ways in which colonial histories were shaped by colonial prehistories, and the difficulty of drawing a sharp line between "the indigenous and the colonial."[6] Exploring colonial Swahili-language print media in East Africa reminds us of the impossibility of generalizing about the new textual cultures that emerged in the colonial world. Just as a contrast can be drawn between the evolution of textual cultures in New Zealand and colonial Australia, so there is a sharp contrast to be drawn between the evolution of textual cultures of print in Tanzania and in Kenya, the former framed around a lingua franca and the latter dominated by vernacular textual production. These different textual cultures were the product of diverse historical contexts and were produced through interaction between colonial powers and colonized societies.

But, and this is the second element of this chapter, this case study also raises bigger questions about the types of textual cultures forged in the colonial world and what we might understand by "indigenous textual cultures." Ballantyne and Paterson make the case for "returning Africa to the fold of indigenous studies, especially given the centrality of the native as an organizing category in colonial thought in Africa, a powerful commonality with the Pacific, Australasia, and North America." In a similar vein to the pidgin-language newspapers of Papua New Guinea explored by Evelyn Ellerman in this volume, the periodicals I focus on here were published by missionaries and the government with didactic intent, aimed at an African audience. As a result, they have often been ignored by historians, who have instead focused on African independent newspapers and periodicals.[7] Yet, I argue, this case study shows that even in top-down creations such as these, the textual cultures and "feeling of mutual attachment" that resulted were shaped from below as well as from above.

VERNACULAR OR LINGUA FRANCA? PRINT, LITERACY, AND SWAHILI

While the colonial period has often been seen as marked either by the expansion of colonial languages such as English, French, and Portuguese or by the standardization in written form of vernacular languages that had previously not been written down, the language ecology of both precolonial and colonial sub-Saharan Africa was far richer than such schematic typologies suggest. Across Africa, missionaries and colonial powers encountered languages that transcended localities, particularly Arabic but also languages such as Hausa, Somali, and Swahili.

These languages were not simply oral: they had long-standing textual traditions that were once overlooked by historians, who assumed that writing in Africa arrived with colonialism.[8] But if text had long been important, its place in social, intellectual, and religious life changed over time. In nineteenth-century West Africa, the leaders of the Sokoto Caliphate placed great importance on education in pursuit of Islamic reform. The scholar Nana Asma'u (1793–1864) translated key texts into Hausa and relied on a new literate group of women to go out into the villages and educate women about Islam using oral techniques.[9] In Zanzibar and coastal East Africa, the late nineteenth century saw literacy in Arabic and Swahili becoming increasingly important, a process shaped by dynamics in the wider Islamic world.[10] Zanzibar became an important node in an Arabic-language intellectual network spanning the Indian Ocean.[11] Within East Africa, where the transmission of knowledge had previously been predominantly oral, and books rare, knowledge of Islam was increasingly conveyed in written form, either in Arabic or translated into Swahili.[12]

It was in this context that the nineteenth-century resurgence of Christian missionary activity in Africa took place. But while missionaries did not straightforwardly introduce text to Africa, they did introduce one important element of novelty, which was printing. In many parts of Africa, missionaries, particularly Protestants, brought the first printing presses. In the Congo, the Baptist Mission Society set up its first press in 1886, and there were sixteen printing presses by 1908.[13] The Universities' Mission to Central Africa in Zanzibar established the first printing press in East Africa in 1865. Possession of a printing press enabled the mission to produce printed religious texts to help attract new converts in the religious marketplace of nineteenth-century East Africa.[14] The growing importance of literacy and the growth of printing in turn sparked new initiatives from Zanzibar's precolonial rulers. In 1875 the sultan of Zanzibar, Sayyid Barghash b. Sāīd, returned to Zanzibar with a printing press in his possession and established a press to publish religious and legal texts.

For the German colonial government, which claimed possession of mainland Tanzania in 1885, the existence of Swahili as a language that transcended localities was an advantage. The German colonial government in mainland Tanzania appointed Swahili-speaking *akidas* (colonial administrators) from the coast as their initial intermediaries to rule over their new subject population, and this in turn encouraged the spread of Swahili. The use of Swahili by the army also played a role.[15] Even in inland regions such as Kilimanjaro, which were on caravan trading routes but where Swahili was in no sense a vernacular language, the German government used Swahili as its language of political communication, conducting public meetings in the region in the language. The argument has even been made that the use of Swahili served to create a "colonial public" in Tanganyika during the 1890s.[16]

The German colonial government not only made pragmatic use of existing language skills to employ Swahili as a language of government but also sought to use Swahili as the language of education. Already in 1890 the first governor of German East Africa insisted that all official teachers must know Swahili.[17] In doing so, the government was in part motivated by fears that teaching German would lead to the radicalization of their colonial subjects. However, if Swahili offered practical advantages for the German colonial government, the use of Swahili posed more problems for German missionaries, and particularly Protestant ones. For Lutheran missionaries in particular, central to their approach to mission was that the word of God should be heard in converts' and potential converts' own language, which in inland Tanganyika would have meant a number of local Bantu languages such as the Chagga or Sukuma language. The added problem that Swahili posed to Christian missionaries was its perceived association with Islam and the preponderance of Arabic-derived words.

Yet on arriving in a new area, missionaries would often find that Swahili was essential as a means of communicating: if they did not know the local language and locals did not know German, Swahili at least provided a point of contact as there would often be somebody who could communicate in the language. Thus, for example, the German missionary Gerhard Althaus recounted the difficulties he faced when he arrived at his mission station in Mamba in northeastern Tanzania in 1894 because neither Chief Koimbere "nor his people understood the language of the coast, Swahili." The missionaries were saved by the arrival of an elderly man who had learned Swahili on the coast and could serve as an interpreter.[18]

Using Swahili as a language of print was also in part a function of economics and the practicalities of printing, as the story of attempts by German missionaries in Kilimanjaro to establish a vernacular-language newspaper suggests. Texts were already available in Swahili, and publishing in Swahili meant that texts could reach a wider market than would be the case for texts published in the vernacular. As already mentioned, Protestant missionaries were committed to working in the vernacular where possible, but the use of Swahili was often a pragmatic and acceptable compromise. In Kilimanjaro, where missionaries had not succeeded in standardizing the Chagga language, a first attempt in 1904 to publish a newspaper in the three different dialects used on the mountain—Machame, Moshi, and Vunjo—encountered practical difficulties, including complaints that one dialect was being unfairly privileged in the newspaper's pages. In 1906 the newspaper became a quarterly publication before finally ceasing publication altogether in 1910.[19] It was replaced not by another vernacular-language newspaper but by the Swahili-language *Pwani na Bara* (Coast and Hinterland).

Yet if the use of Swahili for administration, education, and even evangelization was in part dictated by pragmatic concerns, neither the missionaries nor the German, and then later the British, colonial government simply used the Swahili language as it already existed: both engaged in efforts to reform the language, taking initiatives to render it in Roman rather than Arabic script and even seeking to revise the standard Swahili Bible translation to reduce the number of Arabic-derived words.[20] The Swahili language therefore evolved rapidly in the late nineteenth and early twentieth century. The development of print media both took place in this context and contributed to this process.

PRINT MEDIA IN MAINLAND TANZANIA

In this context, it is unsurprising that when newspapers and periodicals began to be published in mainland Tanzania from the late nineteenth century, the most common language to be used was Swahili, even for newspapers intended for an inland African readership for whom Swahili was not a first language.

As elsewhere in East Africa, it was the missions and government that published the first newspapers. Of the four most important newspapers in

German East Africa in the colonial period, three (*Msimulizi* [The story-teller], *Pwani na Bara,* and *Rafiki Yangu* [My friend]) were published by missions and one, *Kiongozi* (The leader), by the government school in Tanga, eventually with financial support from the colonial government.[21] Their circulation was small, in the low thousands, but grew rapidly in the early twentieth century, which in itself constitutes a dramatic change in reading habits, as Juan R. I. Cole argues for Egypt in a slightly earlier period.[22] In the case of *Kiongozi,* which began publication in 1904, its intended readership was at first limited to those connected to the government school, often former pupils who were now working as teachers elsewhere, but over time it grew to include those with no connection to the school.

Although missions published three of the four newspapers, missionary editors quickly learned that to attract a wide readership, they had to include secular material too.[23] All hoped to attract Muslim readers and readers belonging to neither the Islamic nor the Christian faiths. When *Pwani na Bara* was established by the Protestant evangelical missions in 1910, it was explicitly noted that the fight against Islam should not be a primary aim of the newspaper, although it was a matter preoccupying German missionaries at the time.

By the time World War I began in 1914, a number of newspapers were being published, both by missionaries and by the government, and mostly in Swahili. Newspapers ceased production during the war, but as the British established their rule in the territory (now renamed Tanganyika) after the war, the new government moved quickly to develop a replacement for the government newspaper, *Kiongozi.* That successor was *Mambo Leo,* which started publishing in 1923 and over time became the most important Swahili-language newspaper in East Africa.

If it was common for the first newspapers to be published by missionaries and the government, mainland Tanzania stands out within East Africa for the way in which the print media landscape remained dominated by these publications edited by Europeans with a particular sort of didactic intent. While elsewhere African intellectuals trained on mission presses went on to set up their own newspapers, Tanganyika did not see the emergence of an African independent press until after 1945.

Mambo Leo was produced from within the Tanganyikan Education Department, and it was intended as a tool of education and propaganda, a means of binding new subjects to the British Empire, even if their precise constitutional status, given Tanganyika's formal status as a League of Nations mandate, put them at one remove from the empire. In this sense it had much in common with government newspapers elsewhere in the British colonial world, notably the nineteenth-century Māori-language newspapers about which Lachy Paterson has written.[24] In contrast to newspapers edited and run by Africans, *Mambo Leo* was edited by European officials, and, strikingly, the editor was anonymous, rejecting repeated requests to reveal his name.

Mambo Leo was also produced in the context of wider policies of Swahili-language reform. The British government had initially been reluctant to use Swahili; the very ease with which it was learned was taken by some as a sign of its inferiority as a language. But by 1925 it had been accepted that in Tanzania Swahili would be treated as the vernacular, and moves began, under the leadership of the Inter-Territorial Language Committee, to determine which dialect would be used and how it would be spelled.[25]

Although the British chose the Zanzibar dialect as the basis of standardization attempts, they emphatically did not envisage the imposition of coastal Swahili on up-country areas. In the first place, they denied the claims of Swahili scholars on the coast to be the true arbiters of correct Swahili. When in 1932 the Mombasa newspaper *al-Islah* argued, "It is great harm which we suffer in speaking this Kiswahili which has been ruined by Europeans. Kiswahili is the language of the coastal people, and it cannot be correct unless it is written in Arabic script," the European editor in charge of reprinting the letter in Roman script in the *Inter-Territorial Language (Swahili) Committee Bulletin* responded curtly that it was not standardized Swahili that was incorrect but rather the Swahili of the essayist.[26] The argument itself was deemed worthy of little comment, beyond the observation that "there are several obvious misprints in the above."[27] Thus, not only were coastal Swahili speakers not necessarily the true arbiters of the Swahili language, they could even be judged inferior. At the same time, developing and expanding the linguistic competence in Swahili of those living far from the coast was an important aspect of the committee's work, and there was an obvious role for newspapers like *Mambo Leo* in this process.

The Lutheran Bethel Mission's *Ufalme wa Mungu* too was edited by European, rather than African, editors in the interwar period, though in contrast to *Mambo Leo* the editor was named and had a clear editorial voice. *Ufalme wa Mungu* was also shaped by a context of language reform.[28] It was launched in 1927, and by 1931 its initial circulation of two hundred had risen dramatically to four thousand subscribers.[29] As was the case with *Mambo Leo*, *Ufalme wa Mungu* was linked to wider projects of developing and reforming the Swahili language, though its motivation was slightly different. While German Protestant missionaries adopted the Swahili language on pragmatic grounds, by the first decade of the twentieth century they remained unconvinced that the Swahili of the coast was suitable for use in inland East Africa.[30] This was partly a question of vocabulary and a concern that the Arabic loanwords of the coast were less comprehensible in inland areas. But it was also driven by a concern that the Arabic words used to translate key theological concepts risked confusing the two religions.

In 1912 Martin Klamroth of the Berlin Mission was asked to undertake the work of producing a new translation of the Bible less reliant on Arabic loanwords. After Klamroth's death in 1918, the work was taken over by Dr. Karl Roehl.[31] Roehl's project was an appeal for recognition that Tanganyika's shared religious language should be based on what was perceived to be the shared culture and linguistic heritage of the interior, not those of the coast. While the focus of the project was the translation of the Bible, *Ufalme wa Mungu* can be situated in this wider context. The periodical worked to promote the new translation, describing it as "our" translation, and Roehl was himself briefly editor of *Ufalme wa Mungu* in the early 1930s.

CREATING TEXTUAL PUBLICS IN *MAMBO LEO* AND *UFALME WA MUNGU*

Contemporary observers sought to draw a clear distinction between the mission periodicals and other publications. The journal *Africa*, discussing *Ufalme wa Mungu* in its "Notes and News" column, described its contents as "mainly religious."[32] *Mambo Leo*, in contrast, was avowedly nonreligious in its subject matter. The editors of *Mambo Leo* were adamant that the periodical would not become a forum for religious debate, despite attempts by some of its readers to make it so. A monthly column that published responses to readers' questions explained why some contributions would not be published, and often their religious content was the reason.[33] In contrast, *Ufalme wa Mungu*'s editors celebrated its role in spreading God's word, and this distinctive mission was welcomed by readers. As one reader of *Ufalme wa Mungu* wrote in 1928, it constituted a noticeable improvement on the government newspaper, since in *Mambo Leo* no traces of God's word were to be found.[34]

Mambo Leo differed from *Ufalme wa Mungu* in its attitude to the past as well. The working principle of *Mambo Leo* was that the periodical provided an opportunity for knowledge about the past to be preserved in new ways. In a 1929 editorial, the editor reminded readers of the importance of exploring "the past in order to compare it with the present."[35] Indeed, the journal *Africa* recommended a similar path to *Ufalme wa Mungu*'s editors, writing that while "it is natural that generally Christians should wish to draw a definite line between their present life and their pagan past . . . it is nevertheless the missionary's duty to show his pupils that not everything in their people's history is contemptible and carefully to be avoided."[36]

Yet for all that, the two papers had much in common. There was a clear didactic agenda in both. Knowledge about the past was important as a foundation for progress, the governing philosophy of both newspapers, not as something to be celebrated in and of itself. Both steered clear of explicitly anticolonial topics, which, for some observers, was all to the good. As a report in the journal *Africa* on *Ufalme wa Mungu* stated in 1931, "happily political and race questions are never touched."[37]

Mambo Leo took standardization, and its role in policing "correct" Swahili, seriously. As the editor wrote in response to a reader's question in 1938, now that Swahili was an official language it benefited from having its own guardians, and while swapping the letters *r* and *l*, or *p* and *b*, might be acceptable in speech, in written Swahili it was now simply a mistake.[38] More generally, the editorial team behind *Mambo Leo* understood the newspaper to occupy the role of an educator, bringing important information to the attention of its readers and answering the questions they brought to the editor. As a note from the editor explained, readers should "send your important questions in order for us to learn and to increase knowledge. We want questions which can make people think and which can help and teach readers with the desire to achieve progress."[39]

But for all that there was a clear editorial line and clear didactic intent, these newspapers were not simply a mouthpiece for missionaries or colonial officials—had they been, they would not have taken root in African society in the way they did. Much of the content was written by Africans, though the identity of the authors was often masked by the combination of the print form and the use of anonymity or pseudonyms.[40] They are better understood as a coproduction, albeit one in which power was heavily weighted on the side of those with editorial control.

As the *Africa* report on *Ufalme wa Mungu* made clear, the second section of the journal largely consisted of "contributions from the Africans themselves," which were of "great variety, centring mostly around experiences of their personal lives; important events in Christian communities and in the country at large; the progress of Christianity, the fight against witchcraft; and superstitions; and the Christianization of native customs, as e.g. cattle marriage," with occasional forays into "questions of hygiene, child welfare, and mothercraft."[41]

The same was true of *Mambo Leo*, which had far more space to fill but even so could never print all the letters, poems, and questions it received.

While this was often a source of frustration to aspirant writers whose work was not published, it reminds us that in the 1920s and 1930s, the line between those employed by the newspaper to write for it and others who considered themselves to be writers was blurred.

Mambo Leo typically contained a body of material that was unsigned and that was, in a sense, the "official voice" of *Mambo Leo*, including editorials and "Habari za Dunia" (World news). There were also educational articles written by recognized experts, on matters such as animal husbandry. There were also translations by writers who had a long association with *Mambo Leo* and moved between official and unofficial roles, such as the Swahili-language experts Frederick Johnson or Samuel Chiponde, who produced serialized translations of novels and stories such as *Gulliver's Travels*, *Cinderella*, or *One Thousand and One Nights*.

But there was also considerable space for contributors who were in no sense formally employed by the newspaper, particularly in the section "Habari za Miji" (News of the towns), in the poetry section, in the letters pages, and in the section where the editor gave his response to readers who had submitted material that for one reason or another would not be published.[42] Many poets and writers initially published their work in *Mambo Leo* and developed reputations as respected writers on the basis of these contributions. Aspirant poets were sent away to hone their skills before they would be published in *Mambo Leo*, while the next contributions from celebrated poets were eagerly awaited.[43] While some complained that their work was not published, other correspondents defended the editor's right to choose to print the writings of talented writers such as the poet Mzee Waziri Kijana, rather than the output of less talented writers such as themselves.[44]

The form that *Mambo Leo* took was therefore, to a limited extent, shaped by readers as well as by editors. An attempt early in the 1920s to introduce a spelling reform through the pages of *Mambo Leo* was resisted by readers and ultimately abandoned.[45] In the 1930s, when proposals to use standardized Swahili in *Mambo Leo*'s pages were again put forward, this time for the benefit of school students sitting examinations in standardized Swahili, Martin Kayamba, a frequent contributor in *Mambo Leo*, wrote to oppose the move, reminding the editorial team that "Mambo Leo once became most unpopular with Africans because they complained that the Swahili used in this paper was not pure Swahili but 'Kiswahili cha Kizungu' [European Swahili] which they did not relish."[46] For Kayamba, *Mambo Leo* was "a newspaper for all Africans regardless of age. If standardised Swahili spelling is required for school examinations it can be used in 'Mwanafunzi' school paper."

The importance of producing a newspaper that readers actually wanted to read thus trumped wider considerations of Swahili-language reform. A proposal in 1934 for *Mambo Leo* to become the main Swahili journal for East Africa was rejected by Tanganyika's government on the grounds that "'Mambo Leo' is an established periodical with a character and function of its own, to the maintenance of which great importance is attached," though "no objection would be made to the inclusion of matter submitted from other East African Dependencies."[47] Ultimately, as the chief secretary explained, "a local basis of interest and appeal is essential for a paper of this nature; it is 'Habari ya Miji' and the correspondence columns that sell the paper."[48]

The same push and pull between editorial policy and the demands of readers and writers was evident too in the letters pages in *Mambo Leo*. Many letters were received each month, three hundred to four hundred by the mid-1930s. In this context, it was deemed particularly important that "care must be exercised that the useful ones are selected," for "it is essential that this selection should be made by the editor, otherwise interesting letters are discarded and others not answered." Yet the same letter emphasized the importance of these letters, as the only means the editor "has at present of making contact with native thought."[49]

The tension between the constraints imposed by editors and the demands of readers was particularly apparent in the field of literary production and the development of new bodies of literary work in Swahili. When the final installment of a poem failed to appear, readers were quick to write asking what had become of it and when it would be published.[50] The editor was reassuring—it had been held over because there was too much news to include, but the poem would appear in full. Readers wrote in with their suggestions of books that they would like to see translated into Swahili in the pages of *Mambo Leo* and asked for news of the progress of translations. In July 1928 the editor reassured W. M. O. Ngurau Sultani that while *One Thousand and One Nights* was not yet available in full in Swahili, translators were hard at work and one or two books would soon be available.[51]

THE DISTINCTIVENESS OF PUBLISHING IN A LINGUA FRANCA

The development of Swahili as a language of print culture that went far beyond the coast of Tanganyika under German and British rule was thus in part a product of print media. The Swahili that developed was shaped by colonial and missionary language policies, but it was also shaped by the

African readers and writers who bought copies of Swahili-language periodicals and contributed to their columns. But can we go further and reflect on the implications of using a regional language for the types of publics created through print?

The use of Swahili meant that *Mambo Leo* was open to all who had learned the language. In 1925, in response to Feruzi Habibu of Dar es Salaam's question as to why *Mambo Leo* could not be published in English and Swahili, the editor said that if a European wanted to read *Mambo Leo*, then he could simply learn Swahili; otherwise, he would have to make do with English-language newspapers.[52] And as the editor reminded readers in responses to questions posed, Europeans did read *Mambo Leo* in the Swahili language, and some even ordered copies to be sent to Europe.[53]

If colonial regimes at times imagined Swahili as a means of cutting East Africans off from the wider circulation of ideas, print media situated East Africa firmly within the world. The world news published within both *Mambo Leo* and *Ufalme wa Mungu* ranged widely. While there was much news of political events in the pages of *Mambo Leo*, particularly toward the end of the 1930s as the world moved closer to conflict, there was also cultural and social news, from the death of the famous Turkish poet Abdulhak Hamid Bey, to reports on the rapidly growing size of Japan's population, to news of a forthcoming book containing the work of the great Indian mathematician Srinivasa Ramanujan.[54] Such news reports drew out the contrasts between different parts of the world. Polo, *Mambo Leo* explained in October 1932, could easily be played in Kashmir, where most people owned horses, but not in East Africa, where people instead owned cows.[55] The same was true of *Ufalme wa Mungu*, where alongside news of Christians across the world there was more straightforwardly political news of conflict between China and Japan or contrasting responses to the economic depression of the early 1930s.[56]

Writing in a regional language also meant that news of happenings elsewhere had to be translated. Some articles were directly translated from English-language newspapers, as in the case of an article about soil erosion in the United States published in *Mambo Leo* in January 1936 that had previously been published in the London *Times* some five months earlier.[57] But even where articles were not directly translated, conceptual translation was required, as concepts such as the gold standard or the League of Nations, or more abstract concepts such as citizenship, were rendered into a language that for many was a second language.[58] What we see in such cases is a push and pull between the older meanings of the words and the new meaning that the editors and writers sought to impose.[59]

Translation was important in other senses too. The power of print to cross space and time, coupled with the use of a language that crossed ethnic or religious divides, meant that the local dynamics that shaped social or cultural life could not simply be assumed but had to be explained. As one reader argued in the pages of *Mambo Leo* in 1936, the advantage of Swahili was precisely that it enabled people to talk to each other across distances and to publish books and that it was not the language of any one *taifa* (nation) or ethnic group. It was, in short, a language of print. But, he continued, this did not mean that the mother tongue was not important, for it too had an important role in social life.[60]

On one level, then, the use of a regional lingua franca as a language of print seems to suggest the creation of a relatively open intellectual culture in which ideas could be exchanged. Yet there are signs here of the tensions that persisted as to how far Swahili *could* be open to all. And while Swahili allowed for communication across distances, it did not simply create one large and undifferentiated textual public. In the first place, some continued to argue that the Swahili language properly belonged only to the people of the coast. The pages of *Mambo Leo* provided a site for arguments as to what form the language should take, and in particular whether it should incorporate words from other languages, arguments that often defended the claim that only those who spoke Swahili as a first language and who claimed a Swahili identity truly possessed the language.

Others sought to construct different sorts of print communities that included some and excluded others. For the Lutheran missionaries who edited *Ufalme wa Mungu*, its purpose was clear. Print media, published in the Swahili language, provided a way of bringing together Christians who might otherwise have little opportunity to meet their coreligionists. As the first editor, Ernst Johannssen, explained, the periodical was intended to function as a "cord" binding together Christians across East Africa.[61] The letters pages and the news of the experiences of Christians across the region created a virtual connection and allowed individual readers to imagine themselves as members of such a wider community. As Abraham Mdoe wrote to *Ufalme wa Mungu* in April 1928, the newspaper demonstrated the "huge difference between the Africa of the past and the Africa today," and the way in which Africans had been joined together as "limbs of one body" with countries too drawing closer together and becoming like the "districts of one town." For, Mdoe continued, the newspaper provided an arena that enabled "we Christians of East Africa, that is, Tanganyika Territory and Kenya, to gather together once every month."[62] In the past, he suggested, things had been very different, with relations between people defined by hatred and fear.

The theme that the newspaper's function was to bring unity to the Christians of East Africa was frequently heard in the pages of *Ufalme wa Mungu*, as the editors took advantage of any excuse to take this message to their readers. Thus, for example, in January 1934 the adoption of a new format provided an excuse to remind readers that the newspaper was intended to be read not just in Kenya and Tanganyika but even as far away as Italian Somaliland, its aim to create one Christian community.[63] But it also gave readers an opportunity to insert themselves into a wider transnational community of Christians. When *Ufalme wa Mungu* ran a series of articles on the fate of Christians in Russia, readers were quick to offer donations to support persecuted coreligionists.[64] Yet in drawing together the Christians of East Africa, *Ufalme wa Mungu* also served to define Christians as a distinct body and separate them from non-Christians. It was in this vein that readers were advised to read the Quran in Swahili as a way of understanding the beliefs of their Muslim neighbors and equipping themselves for theological argument.[65]

Just as print media could challenge the physical boundaries that kept Christians separate from each other while also creating new boundaries between religious communities, the same was true of geopolitical boundaries. For all that print media transcended territorial boundaries, including the boundaries of individual empires, such divides were reinforced in the realm of political imagination. Those who lived beyond the borders of the British Empire were reminded that if they wished to subscribe to the newspapers, they had to send their subscription fees in a form of currency acceptable within the British sphere of rule. Thus, while a reader in Kenya was told that he could send Kenyan shillings to pay his subscription fees, a reader in Bujumbura in modern-day Burundi was reminded that Belgian currency was not accepted in Tanganyika.[66] And while *Ufalme wa Mungu* was intended to bring together all Christians in East Africa, the editorial voice at times carried a hint of a nationalist edge, as in then-editor Karl Roehl's uncritical account of the referendum held in Germany in late 1933 to decide whether or not Germany should withdraw from the League of Nations. Similarly, his discussion of the contrasting government policies of Germany and Britain in response to the depression of the early 1930s praised the measures Hitler's government was taking to reduce unemployment and noted that in Germany the numbers of the unemployed were falling faster than was the case in Britain.[67]

And while on one level the imagined reach of *Mambo Leo* extended to all those who understood the Swahili language in the Roman script, wherever they might be in the world, this explicitly excluded those who preferred the Arabic script, who were informed in no uncertain terms that progress demanded the use of the Roman alphabet.[68] Less concretely, letters from contributors suggested that print was understood differently if it appeared in the Roman script. One correspondent asked why books written in Arabic script were conserved carefully, whereas those in the Roman script were swiftly discarded, and whether this was because Roman letters were not understood as godly in the way that Arabic letters were.[69]

Yet while the various Swahili-language newspapers of the interwar period sought to create their own specific publics of readers, addressed purposively by editors, readers often understood them interchangeably, much to the frustration of the editors in question. In 1934 Roehl, the editor of *Ufalme wa Mungu*, chastised his readers for copying their letters to the editor of *Mambo Leo*. Letters to be published in *Mambo Leo* should be sent to *Mambo Leo*, he insisted, and letters to be published in *Ufalme wa Mungu* should be sent to *Ufalme wa Mungu*.[70] The editor of *Mambo Leo* was similarly irritated by the habit of copying letters, using the column in which the editor responded to readers to tell one reader, K. M. Sikeria Nyamuko of Musoma, that if he had a question for the editor of *Rafiki Yetu* (Our friend), he should send it to *Rafiki Yetu*, not to *Mambo Leo*.[71] This perhaps suggests that what the existence of a lingua franca made possible was a set of overlapping publics, characterized by distinctive contours rather than hard boundaries.

This case study encourages us to rethink some of our assumptions about text, print, and writing in colonial Africa. Once seen as the creation of European missionaries and colonial officials, the textual cultures of print that developed in East Africa in the first half of the twentieth century were built on precolonial foundations, and the forms they took were shaped by those foundations. This helps explain the marked differences both between East and West Africa and within East Africa itself. Cultures of print were never simply imposed by missionaries and officials, even in cases such as Tanganyika, where there was a clear colonial language policy to promote a particular form of standardized Swahili, supported by both the government and the missions. The divergent textual cultures that developed across colonial Africa were always forged through dialogue from above and below, and between the demands of the present and the patterns of social, political, and economic life inherited from the past. These textual cultures were therefore not straightforwardly indigenous but were shaped by African readers and writers as well as by colonial powers.

But at the same time, the colonial era also marked a break. Swahili had a long history as a written language, but it was used in new ways and by new people in the colonial period. This was partly a function of print. Print made communication across wide distances possible, and it turned writing into a form that many more people could make use of to construct new sorts of communities. Yet for all that print had a marked effect, its effects were not predetermined. In colonial Africa, print media did not straightforwardly lead either to adoption of colonial or other global languages or to the promotion of small-scale vernaculars.[72]

If the use of imperial languages allowed some African writers to insert themselves into a wider anglophone or francophone community, what did it mean to write in a lingua franca such as Swahili? For some, the use of Swahili by people for whom it was not a vernacular, in the sense of a first language or mother tongue, was threatening or undesirable. For others, the development of a standardized written language offered exciting opportunities to communicate across space and to make sense of new ideas from around the world. This was particularly true in the relatively democratic space of newspapers and periodicals, in which anyone who could read and write, and who was willing to conform to the rules of engagement that structured the arena of print media, could participate. Where, as in this case, these public forums took place within a lingua franca to which growing numbers of Africans and non-Africans had access as a second language, new publics were created that extended widely across space.

In this way, the twin story of language and print provides a counterweight to a perspective on the interwar period once dominant in the history of East Africa that sees it as a time when connections were closed down and ethnic and religious identities accentuated at the expense of alternative connections that transcended locality. It also complicates a narrative that links the spread of Swahili to a story of Tanzanian nationalism. The existence by the 1950s of a shared language of print *did* make some forms of nationalist organization possible, but it also encouraged the creation of alternative publics. These overlapping swahiliphone publics transcended both the colonial borders of Tanganyika and any single political allegiance, and it is perhaps here that their lasting importance for the intellectual and cultural history of eastern Africa lies.

NOTES

1. "Notes and News," 499.
2. Achebe, "English and the African Writer," 342–49; and Ngũgĩ wa Thiong'o, *Decolonising the Mind*. There are of course difficulties with this broad-brush

approach, and there were important vernacular-language textual publics in West Africa as well, from the Ewe-language print communities studied by Kate Skinner to the Yoruba-language print communities explored by Karin Barber. For example see Komedja, *Writing the New Nation in a West African Borderland* (coedited by Skinner); Barber, *Print Culture and the First Yoruba Novel*.

3. Peterson, "Language Work and Colonial Politics in Eastern Africa," 185–214; and Peterson and Hunter, "Print Culture in Colonial Africa," 1–48.

4. Peterson, "Language Work and Colonial Politics in Eastern Africa," 190.

5. As was also the case with the Māori-language newspapers discussed in Paterson, *Colonial Discourses*, 19.

6. Ballantyne and Paterson, this volume.

7. See Ellerman, this volume.

8. Jeppie, "Writing, Books, and Africa," 96; see also D. Johnson and Davis, "Introduction," 4; and Reese, *The Transmission of Learning in Islamic Africa*.

9. Mack and Boyd, *One Woman's Jihad*, 76, 84.

10. Bang, *Sufis and Scholars of the Sea*, 6; and Pouwels, *Horn and Crescent*, 131.

11. Ghazal, *Islamic Reform and Arab Nationalism*.

12. Pouwels, *Horn and Crescent*, 131–32, 147.

13. Yates, "Knowledge Brokers," 315.

14. Pouwels, *Horn and Crescent*, 187.

15. Brumfit, "The Rise and Development of a Language Policy in German East Africa," 262.

16. Wimmelbücker, *Kilimanjaro—a Regional History*, 287.

17. Brumfit, "The Rise and Development of a Language Policy in German East Africa," 262.

18. Althaus, *Mamba—Anfang in Afrika*, 12–13. This draws on material discussed in Hunter, "Languages of Politics in Twentieth-Century Kilimanjaro," 48.

19. Hunter, "Languages of Politics in Twentieth-Century Kilimanjaro," 52.

20. Brumfit, "The Rise and Development of a Language Policy in German East Africa," 274.

21. Lemke, "Die Suaheli-Zeitungen und Zeitschriften in Deutsch-Ostafrika."

22. J. Cole, "Printing and Urban Islam in the Mediterranean World, 1890–1920," 351.

23. Lemke, "Die Suaheli-Zeitungen und Zeitschriften in Deutsch-Ostafrika," 19.

24. Paterson, *Colonial Discourses*, 12–13; and Paterson, this volume.

25. Brumfit, "The Rise and Development of a Language Policy in German East Africa," 278. On the history of the committee, see Whiteley, *Swahili*, esp. 79–94. See also "Kutengeneza namna moja ya kuandika Kiswahili katika nchi hii," *Mambo Leo*, December 1925, 1.

26. "Madhara ya Harufu za Kizungu kwa Lugha ya Kiswahili: Extract from *Al-Islah*, 20th June, 1932," printed in *Inter-Territorial Language (Swahili) Committee Bulletin*, no. 7 (1934): 9–10. More broadly, this piece can be seen as an attack by the editor, Sheikh al-Amin Mazrui, on the triumph of the Kiunguja over the Kimvita dialect at the territorial level. See Pouwels, "Sh. al-Amin b. Ali Mazrui and Islamic Modernism in East Africa, 1875–1947," 329–45.

27. *Inter-Territorial Language (Swahili) Committee Bulletin*, no. 7 (1934): 10. The *Bulletin* was the journal of the Language Committee responsible for Swahili research.

28. *Inter-Territorial Language (Swahili) Committee Bulletin*, no. 7 (1934): 70.

29. "Notes and News," 498.

30. Brumfit, "The Rise and Development of a Language Policy in German East Africa," 300–306.

31. Broomfield, "The Re-Bantuization of the Swahili Language," 83.

32. "Notes and News," 498.

33. For example, in *Mambo Leo* in October 1932, an aspirant poet was told that his poem included too much religious material and so would not be published.

34. Letter from Titos Mahushi, "Upendo wa Mungu,'" *Ufalme wa Mungu*, August 1928, 4.

35. Editorial, *Mambo Leo*, September 1929, 1133.

36. "Notes and News," 499.

37. "Notes and News," 499.

38. Editor's response to Abdallah M. Chamajaha, Mngoni, *Mambo Leo*, September 1938, 149.

39. Editor, "Sanduku ya Posta," *Mambo Leo*, February 1927.

40. As was also common in West Africa, on which see Newell, *The Power to Name*.

41. "Notes and News," 498.

42. See, for example, Askew, "Everyday Poetry from Tanzania," 179–223.

43. Editor's response to Mki bin Mzee Nasoro, *Mambo Leo*, October 1924, 19.

44. Letter from Bilali Ali Mshoro, *Mambo Leo*, November 1938, 183.

45. Editorial, *Mambo Leo*, April 1925, 73.

46. Kayamba to Hutt, minute, 13 August 1935, Tanzania National Archives (TNA) 12871, vol. 2, f. 404, London.

47. Extract from letter to Sec. Governors' Conference, Nairobi, TNA 12871, vol. 2, f. 236.

48. Ag. Chief Secretary to Hon. Director of Education, 9 April 1934, TNA 12871, vol. 2, f. 238.

49. "Review of Mambo Leo Activities, July 1932 to October 1933," TNA 12871, vol. 2, f. 202.

50. Editor's response to Zubeir Aboubakar, *Mambo Leo*, June 1928, 903.

51. Editor's response to W. M. O. Ngurau Sultani, *Mambo Leo*, July 1928, 919.

52. Editor's response to Feruzi Habibu, *Mambo Leo*, October 1925, 231.

53. Editor's response to Issa Kabale, *Mambo Leo*, October 1938, 165.

54. "Kifo cha Mtunga Mashairi," *Mambo Leo*, January 1931, 2; "Maongezeko ya watu," *Mambo Leo*, March 1931, 38; and "Fundi mkubwa wa hesabu," *Mambo Leo*, March 1931, 38.

55. "Mchezo wa Polo," *Mambo Leo*, October 1932, 251.

56. "Yafanyikalo ulimwenguni," *Ufalme wa Mungu*, January 1934, 7.

57. "Uharibufu wa ardhi katika nchi ya United States of America," *Mambo Leo*, January 1936, 9.

58. There are interesting parallels with the Papua New Guinea newspaper *Wantok*, which "introduced the newly coined pidgin words for parliamentary procedure (*mosen, sekenim mosen, muvin mosen, votim mosen*)" in the run-up to independence. Ellerman, this volume.

59. Hunter, "Dutiful Subjects, Patriotic Citizens, and the Concept of 'Good Citizenship' in Twentieth-Century Tanzania," 257–77.

60. Letter from Luxford O. Issa, *Mambo Leo*, March 1936, 49.

61. Editorial, "Karibuni watu wote," *Ufalme wa Mungu*, March 1927, 1.

62. Letter from Abraham Mdoe, "Tukisahau yaliyopita ni vizuri," *Ufalme wa Mungu*, April 1928, 3.

63. Editor, "Kwa wasomaji wote!," *Ufalme wa Mungu*, January 1934, 7–8. The editor also reminded readers that while he hoped the new format would help attract a wide readership, the aim of *Ufalme wa Mungu*, its priority, would remain spreading God's word, and it would not turn into a newspaper solely concerned with worldly stories and lessons, for that was *Mambo Leo*'s province.

64. "Maulizo," *Ufalme wa Mungu*, March 1934, 20; and editor, "Kuagana," *Ufalme wa Mungu*, September 1934, 40.

65. Mikael Samson, "Kurani ya Kiswahili na faida yake," *Ufalme wa Mungu*, August 1931, 153–55.

66. Editor's response to Simeon Shigela, *Mambo Leo*, September 1924, 19; and editor's response to B. Abdurahmin Schaidor, *Mambo Leo*, December 1924, 29.

67. "Yafanyikalo ulimwenguni," *Ufalme wa Mungu*, January 1934, 7.

68. Editor's response to Mbwana Mbaruku, *Mambo Leo*, January 1929, 1018.

69. Letter from S. A. Nambamba, "Kudharau herufi za kizungu," *Mambo Leo*, May 1938, 85.

70. Editor, "Mfuko wa Posta," *Ufalme wa Mungu*, March 1934, 24.

71. Editor's response to K. M. Sikeria Nyamuko, *Mambo Leo*, July 1938, 117.

72. Ballantyne, "What Difference Does Colonialism Make?," 342–52.

CHAPTER EIGHT

Going Off Script:
Aboriginal Rejection and Repurposing of English Literacies

LAURA RADEMAKER

IN MANY PLACES where missionaries introduced the written word, Indigenous people eagerly adopted it. This is just what missionaries hoped, but also just what many might expect Indigenous people to do. Western narratives of modernization would suggest that societies emerge out of orality, casting aside previous traditions, when they encounter the power of literacy. Walter Ong wrote, for example, that "orality is not an ideal," arguing that although oral societies value their traditions, when introduced to writing they inevitably "want to achieve literacy as soon as possible."[1] Similarly, social anthropologist Jack Goody claimed that writing "underpins civilisation" because its permanence fosters critical thought.[2] The dichotomy of "orality" and "literacy" has been used to draw a line between "modern civilizations" and "premodern societies" based on writing, implicitly preparing a script for Indigenous people to follow.

On Groote Eylandt off the coast of the Northern Territory of Australia, Anindilyakwa people left that script. Despite constant missionary encouragement to do so, many Anindilyakwa speakers never became literate in either English or Anindilyakwa. For various reasons, they understood writing as not in their interests. Some did learn to read and write in English, expecting these skills to bring new opportunities. But opportunities did not always eventuate. When they did write, they used writing in English in ways that challenged the missionary narrative that anticipated a movement from traditionalism to civilization to accompany a move from orality to literacy.[3] Refusing to perform evangelical scripts of literacy, conversion, and civilization, they instead repurposed writing in their own ways. For many, this meant not writing at all.

INDIGENOUS ENCOUNTERS WITH WRITING

Closer examination of Indigenous literacies around the globe shows that when Indigenous people took up writing, this did not mean abandoning their traditions or identities. Writing was not a knockout punch to existing Indigenous interpretive practices.[4] Instead, Indigenous people have understood and embraced writing in different ways, even using it to uphold and assert Indigenous identities.[5] In New Zealand, for example, Māori embraced writing as a tool for recasting Indigenous identities in the face of rapid changes.[6] Several *iwi* (tribes) created a "Māori modernity" that included English literacies as a modern resource for Indigenous people rather than simply an instrument of cultural destruction.[7] Literacy could also draw together anticolonial thinkers and create new networks of Indigenous dissent.[8] The durability of orality in Indigenous societies as well as the diverse ways Indigenous people used literacy, sometimes to complement or incorporate existing oral practices, challenges the Western binaries of orality and literacy, civilization and savagery, as well as Western narratives of modernity.

For other peoples, writing was not so attractive. Penny van Toorn showed that when Aboriginal people in colonial Australia first encountered writing, it came entangled in colonizers' ideologies of literacy and civilization. This entanglement shaped Aboriginal peoples' varied engagements with writing.[9] Mindy J. Morgan likewise found that for some Native American communities, English literacy and the institutional power of colonizers were inextricably linked.[10] The use of documents as mechanisms of control shaped how Indigenous people perceived the use and purpose of literacies. Literacy could become laden with cultural meanings associated with colonizers, not always readily reconcilable with Indigenous identities, especially where associated with the colonizers' language.[11]

In Australia, Aboriginal education policy, especially regarding approaches to English literacy, is a contested issue. Yet the history of Aboriginal writing cultures and of the ways Aboriginal people have related to writing in English

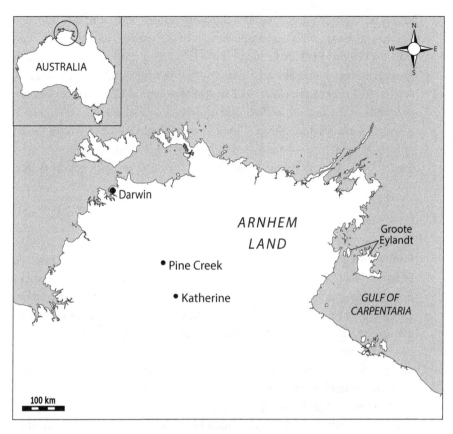

MAP 8.1 Location of Groote Eylandt. Data from Open Street Map contributors.

is not well understood. A number of historians have documented the long Aboriginal tradition, dating back to nineteenth-century petitioners in colonial Victoria and Tasmania, of using writing to demand rights, particularly to land.[12] Long represented by colonizers in script or images, Aboriginal authors are using writing in English to craft their own identities, representing themselves in ways they wish to be seen.[13] Existing studies of Aboriginal writing largely focused on these published works by Aboriginal people (most of whom speak English as a first language) rather than the role of writing in English in Aboriginal people's lives, including among those for whom English is not a first language or those who do not speak English at all.[14]

This chapter turns, therefore, to the history of the Anindilyakwa-speaking people of Groote Eylandt and their engagement with writing in English from the 1940s to the 1960s. The Anindilyakwa language is strong; children from the Groote Eylandt archipelago still speak it as their first language. Anindilyakwa people's ongoing contact with English-language documents began with the establishment of the evangelical Angurugu mission on Groote Eylandt in 1943. This means their early engagement with English literacy is still in living memory. Unlike other studies of colonial literacies, this very recent experience of colonization has allowed me to escape the limits of the mission archive and undertake oral history interviews with Aboriginal people themselves. I look at what English literacy meant in the mission community—both to Anindilyakwa people and to the missionaries themselves—to understand Anindilyakwa responses to writing in English.

ANINDILYAKWA PEOPLE AND THE ANGURUGU MISSION

Long before European writing came to Groote Eylandt, Anindilyakwa people encoded meaning in images and objects. Senior people used message sticks to communicate from afar, often for announcing a ceremony. The notches and pictures on message sticks are mnemonic devices. The markings also confirm the genuineness of the message and the authority of the messenger.[15] The message stick tradition continued into the twentieth century for new purposes. For example, in the 1950s message sticks were used in Arnhem Land as invoices. Circular markings signified the money desired, and other marks represented the groups to be paid.[16] Anindilyakwa people also have their own artistic traditions. They have been painting on rock for millennia, and their bark paintings are famous for their iconic black backgrounds.[17] In Aboriginal art, levels of meaning are encoded in paintings.[18] There are no meaningless marks, dots, or doodles: everything has meaning.[19] It cannot be "read" by strangers; even those with some knowledge of symbols and stories represented in art cannot read its deeper layers of meaning unless granted access by senior people.[20] The messages are secret, impossible to decode on their own, open only to those who have a legitimate right to know.

Missionaries from the Anglican Church Missionary Society (CMS) were the first English speakers to settle on the island. In 1920 the missionaries proposed to transfer the Aboriginal population from their existing Roper River Mission to Groote Eylandt, beginning with the "half-caste" children. The Commonwealth government subsequently declared the whole of Groote Eylandt an Aboriginal reserve to facilitate this transfer. The reserve system barred anyone but the children, CMS staff, government officials, and Anindilyakwa people themselves from visiting the island. The children spoke various Aboriginal languages, so English became the lingua franca of the mission, but the children spoke Kriol among themselves. From there, the missionaries made contact with local Anindilyakwa people, but their interactions were limited mainly to medical treatment and trade.

From around 1932 Anindilyakwa people moved into camps around the mission. Some Anindilyakwa children attended the mission school and began learning English. During World War II, the half-caste children were evacuated from the island. The Australian Air Force established a temporary base on the island, giving Anindilyakwa people further exposure to English.[21] With the half-castes gone, the CMS established a new mission station—Angurugu—specifically for Anindilyakwa in 1943. The mission was staffed by a cluster of white families and a few single women from the southern states of Australia: the superintendent, with his wife and children; the chaplain, with his wife and family; a mechanic or agriculturalist, with his family; and some nurses and teachers. They were typically middle- or working-class people, depending on their occupation. The new mission adopted a policy of assimilation for Aboriginal people. Christian conversion and training in "civil" behavior would, they hoped, allow Aboriginal people to realize the status of Australian citizens and be absorbed into white Australia. In pursuit of this end, the missionaries brought the children into dormitories, established a school, and enforced church attendance and work through provision of rations.

ENGLISH-LANGUAGE DOCUMENTS AND SURVEILLANCE

The missionaries used English script in the hope of keeping things under control. Westerners often presume writing is reliable because the content does not change. It is supposed to create rational order and pin down knowledge. So the missionaries wrote almost everything down, with Saturdays spent attending to correspondence and writing reports.[22] They kept statistics on school attendance; pawpaw and peanut produce; hospital treatments; and births, deaths, and marriages, all with a vision of improving their work to assimilate and convert Aboriginal people. Missionary records extend from formal reports for governments to the more trivial: the minutes of the Angurugu table-tennis club. Their writing routine was a ritual performance, pointing to their authority and their self-discipline as well as to the significance of their work (which would, they believed, be of interest to future generations).[23] Written reporting also served a CMS bureaucracy and enabled centralized control of the missions from Sydney. Through insisting on regular updates, statistics, and reports, the CMS Aborigines secretary, J. B. Montgomerie, gained intimate knowledge of Angurugu mission and its success in Christianizing and "civilizing" (or lack thereof) and rebuked or rewarded the missionaries accordingly. Anindilyakwa people encountered writing as a means of supervision, both of themselves and of the missionaries.

Rather than delivering the clarity they promised, English-language records could be a source of confusion and contention. Instead of ordering Aboriginal lives according to missionary expectations, attempts at representing them in writing only exposed to missionaries how Aboriginal people continued to uphold their own systems of family life and naming. The number of children at Angurugu was often in doubt, since many were under the care of their aunties or "other mothers" (according to Anindilyakwa family norms), making miscounts likely.[24] Missionary and government systems for recording family relationships, which presumed Western biological conceptions of family, motherhood, and fatherhood, proved inadequate.[25]

There were further problems with the roll books. In 1958 the chaplain complained about "adamant 'linguists'" who adopted the "that's what I think it is" method of spelling Aboriginal names.[26] The lack of standardized spelling for Aboriginal names was a recurring dilemma. Another missionary explained her approach in 1968: names should be written "in such a form that the ordinary Australian can pronounce them."[27] Aboriginal people were, to her, still not "ordinary Australians" until their lives conformed to her European systems of knowledge and record keeping. Her attempt to present people as "ordinary Australians" was an attempt to present Aboriginal people as citizens, if only on paper. But missionaries' reports and spellings were unable to convey the reality of Anindilyakwa life. That they could not agree on a common orthography indicates that their faith in writing's ability to convey reality was misplaced. Similarly, Anindilyakwa family life, where children have numerous mothers, and aunties and uncles who share responsibilities, did not easily fit into the schema for government child endowment payments. Writing proved to be ambiguous, inadequate, and particular to the missionary culture rather than a universal authority on the world.

Although writing can be an instrument of authority, it is also risky. Unlike speech, which occurs as an event—an encounter shared between speaker and listener—writing is disembodied, disconnected from the original author, and can be recontextualized and reinterpreted, without reference to the author's intentions. In 1960, when the newly arrived chaplain, Taylor, was appointed acting superintendent over the older and more experienced Arthur Howell, the two disagreed on their responsibilities. A poorly written letter from a

CMS official was the source of the confusion. Taylor read it as simply "a pep talk" to Howell, but Howell believed it gave him oversight of the mission.[28]

Taylor's appointment angered many Anindilyakwa people, who believed he was too young to be their "boss." Taylor became superintendent based on his interpretation of writing. To Anindilyakwa people, perhaps it seemed that writing encouraged self-interested interpretations. Writing, it seems, fostered dishonesty because its disconnectedness from the speaker meant it could be twisted to suit personal needs. Historian Minoru Hokari recounted how Old Jimmy, a Gurindji Elder, complained that "paper"—European laws and letters—could be changed, reinterpreted, thrown away. His Aboriginal law is in the earth, which "never change . . . (law) still there."[29] Old Jimmy's word challenges Goody's thesis of the permanence and subsequent superiority of writing. Whereas writing is "just paper"—subject to editing, reinterpretation, damage, or loss—Aboriginal oral traditions literally have a solid foundation: land.[30] Though writing was, to missionaries, a symbol of their control and surveillance over Anindilyakwa people, to Anindilyakwa people missionary literacy could also seem an unreliable and weak instrument, in many ways inferior to their own oralities.

CHRISTIAN CITIZENSHIP AND ENGLISH LITERACY

Writing had other meanings for missionaries; it was, to them, the foundation of both their religion and their civilization. Protestantism has its origins in a Western literary culture in the sixteenth century and the distribution of the printed Bible. Personal knowledge of scripture was considered the avenue to truth and salvation, so Protestants took care to study the pages closely. Over the course of the twentieth century, evangelicals faced challenges from liberal theologies, so increasingly emphasized their biblicism over pietistic traditions.[31] They honored it in nearly all of their communal activities as well as in their private devotional practice. The CMS missionaries proclaimed themselves a "people of a Book, and that Book the Bible."[32] To them, to be Christian was to read. As the CMS newsletter explained, converts could not be baptized until they could read because "every Christian should be a reader."[33]

The missionaries' spiritual and ritual life depended on texts. They performed the "Quiet Time" (that is, daily private reading of scripture, prayer, and introspection), "Bible Study," and Sunday services (using the prayer book, hymnbook, and Bible). The missionaries' reading and writing was not so much about learning information (they had read the Bible many times before) but was a ritual act, a participation in evangelical culture and reaffirmation of their identity and community.[34] So dependent was their community and spiritual life on reading these texts that one commented in 1962 that she found it difficult to form friendships with Anindilyakwa people who could not read the Bible.[35]

For missionaries, English literacy was also a symbol and precondition of citizenship. Alan Atkinson told the history of Australia as a history of voices and communication. For him, the spread of literacy among the non-Indigenous population in the nineteenth century was a "revolution in communications."[36] Though literacy did not achieve everything nineteenth-century visionaries imagined, it fundamentally reshaped white Australian society—its governance, culture, identity, and even patterns of thinking—opening up new opportunities to those who could read but aiding the dispossession of Aboriginal people who did not.[37] Through the late nineteenth and early twentieth centuries, literacy (particularly in English) became a key marker of being "civilized."[38] The citizen of a democracy must be an informed participant in debates, so literacy was essential.[39] In mid-twentieth-century Australia, English-speaking policymakers and missionaries alike considered English literacy essential for citizenship. The director of the Commonwealth Office of Education wrote in 1949 that reading was a necessary skill for Aboriginal children if they were to become fully functioning citizens. They must be equipped for "newspapers, public notices and documents with which they will have to cope" in order to participate in national discussions.[40] Methodist missionary Arthur Ellemor wrote in 1956 that to be "meaningful," "full citizenship" of Aboriginal people required literacy.[41] Likewise, Montgomerie explained in 1958 that Aboriginal people could not function as citizens without English literacy: "they cannot vote at an election for parliament because they cannot read or write."[42]

In the early years of the Angurugu School, it seems some Anindilyakwa people were eager for their children to acquire English literacy. Superintendent Dick Harris reported in 1945 that on his wife's arrival, the Angurugu people immediately asked, "Are the children having school to-day?" because they were "anxious that their children learn to read and write."[43] His report may have been an exaggeration, as some parents subsequently resisted sending their children to school (though even these children eventually made it onto the school roll).[44] Missionaries introduced the government's English syllabus for Aboriginal schools in the Northern Territory to Angurugu in 1953.[45] Its Bush Book series taught assimilationist messages: education and employment.[46] Children also copied Bible verses and decorated them with drawings.[47] Teachers drilled the children in dictation, which, according to the teachers, was "much enjoyed."[48] Children were, perhaps, more likely to be excited about English literacy, as they had not yet been fully educated in their own law. Nancy Lalara spoke to me of her love of reading: "I used to like reading Enid Blyton books, climb up on the mango tree, get away from my little sisters' hassling."[49] Nancy's younger sister, Rhoda Lalara, explained that she too enjoyed her new literacy: "I really wanted to learn more. I did a lot of exercises like doing arithmetic, writing stories. On the weekend when we used to go out and came back to school on the Monday, 'Can you write a story about what you used to do on the weekend?' and we used to do it."[50]

Although the missionaries focused on children, they also hoped to socialize adult Anindilyakwa people into their culture of English literacy, where adults showed an interest. In 1945, as missionary wife Nell Harris was teaching her son to read, she also taught her "house girl," Gudjiba. Eventually she lent Gudjiba a book: "she brought it back eventually, very dirty, but could read it all." Gudjiba's eagerness convinced Harris of the need for more reading material: "I have never allowed natives to take away Primers to their camp or hut before, but I believe the children, who are really anxious to read, would learn much from these primers if we had them to give."[51] The virtue of reading, for missionaries, surpassed other concerns about regulating mission space and civilized cleanliness. A book was better read than clean. Later, missionaries combined Christian instruction with literacy lessons, gathering women together to read Bible passages aloud in turn.[52]

With the establishment of the school, the missionaries encouraged adult Anindilyakwa people to become teaching assistants to help manage the classroom but also to improve their English literacy. A number of Anindilyakwa people took up positions, reading storybooks to the girls or the boys in the mornings.[53] Through the 1960s, missionaries continued to encourage Anindilyakwa people to use writing at work and participate in the CMS's extensive documentation of mission life. In 1963 the missionary builder praised "men like Ken" who "wanted me to write out the names of the men so that he could learn to write them out in the paybook. I found myself a little amused at his earnestness when he said how much he enjoyed 'thinking'—and he wanted to get some more practice!!!!"[54] Missionaries subsequently encouraged other men to "keep a daily diary and write monthly reports," promoting both their work culture and evangelical introspection through a single act of writing. Spelling was a "heavy job," yet some persisted.[55] By encouraging Anindilyakwa people to use writing at work, missionaries hoped to extend their own vision of modernity into Anindilyakwa lives. The possibility of scrutinizing a written record, they believed, would encourage people to make modernizing adjustments and increase efficiency.

Though missionaries read Aboriginal writing as a sign of conversion and civic behavior, Anindilyakwa eagerness to become literate in English did not necessarily represent submission to a missionary vision of Christian citizenship. Learning to write had many benefits. A number of Anindilyakwa people wrote letters to communicate with family who were away in Darwin.[56] Writing could represent an embrace of modernity: new skills and new opportunities. In 1973 Jambana Lalara asked the missionaries to teach him because he was increasingly required to negotiate with mining and government officials.[57] In light of many Anindilyakwa speakers' familiarity with cross-cultural communication and their fluency in other languages, it is little wonder many were ready to experiment with new modes of communication.

English literacies could be used to foster mutually productive relationships with missionaries. Jabani Lalara, for example, enacted evangelical conversion scripts through letter writing. He had ceased attending fellowship meetings. But in 1963 writing enabled him to regain the missionaries' trust without the shame associated with an apology in person. "A splendid letter came from Paul Jaboni [sic] Lalara. . . . He writes 'I think back to my life before, for what God had done for me. I was shamed of myself so God speak to me in my heart to write this letter. I was lot thinking of you all brothers and sisters in Christ. I was lost and I was found again.'"[58] Jabani performed an evangelical narrative of repentance and reconciliation, communicating to missionaries in their own forms through writing. Anthropologist Rosemary S. O'Donnell found that Aboriginal people learned to "talk Christian way" to maintain cohesive, constructive relations with missionaries.[59] In this case, Jabani had learned not only to talk but to "write Christian way." This writing could move missionaries to action. Jabani was a master of it. The missionaries also printed a conversion story about Jabani in an Angurugu newsletter, entitled "My Story by Djabani":

> If anyone likes to read this story about what I have done in the old time, first I didn't know the Lord Jesus. I didn't read the Bible because I didn't know anything about it. Then from that Time I went to school and learnt lessons there. Then I learnt about the Lord Jesus, the word in the Bible and some other things. I didn't learn yet the big words from the Bible but I like to learn more about the Book. Then I thought about myself, to follow Jesus and I went to Mr Warren. Mr Warren questioned me there and he said to me, "You really want to follow Jesus?" And I said, "Yes."[60]

Jabani's article is an entangled text, produced by engagement between two cultures. Missionaries probably edited Jabani's story, though it does seem to be largely his. It fits within a genre of evangelical conversion stories, common in missionary publications. Perhaps he had read other conversion stories before and so learned how to communicate in this genre. It reflects the deep connection of English literacy and Christian conversion at Angurugu; he needed to learn about the "Book" to "follow Jesus." For Arrernte people of central Australia, "paper" has come to mean Lutheran liturgy, buildings, prayers—anything associated with missionary religion.[61] Lutheranism was paper. Similarly, to Jabani, the "Book" symbolized Christianity itself but also represented schooling and education. He felt he would "like to learn more about the Book" and was open to learning new things from the missionaries. In doing so, he demonstrated his appreciation for the missionaries' teachings and a willingness to work with them, engaging with their stories, symbols, and culture.

Though missionaries expected literacy would inevitably lead to conversion and participation in Christian citizenship, it could have unexpected consequences. Nancy Lalara told of how her high opinion of the missionaries changed in the late 1960s because she read widely. She was "really into Christianity" in her youth. By the 1960s she began to understand more of the history of colonization in Australia and to question the missionary project. Her education enabled her to judge the missionaries' sacred text in light of her own experience and broader knowledge. I asked what changed for her. She replied:

> Just getting older and reading, thinking. Reading about what happened to my people in all of them days. . . . I changed because of the way that when things, looking at it in the Bible version of the way that everything was pure. . . . But the more that I grew up with that way, that wasn't a better life. Reading the Bible twenty times a day, saying thank you for our food when we had it on the table. Other things, reality, sort of crept into me about "that wasn't like that in the Bible," "how come it's like this?"[62]

English literacy alone could not guarantee the transformation of Anindilyakwa people into the Christian citizens envisaged by missionaries.

English literacy was so bound up in missionary visions of Christianity and civilization that when it was used in ways that contradicted this narrative, missionaries became puzzled or angered. Missionaries rejected Aboriginal writing, even punishing writers whose writing did not conform to their hopes. At Angurugu, dormitory girls used writing to contact their promised husbands or sweethearts, undermining missionary attempts to abolish child marriage and polygyny.[63] The punishment for a dormitory girl discovered "writing letters or giving presents" to a young man was "the strap."[64] The girls embraced English literacies but used writing to undermine the very citizenly behaviors that missionaries hoped it would instill. Men discovered writing "sweetheart talk" letters faced exile from the island. Unfortunately for one in 1961, his "sweetheart" rejected his advances and handed his love letter over to the missionaries.[65] He was subsequently banished from the island and then (for other reasons) imprisoned in Darwin.[66] But the rumor circulated on Groote Eylandt that, in his brother's writing, he had "been sent away by counsel for two years punishmen hes in ploce station now [sic]" simply because of "one letter he write a letter . . . no other thing just for one letter."[67] Anindilyakwa people came to believe that unauthorized letter writing was a terrible offense to the missionaries. Despite this, they continued to write sweetheart letters; Anindilyakwa people insisted on using writing for their own purposes.[68]

They also used English literacy against missionaries by petitioning, turning English documents against the authorities. Through writing, Indigenous people could lodge their complaints "on the record" of the CMS Aborigines Committee minutes, making them harder to ignore.[69] Aboriginal people had used writing in the colonizer's language as a means of protest for many years.[70] Anindilyakwa people also came to recognize that, in the cultural logic of the missionaries' world, political claims were only legitimate or remembered when made on paper. In 1960 a number of Anindilyakwa people wrote letters petitioning Montgomerie to uninstall the new superintendent, Taylor, in favor of Howell:

> Dear Mr Montgomerey. Just a few words from us and to you saying that all the people doesnt want Mr Taylor because we have find out that he is no good. All ready we dont wont him to be our boss put somebode as man please not young boy please. A lik mr Harris and Mr Howell a big man got lots of under-standing and knows for people more about this place.
>
> So I am tell to do something for us pleas if you dont well he is looking for a belting from the peopl here in this mission . . .
>
> May God bless and keep you all ways and tell wee meet in haven
>
> Letter from all the people
> At Groote Eylandt[71]

In writing letters like this one (there were many), Anindilyakwa speakers performed the role of the modern literate citizens the CMS was training them to become. They positioned themselves within a shared moral order with the missionaries such that their claims could be considered legitimate.[72] Anindilyakwa people, for example, acknowledged their mutual interest in the quality of the mission and the legitimacy of the office of superintendent. They implicitly acknowledged writing as the appropriate means to appeal decisions. In fact, they did so in direct imitation of the missionaries. Only a year previously, the missionaries had circulated a petition "signed by all the single women on staff" calling for Montgomerie to retain the previous superintendent.[73] Through petitioning, Anindilyakwa speakers, like missionaries, participated in the literate, English-speaking culture of white Australia.

Yet the CMS did not welcome these letters as evidence of progress toward Christian citizenship. Instead, the Aborigines Committee doubted their authenticity. They consulted their most experienced missionary, Harris, regarding the letters. He found it was inconceivable that Anindilyakwa people would threaten violence. This objection is questionable since Anindilyakwa people had used violence against missionaries on numerous past occasions. Harris inferred that Howell had prompted the letters: "Arthur's conduct is not Christian and is not 'cricket.'"[74]

Silencing Indigenous claims by questioning their authorship has been a common strategy of paternalistic authorities.[75] The CMS had not always discounted Aboriginal petitions. In 1934 the CMS Aborigines Committee warmly received a "~~splendidly~~ emphatically worded petition" from Aboriginal people at the Roper station calling for that mission to remain open. The role of missionaries in eliciting those signatures went unquestioned, but of course such a request is exactly what the CMS hoped Aboriginal people would make.[76] It is not clear whether or how Howell was involved in the petitions from Anindilyakwa people, but for the CMS, the question was, how could a Christian mission have produced these unorthodox and subversive letters? How could civilized writers threaten such violence? Missionaries were uncomfortable with the Anindilyakwa cultures of modernity and the literacies developing on Groote Eylandt. Though the CMS hoped to create writers, only a particular kind of writing was welcomed or expected.

REJECTING AND REPURPOSING WRITING

For Anindilyakwa speakers, the rejection of these letters, combined with the ineffectiveness of writing in other contexts, could only confirm that the English literary culture of the missionaries did not deliver the benefits it promised. When they participated as modern citizens and submitted their concerns, their writing was questioned and rejected as inauthentic. Oral communication cannot have its authorship rejected and be dismissed in this way. To some Anindilyakwa people, it could seem that learning to read and write would never be rewarded unless they fully embraced the broader culture and practices of the missionaries' literacy. Many were not willing to do so.

Subsequently, many Anindilyakwa people were ambivalent about learning to read. In 1960 the acting head teacher ran adult-education reading classes. "Those interested are small in number"; he averaged twelve pupils. The lack of interest, in his mind, was due to a lack of appropriate literature.[77] "Why learn English when there's nothing to read?" questioned the CMS in 1963. Their solution was "to produce booklets in simple English dealing with Bible topics."[78] Secular reading was scarcer still. The teachers reported that their adult Bible-reading classes included only "those who can already read, those unable to read not wishing to learn."[79] Some showed an interest but did not, or could not, conform to missionaries' expectations. Missionary Norma Farley noted that "quite a number" of Anindilyakwa people, mostly women, purchased Bible study materials, but she found in 1971 that "only very few seem to read them."[80] "Very few . . . have persevered," Farley commented the following year.[81] Despite constant missionary efforts to encourage reading, as late as the 1980s Judith Stokes complained, "Reading is still not a normal Aboriginal occupation!"[82]

Not reading could be a means of evading missionaries' influence. Those who did not read English could claim ignorance of church teaching. They could limit their participation in Christian ritual, not reading either the prayer book or the hymnbook. Whereas the missionaries posted community rules on a public noticeboard—ordering Anindilyakwa people to keep quiet at night or keep their houses clean—not reading rendered the missionary laws powerless and invalid. The missionary culture, which depended so much on the power of the letter, could be marginalized to some extent where Aboriginal people refused to read.

The missionaries did make some attempt to introduce writing in Anindilyakwa, but this attempt met with similar ambivalence. Writing in Anindilyakwa came decades after writing in English, so, for Anindilyakwa people, it was colored with the same connotations of Christian civilization as writing in English. By the late 1960s, the CMS was committed to bilingual education. Reading the Bible in one's own "heart language" was the "ultimate goal" of its linguistic work.[83] Becoming literate in Anindilyakwa, therefore, was another means to perform evangelical conversion.[84] From 1967 the CMS employed Judith Stokes as a missionary linguist at Angurugu. Despite early enthusiasm, progress soon slowed. By 1970 Stokes had only three regular pupils.[85]

She constantly asked supporters of the mission to "pray for increasing interest in learning to read."[86] For most Anindilyakwa people, this interest never developed. The bilingual education program, formally introduced in 1973, was suspended by 1976 owing to a shortage of Aboriginal teaching assistants, high staff turnover, lack of resources, and an unresolved orthographic dispute.[87] By the late 1970s, Stokes faced criticism that not a single Aboriginal person at Angurugu was fluent writing in Anindilyakwa, and only a handful had ever written in Anindilyakwa at all.[88] To Stokes, this was inexplicable. Anindilyakwa people had not followed the script. But when I asked Jabani Lalara if he wanted to learn to read Anindilyakwa, he said no: "I didn't want to learn Anindilyakwa, because I could speak Anindilyakwa."[89] It was already his language, an oral language; a missionary had no place in teaching it to him in writing.

Though many were reluctant to adopt the missionaries' literacies, Anindilyakwa people were developing their own new Anindilyakwa writing cultures, incorporating literacies into their own frameworks of knowledge. For them, oral and literate cultures did not need to be mutually exclusive. Anindilyakwa parents used the missionaries' record-keeping culture to uphold their own oral naming traditions. It is rare for Anindilyakwa people to use each other's names in conversation, especially their most important names (people have many names, some secret). Anindilyakwa names come from their clan songs.[90] Names therefore have spiritual implications, linking individuals to country, to kin, and to their songs. They carry such spiritual power that to speak them lightly is disrespectful. In some relationships, speaking each other's names is prohibited. Names of deceased people are also taboo for extended periods. Generally, Anindilyakwa people prefer to use kinship terms or nicknames. By the 1970s parents were asking missionaries to "write down the Aboriginal name" and its meaning "correctly" for their babies.[91] By recording the names, Anindilyakwa people could uphold their own oral practices around naming (or not naming), while also ensuring the names were kept safe.

Anindilyakwa writing complemented orality by providing access to the words of the old people who had passed away, but it did not replace oral systems of knowledge or authority. In 1969, when anthropologist David Turner began fieldwork on the island, Nandjiwarra Amagula asked him to "write their Bible." Anindilyakwa people were willing to use writing as an authority, if done in the right way. The "Bible" Turner produced from his research recorded various clan territories in print and, inadvertently, played into an ongoing Anindilyakwa territorial dispute. When Turner returned to the island years later, he found a man using his book to justify his claim to land, claiming that Turner had "asked the old people and wrote it down."[92] Yet this is not to say that Anindilyakwa knowledge systems were abolished with the arrival of the book. Existing methods of resolving disputes were disrupted but not overturned. According to Anindilyakwa methods of interpretation, writing was contestable. Turner noted that if his book had not suited clan interests, the remark would be simply, "What could a white man know about our ways?"[93] The book's authority came from the old people, not from the script it contained. Contrary to Goody's thesis regarding the permanence of writing and thus its effect on cognition, Anindilyakwa people here integrated literacies into their existing cultures.[94]

Even Anindilyakwa people who did not embrace the missionaries' literacy used books to convey meaning. The book as a ritual and symbolic object could communicate shared meanings. Although missionaries believed their faith and practice rested on the written word, theirs was perhaps not as entirely literate a culture as they believed. Even in literate societies, patterns of orality exist.[95] For evangelicals, the Bible was used in nonliterate symbolic ways— not as text but as object—to affirm a Christian identity. The tradition of keeping a family Bible, with names and significant dates inscribed inside, pointed to a faith in family unity and continuity within a Christian framework; it was a tangible symbol of faith in divine providence across generations.[96]

Anindilyakwa people observed how the presence of books was necessary in missionaries' ceremonial life, and they used the missionaries' own symbolic object to assert themselves and negotiate with the missionaries. Nangwarra, for example, used the Bible to reconcile himself with the missionaries in 1959. He placed his Bible between himself and the superintendent. The missionaries interpreted this symbolic gesture as Nangwarra's suggestion that "God was his witness and that he had put the trouble out of his life."[97] Though Anindilyakwa children could not read, they asked for hymnbooks at evening prayer. "In walked Simon (age 6)," wrote Farley, "and said in perfect English, 'Please may I have a paper (hymn-book)?'"[98] Farley was delighted. She also reported an old woman who treated her Bible as a sacred object. "She can't read and understands only a little English, but the Bible is very precious to her." Farley' interpreted the woman's attachment to the book as the woman's way of reminding herself "of a strong God whom she loves."[99] The old woman may have considered the book to be a powerful spiritual object. By displaying her protection of the Bible to the missionary, the old woman communicated a respect for the missionaries' spirituality using the missionaries' own oral practices and symbols, even if she did not participate in the same literary culture or mode of Christianity Farley propagated.

Occasionally the missionaries encouraged Anindilyakwa speakers to speak freely in the church, without the guidance of writing. But, to their surprise, a number of Aboriginal people rejected these moves. At the nearby CMS Roper River mission, for example, James Japanma, though nearly blind, felt it was important to hold the prayer book. The book became a prop for performing and claiming the missionaries' authority. As missionary Perce Leske remembered, "James was a very good lay preacher, knew just about everything, the prayer book off by heart. He'd put on his glasses and hold the book. It didn't matter if he'd hold the book upside down, it's just that's what you'd do, you'd hold the book."[100] Similarly, at Angurugu, Aringari Wurramara claimed he could not pray in church if the prayer was not written down; he wanted the prayer written down for him to read, just like the chaplain.[101] Seeing that missionaries used texts as a symbol of authority, Aringari did likewise. The Anindilyakwa evangelists claimed equal status to the missionaries through the use of the missionaries' own ritual symbolic objects: books. Anindilyakwa people took hold of the books' symbolic meanings, using practices associated with the book and writing to assert their own authorities to missionaries.

Aboriginal people around Australia have used writing to make claims and assert their interests and distinct identities. But in the Anindilyakwa case, sometimes this meant not writing at all. Anindilyakwa people both rejected and repurposed the missionaries' writing. Their experience reveals that not learning to read can coexist with repurposing writing for unexpected, local Indigenous purposes. For some Anindilyakwa people, who did not always accept or welcome the missionaries' agenda, learning to write could represent a concession they were not willing to make. Refusing, at times, to perform literacy according to evangelical scripts of conversion (though these also had their own usefulness at times), they continued to use books and texts in ways suited to their own priorities, without reference to the missionaries. The new Anindilyakwa literacies at Angurugu were embedded in Anindilyakwa cultures and priorities and upheld oral systems of knowledge. They confounded the missionaries' binaries—orality and literacy, pagan and Christian, traditional and modern, savage and civilized—and frustrated expectations of progression from one to the other. Anindilyakwa people used written texts in diverse, oral, and more Aboriginal ways, sometimes to subvert the very "Christian civilization" offered by missionaries.

For missionaries, English literacy was a foundation of civilization and Christian practice. Yet missionaries were uneasy with the very Anindilyakwa literacies that arose from the mission encounter. In failing to follow the missionary script, Anindilyakwa people themselves could no longer be read by the missionaries. Missionaries struggled to understand why and how Anindilyakwa people would not embrace literacy in the ways they expected. Where they did write, the growth of distinct Anindilyakwa writing practices was unsettling for missionaries; they could no longer have such faith in English literacy as the seed of Christian civilization. Literacy was out of their control.

NOTES

I am grateful to Ann McGrath and Martin Thomas, who commented on earlier drafts of this chapter. I am also indebted to the Anindilyakwa community for welcoming me to their country and allowing me to undertake research. I wish to acknowledge the support of the Northern Territory government through the Northern Territory History Grants Program of the Department of Natural Resources, Environment, the Arts and Sport. An extended version of this chapter is available in my book *Found in Translation: Many Meanings on a North Australian Mission* (Honolulu: University of Hawai'i Press, 2018).

1. Ong, *Orality and Literacy* (1982), 172.

2. Goody, *The Interface between the Written and the Oral*, 298–300.

3. See also the chapters in this volume by Keith Thor Carlson, Michael P. J. Reilly, and Bruno Saura.

4. Newell, *Literary Culture in Colonial Ghana*, 3.

5. Peterson, *Creative Writing*, 5.

6. Ballantyne, *Orientalism and Race*, 146.

7. M. Stevens, "Kāi Tahu Writing and Cross-Cultural Communication," 130–31.

8. Ballantyne, "Contesting the Empire of Paper," 219.

9. Van Toorn, *Writing Never Arrives Naked*, 13.

10. M. Morgan, *The Bearer of This Letter*, 5.

11. M. Morgan, *The Bearer of This Letter*, 11.

12. Curthoys and Mitchell, "'Bring This Paper to the Good Governor,'" 183; Reynolds, *Fate of a Free People*; Horton, "Rewriting Political History," 157–81; Attwood and Markus, *The Struggle for Aboriginal Rights*; and McGregor, "Protest and Progress," 567.

13. Shoemaker, *Black Words, White Page*, 4–5; and Ariss, "Writing Black," 132.

14. See, for example, J. Davis and Hodge, *Aboriginal Writing Today*; and Narogin, *Writing from the Fringe*.

15. Mathews, "Message-Sticks Used by the Aborigines of Australia," 288.

16. Sweeney, "An Experiment in a Mission Trading Outpost"; and Baker, "Indigenous Workers on Methodist Missions in Arnhem Land."

17. Sutton, *Dreamings*, 56.

18. Morphy, "Too Many Meanings," vii.

19. Sutton, *Dreamings*, 13.

20. Morphy, "The Art of Northern Australia," 17.

21. Riseman, "Disrupting Assimilation," 245.

22. Angurugu Journal, Northern Territory Archive Service, Darwin (hereafter NTAS), Northern Territory Record Series (hereafter NTRS) 704.

23. James Carey, *Communication as Culture*, 33.

24. Dulcie Levitt Memoirs, provided by Julie Rudder (née Waddy), n.d.

25. D. Turner, *Genesis Regained*, 12.

26. Earl Hughes to J. B. Montgomerie, 13 March 1958, Mitchell Library (hereafter ML) MSS 6040/33, Sydney.

27. Callon Moore to A. Campbell, 3 October 1968, NTAS NTRS 869, box 1.

28. Jim Taylor to Dick Harris, 28 September 1960, ML MSS 6040/33, box 28.

29. Old Jimmy, quoted in Hokari, "Cross-Culturalizing History," 96.

30. Goody, *The Interface between the Written and the Oral*, 298–99; and Newell, *Literary Culture in Colonial Ghana*, 4.

31. Bebbington, *Evangelicalism in Modern Britain*, 4.

32. Oliver Allision, "That They May Have Life," *Open Door*, May 1950.

33. "What Are You Reading," *Open Door*, April 1963.

34. James Carey, *Communication as Culture*, 15.

35. Norma Farley, "Breaking the Language Barrier," *Open Door*, July 1962.

36. Atkinson, *The Europeans in Australia*, vol. 3, *Nation*, xiii.

37. Atkinson, *The Europeans in Australia*, vol. 2, *Democracy*, 24, 157.

38. Damousi, *Colonial Voices*, 2.

39. A. Taylor, "Education for Democracy," 427.

40. R. C. Mills, 10 October 1949, National Archives of Australia (hereafter NAA) A431 1951/560, Canberra.

41. Ellemor, *Can the Aboriginal Be Assimilated?*, 11.

42. J. B. Montgomerie, "That They Might Have Life," 1958, NTAS NTRS 1105. At this stage, even if Anindilyakwa people were literate in English, they were not permitted to vote since they were wards of the state. Aboriginal people in the Northern Territory were given voting rights in 1962.

43. G. R. Harris, 5 March 1945, NTAS NTRS 1098, box 1.

44. N. Farley and J. Stokes, Groote Eylandt Mission Reports, June 1952, NTAS NTRS 1098, box 1.

45. J. Stokes and D. N. Farely, Groote Eylandt Mission School Report, July 1953, NTAS NTRS 1098, box 1.

46. Katherine Morris, *Nari and Minala Go to School*; and Katherine Morris, *Nari and Minala Go to Work*.

47. N. Farley and J. Stokes, Groote Eylandt Mission Reports, August 1952, NTAS NTRS 1098, box 1.

48. N. Farley and J. Stokes, Groote Eylandt Mission Reports, July 1952, NTAS NTRS 1098, box 1.

49. Nancy Lalara, oral history interview with author, 29 April 2012.

50. Rhoda Lalara, oral history interview with author, 23 April 2012.

51. Extract from letter from Mrs. G. R. Harris to CMS Aborigines Committee, Groote Eylandt Missions, 27 June 1945, ML MSS 6040/6.

52. N. Farley and J. Stokes, Groote Eylandt Mission Reports, July 1952.

53. N. Farley and J. Stokes, Groote Eylandt Mission Reports, August 1952.

54. R. B. Dent, Groote Eylandt Mission Builder's Report, August 1963, NTAS NTRS 1098, box 1.

55. R. B. Dent, Angurugu Groote Eylandt Building Report, October 1965, NTAS NTRS 1098, box 2.

56. N. Farley, Supplement to Chaplain's Report, January 1972, NTRS 1098, box 2.

57. Angurugu Journal, 22 May 1973, NTAS NTRS 704, box 3.

58. Ben Moore, Chaplain's Report, October 1963, NTAS NTRS 1098, box 1.

59. Rosemary S. O'Donnell, "The Value of Autonomy," 96.

60. "My Story by Djabani," *Anindilyaugwa Agarragarra*, February 1961, Australian Institute of Aboriginal and Torre Strait Island Studies (hereafter AIATSIS) MS 3518, box 2, folder 9.

61. Austin-Broos, "The Meaning of Pepe," 311.

62. Nancy Lalara, oral history interview with author, 28 April 2012.

63. On "sinful" letter writing, see also Keith Thor Carlson in this volume.

64. Angurugu Superintendent Diary, 1 February 1961, NTAS NTRS 704, CMS, box 1.

65. E. Lawry, Re Gagima—Groote Island, n.d., NAA E460 1979/635.

66. H. C. Giese to J. Taylor, 23 October 1961, NAA E460 1979/635.

67. Galima to Kevin Gaŋgulena, 26 August 1961, NAA E460 1979/635.

68. Nandjiwara Amagula, Aboriginal Welfare Officer's Report, October 1965, NTAS NTRS 1098, box 2.

69. Van Toorn, *Writing Never Arrives Naked*, 135.

70. Perhaps most famous are the Aboriginal petitions from Coranderrk Mission in the 1870s and from the Cummeragunja Reserve in the 1930s. See also Grimshaw, Nelson, and Smith, *Letters from Aboriginal Women in Victoria, 1867–1926*.

71. All the people at Groote Eylandt to J. B. Montgomerie, n.d., ML MSS 6040/33.

72. De Costa, "Identity, Authority, and the Moral Worlds of Indigenous Petitions," 670.

73. Arthur Howell to J. B. Montgomerie, 14 August 1959, ML MSS 6040/33, box 28; and Aborigines Committee Minutes, 10 September 1959, ML MSS 6040/5.

74. G. R. Harris to J. B. Montgomerie, 3 November 1960, ML MSS 6040/33, box 28.

75. Belmessous, "Introduction," 7; and de Costa, "Identity, Authority, and the Moral Worlds of Indigenous Petitions," 680.

76. Roper River Mission Report, February 1934, ML MSS 6040/7.

77. L. D. Fry, CMS Groote Eylandt Mission School Report, November 1960, NTAS NTRS 1098, box 1.

78. "Literature in Simple English," *Open Door*, October 1963.

79. N. Farley and J. Stokes, Groote Eylandt Mission Reports, July 1952.

80. N. Farley, Angurugu Groote Eylandt November 1971 Supplement to Chaplain's Report, NTAS NTRS 1098, box 2.

81. N. Farley, Angurugu Groote Eylandt November 1972 Supplement to Chaplain's Report, NTAS NTRS 1098, box 2.

82. Judith Stokes, "Prayer Letter," January 1986, ML MSS 6040/94.

83. Church Missionary Society Linguists' Conference Groote Eylandt, 7–10 April 1970, NTAS NTRS 1106, box 1.

84. Rademaker, "'Only Cuppa Tea Christians,'" 228–42.

85. Judith Stokes, Angurugu Groote Eylandt Linguistic Report, August 1970, NTAS NTRS 1098, box 2.

86. Judith Stokes, Angurugu Groote Eylandt Linguistic Report, August 1969, NTAS NTRS 1098, box 2.

87. Judith Stokes, "Prayer Circular," April 1976, ML MSS 6040/203.

88. Velma J. Leeding to Judith Stokes, 23 May 1978, AIATSIS MS 3518, box 3, folder 9.

89. Jabani Lalara, oral history interview with author, 15 June 2012.

90. D. Turner, *Return to Eden*, 49.

91. Rhoda Lalara, oral history interview with author, 23 April 2012; and "Linguistic Duties Angurugu," June 1978, AIATSIS MS 3518, box 4, folder 17b.

92. D. Turner, *Return to Eden*, 137.

93. D. Turner, *Return to Eden*, 21.

94. Goody, *The Interface between the Written and the Oral*, 298–99.

95. Atkinson, *The Commonwealth of Speech*, xii.

96. Lyons and Taksa, *Australian Readers Remember*, 30.

97. J. B. Montgomerie to John Mercer, 21 January 1959, NTAS NTRS 868, box 10.

98. Ben Moore, Umbakumba Mission Chaplaincy Report, June 1965, NTAS NTRS 873, box 28.

99. Norma Farley, "Prayer Letter," July 1979, ML MSS 6040/176.

100. Perce Leske, oral history interview with author, 10 December 2011.

101. Transcript of interview with Lois Reid, 30 April 1975, CMS South Australia Office, Adelaide, box 42.

CHAPTER NINE

"Read It, Don't Smoke It!":
Developing and Maintaining
Literacy in Papua New Guinea

EVELYN ELLERMAN

IN 1962, the *New Guinea Times Courier* at Lae began to publish a supplement in Tok Pisin for a Melanesian audience. Called *Nu Gini Toktok* (New Guinea talk), this one-page supplement was edited by Muttu Gware, the first Melanesian to edit a commercial newspaper in the colony. It was one of a number of pidgin-language publications, most of them short-lived, that appeared during the decolonizing years before self-government (1973) and independence (1975) in the colonies of Papua and New Guinea.[1]

Nu Gini Toktok was often casually referred to as the most smoked newspaper in the world.[2] The joke about a newspaper that people would rather smoke than read was not made in isolation. In 1970 the newly established *Bougainville Nius* (Bougainville news) included this admonition on its front page:

> Dispela niuspepa emi ni bilong smok na tu emi ni bilong rabim as. Taim yu pinis long ritim yu putim gut na bihain bai yu inap long ritim gen.

> The newspaper is not to roll cigarettes with, nor is it for wiping your ass. When you have read it, put it away and later you can read it again.[3]

So, in 1970, when Father Frank Mihalic inaugurated the weekly Tok Pisin newspaper *Wantok*, he is said to have commented:

One of the things we are going to have to settle before we even start printing is the smokeability of the paper we are using. That will help to sell papers. People here have the custom of rolling their home-grown tobacco into cigarettes with newsprint. They don't like the usual thin tissue paper for roll-your-owns. It burns too fast. They like newsprint—but not every kind—it must burn a certain way and produce a white ash. So we are experimenting among our staff with various samples from the paper manufacturers. We want to make sure that we have the best smoking paper in the country. Then we can advertise it that way. And we'll have to print a warning on the front page stating: PLEASE READ THIS PAPER BEFORE YOU SMOKE IT.[4]

How was it that the technologies of literacy were so opaque to potential readers in the colonies of Papua and New Guinea in the 1960s and 1970s that such statements were a necessary part of publishing a newspaper? What involvement did missionaries have in the attempted transfer of Western-style literacy to Papua New Guinea (PNG), and why, in the 1960s and 1970s, were those same missionaries suddenly so intent on publishing secular material that Melanesians would read? Why was the indigenous reaction to these efforts so tentative, one might even say indifferent? Among the general public in PNG there seems to have been a failed transfer of values with respect to print literacy skills—people would rather smoke the newspaper than read it. But, more interestingly, there developed a range of compensatory literacy skills and activities, including the enthusiastic adoption of radio as a means of consuming literature.

In this chapter, I explore the multilingual, multimodal response to the introduction by missionaries of foreign literacy technologies and practices to the peoples of PNG.[5] My investigation is guided by the possibilities offered in theoretical frameworks located in two different disciplines: the literacy sponsorship concepts developed by Deborah Brandt (1998) and the Diffusion of Innovation model first proposed in 1962 by Everett M. Rogers for the field of communication studies.[6]

Literacy sponsors are the people and organizations who, for a variety of reasons, have tried to promote literacy in specific contexts. Brandt is interested in whether and how sponsors provide access to media-rich, information-rich environments and for whom. In doing so, Brandt examines the sponsor's role in creating and then bridging the gap between older and newer standards of literacy. As part of the sponsorship process, Brandt then looks at the intentional misappropriation of literacy resources by the sponsored for the purposes of self-interest or self-development.

Rogers proposes a typology of adopters for ideas and technologies that is tied to their reactions to innovation, which in turn is linked to their perception of the benefits that might accrue from adoption. His model is more suggestive than prescriptive for this chapter, since he ignores degrees of adaptation or rejection as possible responses. Nevertheless, a wider range of responses to literacy as a sociocultural innovation could easily be patterned on Rogers's original acceptance model. Each of these approaches moves us past simple questions of whether skills and ideas have been transferred or not, of whether people are literate or illiterate, to a more nuanced discussion of context and process where we can ask what people are doing with literacy and why. Together, these two frameworks could assist us in understanding the interactions between sponsor and target in attempts to transfer certain European-based social practices to colonial settings.

The chapter focuses on two things. First, it discusses the sponsorship efforts of Protestant and Catholic missionaries to introduce literacy, not just for functional purposes connected with religious practice, or for employment and the writing of letters, but for the sociocultural purposes of intellectual growth and personal and social empowerment. Second, the chapter addresses the reactions of the general public to this sponsorship. In doing so, it describes an incomplete process in which literacy programs were established, evolved, and then persisted or failed. But, mostly, it documents a region and a time in which few literacy programs succeeded as planned.

The specific context of PNG is crucial for understanding literacy development there.[7] Whereas literacy schemes had been in place in some British colonies in the interwar years and in many others in the 1950s, literacy campaigns were basically unheard of in PNG as late as the mid-1960s, ten years before independence. Indeed, colonization itself was relatively new to most people living in PNG. Although coastal peoples had had regular contact with missionaries since the nineteenth century, the bulk of the population lived in the New Guinea Highlands, where their first contact with Europeans had been during the 1930s. Given the disruptions of World War II, this meant that few islanders had experience with Western technologies of any sort, let alone the technologies of writing and reading, in the years leading up to independence.

Formal schooling in PNG was largely in the hands of underfunded missionaries, few of whom were trained to Australian teaching standards. What is more, their first educational aim was sociocultural: to promote Christianity. A secondary, functional, aim arose between the world wars when the colonial administration needed indigenous literates who could work as clerks and assistants in the colonial service.[8] But it was not until the early 1960s that the first three high schools were established. Afterward, during a period of frenetic decolonization from the mid-1960s to the mid-1970s, missionaries hoped to produce graduates who would then train in such professional fields as law, journalism, medicine, and education.[9] Even so, in pursuing these laudable if unrealistic goals, missionaries were conflicted: they preferred primary education to be in a vernacular, while government service and professional occupations required literacy in English.

The difficulty in choosing a language of primary instruction was further complicated by the linguistic density of the two colonies. In total, PNG has over eight hundred, or about 12 percent, of the world's languages. Because of its mountainous terrain, most of these languages have fewer than a thousand speakers.[10] Early in the establishment of formal schooling, there were no commercially available vernacular teaching materials; these had to be invented by missionary teachers on the spot. In addition to the wealth of vernaculars, two pidgin languages were widely used orally: Hiri Motu in Papua and Tok Pisin in New Guinea. Nevertheless, missionaries were loath to use such nonindigenous trade languages for instruction. Missions wanted literates who could read the Bible in their own language. Melanesian children in primary schools were therefore taught either in vernaculars or in English, depending on the era and source of their schooling. The very few who could find a place in high school were taught in English at that level.

Adult Melanesians who wanted to read had choices to make. During decolonization, English was the only language that could lead to success in a Western profession. But for the bulk of the population, reading and writing in English was of little importance. Kevin Walcot, editor of *Wantok*, once remarked that learning to read English meant that you could read the income tax form, and who would ever want to do *that!*[11] Most Melanesians, then, might be exposed to English in elementary school but were at best functionally literate in that language after leaving school. Walcot writes that English was used for "talking with foreigners and for formal and administrative matters"; people might purchase an English-language newspaper that they could barely read for prestige value or for reading the daily news.[12] For those people who had received their primary education in *plestok* (vernaculars) and received no further schooling, reading materials for maintaining literacy were generally restricted to a grammar, a dictionary, church-related publications, and translations of religious texts. In other words, most people lost whatever literacy they had achieved soon after leaving school, because there was no perceived need to be able to read and very little material to read in their own language should they wish to.

The two pidgin languages were used informally in colonial administration. Missions did not use pidgins in the schools; however, they used Tok Pisin widely and informally as a means of communication on the mission stations. Tok Pisin had the advantage over Hiri Motu in having been standardized by Father Mihalic with a dictionary and grammar. This enabled its use in a number of church newsletters, secular newspapers, and government publications.[13] Mihalic's efforts to promote this lingua franca were bolstered by the 1969 Bible Society translation of the New Testament into Tok Pisin, which he described as a best seller, with over 400,000 sold by the mid-1980s. He wrote that its "wide dissemination has greatly influenced the acceptance of standard Tok Pisin spelling."[14]

The colonial administration's clear preference was for English. But in the absence of any official national language, Tok Pisin was the most likely choice for literacy among most Melanesians. In the 1971 census, 43 percent of the population claimed to speak the language, while 20 percent spoke English and only 9 percent Hiri Motu. The literacy rates of 1971 confirm these figures. Nearly 19 percent of the population over the age of ten was literate in Tok Pisin, 17 percent in English, 4 percent in Hiri Motu, and 13 percent in other languages.[15] The school enrollment figures and completion rates were abysmal. In 1975, the year PNG achieved independence, only half of all children aged seven to twelve were in school, and only five out of a hundred were expected to complete high school.[16]

This meant that a majority of the population in PNG was illiterate on the eve of independence even though both the colonial administration and the missions saw literacy as crucial to national development and the development of an informed electorate. The question was how to bring literacy up to acceptable levels. By the 1960s and 1970s, the colonial administration had finally attempted to exert more control over the education system by funding only those mission schools that met Australian standards. Since the secondary system was almost nonexistent, the administration decided to provide scholarships for indigenous students to study in Australia. By 1961 only seventy-six students were receiving the scholarships; these young people were meant to serve leadership roles in the new nation, which they did.[17] Unfortunately, there were just so *few* of them. The adult electorate was another matter. The administration had no viable plan for mass literacy. So the missions assumed advocacy, beginning what was to become a decades-long campaign to raise adult literacy rates in PNG. But what kind of literacy did the missions aim for? How did they approach adults who could see little use in learning to read and write? And what was the reaction?

THE PROTESTANTS AND LITERACY

In 1990, the International Literacy Year, Dennis Malone, a literacy consultant for the Summer Institute of Linguistics (SIL) who was seconded to PNG's Department of Education, defined literacy as the "skills that give people the ability to read and write a language that they speak and understand."[18] In addition to this well-established notion of literacy, Malone emphasized a newer idea that literacy should be extended to most people, not just a privileged few. Malone's approach to literacy is necessarily general, but the decolonizing climate of the 1960s and 1970s in PNG required further refinement.[19] Aside from tricky questions about language, equal access, funding, and support, literacy in PNG and many other colonies was marketed to colonized peoples as an instrumental accomplishment. Its technologies allowed people access to information and education that would make their lives better. Many early SIL publications for Melanesians, for instance, focused on practical matters like how to grow better gardens and how to write a letter. Even the mission sphere's first two literary journals of the early 1970s, *Nobonob Nius* (Nobonob news) and *TokSave* (Information), shared this masthead: "Rit Moa na Save Planti" ("Read More and Learn a Lot").[20]

Although much of the content of mission publications from this period can be characterized as one-way communication intended to inform and educate, there was a serious effort on the part of expatriate editors to encourage Melanesians to write creatively, share traditional stories, send letters to the editor, or contribute to the news. Writing was often framed as a duty. For instance, the highest functioning of the indigenous mission writers of this era—teachers, church workers, journalists—were asked to write for their people in the inaugural issue of *Precept* (1972), the literary journal established for the Christian Writers Association of Melanesia (CWAMEL). In the journal's opening article, the editor, Glen Bays, compared Helen Keller's experience of learning to read and write to that of indigenous people learning through print about the world around them:

> How are you going to awaken people, to make them want to live and be happy and be joyful? One of the best ways is for them to read a lot about themselves.
>
> Where DO adults—and where do the children in school—get the material they read today? Where does it come from? Overseas mostly. They read nothing—or very, very little—written by Papua New Guineans. . . . Your children reading books by foreigners have never known what that foreign person is writing about. So the children are living in a world where there's no light and where they can't hear anything.
>
> THEREFORE WRITERS in this country have got to get busy so that they produce something in languages used here. So that's why we need to learn about creative writing.[21]

As a means of coping with the substantial demands of establishing mass literacy in a short period of time for hundreds of preliterate cultural groups, missions established a series of institutions and programs that were intended to be as open and welcoming as possible. The most organized of these was the SIL, which had come to New Guinea in 1956 and remains in PNG to this day.[22] Since the two colonies could never claim more than a 50 percent participation rate in primary school, the main targets of the SIL's literacy programs have been adults and teenagers. The SIL mounted a continuous appeal to the colonial administration and then the independent government of PNG to include indigenous content in the curriculum and vernacular languages in instruction.

Originally formed in the United States in 1934, the SIL (and its associated agency, the Wycliffe Bible Translators) is a Christian change agency whose goals are to permeate a culture without destroying it. Members of the Wycliffe Bible Translators and of the SIL are at pains to encourage indigenous peoples to retain aspects of their original culture like musical forms and folklore, to write their own words to Christian songs, and, above all, to retain their own language.[23] The SIL's members are trained linguists and cultural anthropologists. Their production of language resources like grammars, dictionaries, and functional literacy texts is impressive. Charles Dominic Lynch indicates that, of the mission organizations in PNG, the SIL has been the most successful in producing the largest number of nonreligious literacy texts. In 1977, of the eighteen languages that had ten or more publications, nine were from the Eastern Highlands Province where the SIL is based. However, after quoting these figures, Lynch then castigates the SIL and other missionary organizations for dereliction in their duty to provide *interesting* secular literacy materials. In Lynch's opinion, "How the Jews Lived," "Houses of the World," "Stone Age Men in Britain," and "Flies Are Your Enemy" do not constitute a "body of literature."[24]

To be fair to the SIL, it was quite vigorous in eliciting folklore, short stories, and poetry from its burgeoning writers. In addition, Lynch, a newcomer to the colony, may not have known that the SIL supported the annual literature competitions run by the administration's Literature Bureau, especially the categories for writing in Tok Pisin.[25] It also actively promoted writers' workshops, whether initiated from within or outside the Christian community. What is more, it supported demands from CWAMEL, the Christian writers' union, for copyright legislation.[26] On the other hand, the list that Lynch presents is actually quite typical of the informational and educational material supplied under the category of "General Literature" by missions throughout Africa and the South Pacific at this time.[27]

Lynch's figures were synthesized from a 1975 survey conducted by the SIL in cooperation with the Educational Research Unit of the University of Papua New Guinea (UPNG). The author of the SIL report on the survey, Joice Franklin, states that although the government's Adult Education Department "has been experimenting with literacy programmes in some areas ... literacy programmes for unschooled adults and teenagers have largely been the responsibility of missions and SIL."[28] In 1975 Franklin could report that the SIL was producing literacy materials in over forty languages, half of which had never had print materials before. By 1988, when the decolonizing frenzy had cooled down, the SIL was still active but at a more measured rate, producing eighty-one titles that year in twenty-nine languages.[29]

Once the SIL linguists understood each vernacular well enough, they prepared literacy materials, primers, and readers. They actively promoted vernacular literacy classes and began to train indigenous teachers. The fundamental principle behind this highly organized and extremely effective sector of colonial subculture was that language and culture were considered indivisible.[30] "Although it is desirable for indigenous peoples here and elsewhere to speak, read and write the national language of their country, long experience has shown that the most effective means of communication with any people is through their native tongue."[31]

Once the structures were in place for SIL workers to promote literacy in local communities, the SIL embarked on a much more ambitious program. Materials for literacy were produced at an increasing pace after 1965 and took another surge forward after 1973.[32] In the mid-1970s, the SIL conducted a series of vernacular literacy seminars for staff and students at the UPNG and at several teacher colleges.[33] Beginning in 1983, the SIL began to hold National Literacy courses at its headquarters at Ukarumpa. The idea was to work for eight weeks with Melanesians, who would return to their own villages to continue literacy classes there.

It seems ludicrous to say that the SIL viewed writing as a means not only to translation but also to the reintroduction of coherence in oral cultures damaged by contact with Europeans. And from one point of view it was ludicrous. How, we might ask, was more interference in the form of a foreign technology going to correct the problems that the technology created in the first place? But, from an SIL view, writing was now a permanent feature of indigenous daily life. The sooner that all people had access to it, the more equal and fair daily life would become. Therefore, the SIL could state that literacy "helps the older people to respect the literate, who are usually the youth. The literates' knowledge of how to communicate with people outside the village and how to trade develops this respect. As culture preservation becomes increasingly emphasized, the educated can also write and record the traditions of the people for future generations."[34]

The SIL's workers understood why some people in PNG wished to become literate. Franklin's 1975 survey indicated that adults mostly wanted to be able to read and write personal letters. Other reasons were "to get better jobs, to run businesses, to gain prestige, to read the Bible, and to read news. In Papuan areas another frequent reason given was to keep up with the children."[35] These practical desires on the part of the illiterate generated much of the "how-to " secular texts that Lynch denigrated. For instance, Roy Gwyther-Jones, an SIL missionary, produced a number of pamphlets in the 1970s telling people how to write letters and how to make use of the postal service.[36]

The campaign in the SIL's literacy publication, READ: The Adult Literacy and Literature Magazine, was relentless. Ann Cates, in a January 1975 article, asked "Why Teach First in the Vernacular?" The answer was that literacy is easier to obtain when the language of literacy is the same as that in which the student "verbalizes all reality."[37] If books speak to the students in their own language, then the value of literacy is solidly embedded in their minds. Cates added that as experience in Vietnam's Highlander Education Project had demonstrated, the school dropout rate (a persistent problem in PNG) had been greatly reduced because of vernacular literacy. In that same issue of READ, C. Collins actually provided a manual for teaching the vernacular. It offered step-by-step instructions for teachers who wished to subvert the national education system's preference for English-language instruction by expanding the use of vernaculars in the classroom. There is even a section on how to involve parents and community members in this subterfuge.

From its inception in 1966, READ has provided an engrossing diary of the concerted attempts by SIL members in their fight for literacy. What is clear from the journal is that the editors see the literacy campaign in part as the sort of program the government should have adopted but had not.[38] In a special issue of READ in 1976, entitled "Providing Literature for New Literates," the editor says, "In most developing countries one aspect of development is a national literature which is written not just for the people but by the people of that developing country. The opportunity to write for one's own people should not be the privilege of an educated elite only."[39] It is quite clear from this editorial, and from the magazine as a whole, that READ saw itself as an advocate for *all* people in PNG, an organ of true democracy through mass literacy.

The SIL members also used READ as a vehicle for information sharing among themselves. Articles abound on how to set up and maintain all aspects of print production and consumption. A list of titles from the retrospective special issue of 1976 gives a clear indication of the scope of these concerns:

- What Is a New Reader
- How to Write for Inexperienced Readers
- First Writers Training at Nobonob
- Who Shall Write for New Guineans
- Writers and Readers for Papua New Guinea
- Indigenous Writers in the Making
- Purposes and Problems in Producing Periodicals
- Training National Editors
- A Book Market for New Guineans

Contributors to READ were also concerned with matters of creating a written style in languages where writing had never before existed.[40]

But more than any other problem, contributors puzzled over how to keep new literates reading. In a perceptive article from 1974, Helen Marten reviewed attempts that had been made by SIL members to produce materials interesting enough to keep literates literate. Her observations were that "helpful" literature like *How to Grow Good Coffee* and natural-history books like *Animals of the Bible* were "not bad" as a beginning but needed to be supplemented with books written by indigenous people on subjects that interested *them*. She recommended change agents closely observe Melanesians to see what kind of story, subject matter, and illustrations they reacted to best. *Kovave*, the UPNG literary journal established by Ulli Beier, and the Literature Bureau's *New Guinea Writing* were specially mentioned as good examples of indigenous writing.[41]

Marten was careful to note that literature "for new literates should include some fiction so that they don't think that everything in print is true."[42] For fiction sources she suggested folklore unless it might be equated with scripture or even come into conflict with it. Other dangers of using folklore might be that it contained content that natives themselves considered immoral (i.e., stories they might tell orally but would not like to see in print), competitions between villages over the "true" version of a given story, and copyright problems over previously translated and published versions of the stories. Marten also felt that "failure" stories should be included since "life is not all success."[43]

In sum, her article demonstrates a keen awareness of the issues involved in producing reading material for people of other cultures. Furthermore, it demonstrates an active willingness to search beyond the world of the Christian church for resource material for her purposes. But at the same time, her article contains the assumption that the material absorbed into the mission system must be filtered through Christian ideas. Marten's article ends with comments on the efficacy of writing courses. The short courses were not producing writers. She pointed to African experience where concentrated time spent with individual students over a long period had been more productive. She concluded that the literacy program was now at the stage where developing a "tribal literature" should be a major goal.[44] Her conclusion went unheeded.

Marten made a habit of posing uncomfortable questions. In a 1969 READ article entitled "Literacy for Those Who Don't Want It," she asked, "Do you have any ideas of how to get people to do what they don't seem to want to do?"—that is, read.[45] She reported that members of the Yessan-Mayo tribe, to whom she had been trying to introduce literacy classes for *five* years, just were not interested. After only thirty years of contact with Europeans, these nine hundred people living in seven villages much as they had always lived just did not see the point. Marten's question went unanswered by her colleagues in READ magazine.

THE CATHOLICS AND LITERACY

If the main Protestant efforts in aid of literacy can be demonstrated by the aims and practices of the SIL, advocacy on the part of the Catholic Church can be examined through the work of Father Frank Mihalic and *Wantok*. It was through the establishment of this newspaper, along with the relentless campaigning of missionaries, that Tok Pisin became a viable instrument for literacy among the general public. The Society of the Divine Word, the chief Roman Catholic mission organization in former New Guinea, established the fortnightly (and then weekly) Tok Pisin newspaper *Wantok* on 5 August 1970 in Wewak.[46] The Catholics had always championed pidgin over the vernaculars, primarily because their operations were so strong in New Guinea, where Tok Pisin was prevalent.[47] The aim of *Wantok* was not religious, but the paper operated with a Christian philosophy. Its particular goal, in which the paper was successful, was to create "a forum for the Pisin writer."[48] Pidgin translations of legends have been part of its Melanesian identity-building program. By 1986 *Wantok* had published over six hundred ancestral stories, and its editor was receiving over a hundred letters each week. Over the years its weekly format has included poems, the *Kaunsila Traim* comic strip, "Stori Tumbuna" (a folklore feature), and the all-important letters-to-the-editor section that serves as the heart of PNG newspapers. Indeed, letters to the editor have been just as popular in PNG's literary journals; the whole phenomenon remains a fertile, if unstudied, area.[49]

After five years, Mihalic turned the editorship of *Wantok* over to Kevin Walcot. With his arrival, the paper was moved to Port Moresby, where it could take advantage of cheaper air freight, reach a wider public, attract the services of trained journalists, and be closer to the sources of national news. *Wantok*, which is still publishing, has been very successful. In 1984 its weekly sales were at fifteen thousand, with an eight-to-one ratio for readership (i.e., 120,000 people "read" it each week).[50] By 1986, Mihalic gave the figures as twenty thousand copies (and 160,000 readers) with the entire newspaper operation indigenized.[51] Renée Heyum, in her survey of PNG publishing, stated that during the period of decolonization, *Wantok* was the best source of information in PNG.[52] And certainly *Wantok* writers have produced more Tok Pisin copy than any other source in the country.

Wantok was a useful tool for the decolonizing manufacture of the nation-state. During the 1970s it regularly carried features on how to deal with money, the postal service, voting, and so on. It introduced the newly coined pidgin words for parliamentary procedure (*mosen, sekenim mosen, muvin mosen, votim mosen*; motion, seconding the motion, moving the motion, voting on the motion) and gave wide coverage of the run-up to independence.[53] *Wantok* was published by Word Publishing, which extended its range to the well-received youth magazine *New Nation* (written in controlled English with a limited word stock and syntax), the *Times of Papua New Guinea* (the only nationally owned weekly in English), and then WEB Books (Word Educational Books).

In his development of *Wantok* and then Word Publishing, Walcot took a pioneering approach. He decided that the more services the organization could supply for itself, the more viable it would be. This was confirmed to him when he looked at the printing costs for *Wantok*. When Word began to consider publishing the English-language paper, the *Times of Papua New Guinea*, Walcot went to Misereor, the German Catholic bishops' agency for development, and obtained the money to buy a press. Once Word owned a press, Walcot realized he needed to keep it busy. This resulted in a third newspaper venture, the commercial printing of *Niugini Nius* (New Guinea news).[54] With its outside funding, Word was able to subsidize those ventures that did not make money.

If *Wantok* and the other publishing ventures of Word Publishing were successful, why did Tok Pisin not garner more readers?[55] Although there were over one million speakers of Tok Pisin in 1984 and although the language was spoken daily in eighteen of the country's twenty provinces, PNG still had one of the lowest literacy rates in the world. Walcot's observations about language use are important to follow. In the first place, literacy was not a priority for most people. PNG was still primarily an oral culture where reading was considered antisocial and useless. What is more, agricultural workers, miners, and many businessmen could make very good money even though they were illiterate, so their individual motivation to read was low. Add to this the high number of "literate" elementary school leavers who could obtain no work, and the white man's literacy had very little currency.

Walcot also observed that islanders used a variety of languages for a variety of purposes: Tok Ples when talking to *wantoks*, English for talking to foreigners or for formal/administrative matters, and Tok Pisin out of the classroom, on the telephone to friends, for sports or for fun, on the bus, and on the police radio. He noted that his own readers bought *Wantok* for sports and the letters.[56] His observations confirmed those of Elton Brash, who claimed that multilingualism was both normal and unremarkable for Melanesians. Brash wrote that in PNG most people moved easily among their own vernacular, church languages, and Hiri Motu or Tok Pisin. Two-language conversations were common with or without an interpreter. Brash's conclusion regarding "the language issue" in PNG was that it became an issue only once the European notion of the nation-state was introduced. By and large, most islanders continued to do what they had always done—use several languages to suit their practical daily purposes.[57]

From the SIL working with new literates in vernaculars, to the Catholic Church producing a popular newspaper in Tok Pisin, to the establishment of the Creative Training Centre (CTC) in 1970 for training journalists, the missions tried to cover a wide range of literacy levels and types during decolonization and in the early years of independence. The CTC represented an attempt on the part of several mission agencies to coordinate their efforts to train writers of vernacular and Tok Pisin texts through short workshops.[58] One of the greatest difficulties for these trainers was time: none of them could devote enough of it to the task. Their solution was to hire a full-time trainer. The CTC was an ecumenical operation; before independence, churches in PNG had united in a number of such joint ventures. In this case representatives of the SIL, the predominantly Lutheran publishing house, Kristen Pres, the Evangelical Alliance, and the United Church had contacted the Agency for Christian Literature and Development of the World Council of Churches requesting a survey into the possibility of establishing a fully developed program for indigenous writers. The agency sent Dr. Charles Richards, who had started the East Africa Literature Bureau, and Doris Hess of the Methodist Mission Board. Their report recommended the establishment of the training centre on a full-time basis, using Kristen Pres as its publishing outlet. Funding was to be supplied by the Christian Literature Fund of the World Council.

With this cooperation and financial support, the missions were able to recruit and hire Glen Bays, who was then serving as the director of the African Literature Centre at Kitwe in Zambia, to serve as the first director of a new institution, the CTC at Madang. Through trial and error, Bays adapted his African experience to the PNG context. His students were high-functioning literates—teacher trainees, high school students, and employees of the mission presses. He began instruction in English but soon realized the necessity for instruction in pidgin, learned the language, and used it afterward.

Using a variety of writing models—from Africa (e.g., Kenneth Kaunda) and from Western writers (e.g., Leo Tolstoy), samples of folklore from around the world, and well-established writing handbooks (e.g., William Strunk and E. B. White's *Elements of Style*)—Bays set about trying to develop professional writers.[59] He felt that students were developing their own PNG style of writing, something he described as "rambling, folksy," with "feelings mixed with facts." Instead of imposing his African-based model on them, he decided to let them be themselves and do their best, but most of all he encouraged them to keep writing. Bays felt that what Melanesians needed most was encouragement, to feel good about who they were and what they were doing.

Bays's courses were very popular. Although the first course attracted only six people, soon requests were coming in regularly, and in the first year and a half, he taught over 120 people. Many of those students then went into careers in national journalism and radio, or with the government as well as with church organizations. He was particularly proud that many women attended the courses. The churches apparently were more willing to send women, whom they considered more competitive than the men. After the course ended, they would return to write at home or for their churches, or they would carry on in the same careers as the men. Students mostly wrote legends and folktales for Bays's workshops.

The PNG model that eventually developed out of Bays's writing courses was adopted by SIL workers, whose indigenous writers had much lower levels of literacy than Bays's students. The SIL complemented Bays's work with teachers by offering a series of two-week-long annual National Writers Courses at Ukarumpa. The first of these was held in September 1972, comprising men who were language informants for trainers. "The only conditions for entry were oral fluency in Melanesian Pidgin and the ability to read and write in a vernacular language." Bays's method of using field trips to provide subject matter for creative stories was used in these courses, as well as the discussions and rewrites. Style was never a concern in these workshops. The SIL missionary Roy Gwyther-Jones felt a vernacular style would develop naturally and could not be taught by a foreigner. The students were simply to write as they would speak. [60]

Bays had three tours of duty in PNG. From 1970 to 1973, he had not only established the CTC but also helped his students to form a writers' union (CWAMEL) and writers' clubs for union members. The writers' union operated as a sort of Christian literature bureau: it published *Precept*, a "journal containing articles of help and encouragement to writers, maintain[ed] a manuscript counselling and placement service, and help[ed] in getting educational materials to those studying writing methods at home." The organization was to be ecumenical and open to anyone who "writes, edits or translates religious matter for print, broadcasting or film."[61]

Precept was written in English and first appeared in May 1972. Bays presided over its first issue before returning to the United States, but after his departure, the United Church took it over, along with its sister Tok Pisin publication *Singaut Strong* (first issued 1 November 1972). *Precept* assumed most of its audience were beginners and rural teachers who would encourage writing among their students. It urged them to obtain the best writing possible as models: "not cheap, exciting-but-worthless romance, cowboy or war stories. Get outstanding literature. Write to librarians—at your college, the university, the Public Library in the capital city. Ask them to list the 50 or so best short novels, biographies, histories and travel books from the libraries."[62]

The pages of *Precept* were filled with confessional literature and parables, exempla, and patriotic poetry. Yet the journal encouraged translators to write myths and legends, as well as collect them from their students. For publication possibilities they were encouraged to contact the Education Department, the Department of Information and Education Services, or the Literature Bureau.

Clearly the attempt in *Precept*, as in the SIL courses, was to assist Melanesians to reach beyond Christian ideology in their creative writing. The chief means of doing this was intended to be through indigenous oral culture. Not surprisingly, these newly literate authors, for whom the whole process must have been fraught with paradox, seldom produced texts that emulated the "high" literature of the West.[63] Nevertheless, when Marjorie Crocombe edited the special PNG issue of "Mana" in *Pacific Islands Monthly* (1973), she included work by Bays's students.[64]

In addition to shaping the template for short writers' courses in the mission sphere and establishing a writers' association/literature bureau clearinghouse, Bays published several anthologies gathered from individual workshops. One example is *New Voices*, a Tok Pisin/English collection of about fourteen, legal-sized, mimeographed pages.[65] Publishing these inexpensive local anthologies, usually run off at the school or college where the workshop had taken place, was another practice he had found successful in Africa. Authors saw immediate results for their labor. Copies of the anthology were immediately available to use as teaching materials. Teachers and students gained prestige in the community through these results-oriented practical demonstrations of appropriate technology. And they were easily continued by teaching staff once the expatriate change agent had gone.

Bays also established a number of periodicals devoted to writing. *Nobonob Nius*, a precursor to *Precept*, dates from his 1970–73 tour at the CTC. Its readers were previous course participants, and occasionally one of the students would edit it. The content of *Nobonob Nius* included poems, plays, short stories, and essays, mostly in English with the odd one in Tok Pisin. Issue 2 (1971) consisted of letters from former participants. Most indicated that they were not only writing but also submitting manuscripts to Kristen

Pres, Kristen Pres's literature competitions, the Literature Bureau's literature competitions, local drama festivals, and the like. Many had also started publications in their own areas. In issue 4 (1971), Bays was able to announce that two former students, Joseph Nidue and Paul Kavon, were the first- and second-place winners in Kristen Pres's drama competitions. Nidue also won a special prize for his pidgin play in the 1971 Literature Bureau Competition, and A. K. Waim (who worked for Kristen Pres) won a commendation from the Literature Bureau for a play entered in the same contest.

However, not all was well at the CTC. Members of the board of Kristen Pres felt that the writing produced by Bays's students was not Christian enough. Bays countered that he was meant to be training good writers, not good *Christian* writers. The board responded by refusing to issue him the money he required for high-quality publications, which forced him to use Gestetner machines as a low-cost alternative to publish his journals. Bays pressed the issue with the board, but they would not budge. There was nothing for it but to leave, and when Bays left the colony, the World Council of Churches money left with him. Many people in the mission sphere were at a loss as to how to recover from the failure of the CTC. The SIL continued its own writing courses. To some extent the efforts to create writers and structures that would support them simply diffused back among the different churches. Some of the work was channeled into the Melanesian Institute, the research and publishing arm of the Melanesian Council of Churches.[66]

RADIO AND LITERACY

An important part of the colonial literacy landscape in PNG was the presence of radio as a means of production and dissemination. Radio was, and is still, hugely popular, not only for its history of broadcasting plays, stories, and Melanesian songs, but also for its music and talk-back shows (an equivalent to letters to the editor). In an effort to encourage critical participation in government, the minister of information had openly endorsed talk-back programs on provincial radio stations in 1976.[67] But these programs had been operating for several years. Keith Jackson has reported on the experiences of talk-back in Bougainville. *Kivung Bilong Wailis* (Radio forum) had begun in 1972 as a ten-minute question-and-answer segment that aired five times each week. People wrote in requesting answers to specific questions; the responses were read over the air. It was enormously popular. The first year, the station received 250 letters each month. By 1973 the project had been extended to fifteen-minute segments seven times each week and was the second most popular out of forty-two programs. Jackson concluded that "Kivung contributed perhaps more than any other single programme to aligning Radio Bougainville with the needs of its audience."[68] The success of *Kivung* prompted the station to broaden this type of program. The information service was separated out into *Askim na Bekim* (Questions and answers). A telephone talk-in on pre-arranged topics, *Wanem Tingting Bilong Yu* (What do you think?), was so popular that staff could not handle the volume of calls, and the station was forced to take the program off the air after only two weeks.

Missionaries had similar experiences. From the early 1960s onward, missions in PNG had been vigorously involved in establishing radio stations. However, unlike their experience with the technologies of print, missions could not at first find common ground for cooperation. The result was a wide array of fragmentary radio and audiovisual services developed over time among a variety of mission agencies. During the 1960s, the missions in PNG operated some three hundred radio stations.[69] In the 1970s an attempt was made to coordinate these radio stations into a single system under an umbrella organization, the Christian Communications Commission. Bays was elected its first director. One of the main aims of the Commission was to act as a clearinghouse that could distribute Christian messages quicker and cheaper than in print. This meant pressing the small evangelical broadcasting outlets in the Highlands to cooperate and improve their operations. It also meant coordinating the publishing efforts of Kristen Pres and the Catholic Church. But just as Bays was beginning this work, the funding situation at CTC deteriorated, ending his first PNG contract.

On Bays's second tour, from 1979 to 1981, he was attached to the United Church's Christian Education and Communication Centre at Rabaul, the successor to the CTC. On his return, he found an expanded communications network, with a focus on broadcasting. During this second period he realized how shallow the penetration of writing into PNG society had been and how strong the tradition of music. One of his chief activities from 1979 to 1981 was to develop and distribute a large catalog of cassette tapes. The tapes were produced in English, Tok Pisin, and several vernaculars. Many of them were recordings of local choral groups. Some were recordings of sermons and readings. Poet Apisai Enos was featured on one tape reading poems he had written for children. The tapes were hugely successful, especially the music. Their reception prompted Bays to reassess the period of decolonization in which he had played so crucial a part; he concluded that in bringing literacy and creative writing to a nonliterate society, he had brought the wrong technology.

In PNG, a place of rich oral culture, Bays finally realized that people would rather listen than read. In his view, radio was the appropriate Western technology for the transmission and reception of stories and song, not the printed word. And, in fact, Mihalic's personal opinion had been similar. Philip Cass recounts that Mihalic knew of failed publishing attempts in Africa where widely scattered illiterate peoples were best reached through radio. He quotes Mihalic as saying, "In view of this trend . . . anyone who was planning to start a newspaper in a virtually illiterate Third World country as primitive as New Guinea was deemed psychologically suspect. To complicate the plot still more [I] had no property, no staff, no journalistic experience and no promise of any funds from the bishops."[70]

Mihalic established *Wantok* because he was asked to do so by the church, not because he believed it to be the right technology. Yet, oddly enough, it *was* an appropriate technology because many people read it in their own way: that is, they listened to others read it aloud. *Wantok* was popular because it was written in a language that was uniquely Melanesian and because it focused on local people and events. It could be kept and "read" more than once before anyone smoked it. What is more, it published a very large letters-to-the-editor section where readers could voice their opinions, whether they wrote the letter themselves or asked someone else to write their ideas down. In short, in the years leading up to independence, radio and the letters to the editor provided an intellectual forum for Melanesians, a goal never articulated by the many well-meaning and experienced literacy change agents at the SIL, *Wantok*, or the CTC. Walcot once commented that the problem for the publishing industry in the United States was to find the gap in the market. The problem in PNG, on the other hand, was to find the market in the gap.[71] Clearly newspapers and radio, in allowing Melanesians to participate in public discussion as an extension of the technologies of oral culture, had found that market.

CONCLUSION

PNG has been called one of the most "missionized" places on earth. Clearly, this case study of literacy as a development tool in PNG demonstrates that the many religious sponsors of literacy were as active and diverse in their motives and methods as the targets of literacy campaigns were in their responses. What is more, the unparalleled linguistic diversity of PNG, when added to its very brief colonial contact with the technologies of reading and writing, complicates an already dense and confusing picture of human action, reaction, and interaction. If we choose to take an institutional approach to understanding such complex cases in the colonial field, we have very few tools at our disposal. Two of the most interesting, in cases where literacy was introduced as a development tool, are the sponsorship model proposed by Brandt, which presents a useful method for untangling the web of intentions and actions among various change agents, and Rogers's typology of change targets.

As the main educational sponsors in the colonies of Papua and New Guinea, missionary change agents had as their primary task the education of children to whatever levels were acceptable to colonial administrations in any given colonial era. As far as literacy was concerned, until the 1960s this meant at least functional literacy in either English or a vernacular in the primary grades; from the 1960s onward, literacy in English was required where senior grades were offered. For the most part, as the literacy rates reveal, the missions failed in this task. However, they did not fail with all students. The young men who were among PNG's first high school and university graduates had high rates of literacy; in fact, several of them are numbered among PNG's first playwrights.

In describing the dynamics of literacy sponsorship, Brandt writes that when people have frequent, high-quality access to powerful sponsors, they have a much greater proficiency than do people without that access.[72] Furthermore, when the ties are strong enough, the sponsored tend to develop affinities with the sponsors. Eight of PNG's first generation of thirteen writers were related to churchmen or had spent their first years as children of the manse. None of these authors adopted a critical stance toward the missions in their writing.[73]

Among PNG's second generation of elite writers was Anna Solomon, whose mother purchased a copy of *Wantok* each week and saved them for Anna to read when she came home from boarding school at the end of the month. Anna, who was born in Port Moresby in 1955, was a native speaker of Tok Pisin. After her father's death, the family moved back to her mother's village. There, among a largely illiterate community, her mother would read the newspaper for the folktales, which she would then "tell" to an audience of friends and family. Anna's mother might fit into Rogers's "early adopter" category: she had read *Wantok* since it was first published and made sure that her daughter read the paper as well. For Anna, the future editor of *Wantok*, the newspaper was full of exciting news about independence and about the first publications by PNG writers. It had always been in her home, and it was in her own language and about the future of her country, so there was no decision to make.[74]

Brandt writes that a second important feature of literacy sponsorship lies in the strategies that sponsors adopt as they attempt to bridge the gap between the literacy practices they have upheld and the new standards they establish as they adapt to the times and compete with other sponsors. In the colonial world, for example, there is a gulf between the literacy expectations before World War II and those after the war. The argument in colonies about whether education should be more classical or more technical is one indicator of the tensions around what kind of literacy was required and for whom. In PNG the failure of the missions to produce a literate school-age population led organizations like the SIL to engage in mass adult literacy campaigns to rectify a problem the missions had, in fact, created. The difference was that, with adults, the SIL was able to make its own choices about the language used. Nevertheless, the SIL continued to work with administration agencies to encourage literacy for civic participation at a time when the government was trying to prepare the population for independence. This is likely the most conflicted dynamic of literacy sponsorship and therefore the most interesting.

Finally, Brandt looks at the relationship between sponsorship and appropriation of literacy by the sponsored. It is at the point of transmission that the sponsored have the opportunity to reject the innovation entirely, as so many people in PNG have done, or adapt the innovation to their own purposes. Rogers tells us that people will do this by assessing the relative advantage of the innovation, looking at how compatible it is with the previous system, deciding whether it is too complex to adopt, testing to see whether it can be adopted gradually, checking its possibilities for reinvention, and observing its real-world effects.[75]

For the elite writers of PNG, the choice to develop strong literacy skills in English was clear. But what of the general public? The oral tradition in PNG was still strong enough during the independence era that people would reinvent aspects of print culture to replicate or strengthen what they already knew. One person would read the newspaper out loud to up to twenty others; Anna Solomon's mother would read the newspaper for the folklore and then "tell" the tales to people she knew; people would send letters to the editor of *Wantok* so that they could participate in a community discussion on important issues; and they used letters to radio stations for the same purpose. This self-interest is what Brandt is referring to when she writes about diverting the resources of the sponsor for individual gain.[76]

The preparations for independence in a colony tended to magnify development practices, sometimes out of all proportion. For that reason, they are particularly fruitful for study. Processes that ought to have developed more organically over time were established too quickly and with very little long-term planning or support. In choosing a language for literacy or participating in mass literacy campaigns such as those operated by the SIL or in development programs like *Wantok* and the CTC, people were making some of the biggest decisions of their lives. In choosing to ignore this new technology of reading and writing, other people indicated that they could find no practical use for literacy.

Missionaries altered their own practices and expectations to accommodate this range of response from Melanesians. Bays eventually abandoned promoting print literacy in favor of participation in the aural culture of radio. Father Mihalic, on the other hand, pragmatically covered all options by producing his newspaper with newsprint that made a good cigarette. One wonders if he wasn't tempted at some point to change the masthead of *Wantok* to "Read it . . . *then* smoke it!"

NOTES

1. The two colonies were finally united as a single nation called Papua New Guinea on independence. New Guinea had originally been a German colony and was ceded as a League of Nations mandate after World War I. It was given to Australia to administer, along with Papua, which Australia had been governing for Britain since 1888. Australia kept separate administrations for each of the colonies until after World War II.

2. Patrick Matbob, "Mihalic—wantok tru bilong PNG," *Yumi Blogspot*, 6 April 2013, http://yumistori.blogspot.ca/2013/04/mihalic-wantok-tru-bilong-png .html.

3. My translation; the pidgin is taken from the masthead of the first issue of the newspaper in 1970.

4. Matbob, "Mihalic—wantok tru bilong PNG." Philip Cass also discusses how employees of *Wantok* experimented with newsprint that could be smoked. Cass, *Press, Politics and People in New Guinea, 1950–1975*, 127. *Wantok* can be translated as "people who speak the same language as you do."

5. The concept of multimodal literacy is particularly important in colonial settings from the mid-twentieth century onward, when the introduction of radio as a means of producing and disseminating plays, folktales, and modern fiction played an important role in the development of many new literatures. Authors found that they needed to work in radio to reach their audience in situations where print literacy rates were low or where printed text was expensive or unavailable. Debra Spitulnik discusses how saucepan radios contributed to this phenomenon in Zambia. Spitulnik, "Documenting Radio Culture as Lived Experience," 144–63.

6. Brandt, "Sponsors of Literacy"; and Rogers, *Diffusion of Innovations.*

7. The importance of examining the particulars of each colonial situation, despite common experiences across the colonial world, has been amply demonstrated by Frederick Cooper in his discussion of African colonialisms as distinct from the colonial experience in India. See Cooper, *Colonialism in Question.*

8. These two types of literacy—sociocultural and functional—are examined by Corinne M. Wickens and Jennifer Sandlin for their goals and effects in colonial and neocolonial environments. Their argument is that colonial schooling tended to emphasize functional literacy, geared to the job market and productivity, and not enough sociocultural literacy, which focuses more on personal and social betterment. See Wickens and Sandlin, "Literacy for What? Literacy for Whom?," 275–92.

9. Megarrity, "Indigenous Education in Colonial Papua New Guinea," 50.

10. The Summer Institute of Linguistics has worked on 389 of these languages to date. Their website provides a detailed mapping of that work: "Languages of Papua New Guinea," accessed 4 January 2020, https://pnglanguages.sil.org/resources.

11. Walcot, "Perspectives on Publishing, Literacy and Development," 20.

12. Walcot, "Perspectives on Publishing, Literacy and Development," 17.

13. Different versions of Tok Pisin could be found in the *Bougainville Nius* (Bougainville news), *Toktok bilong Haus ov Assembli* (Talk from the House of Assembly), *Nius bilong Yumi* (Our news), *Nu Gini Toktok* (New Guinea talk), and *Kundu* (Drum), among others. With the eventual publication of the New Testament in Tok Pisin and the weekly newspaper *Wantok,* each of which was very successful and followed Mihalic's standardized usage, the variants of Tok Pisin melted away. By the 1960s this pidgin language was becoming creolized, as generations of young people in urban areas began to speak it as their native tongue.

14. Mihalic, "Tok Pisin," 90.

15. These figures were retrieved from the PNG Bureau of Statistics by Rodney V. East and appear in his master's thesis, "The Development of a Papua New Guinea National Information System," 45–46.

16. PNG Central Planning Office, *Programmes and Performance, 1975–76,* 162.

17. Megarrity, "Indigenous Education in Colonial Papua New Guinea," 46.

18. Malone, "International Literacy Year—1990," 2. The SIL is a worldwide missionary organization that specializes in Bible translation. In Papua New Guinea, it operates mainly in the Highlands, where they have since reduced dozens of indigenous languages to print. In addition to this "core business," the SIL has been extremely active in PNG in promoting adult literacy through mass literacy campaigns and through the production of practical manuals and general literature for Melanesians.

19. Many people were able to analyze the hectic decolonizing years from an intellectual distance in the 1980s and 1990s, realizing that the colonial situation required a redefinition of many concepts they had previously taken for granted. See Faraclas, "Literacy, Awareness, Development and Communication in Papua New Guinea," 52–61.

20. Both journals were written mostly in English, with some pidgin.

21. Bays, "Creative Writing," 1.

22. Hooley, "SIL Research in New Guinea," 64.

23. See Robert Taylor, "The Summer Institute of Linguistics/Wycliffe Bible Translators in Anthropological Perspective," 93–116, for an informative view of this missionary organization.

24. Lynch, *Church, State and Language in Melanesia*, 12–13; Lynch's opinion is supported by the director of the Institute of Papua New Guinea Studies, Don Niles, who told the author in 2008 that the SIL has warehouses of this material that no one wants to read.

25. The Literature Bureau was an institution of the British Empire first developed in West Africa between the two world wars. The Literature Bureau in PNG was the last of these to be established, in the late 1960s. The general purpose of these bureaus was to encourage the production, dissemination, and consumption of texts written by indigenous authors.

26. "What is CWAMEL?," *Papua New Guinea Writing* 8 (1972): 19.

27. A survey of *Books for Africa* (1931–63), the journal edited by Margaret Wrong for the International Committee on Christian Literature for Africa, yields a "General Literature" section that is similar to Lynch's list. Missionaries meant "something to read" when they used the term *literature*. The missions were not averse to including imaginative fiction on their lists. It was just extremely hard to come by in indigenous languages.

28. Franklin, "Towards a Language and Literature Directory of Papua New Guinea," 7.

29. Franklin takes these figures from the SIL *Annual Report for 1988*, 23. Franklin's subtext is that the number of children wishing places in the education system vastly outnumbered the number of places. Bishop Jeremy Ashton noted in 1977 that only one-third of the Standard 6 class could go on to high school. A further 40 percent of the Standard 8 students had to leave the system because of lack of places. In his opinion only eighteen out of every hundred students who started school could obtain places in a national high school. Ashton, "Some Thoughts on Community Education," 139–46.

30. As Jürgen Osterhammel points out in his typology of colonial states, such practices are more typical of colonies of exploitation, where the indigenous populations vastly outnumber the expatriate. However, a different set of principles appears to operate in settlement colonies where overwhelming numbers of expatriates can eventually expect (or require) that indigenous peoples assimilate. See Osterhammel, *Colonialism*, 10–12.

31. Hooley, "SIL Research in New Guinea," 67.

32. SIL *Bibliography 1956–90*, 75.

33. East, "The Development of a Papua New Guinea National Information System," 140; and R. Johnson, "Bilingual Education and Teacher Training in Papua New Guinea."

34. SIL *Annual Report 1988*, 14.

35. Franklin, "Towards a Language and Literature Directory of Papua New Guinea," 6.

36. Gwyther-Jones, "Pasina Ätre'amofo näneke," 10.

37. Cates, "Why Teach First in the Vernacular?," 2.

38. Note that the government's adult education budget in 1973 was only 0.02 percent of all moneys spent on education. See Leadley, "Emancipating Relevant Education," 5–6. Leadley claimed that "a national plan for adult out-of-school education has never been a part of the colonial pattern, and hence not an integral part of the new nation and its leadership" (12).

39. Editorial for Special Issue, "Providing Literature for New Literates," 7.

40. Johnston, "Devising a Written Style in an Unwritten Language," 66–70.

41. The journal's title, *Kovave,* is taken from the name of a first initiation ceremony in Orokolo, Papua.

42. Marten, "Keeping Literates Literate," 113.

43. Marten, "Keeping Literates Literate," 113.

44. Marten, "Keeping Literates Literate," 116.

45. Marten, "Literacy for Those Who Don't Want It," 13–14.

46. See Mihalic, "Tok Pisin," 90ff., for an overview of the history of this lingua franca in print.

47. See Frazer, "A Study of the Development, Format and Content of the *Niugini Toktok*," 63ff.

48. Mihalic, "Tok Pisin," 90.

49. *Kaunsila Traim* was a spoof on trying out development technologies with a main character who never quite figured out how anything worked.

50. See Walcot, "Perspectives on Publishing, Literacy and Development," 24ff. Literates would pass the newspaper to one another and would read it aloud to their illiterate friends and family.

51. Mihalic, "Tok Pisin," 90.

52. Heyum, "Publishing in the Islands," 19.

53. Mihalic, "Tok Pisin," 91.

54. Walcot, "Perspectives on Publishing, Literacy and Development," 33.

55. Although *Wantok* was at one time considered a Catholic paper, it has managed to grow over the years into an ecumenical organization. Similarly, although Word Publishing began as a Catholic-funded institution, in 1982 the board was broadened to include representatives of the three other main churches in PNG: the United, the Lutheran, and the Anglican. Word Publishing has been for some years now associated with the Melanesian Christian Council.

56. Walcot, "Perspectives on Publishing, Literacy and Development," 17.

57. See Brash, "Tok Pisin!," 321ff.

58. Unless otherwise indicated, the information contained in this section was gathered during telephone interviews with Glen Bays in March 1993 as well as written correspondence.

59. See Schild, *Literaturen in Papua-neuguinea,* 84ff.; some of this information was also garnered from the Bays interviews in 1993 and from correspondence with

Bays in the same year. Note that Bays would accept writing in English, Tok Pisin, or the vernaculars. However, most of the submissions to his journals were in English.

60. Gwyther-Jones, "How to Get Writers Writing," 12–15.

61. *Papua New Guinea Writing* 8 (1972): 19.

62. *Precept* 1 (1974): 5.

63. That is not to say they did not write. The church, school, mission, newspaper, and national archives of PNG are well stocked with anthologies from writers' workshops and the like. They form an untouched reservoir of early PNG literature in English, Tok Pisin, and the vernaculars.

64. M. Crocombe, "Mana: Papua New Guinea," 61–67.

65. Glen Bays gave me a copy of *New Voices* 2 about twenty-five years ago; I have digitised it and placed it on the website Creating Literature in Papua New Guinea (1966–1986): The First Twenty Years. The journal can be found on this page: http://png.athabascau.ca/docs/new_voices_2.pdf. I am unaware of any other copies in libraries or archives. These "publications" of student writing were produced for the use of the students and their sponsor/ teacher, rather than for general distribution.

66. The Melanesian Council of Churches was an umbrella ecumenical organization supported mainly by the four largest churches in PNG: the Anglican, the United, the Roman Catholic, and the Evangelical Lutheran. The Melanesian Institute parallels the secular Institute of Papua New Guinea Studies and the academic journals based at the UPNG. The Institute focuses on cultural studies and serves as an information clearinghouse linking member churches and their programs.

67. "Taureka Talks about Radio," *Transmitter*, July 1976, 1, 6.

68. Keith Jackson, "Radio and Development: The Importance of Listener Access," Information Paper 9 (Port Moresby, PNG: National Broadcasting Corporation, n.d. [probably ca. 1973–75]), 6.

69. Mackay, *Broadcasting in Papua New Guinea*, 75.

70. Frank Mihalic, undated manuscript, quoted in Cass, *Press, Politics and People in Papua New Guinea, 1950–1975*, 217.

71. Walcot, "Perspectives on Publishing, Literacy and Development," 11.

72. Brandt, "Sponsors of Literacy," 172. Wickens and Sandlin found strong ties between the agendas of powerful sponsors and the types of literacy achieved. Wickens and Sandlin, "Literacy for What? Literacy for Whom?"

73. Kirsty Powell feels that this context explains not only their choice to further their education but also their demonstrated superiority with the English language. See Powell, *The First Papua New Guinea Playwrights and Their Plays*.

74. This information was garnered through an interview with Anna Solomon in Sydney in 2002.

75. Rogers, *Diffusion of Innovations*, 219–66.

76. Brandt, "Sponsors of Literacy," 178–79.

Part IV
Writers

CHAPTER TEN

Colonial Copyright, Customs, and Indigenous Textualities:
Literary Authority and Textual Citizenship

ISABEL HOFMEYR

ON 8 AUGUST 1912, the *Gold Coast Nation* "hail[ed] with delight" the governor's proclamation that the Copyright Act would now apply within the colony. "The Copyright Act should have been applied to the Colony long ago; its absence has for some years worked a hardship on many natives blessed with the gift of literary taste and who have been embodying their thoughts and ideas on paper in more or less permanent form." The paper went on to summarize the major sections of the act and covered infringement, duration of copyright, civil remedies for infringement, and delivery of books to deposit libraries.

When I first read the story, I must admit that I was somewhat taken aback. Rather inchoately, and influenced by my work on Gandhi (who generally rejected intellectual property law), I had imagined copyright as an imperial imposition that might be resisted rather than welcomed.[1] The contemporary situation where international intellectual property regimes like TRIPS (Trade-Related Aspects of Intellectual Property Rights) function in the interests of large and quasi-imperial multinational corporations had no doubt also colored my assumptions, which had then been projected into the past.[2]

A second contemporary factor, namely, the general disregard for intellectual property law that apparently characterizes much of the "developing world," had likewise crept into my thinking and had acquired a retrospective gloss.[3]

However, even a superficial investigation into imperial copyright law soon revealed that far from being imposed on colonial subjects, this legislation ignored and excluded them. As several scholars have demonstrated, imperial copyright law was initially designed to protect the rights of metropolitan authors whose work traveled out into empire with little interest in material produced in the colonies.[4]

The trajectories of colonial copyright are hence more complex than first meets the eye. Yet, attempting to delve into the workings of imperial and colonial copyright on the ground is at present difficult as we lack serious histories of intellectual property (IP) written from the perspective of the colonial world. There is a rich body of work on the eighteenth- and nineteenth-century histories of Euro-American copyright.[5] There is also a sophisticated body of work on the effects of twenty-first-century IP law in the postcolonial world (whether for patenting plants, trademarking "native" culture, or commoditizing ethnicity).[6] The field of IP law hence has a Western past and a postcolonial present but little sense of anything in between.

Yet, to grasp the issues at stake, it is precisely this part of the picture that we need. Legal scholars have authored fine accounts of the spread of international IP law, but these take a view from above and provide little sense of the social life of IP law in the colonial world.[7] Without this missing middle colonial section, our view of IP regimes in the postcolonial world remains stereotypical: either a tale of evil cartels oppressing peasants in the third world commons or a vision of laudable U.S. multinationals reforming zones of IP delinquency and marauding piracy. To debate the topic adequately, we need to understand the meanings that IP has accrued in the colonial world and the ways in which these have shaped contemporary practice in the postcolonial arena.

This chapter attempts to provide some preliminary accounts of colonial copyright from a social and cultural, rather than a legal, perspective. The setting is late nineteenth- and early twentieth-century southern Africa. The chapter offers two vantage points on the topic, namely, the colonial state on the one hand and black writers on the other. As regards the former, the focus is on Customs and Excise, the section of the colonial state to which questions of copyright were entrusted. Yet dealing with this instrument was not straightforward since customs officials faced a crow's nest of imperial, international, and colonial copyright legislation and had to develop their own protocols to deal with copyright. In elaborating such "homemade" procedures, customs officials followed the racialized logics of the Immigration Department, alongside whom they worked. Intent on policing the global color line, the Immigration Department followed a logic of exclusion and inclusion based on race. With regard to copyright, Customs and Excise applied the same logic, treating British copyright as a sign of British manufacture and as a respectable mark of origin. In pursuing such protocols, Customs and Excise interpreted copyright as a type of racial trademark.

However, to tell the story of colonial copyright solely from the perspective of the colonial state is to present a partial picture. The second part of the chapter examines the case of black writers, who were generally keen users of copyright since it represented an opportunity of claiming rights and constituting oneself as a rights-bearing subject and a citizen of empire. One route into being a rights-bearing subject was to become a book-bearing one (an act that ironically reflected on, and balanced out, other forms of forced book bearing, like passes).

The chapter speaks to the larger concerns of the volume by exploring indigenized ideas of authorship and the book. It argues that writers construct a portfolio approach to authorship, adding new possibilities to existing ideas of cultural and oratorical authority. Rather than just the Western idea of the individual genius (which is at times invoked), the writers discussed in this volume experiment with different forms, creating notions of authorship that can encompass changing ideas of community. The chapters by Arini Loader and Ivy Schweitzer resonate with this theme, showing how any book is in fact a dispersed event that takes in the networks and social relationships from which the text emerges. Reinterpreting textual practices in this way allows the full range of authorship practices to become visible.

COPYRIGHT AT THE COLONIAL CUSTOMS HOUSE

I turn now to the customs house, but before doing so will make a quick stop at the Royal Copyright Commission, which met in London from 1876 to 1878. Fairly early on in its proceedings in 1876, Frederic Daldy, London publisher and subsequently secretary of the English Copyright Association, addressed the commission. Daldy was an expert on colonial and international copyright law, a subject on which he would subsequently publish various handbooks. Daldy's evidence focused "on the question of copyright as it affects the colonial aspects of the subject."[8]

The discussion soon entered the byzantine terrain of which copyright law applied where in different parts of the British Empire. One of the commissioners, Anthony Trollope, weighed in with a hypothetical Australian problem and posed the following question: "Is not any property which I may take into Victoria [in Australia] guarded by the laws of Victoria?" "Yes," replied Daldy, "as far as the laws of Victoria can operate upon it."[9]

Daldy's comment ("as far as the laws of Victoria can operate upon it") hones in on a central problem in copyright, and indeed more generally. How does the law gain traction on an object? In the case of copyright, such traction apparently inhered in a repertoire of mechanisms—statutory legislation, an entry into a register, and a mark in the book itself. Yet how does one know that the book is what it says it is? This of course is a problem inherent in any purchase and indeed in much of daily life. Yet, add in the factor of distance, and the puzzle deepens. When an object has traveled across oceans, languages, and empires, how can one know that it is what it pretends to be? Put in simple terms, how does one know that a book is copyrighted? Can one detect a pirated reprint? How would one do this?

This problem was one that concerned not only Trollope and his fellow commissioners. It also affected most customs officials across the British Empire since it was they who stood at the front line of policing the imperial IP frontier. To these officials fell the task of implementing a confusing variety of copyright legislation that derived from three domains: imperial, colonial, and international law. The first—imperial copyright law—emanated from the metropolis; it prioritized the defense of British rights holders and promoted British publishing in the international arena. The second level—colonial copyright—covered material produced in the colony itself and was generally introduced into settler colonies from the 1850s. The third—international copyright law—was inaugurated by the Berne Convention of 1886 and was largely designed in the interests of large European exporters of copyrighted material.

Unsurprisingly, most officials had little grasp of these various laws, and when illegal reprints were detained or arrested (to use the language of Customs and Excise), no one knew how to proceed. In Durban in 1915, officials seized a consignment of foreign reprints that included copies of *Treasure Island* and *Kidnapped*. The collector of customs dithered—should he seize the books in terms of the colonial copyright legislation or the imperial law? While the books languished in the dockside warehouse, this query was batted between Customs and Excise and the Justice Department with no clear answer emerging.[10]

In another instance, this time in 1930, a customs official at Windhoek in what was then South-West Africa, now Namibia (a German colony placed under South African mandate after 1918), seized copies of *Lady Windermere's Fan* that had been reprinted in Germany. Again no one seemed sure what to do. After much bureaucratic toing and froing, the books had to be released: imperial copyright legislation apparently did not apply in mandated states.[11]

This level of confusion is not surprising especially if one remembers that for the second half of the nineteenth century, the importation of foreign reprints of British copyright works had been entirely legal across much of the empire. British possessions (or at least those who signed up for the system) could quite legally import pirated editions of British copyright work provided a duty of 10 to 15 percent was paid by the importer—the duty in theory being remitted back to the publisher in Britain. These circumstances were enabled by the Copyright Act of 1847 (or the Foreign Reprints Act), and most colonies, with the notable exception of the Australian colonies, subscribed to its terms. Driven by the ubiquity of cheap U.S. reprints, especially in Canada and the West Indies but also beyond, and the inability of the British publishing industry, at least initially, to meet the needs of these markets, the 1847 act remained in place until 1911. The system both then and now has been characterized as farcical.[12]

As an aside, it is worth noting the role that cheap American reprints played in shaping ideas of print and copyright in the British Empire. By providing a steady stream of books for both a domestic and an international market, the U.S. reprint trade offered a model for what the book as an educational instrument should be—cheap and accessible. In a context where printed books represented a form of soft imperial power (as instruments of civilization and calling cards of Englishness), the U.S. model was often invoked by imperial enthusiasts. Speaking to the Royal Copyright Commission, Charles Trevelyan advocated the reprinting of English copyright works in India (and elsewhere) as a means of "civilizing" the exponentially expanding number of readers.[13]

The system enabled by the Copyright Act of 1847 not only created considerable confusion but also generated a lumbering bureaucracy. Forms listing British copyright works were sent from London on a three-monthly basis to every customs post in those parts of the empire that signed up for the system.[14] This blizzard of documents was meant to be filed and then consulted, page by laborious page, to discover whether a work was legitimate or not. Thousands upon thousands of such pages must have accumulated in entirely unused files, slowly moldering in the humid atmosphere of the foreshore.

Given the cumbersomeness of these procedures, what did customs officials on the ground do? In the southern African case, they formulated their own methods, subordinating the question of copyright to their normal routines for dealing with objects. These procedures were in turn governed by the larger logics of imperial trade that from the early twentieth century regulated the workings of the Customs House. This trade was divided into three categories: goods from Britain, goods from other British colonies, and foreign goods. The first two items enjoyed a sliding scale of preferential rates; the latter did not. Within this larger grid, every item that passed the border had first to be assigned to one of these three categories and then to a further set of subcategories so that an exact tariff could be determined and duty charged.

In being categorized, commodities entered a byzantine system of classification adjudicated according to a tariff handbook of several hundred pages. Such handbooks hubristically promised to account for every object in the British Empire but in their very form acknowledged the impossibility of this task: tariff books were generally interleaved—every second page was blank to allow officials to write in comments and recommendations for changes, which were then forwarded to the head office for inclusion in the next year's edition.[15]

Much of the Customs and Excise officials' time was taken up trying to decide into which category items fell. One only has to flip through these volumes to grasp the complexity of customs operations. With dizzying speed, one moves from haberdashery, to haggis, to hair, from palisade fencing to pancake flour (always of course with a get-out clause "EOHP"—"except as otherwise herein provided"). Disagreements were routine, both among customs officials and between officials and importers keen to obtain the lowest tariff for their goods. Each such dispute generated a file, and the state archives in South Africa abound with such material as committees attempted to adjudicate how objects should be categorized. Was a substance butter or margarine? Could medicinal herbs be classified as tea? Were soup squares the same as stock? Was there any difference between poppy seed in a packet (which could be detained under the opium laws) and poppy seed for culinary use? Fabric proved particularly tricky as officials debated whether a particular bolt of cloth should be entered as printed tartan or gingham with swatches included in the file itself to aid discussion.[16] These dockside nominalists engaged with objects in detail—sniffing, tasting, feeling—attempting to classify and define objects in an attempt to make them real in the world of colonial indeterminacy.

Yet, underlying this activity lay the grammar of imperial trade: British, colonial, foreign. In terms of these categories, all objects had to carry a mark of origin so that they could be sorted in the tripartite schema. In one case, a consignment of pills was turned back because they did not specify that they had been "made in England."[17]

This concern with the mark of origin was equally apparent if one turned to the Immigration Department, which worked on the dockside alongside Customs and Excise (indeed, in some cases the two functions were combined in one person). Immigration officials took upon themselves the task of policing the global color line, inventing protocols to keep out as many immigrants of color as possible. The writing test (in European languages and roman script) created the notion that those with literacy were Europeans and that all Europeans possessed literacy. These procedures become a way of constructing race itself as source or origin.[18]

Objects too were subject to an informal writing test since lettering on commodities generally had to be in roman script and in English. Indeed, in some cases the English language itself was considered as a mark of origin. Or, as one handbook explained, "if any names, trade-marks, or descriptions in the English language or any English words at all appear on the goods, wrappings or containers, they are considered . . . as purporting to be of British origin."[19] Goods produced outside Britain but with English markings had to carry clear signs of what was called "counterindication," showing that despite the English words on the product, the commodity had not been manufactured in Britain.[20] Exporters from the United States were advised that "the words 'Made in the U.S.A.' in letters as large and as conspicuous as any other English wording, should be printed on every article, label, or wrapper bearing any words in the English language."[21] In some cases the mania for inscription went to extraordinary lengths. In the case of writing paper, "if so much as a watermark containing English lettering appears in sheets of paper, a counterindication of origin must also be watermarked into each sheet, wherever the water-mark occurs."[22]

These types of regulations formed part of a mania of marking, enough to sustain several handbooks that instructed exporters on how objects had to be inscribed with marks of origin.[23] The handbooks are veritable thesauruses of inscription replete with instructions on how objects had variously to be impressed, embossed, die-stamped, cast, engraved, etched, printed, applied, stamped, incised, stenciled, painted, branded, molded, punched, cast, along with an appropriate range of adverbs: *indelibly, visibly, conspicuously, durably*.[24] The designers of these regulations had to tussle with the shape of the object itself to determine where best it should be marked: on the stem of pipe, the face of clock, every two yards on the selvedge of fabric, on the address section of a postcard, on the rind of the bacon, on the flange of the printing block, and so on. In the case of chilled beef, each side had to bear an indication of origin "in a continuous series of words . . . extending longitudinally: From the hock joint to the neck . . . provided that . . . if the name of the country of production comprises more than one word, such words may be placed vertically one beneath the other instead of in a continuous line."[25]

"Made in," "produced in," "printed in," and "copyrighted in" all stood as marks of origin; indeed, the English in which they appeared spoke of the source, which was of course implicitly understood as English and white.

To have the wrong mark of origin was to risk exclusion, deportation, or, in the case of books, seizure and banning. During the Anglo-Boer War, Dutch books deemed sympathetic to the Boer cause were seized, customs officials making use of their powers to proscribe seditious or obscene texts. These customs officials established the protocols of reading and censorship that would subsequently inform the larger and more ambitious censorship machine established by the apartheid state.[26]

In dealing with books and questions of copyright, customs officials used these mark-of-origin grids to make decisions. Unable to fathom the various levels of copyright law and faced with unwieldy systems, officials sought evidence that the book had been composed, manufactured, or copyrighted in Britain, subjecting the book to a logic of origin and source. In these procedures they were supported by the Merchandise Marks Act of 1887 (a piece of empire-wide legislation), which specifically indicated that British copyright could "be taken to be [an] indirect indication of British manufacture."[27] Once marked as British, the book became a "white" object trailing a racialized copyright, a mode of commoditized whiteness determined by imperial trade.

This implicit racialization at times became explicit. In the German empire, for example, *Eingeborene* (natives) could not hold copyright.[28] While British copyright law in the dominions did not specify categories of persons, its imagined subject appeared to be presumptively white. In South Africa, whenever Native Affairs Department officials discussed copyright, they debated whether their own internal publications should or should not be registered under the provisions of the law. That their "native subjects" might be affected or wish to partake of such legislation simply never occurred to them—in their mind, it was a white man's right (white women could hold copyright but had to indicate their marital status since this impacted whether they could hold property).[29]

One inclination may be to see this racialization of copyright as a feature peculiar to the colonies: metropolitan law is apparently racially neutral and becomes racialized only as it travels out into empire. In the view proposed here, however, it is more useful to think of this racialization as something that had been inherent in the law all along. Copyright is a form of property, and to claim it, one had to be a person who could hold property, a category that at least until 1834 took its meaning from an implicit contrast with racialized slaves, whose bonded presence and inability to hold property defined the free sovereign property-holding subject.

RESHAPING COPYRIGHT

How did black South African writers enter these imperial and colonial copyright fields? As a way of generating some answers, I begin with a title page of a 1906 book by Mpilo Walter Benson Rubusana (1858–1936), a prominent member of South Africa's black elite. The title, *Zemk'inkomo Magwalandini* ("There go your cattle, you cowards!" or "The cattle are being driven off by the enemy, you cowards!"), is an isiXhosa war cry and call to arms. The term can also be construed more generally as "Defend your heritage."[30] The page itself identifies the author as W. B. Rubusana and provides a miniature CV: he has a PhD, is "the first black member of Parliament in South Africa" (he was a member of the Cape Provincial Council), is a minister of the Presbyterian Church, and is president of the South African Native Convention. Rubusana's other books (*Steps to Christ* [a translation], *Presbyterian Service Book, Jesus Is Coming*, and so on) are listed. The latter half of the title page appears in English and tells us that the book has been entered at Stationers' Hall in London and that it is the second edition printed for the author by a company, Burton and Tanner, operating in Frome (Somerset) and London.

The title page carries what at first sight appears to be an error: the phrase "entered Stationers' Hall" would normally be "entered *at* Stationers' Hall" (namely, entered into the register of the Company of Stationers of London, which was housed at Stationers' Hall, such registration being the statutory requirement for copyright registered in Britain until 1912). Rubusana (or his representative) would have been required to enter the title, date of first publication, and the name and "place of abode" of the publisher and of the proprietor of the copyright and to indicate whether this copyright had been assigned and, if so, to whom.[31]

Since Rubusana was in London at the time of the first publication of the book to oversee the production of the isiXhosa Bible, he may well have completed the registration in person. If so, the phrase "entered Stationers' Hall" would be literally correct, as indeed the page tells us—if we read the page from the top down, it indicates that Rubusana entered Stationers' Hall. He "made an entrance" in both senses of the word: the action of going in and the action of entering in a record. If we consider the title of the book, then we are also being told that an isiXhosa war cry entered Stationers' Hall and was entered into the register.

The type of copyright being asserted here is far from routine. First, the page indicates an active and a passive copyright: the book and its author entered, and were entered into, the space of copyright. Furthermore, this copyright is "strong": it emanates from the imperial capital and derives from Stationers' Hall, the *fons et origo* of all British imperial copyright practice. Rubusana could well have produced the book in the Cape Colony, but there would have been various drawbacks, most notably being subject to the strictures and condescension of the white-controlled Christian mission press, the only printers permitted to typeset material in African languages (a ploy by white printers to keep cheaper African compositors out of "their" domain).[32] With regard to copyright, Rubusana would have had to register his book in the Deeds Office in Cape Town, an act that would technically have secured protection of his rights across the British Empire.[33] Instead, however, he chose to produce the book and register its copyright in Britain. The market for the book lay in South Africa, but nonetheless Rubusana wanted it to bear the imprimatur of the imperial capital, both in its production and in its claiming of the "highest" copyright authority.

Yet, at the same time, this imperial identification is complicated by the isiXhosa war cry. On one level, the call to arms acts as a reminder of the hundred-year war that British imperial expansion visited on the Xhosa. This powerful phrase "entitles" the book. Yet, even as this call enters the space of imperial copyright, it is contained by being entered into the register and hence being turned into a minor piece of property. On another level, the airing of the war cry in the metropolitan capital could symbolically enact an appeal to the imperial authorities over the head of the colonial state in the hope that it might receive a more sympathetic response. Indeed, in 1914 Rubusana formed part of exactly such an appeal to the imperial metropole: he was a member of a black South African delegation to London to appeal (unsuccessfully) against the Land Act of the previous year, which had allocated 13 percent of South African land to black South Africans and the rest to whites.

Like many members of the African elite, Rubusana took notions of imperial citizenship seriously. As Sukanya Banerjee has so elegantly demonstrated, imperial citizenship was less a statutory claim than a process of "thick" credentialing that aimed to "fortify" the colonial subject with a rights-bearing capacity. Professional attainments constituted a major source for such credentialing, which sought to solve the contradiction in which colonized subjects were trapped: as abstractions they were theoretically equal, but as embodied subjects they could never be. As Banerjee indicates, professionalism with its stress on expertise rather than the individual "approximates the formless equality of liberal citizenship" and became one idiom for claims to colonial entitlement even as colonial subjects pursued others that foregrounded their embodiment as a source of oppression and therefore intellectual resistance.[34]

Rubusana's title page "enters" these contradictions in strategic ways. Heavy with credentialing, the title page through its copyright constructs Rubusana as a "legal person" and hence an abstract entity. Yet, at the same time, by uttering an isiXhosa war cry, the page embodies an uprising body politic with Rubusana as its "author." The page presents simultaneous claims for equality, one mediated through liberal frameworks, the other through militarized ethnic assertion. This dual strategy has a further use: it bypasses and disavows the white settler colonial state—by identifying over it (to an imperial authority) and under it (through an ethnic affiliation).

The order of literary property that emerges from these intersections is again far from conventional, something that becomes clearer if we glance through the 516 pages stacked behind the title page. These largely contain praise poems with a range of addressees (chiefs, editors, clerics, institutions, animals); prose pieces dealing with the genealogies, histories, and lineages of the Xhosa polity; and religious verse. Several of the poems plus the prose pieces are extracted from newspapers and books, as the introduction indicates, although the items themselves are presented without any indication of the sources from which they have been reprinted. In some cases the authors are identified by initials or a moniker ("Yimbongi yakwa Gompo"—the Praise Poet of East London, namely, S. E. K. Mqhayi). One author identified by his initials (W. W. G.) is William Wellington Gqoba, with seven of his pieces being included in the collection. As Jeff Opland, Wandile Kuse, and Pamela Maseko's translations of Gqoba's corpus indicate, these pieces are taken from Gqoba's newspaper *Isigidimi sama Xhosa* (The Xhosa messenger). The pieces include religious verse; "A Great Debate on Education: A Parable," with allegorical characters (like Familiar with Learning, Die for Truth, Chatterbox, and Dimwit) who express different views on Western education; and prose pieces outlining lineage accounts and major events of Xhosa history. As Opland points out, in some cases Gqoba's pieces have been changed by Rubusana, a "cavalier editor" in Opland's view.[35] However, perhaps such "editing" can be understood as part of the textual economy of reprinting that characterized Rubusana's world.

Zemk'inkomo Magwalandini is hence a compilation of which Rubusana represents himself as the author. As such, he stands at the intersection of three textual commons: isiXhosa oral literature, the periodical press, and Christian religious writing. I say "commons" since these were all fields that operated largely without reference to ideas of IP. Each certainly had practices of status and authority embedded within it (by gender, lineage, age, race, and so on), but once works from these commons had been printed, they entered a public realm where they could be used and reused. As Antoinette Burton and I have argued elsewhere, these might be thought of as part of an imperial commons: "The right to the resource [of these] is not contingent on obtaining the permission of anyone: 'No one exercises a property right with respect to these resources.'"[36]

As I have suggested in *Gandhi's Printing Press: Experiments in Slow Reading*, the basis of this commons lay in the vast sprawling system of scissors-and-paste journalism by which papers legally culled material from each other.[37] Known as the "exchange system," these decentralized networks produced webs of interpenetrating periodical matter that carpeted the globe. In place by the eighteenth century, this system persisted into the twentieth century, surpassed finally by telegraph, wire services, and the appurtenances of "modern" journalism. Indeed, the Berne Convention recognized reprinting with attribution as legitimate, a provision that persisted into the 1960s.

The exchange system crossed continents, countries, empires, regions, religions, and languages, and for much of the nineteenth century there was probably not a newspaper or periodical in the world that did not rely on legally reprinting material for at least some of its content. Newspapers and periodicals made up the bulk of what most people read most of the time, and so a significant portion of print culture consumed was uncopyrighted material legally republished from elsewhere. There were of course exceptions (copyright could always be asserted over material, and from 1896 fiction in periodicals and newspapers was excluded from the provisions of the Berne Convention), but overall the exchange system propagated an ecology of print media that was uncopyrighted and operated largely without reference to IP law (as indeed did the international trade in U.S. reprints, which reached many part of the British Empire). As an institution that shaped popular ideas of reading and writing across the globe, the exchange commons sits at the heart of what we might call demotic ideas of world literature, which were not centrally pegged to notions of literary property and individual authorship.

While these are not the terms they use, Karin Barber and Stephanie Newell have demonstrated for British West Africa how the confluence of these commons (oral literature and the periodical press) constituted a rich site for experimenting with modes of authorship or, in some cases, antiauthorship. As Newell demonstrates, the British West African press was dominated by anonymous or pseudonymous forms of writing that allowed writers to evade, play with, and thwart the state's desire to classify and name its subjects, to make them legible and hence governable.[38] Anonymity or pseudonymity offered a form of address that foregrounded the message, not the messenger, that severed text from body and hence offered an opportunity to speak as an abstract, disembodied subject.

Oral forms and genres were enlisted in these experiments with "folktales" appearing under cryptic or initialized attributions, the writer experimenting with the possibilities of yoking together a traditional form and an author. As Barber demonstrates, oral forms and the genre of the periodical also "discovered" each other. The use of naming as an elaborated site of meaning and verbal creativity, a seminal component of oral poetry, expressed itself in the experiments with authorship in the press. The use of quotation, or "quotedness," central to Yoruba praise poetry likewise found an equivalent in the form of the periodical. "Both *oríkì* and the Yoruba newspapers assembled texts by quoting and recycling materials already in circulation; both constituted open webs hosting multiple, often anonymous contributions; both were fluid and heterogeneous assemblages of diverse fragments; and both were nonetheless strongly oriented towards permanence, to the constitution of a text out of discourse—a form that would endure."[39] Yet, as Barber and Newell note, even as authors experimented with anonymity, they equally wrote under their proper names backed up by copyright. In Lagos (as elsewhere), such authorial strategies surfaced in relation to books and serials in periodicals that had book potential.[40] In part, these attempts had an eye on making money of course, yet at the same time they were equally aimed at trying to construct permanence out of ephemerality and anonymity.

As Ellen Gruber Garvey has incisively demonstrated, periodical and newspaper readers across the world grappled with how to create value out of ephemeral forms of print culture. Often reproducing the cut-and-paste aesthetic of periodicals themselves, ordinary readers created their own archives of back copies, wrote out quotations by hand, and, most commonly, kept scrapbooks of cuttings from periodicals. As she demonstrates, this "writing by scissors" needs to be seen as a demotic form of authorship in which editing rather than writing becomes the template for textual production.[41]

Rubusana's presentation of himself can usefully be located against this background. The title page indexes oral traditions, Rubusana's religious writings (some of which may in fact have appeared anonymously and were retrospectively claimed here), and Rubusana as a copyrighted author. Yet his authorial status does not depend solely on this last credential but is distributed across these textual traditions. Indeed, Rubusana uses these different forms to credential each other: the monumentality of the praise poem invests the book with authority and vice versa. The book and newspaper work in relation to each other: parts of the book rise up from the newspaper *Izwi labantu* (Voice of the people) and no doubt migrate back into it. The book itself becomes a type of durable container, made momentous both by its bookness and by its epic contents. The title page stands as a kind of engraving or even an epitaph. An abridged edition undertaken in the 1960s preserves the 1911 title page while inserting the new publisher below. The copyright for this edition would have been invested in the new compiler, B. B. Mdledle, and Lovedale Press, yet epitaph-like the older imprimatur still stands.

Rubusana's use of copyright, then, is less about turning text into private property than about constituting it as public property, a "donation to the public sphere," in Newell's words.[42] In 1930 another prominent member of the black elite in South Africa, Sol T. Plaatje, published a novel, *Mhudi*. Its preface indicated that one reason for publishing the novel was to use the royalties to "collect and print (for Bantu Schools) Sechuana- folk-tales, which, with the spread of European ideas, are fast being forgotten."[43] The proceeds of one book were to be donated to create another, something that never happened, in part owing to the very poor sales of *Mhudi*.[44]

These disappointing sales raise the questions of the limitations of the southern African book markets, which were hampered by problems of distribution, tiny markets, and limited literacy (all of which made copyright a precarious right of limited value). These latter constraints on the print culture market have attracted considerable comment.[45] Less noticed perhaps has been the role of readers as purchasers (or nonpurchasers). As many studies have shown, audiences were made up of ardent and inventive readers.[46] Yet, overwhelmingly, they were reluctant buyers—as litanies of complaints from southern African authors, publishers, and editors attest. One way to construe this reluctance to buy commoditized text is via the idea of the commons: oral literary traditions were incommensurate with the idea of turning words into private property; subsidized religious and educational material was free (or very cheap); and the periodical press operated with a self-proclaimed cannibalizing system in which publications subsisted by cutting and pasting copy from each other. Together, these intersecting traditions created a general and deep-seated orientation that printed matter, rather like cheap U.S. reprints, should be easily available. If my initial hunch, namely, that copyright would be resisted, had any substance, then it was in relation to readers rather than writers. But to label this orientation "resistance" is misleading— to most people it probably appeared as common sense, or, alternatively, it could be interpreted as readers holding the British Empire to its promise to educate its subjects by supplying them with cheap reading material.

The limited pockets in which printed material was purchased support this hunch. While figures on book sales are notoriously difficult to pin down, especially in postcolonial situations of fragmented archives, those that are available indicate purchases of what we might call the top and bottom end, the top end being books that could "keep," like Bibles, hymnbooks, and anthologies of praise poetry (like Rubusana's), and the bottom being newspapers and periodicals.[47] Such purchases were possibly regarded less as the acquisition of a commodity than as an investment in a textual commons.

———

What broader conclusions can we draw from these snapshots of different textual economies in the colony? The first is that the material presented here inverts the picture that contemporary debates on IP lead us to believe— these generally hold that the "developing world" ignores IP because of its communal or "traditional" orientations, as opposed to the individualism of Western property law. The southern African picture presented here suggests the opposite: African writers defend copyright, while the settler representatives of the West turn it into a question of racial customs (in all senses of the word). Writers like Rubusana were keen and strategic users of copyright, an instrument by which they could construct themselves as rights-bearing subjects. Customs and Excise, by contrast, wanted to eviscerate such rights, turning copyright into yet a further instrument of racial supremacy.

A recent collection, *Copyright Africa: How Intellectual Property, Media and Markets Transform Immaterial Cultural Goods*, covering a range of periods, supports this understanding of copyright as an experiment in creating rights. The editors of this volume propose an extraversion argument, namely, the idea that African societies are experts at selectively absorbing influences from elsewhere. They suggest that African authors consequently add copyright as another possibility in their repertoire of ways of dealing with literary authority and ownership.[48] In Rubusana's case, copyright as a mode of authority is tacked onto the weight of the praise poetry tradition to create a new repertoire of cultural power.

Rubusana and the writers discussed here of course belonged to a tiny elite, so we cannot generalize their view of copyright too readily or too easily. There are many other nodes from which to consider colonial copyright: the printing and publishing industry, libraries and institutions of reading, legal histories. Such points of view, however, tend to favor a national and legal perspective. To open up a wider vista, I have selected instances that furnish a transnational and extralegal perspective, so as to give us a better sense of the mobile and social lives of colonial copyright. As the material represented here indicates, these lives are surprising and indicate the need to explore the worlds of colonial textualities rather than assuming that we know how they operated.

NOTES

1. Hofmeyr, *Gandhi's Printing Press*.
2. Wirtén, *Terms of Use*, loc. 1235 of 5229, Kindle edition.
3. Also influential in my thinking is Larkin, "Degraded Images, Distorted Sounds," 289–314.
4. Seville, *The Internationalisation of Copyright Law*; Bently, "Copyright, Translations, and Relations between Britain and India in the Nineteenth and Early Twentieth Centuries," 1181–1240; Birnhack, *Colonial Copyright*; and Peukert, "The Colonial Legacy of the International Copyright System," 37–68.
5. For some major beacons in the scholarship, see Johns, *The Nature of the Book and the Book of Nature*; Woodmansee and Jaszi, *The Construction of Authorship*; and Rose, *Authors and Owners*.
6. Coombe, *The Cultural Life of Intellectual Properties*; Michael Brown, *Who Owns Native Culture?*; Comaroff and Comaroff, *Ethnicity Inc.*; Drahos and Braithwaite, *Information Feudalism*; and Sunder, *From Goods to a Good Life*.
7. See note 4.
8. Royal Copyright Commission, *Minutes of Evidence*, 53.
9. Royal Copyright Commission, *Minutes of Evidence*, 55.
10. "Prohibited Imports. Copyright Works," DEA 202, A10/8/X, National Archives of South Africa, Pretoria.
11. "Prohibited and Restricted Imports. Objectionable Literature," DEA 200 A10/6X, vol. 2, National Archives of South Africa, Pretoria.
12. Seville, *The Internationalisation of Copyright Law*, 86–90.
13. Royal Copyright Commission, *Minutes of Evidence*, evidence from Charles Trevelyan, 1.
14. "British Copyright Works," DCU 67, 237/06, National Archives of South Africa, Pretoria.

15. South African Railways and Harbours, *Official Railway Tariff Handbook*.

16. "Contravention Customs Union Regulations. JE Bigwood—Standerton. 2 Cases Margarine . . . ," DCU 76, 670/06; "Underentries of Duty:—Foo Lee and Company. Tea Described as Herbs," DCU 85, 1416/06; "H. Moschke, Pietersburg, Soup Squares, re Classification of," DCU 82, 1091/06; "Importation of Poppy Seed," DCU 74, 574/06; "'Gingham' (Flanelette) Tariff Item 175. Imported by Mosenthal Brothers, Limited," DCU 81, 1032/06, all in National Archives of South Africa, Pretoria.

17. "Customs Detention of Certain Books," LTG 19, 25/54, National Archives of South Africa, Pretoria.

18. For an account of the precise workings of the Immigration Department in Durban and Cape Town, see Dhupelia-Mesthrie, "Betwixt the Oceans," 463–81; MacDonald, "Strangers in a Strange Land"; and MacDonald, "Colonial Trespassers in the Making of South Africa's International Borders, 1900 to c.1950."

19. Wakefield, *Foreign Marks of Origin Regulations*, 82.

20. Wakefield, *Foreign Marks of Origin Regulations*, 83.

21. Wakefield, *Foreign Marks of Origin Regulations*, 89.

22. Wakefield, *Foreign Marks of Origin Regulations*, 83.

23. Wakefield, *Foreign Marks of Origin Regulations*, 82, 83.

24. These are extracts from Wakefield, *Foreign Marks of Origin Regulations*.

25. Wakefield, *Foreign Marks of Origin Regulations*, 22.

26. "Complaint by Mr Speelman Regarding the Detention of Certain Books by the Customs," T 815 1505; "Detention of Book 'Vechten en Vluchten van Beyers en Kemp,'" T 912 2145; "Book Entitled De Dochter van dan Handsuffer [Hensopper]: Detention of," AG 1441 4790, National Archives of South Africa, Cape Town.

27. Payn, *The Merchandise Marks Act of 1887*, 21; see discussion in "Seizure under the Copyright Protection and Books Registration Act of 1895 of Certain Books," T 972 936, National Archives of South Africa, Cape Town, where the attorney general requests evidence that books have been manufactured or copyrighted in Britain.

28. Peukert, "The Colonial Legacy of the International Copyright System," 41.

29. "Copyright Act," NTS 1930, 202/278, National Archives of South Africa, Pretoria.

30. These translations are drawn from Opland, *Xhosa Poets and Poetry*, 64; Opland, *The Greater Dictionary of isiXhosa*; and "Dr Walter Benson Rubusana," South African History Online, accessed 13 June 2014, http://www.sahistory.org.za /people/dr-walter-benson-rubusana.

31. "Copyright Records of the Stationers' Hall, " National Archives (UK), accessed 1 June 2014, http://www.nationalarchives.gov.uk/records/research-guides /copyright.htm.

32. Peires, "Lovedale Press," 71–85; and T. White, "The Lovedale Press during the Directorship of R. H. W. Shepherd, 1930–1955," 69–84.

33. This registry was a small affair. Records indicate that in the 1890s it was recording about ninety titles a year, mostly items of colonial knowledge: manuals on how to deal with servants, maps, advice on agriculture, botanical books, and grammars of local languages. Cape of Good Hope: Transcript of the Copyright

Entries in the Registry Book, Deeds Registry Office, 1894–1901, Deeds Registry Office, Cape Colony, n.d. After the union of the various colonies and ex-republics in 1910, a central Copyright Registry was established in the Deeds Office in Pretoria, but it never carried the same authority as Customs and Excise vis-à-vis questions of copyright. In 1918 a set of regulations was promulgated in the *Government Gazette* to accompany new copyright legislation. The first time the registrar of copyright came to see these was when he encountered them in the gazette, causing him to write a bemused letter asking that in future he be consulted. "Prohibited Imports. Copyright Works," DEA 202, A10/8/X, National Archives of South Africa, Pretoria.

34. Banerjee, *Becoming Imperial Citizens*, 119.

35. The pieces referred to are (in Rubusana's orthography and capitalization, with translations by Jeff Opland, Wandile Kuse, and Pamela Maseko) "Isimangalo Sika-Tixo" ("God's Complaint"), "Icebetshu Lokusinda" ("A Narrow Escape"), "Ingxoxo Enkulu Ngemfundo" ("A Great Debate on Education"), "Imbali zama-Xosa" ("The History of the Xhosa People"), and "Isizatu Sokuxelwa kwe-Nkomo ngo-Nongqause" ("The Motive for the Nongqwause Cattle-Killing"). For Rubusana's versions, see Rubusana, *Zemk'inkomo Magwalandini*, 20–23, 24–25, 63–130, 198–218, and 219–25. For the translations, see Opland, Kuse, and Maseko, *William Wellington Gqoba*, 62–69, 84–209, 248–53, 264–99, and 460–83. The quote about the "cavalier editor" is on p. 18 of Opland, Kuse, and Maseko's volume. For further discussion of Rubusana, see Opland, *Xhosa Poets and Poetry*, 225; and Peires, *The House of Phalo*.

36. Burton and Hofmeyr, "Introduction," 4. Quotation from Lawrence Lessig, *The Future of Ideas*, 19.

37. Hofmeyr, *Gandhi's Printing Press*, 69–97.

38. Newell, *The Power to Name.*

39. Barber, "Authorship, Copyright and Quotation in Oral and Print Spheres in Early Colonial Yorubaland," 125.

40. See, for example, the series on Zulu history in *Ilanga lase Natal* (The sun of Natal) that is copyrighted. It ran from 2 August 1908 to 7 May 1909.

41. Garvey, *Writing with Scissors.*

42. Newell, *The Power to Name*, 105.

43. Plaatje, "Preface to the Original Edition," 21.

44. Willan, *Sol Plaatje*, 361–64.

45. This is a strong theme in southern African literary history. See specifically Peires, "Lovedale Press"; T. White, "The Lovedale Press during the Directorship of R. H. W. Shepherd, 1930–1955"; and Evans and Seeber, *The Politics of Publishing in South Africa.*

46. Newell, *Ghanaian Popular Fiction*; and Newell, *Literary Culture in Colonial Ghana.*

47. The best available figures are in the Lovedale Press archives, Cory Library, Rhodes University, Grahamstown, South Africa, and bear out these trends.

48. Röschenthaler and Diawara, "African Intellectual Worlds in the Making," 1–34.

CHAPTER ELEVEN

He Pukapuka Tataku i ngā Mahi a Te Rauparaha Nui: Reading Te Rauparaha through Time

ARINI LOADER

> Te Rauparaha is a god
> and Kapiti is his backbone
> Even the moon is his ally!
> —Campbell, *Sanctuary of Spirits*

TE RAUPARAHA, of the Ngāti Toa Rangatira and Ngāti Raukawa tribes, is a prominent historical figure whose influence permeates the history of Aotearoa New Zealand. He was a renowned leader, warrior, military strategist, and provider for his people, whose deeds during the tumultuous decades of the early to mid-nineteenth century have long since captured the national imagination. Te Rauparaha is well remembered in *waiata* (songs or sung poetry), *haka* (posture dance—vigorous dances with actions and rhythmically shouted words), poetry, and prose.[1] Additionally, with seven major published biographical treatments of his life, Te Rauparaha is at little risk of being forgotten from the pages of Aotearoa New Zealand's history.[2] Yet all these accounts rely heavily, indeed in some cases entirely, on a manuscript written in the mid-nineteenth century by his son Tāmihana Te Rauparaha.[3] The opening lines of this manuscript read:

He pukapuka tataku tenei i nga mahi a te
Rauparaha nui, o tona itinga kaumatua noa
Na, tana tamaiti tupu ake na Tamihana te
Rauparaha i tuhituhi kei wareware.[4]

This is an account of the deeds of the Great Te Rauparaha from the time of his infancy until his old age written by his son Tāmihana Te Rauparaha lest it be forgotten.[5]

In these brief words, Tāmihana lays out the topic of his narrative, followed by an authorial statement confirming himself as the writer.[6] He furthermore clarifies his reason for writing the manuscript: "kei wareware" (lest it be forgotten).[7] This rather foreboding sentiment echoes an observation made a decade or so earlier by a Hokianga *rangatira* (chief), Mohi Tāwhai, who in 1840, while debating whether or not to put his name to the Treaty of Waitangi, predicted that the written words of the *Pākehā* (European settlers) would "float light, like the wood of the w[h]au-tree, and always remain to be seen," but the sayings of Māori would "sink to the bottom like a stone."[8] Both Tāwhai's and Tāmihana's words suggest a dark future for Māori and prompt the questions, what was at risk of being forgotten, what are the stakes of this forgetting, and what does it mean for us today?

Tāmihana Te Rauparaha was clearly *not* in the business of forgetting his father or allowing his father's memory to be forgotten. His 127-page (unpaginated) manuscript consisting of extended narrative sections, a great deal of what might be termed "battle history," and eight waiata, and ending with nine pages of *whakapapa* (genealogy), though undated, is most likely to have been written during George Grey's first term as governor of New Zealand between 1845 and 1853.[9] Tāmihana's text is held in Grey's collection of Māori manuscripts at Auckland Public Library.[10] The two men corresponded regularly and appear to have been, together with their respective wives, on friendly, personable terms.[11] It is not known where the manuscript was written, how long it took to write, or how many sittings it was written in. It may have been written in Ōtaki, where Tāmihana and his wife, Ruta, lived most of the time, but Tāmihana was also a keen traveler, preaching Christianity in Te Waipounamu (the South Island) in 1843, living with Ruta in Auckland while attending Bishop George Augustus Selwyn's St John's College in the mid-1840s, and visiting England in late 1850, returning in 1852 after securing an audience with none other than Queen Victoria herself.[12] When compared to the great body of Māori manuscripts produced in the nineteenth century that are located in public archival institutions, Tāmihana's manuscript is outstanding not only in terms of its length and its comprehensiveness but also in its biographical dimension. Whereas there is a substantial body of biographical writings that take Māori as their subject, few of the authors were themselves Māori.[13] Tāmihana's manuscript is one of the earliest extant examples of Māori biography by a Māori writer.

Tāmihana Te Rauparaha was a talented writer; he learned to read and write as a young man in the mid- to late 1830s, instructed by a man named Matahau, also of the Ngāti Raukawa tribe (later baptized Hōhepa [Joseph] Ripahau). Matahau had been taken to the Bay of Islands as a captive in his youth; he came to live in Paihia with Anglican missionary Rev. William Williams, studying at the mission station before journeying back to the Kapiti Coast region. Tāmihana and his close relative Mātene Te Whiwhi were interested in Matahau's knowledge of Christianity and the segments of the New Testament and Book of Common Prayer that he brought with him from the Bay of Islands.[14] With a small amount of paper gained from a nearby whaling station, Matahau taught Tāmihana, Mātene, and ten others how to read.[15] By the end of six months' intensive study, the group could read a little. Tāmihana utilized his writing skills to good effect, as evidenced by collections of letters written by him held in various public repositories such as the Auckland Public Library and the Bishop Selwyn Collection of Early Māori Documents housed at Waikato University Library. Tāmihana also wrote to and was published in the *niupepa*, the nineteenth-century Māori-language newspapers, and while visiting England in the early 1850s he wrote a text for the Church Missionary Society outlining his personal introduction to and engagement with Christianity and alphabetic literacy.[16]

Tāmihana Te Rauparaha maintained a lifelong interest in Christianity, traveling with Mātene Te Whiwhi to the Bay of Islands to seek a resident missionary for the Kapiti Coast in 1839 and eventually returning with Henry Williams and Octavius Hadfield, the latter of whom remained permanently on the Kapiti Coast.[17] In 1844 he accompanied Bishop Selwyn on his first overland trek in Te Waipounamu (the South Island), where he carried a message of peace to the former enemies of his father and his people. Tāmihana is also said to have lived "the life of an English gentleman" in a European-style weatherboard house, with European servants. He also took to wearing European-style clothing.[18] He became a successful sheep farmer and a man of considerable wealth, possessing a flock of seven hundred sheep by 1866.[19] Tāmihana's penchant for things Pākehā may have estranged him from his own people.[20] This dimension of Tāmihana's personality in some ways sits in stark contrast to Te Rauparaha, or at least how Te Rauparaha tends to be remembered in the intersection between the man and the myth. Whereas

Tāmihana was quick to embrace many aspects of imported European culture, his father was more circumspect, though certainly not slow to incorporate and adapt new technologies to suit his needs and purposes.

Although the precise date remains unknown, Te Rauparaha was born in the 1760s, right on the cusp of European peoples' earliest meaningful encounters with Māori. As such, Te Rauparaha lived through a time when *te ao Māori* (lit. "the Māori world") underwent radical change and shifts stimulated by contact with Europeans and the greater world at large. Born into the rangatira classes, though not of the most elevated genealogical lines, Te Rauparaha rose to prominence as a military strategist, warrior, and leader within the ranks of Ngāti Toa Rangatira and Ngāti Raukawa, tribes of the Tainui waka (canoe) confederation. He is the visionary leader who spearheaded the major nineteenth-century migratory movements, which saw Ngāti Toa and allied *hapū* (kin group or subtribe) of Ngāti Raukawa and Te Āti Awa move to the southern parts of Te Ika a Māui (the North Island) in the 1820s. Te Rauparaha is celebrated as a master of subterfuge and for his almost supernatural, uncanny ability to survive against seemingly insurmountable odds. Following the migration to and settlement in the south, after leaving the tribal homelands in the rich, fertile Waikato region, Te Rauparaha made Kapiti Island his base, from which he commanded his lucrative maritime trading empire encompassing both sides of Raukawa moana (Cook Strait).[21] Formal colonization in 1840 heightened tensions with Pākehā over land, as discussed later in this chapter. Although Te Rauparaha professed friendship with Pākehā and demonstrated through many actions that he was willing to listen to reason, to trust European processes, and to at least attempt to work out compromises over territory and resources, Governor Grey kidnapped him in 1846 and transported him to Auckland, where he was held indefinitely without charge.[22] Te Rauparaha was finally returned to his people at Ōtaki in 1848, where he died a year later on 27 November 1849.[23]

The first part of this chapter explores the more than hundred-year history of the publication of book-length biographies of Te Rauparaha, in order to draw out the contours of the ways in which Tāmihana's written work, specifically the manuscript he wrote about the life of his father, has been represented to the wider community. This publishing history illustrates some of the ways in which Māori intellectual traditions have been presented back to Māori and the wider community in an example of what New Zealand historian Peter Gibbons has called "cultural colonization," through which Māori, already deprived of lands and resources, were also alienated from their intellectual traditions and histories.[24]

The second part of this chapter takes inspiration from the work of such Māori scholars as Aroha Harris, Melissa Matutina Williams, and Nēpia Mahuika, who are engaged in writing histories "that help Māori escape the past into which they have been written," "writing up from under the great weight of New Zealand historiography" and "the dominant historical discourse which tends to locate Māori history in the context of British colonialism and expansionism."[25] Harris, who is interested in Māori and tribal histories of Māori policy and community development in the twentieth century, draws attention, for example, to the dynamic ways in which the great migratory waves of Māori who relocated into the cities during and immediately following World War II responded to the challenges of an urban environment where European customs dominated and English was the main language.[26] Similarly, in her book *Panguru and the City; Kāinga Tahi Kāinga Rua: An Urban Migration History*, Melissa Matutina Williams *rewrites* and *rights* the history of twentieth-century Māori urban migration by returning it to the tribal and *whānau* (familial) context in which it occurred.[27] Nēpia Mahuika also advocates locating Māori historical scholarship within specific iwi and hapū paradigms and interpretive frames, effectively repatriating Māori history to Māori people, communities, and places.[28] All three historians are engaged in writing Māori histories on Māori terms using methodologies, approaches, and frames that enable us to tell histories that we, that is, Māori, recognize, histories that we see ourselves in, histories that we belong to and that are a part of us. As Harris so eloquently put it: "We are what we write: we are our stories, our histories, our pasts. . . . The histories that Māori historians narrate are rarely—if ever—those of an impersonalised other, or even of an amorphous, generic us. At the base of our histories, are ourselves, however we understand ourselves to be, and whether in familial, tribal or Māori terms."[29] Following Harris's lead, this chapter returns Tāmihana's manuscript to its familial, tribal, Māori (*māori*, that is, "normal") context. It reads up from and out of published biographies, specifying the various ways in which Tāmihana's account has been deployed by secondary writers and often heavily edited, thereby misinterpreting the content and obscuring its authorship.

READING BACK

Te Rauparaha entered book-length print culture through the efforts of William Thomas Locke Travers, who was the first to produce a substantive, comprehensive biographical treatment of him. Travers was an Irish-born lawyer who moved to New Zealand in 1849, with his wife, Jane, and their two children, where he practiced law in Nelson, Christchurch, and Wellington and pursued "a fitful political career."[30] His interest in natural history and his penchant for exploring the natural world led him in 1867 to become one of the founders of the New Zealand Institute (known today as the Royal Society Te Apārangi), and he went on to publish some forty articles on botany, ornithology, geology, and ethnology in the institute's *Transactions and Proceedings*.[31]

Travers first presented his work on Te Rauparaha orally, and then in print in at least three different guises. His series of lectures, "On the Life and Times of Te Rauparaha," was read before the Wellington Philosophical Society on 21 August, 4 September, and 2, 9, and 30 October 1872, and they were then published in 1872 in volume 5 of the *Transactions and Proceedings*, before being repackaged the same year as a book, under the title *Some Chapters in the Life and Times of Te Rauparaha, Chief of Ngatitoa*.[32] Travers's text was released for a third time in 1906 in a joint publication with the Rev. J. W. Stack's book about Te Rauparaha's attack on the Ngāi Tahu settlement of Kaiapohia under the title *The Stirring Times of Te Rauparaha (Chief of the Ngatitoa), also, The Sacking of Kaiapohia*.[33] Travers's work on Te Rauparaha was thus widely disseminated, first to members of the Wellington Philosophical Society, then to subscribers of the *Transactions*, and finally to the general reading public.

In each instance Travers begins by explaining his two main reasons for writing on Te Rauparaha: the first was the chief's association with the New Zealand Company settlement in Wellington. This was a commercial operation designed for investors based on theories developed by Englishman Edward Gibbon Wakefield about solving social distress in Britain, with the view that population growth was related to food production and that the solution to mass starvation was to export surplus population.[34] As his second reason for writing on Te Rauparaha, Travers identifies Te Rauparaha's prominence in significant historic events leading up to the signing of the Treaty of Waitangi. Travers looks to the future when writing on what he imagines will be important "for the future historian of the Colony." He was self-consciously in the business of making history and was keen to leave behind something of his own legacy for future generations of New Zealanders. Travers's publication did indeed go on to have wide-reaching implications, for all subsequent work on Te Rauparaha and his times draws from these early biographical sketches.[35]

Although Travers clearly made extensive use of Tāmihana's manuscript, he was evasive about his sources, providing minimal acknowledgment of the intellectual debt he owed to Tāmihana and obscuring how he obtained access to the manuscript. He attributes two large quotes in his text to Tāmihana: the first totals 394 words concerning the circumstances of the death of the Ngāi Tahu chief Te Maiharanui.[36] Travers introduces this with, "The following is the account given to me by Tamihana Te Rauparaha of the mode in which the unfortunate chief was delivered over to his death."[37] The second is the longest quote to appear in Travers's account, at just over a thousand words.[38] Travers prefaces this quote, which corresponds to the last sixteen pages of Tāmihana's manuscript, with, "I think it is as well to give Te Rauparaha's own view of the disastrous affair at the Wairau in 1843, and of its results as related to me by his son."[39] Both of these extended quotes, which Travers implies were given to him orally from Tāmihana Te Rauparaha, are in fact paraphrases of Tāmihana's manuscript.

Further evidence that Travers utilized Tāmihana's manuscript is provided by George Grey in the form of a note pasted onto its front cover that states Travers saw the manuscript and made an English-language summary of it. Despite his claims of having received a personal account from Tāmihana, there can be no doubt that Travers accessed the manuscript through Grey, who, for all intents and purposes, owned the document. In addition, George Samuel Graham, a New Zealand–born accountant and lawyer with familial ties to Māori who had a lifelong interest in Māori history, language, culture, and artifacts, compiled a large number of manuscripts in these fields, many in Māori accompanied by his translations.[40] Between 1915 and 1918, he completed an English-language translation of Tāmihana Te Rauparaha's manuscript. Graham noted Travers's reliance on Tāmihana's account, stating that Travers "borrowed largely" from the text.[41] Travers's work simultaneously makes Tāmihana's contribution to the literature on the life of his father visible while making the precise nature of that contribution, Tāmihana's *written* contribution, invisible.

Te Rauparaha also appeared in John White's monumental government-sponsored, bilingual (Māori and English) *Ancient History of the Maori*, a six-volume series published between 1887 and 1890. The English-born White emigrated to New Zealand as a child in 1834, with his parents and seven siblings; the family settled in Hokianga in the far north.[42] After embarking on a course of self-improvement involving revising past lessons, taking up music, and reading widely, White became interested in Māori song poetry, which very quickly resulted in his accumulating several hundred songs and traditions.[43] White gained the attention of Governor Grey by sending him manuscripts of Māori material, which led to an appointment as Grey's secretary and translator in 1851.[44] Years of public service followed in, for example, the Land Purchase Department, and as a resident magistrate for the Whanganui region, before White became involved in other ventures, including gold mining in 1867.[45] Between 1874 and 1878, White edited *Te Wananga*, a Māori-language newspaper published by Ngāti Kahungungu leader Hēnare Tōmoana. This experience and the reputation White had acquired as an ethnographer resulted in his appointment in early 1879 as the compiler and writer of an official Māori history.[46]

In the sixth and final volume of *Ancient History of the Maori*, centered on the history and traditions of Tainui (a group of tribal groups connected by shared lineage to the ancestral Tainui canoe), White includes what he titles "an account of the acts of Te Rauparaha from his birth to the time of his old age."[47] The chapter heading in the English-language version reads, "Chapter II. Rauparaha. Ngatitoa: Written by Tamihana Te Rauparaha" and in the Māori-language version, "Upoko II. Te Rauparaha Ngatitoa: Na Tamihana Te Rauparaha i tuhituhi." While he acknowledges Tāmihana as the writer of the account, White made substantial changes to Tāmihana's text without acknowledging or noting where and how he had done so. In effect, White's account is in fact Tāmihana's manuscript, heavily edited and reproduced in a substantially altered form. White, for example, adds his own ideas, interpretations, and understandings to Tāmihana's text despite representing the narrative account as Tāmihana's written work. One particularly glaring example appears on the first page, in which Te Rauparaha's family are introduced. In his text Tāmihana gives a detailed description of the immediate family group and includes, for example, the names of Te Rauparaha's siblings and the order of their birth. Tāmihana also supplies detailed information about Te Rauparaha's parents; in addition to noting that he was the last-born of the family, he writes that Te Rauparaha was also known as Māui Pōtiki:[48]

> Ko te wahine tenei a Wherawera ko Parekohatu
> Ko te whaea tenei o te Rauparaha. Otira tenei
> ano o mua ake i a te Rauparaha me ata tuhi
> o ratou ingoa,
> Ko te Rangikatukuatomua
> Muri iho ko Whaitohi
> Muri iho ko te Kiripaeahi
> Muri iho ko Mahurenga
> Muri iho ko te Rauparaha, te wakamutu
> nga tenei ko tona wakatauki, ko Maui Potiki.[49]

Parekōwhatu was the wife of Wherawera and mother of Te Rauparaha, but there were children older than Te Rauparaha as recorded herewith;

Te Rangikatukua was the eldest followed by Whaitohi, Te Kiripaeahi, then Mahurenga, after whom came the youngest, Te Rauparaha, known as Māui Pōtiki.

White, however, reframes the way in which Tāmihana introduces his father's immediate family:

Tona kainga i whanau ai ko Kawhia, tona matua tane ko Werawera, ko te matua wahine ko Parekowhatu. Ka whanau a te Rauparaha, tokorua ona tuakana, a tokorua ona tuahine. He potiki rawa aia no te whakapakanga. Kahore i whai tikanga nga tuakana, he rangatira anake tona tikanga.[50]

He was born at Kawhia. His father's name was Werawera (heat) and his mother's name was Parekōwhatu (plume of stone). He had two elder brothers and two elder sisters. He was the last born of the family. His elder brothers did not show any superior knowledge or power: they were chiefs of rank, and that is all they could assume.[51]

White presents the text to conform to his own Eurocentric gaze by simply giving the names of Te Rauparaha's mother and father, noting that he had two elder brothers and two elder sisters and that he was the youngest in the family. White's heavy-handed editing of the text glosses over layers of complexity and meaning. Of even greater concern than White's editorial interventions is his additional comment, "Kahore i whai tikanga nga tuakana, he rangatira anake tona tikanga" ("His elder brothers did not show any superior knowledge or power: they were chiefs of rank, and that is all they could assume").[52] Nothing even resembling this statement appears in Tāmihana's manuscript, which suggests White made this addition himself.[53] Not only are Te Rauparaha's siblings rendered nameless in White's version, but White makes a significant mental leap in assuming that Te Rauparaha's brothers "did not show any superior knowledge or power."[54] White furthermore makes no comment at all on Te Rauparaha's sisters, one of whom in particular, Waitohi ("Whaitohi" in Tāmihana Te Rauparaha's manuscript), was a renowned leader of her people.[55]

Many more examples of editorial intervention can be cited throughout White's work. Although he passes the narrative off as a reproduction of Tāmihana's manuscript, he made numerous alterations and changes to the text so as to render it a confused version of Tāmihana's original text.[56] Having the imprint of government sponsorship gave White's version greater legitimacy and ensured it reached a wide audience. Now available online, White's interpretation continues to reach a wider reading audience than does

Tāmihana's original manuscript.[57] While Tāmihana's manuscript is available for those who wish to seek it out, only a handful of copies exist in research libraries.[58] Furthermore, the original manuscript continues to lie in relative obscurity in the Special Collections at Auckland Public Library, far away from its tribal context.[59] In its publication history, Tāmihana's manuscript fits an observation made by Paul Meredith and Alice Te Punga Somerville, who note that "a great deal of the primary writings by tangata mohio [knowledgeable persons] . . . have found their way into the Alexander Turnbull Library, while the published works of Pakeha ethnographers have enjoyed a much wider audience, shaping much of the contemporary discourse around Maori culture and traditions."[60] The same can be said for two other major research libraries in Aotearoa New Zealand: Auckland Public Library and Hocken Library in Dunedin. Tāmihana Te Rauparaha is, within Meredith and Te Punga Somerville's framework, a "tangata mōhio."

In 1911, some twenty years after the publication of White's official history, New Zealand–born Thomas Lindsay Buick produced *An Old New Zealander, or Te Rauparaha, the Napoleon of the South*. During his career as a journalist, Buick wrote twelve books and a small number of pamphlets, many of which he published at his own expense.[61] Buick's first book, *Old Marlborough*, was published in 1900, and his second book, *Old Manawatu*, followed in 1903.[62] After completing *An Old New Zealander*, Buick went on to publish his best-known book, *The Treaty of Waitangi*, in 1914.[63] Of Buick's published work, J. E. Traue notes that as well as having had "a fluent prose style and firm sense of narrative structure," Buick "synthesised a wide range of printed sources and, particularly for his earlier works, sought out eyewitnesses and others closely associated with historical events."[64]

Buick alludes to this "synthesis" of a range of printed sources in the acknowledgments section of *An Old New Zealander* where he expresses his thanks to the authors "of the many existing publications on New Zealand."[65] Gibbons takes Buick's practice of synthesizing printed sources a step further, claiming that he deliberately added "imaginative colour to the documentary framework."[66] Gibbons furthermore asserts, "Though Buick was prepared to challenge popular misconceptions . . . his own interest was in myth-making, and his histories were attempts to depict a glamorous and dramatic past."[67] Patricia Burns is also highly critical of Buick's work and identifies a number of specific instances where Buick distorted the events through the degree to which he expresses his own views and opinions within his text. Burns notes, for example, that Buick took Godfrey Charles Mundy's eyewitness report that Te Rauparaha, on being released from Crown custody, "covered his old grey head with his mat, and remained for hours immovable," and converted it to a preposterous "covered his old grey head with his mat, and for two hours sat and sobbed like a child."[68] Burns here demonstrates how Buick twists Mundy's words to produce an account that belittles Te Rauparaha, and by extension Māori people, culture, and customs.

Following New Zealand's turmoil of the 1960s and 1970s, as Māori urbanization challenged cherished notions of harmonious race relations, as Māori intellectual activities flourished, and as Māori began to protest for civil and land rights, the 1980s were ripe for new, revisionist histories. In 1980 Patricia Burns, a Pākehā freelance writer and researcher who gained her doctorate on the history of the New Zealand press from Victoria University in 1957, published her award-winning biographical treatment, *Te Rauparaha: A New Perspective*.[69] As the word *new* in the title indicates, Burns signals a movement toward alternative ways of thinking and theorizing about Te Rauparaha and New Zealand history more broadly. Burns's biography draws on a wide range of sources including unpublished manuscripts, private papers, letters, published government papers, official papers, and New Zealand Company records as well as a selection of published material including journal articles, newspaper articles, and books. Her work is constructed critically and carefully, resulting in the most in-depth and thorough study of Te Rauparaha to be produced thus far.

Burns has little to say about Tāmihana's manuscript, however. In the brief comments she does include in her book, she mentions the translation made by Graham and acknowledges that Travers and White, whose works were subsequently considered as basic sources for the life of Te Rauparaha, had used Tāmihana's "History." Burns also states that Graham noted that while Travers and White "borrowed largely" from Tāmihana's "History," it had not been translated and that "only parts" had been paraphrased. Burns herself notes that Graham's own translation is uneven and had not been published.[70]

While Burns's comments do shed some light on the translation and publication history of Tāmihana's manuscript, she does not offer any thoughts on Tāmihana's significant written contribution in regard to Te Rauparaha. Despite this, Burns quotes from Tāmihana's manuscript throughout her book and notes where Tāmihana's version of events either agrees with or departs from other published and unpublished sources. For example, Burns describes a pursuit on the sea where some of the men in the overloaded canoe containing Te Rauparaha and his family were frantically baling, jumping in and out of the canoe, and sometimes being thrown out by Te Rauparaha, until they could board the canoe of his kinsman, Rāwiri Pūaha.

Burns writes in a footnote, "According to Tamihana, who had been in the canoe. A Ngati Hau told John White (*Ancient History*, Vol. 6, p. 103) that women, children and aged men were thrown overboard by Te Rauparaha to enable him to escape. This was seized on by later writers, including Buick (*An Old New Zealander*, p. 192), but is not likely to be true. It is not mentioned by Stack and other early sources; Travers did not believe it so and Tamihana's story offers sufficient explanation."[71] Burns takes a considered approach to the conflicting versions of the episode as given by Tāmihana and an unnamed Ngāti Hau source, and compares these to those of Stack and other unnamed "early sources." Burns furthermore notes that Travers did not believe White's version to be true. While it is notable that Burns takes care to reference Tāmihana's manuscript throughout her work, it is unfortunate that she includes quotes only in English-language translation and does not indicate where or whom these translations are from.

In the same year that Burns's book was published, Peter Butler produced an illustrated English translation of Tāmihana's manuscript, *Life and Times of Te Rauparaha by His Son Tamihana Te Rauparaha*. No biographical information is available about Butler although by his own account in his short introduction to his publication he was a keen amateur historian. *Life and Times of Te Rauparaha* appears to be his only published work. Although he does not supply the source of his translation, it is clear that Butler reproduced Graham's translation work, albeit in an extensively edited form. Butler thus does not allow for issues around translation or even his own editing of the text. He equates Graham's English translation with Tāmihana's manuscript and criticizes what he perceives to be Tāmihana's poor standard of writing. Butler suggests that "[Tāmihana] was certainly no scholar and the manuscript had to be extensively edited, but I have not cut anything of substance or interest."[72] Worse still than not acknowledging his use of Graham's translation work, Butler makes no mention whatsoever that his publication is a translation of a text that was originally written in Māori. Butler disregards a raft of issues associated with translation, in particular the relationship between language, culture, and worldview, and assumes that a translation of Tāmihana's manuscript is as good as, or the same as, Tāmihana's original work. Butler's work smacks of a cultural superiority that is incapable of acknowledging its own inherent subjectivity.

Butler's narrative reads as confusingly as does his introduction. Notwithstanding the "extensive editing" that Butler undertook, the prose does not scan well and reads haltingly. As the first of the major publications on Te Rauparaha to reputedly bring Tāmihana's manuscript to print, it is disappointing to say the least. In his editorial interventions, Butler echoes the practices of nineteenth-century ethnographers and collectors of history and tradition, such as George Grey, who over a hundred years earlier embarked on his own editing and publishing of Māori manuscripts.[73] Grey routinely edited out content that he regarded to be of no "substance" or "interest," which resulted in the original Māori manuscript texts being rearranged and re-presented in ways that aligned with his worldview and belief system.

Butler's publication presents a remarkable challenge when read alongside Burns's book: that two works about Te Rauparaha published in the same year are so extremely different can be read as a sign of the changing times. Whereas Burns's work signals a shift in the ways that Māori historical biography might be undertaken, Butler's work reminds us that the Pākehā-centric tendrils of the old guard of two-dimensional, Eurocentric writers and scholars of New Zealand history are reluctant to lose or even loosen their grip on this intellectual territory. This is not to say that Burns's work is a perfect example of scholarship on Māori, but it does take significant steps toward more complex and ethically sound work. When viewed alongside each other, Burns's and Butler's works can be seen to represent, respectively, a step forward toward useful research and a step sideways and perhaps even backward toward work that is of limited use to Māori communities as well as the broader reading public.

Thirty years after Burns's and Butler's work appeared, Hēni Collins published her biography *Ka Mate Ka Ora! The Spirit of Te Rauparaha* (2010). This is the first published book-length biographical treatment of Te Rauparaha by a Māori author. Collins furthermore claims a kinship relationship to Te Rauparaha as a descendant of his uncle, Hapekituarangi. *Ka Mate Ka Ora!* was launched at Takapuwāhia marae, where it was blessed by Matiu Rei, the chief executive of the tribe's governing body, Te Rūnanga o Ngāti Toa Rangatira, and by Te Waari Carkeek, the *tumuaki* (chairperson) of Te Rūnanga o Ngāti Raukawa, a tribe to which Te Rauparaha also belongs.[74] That Collins's book was officially launched by the tribal leadership in a ceremony at the main Ngāti Toa Rangatira marae (complex of buildings usually including a large, often ornately carved meeting house and a dining hall) suggests that it was endorsed by the tribe both to tribal members themselves and to outsiders. Collins, however, a former newspaper journalist, describes the book as "an updated version of [a book by Patricia Burns]" that aims to "provide more cultural authenticity by returning to early manuscripts in te reo, a stronger understanding of our rights as Maori by having looked at Waitangi Tribunal reports, but also attempts to offer the perspectives of other iwi and Europeans."[75]

In her acknowledgments, Collins cites Tāmihana's manuscript as one of the most important sources for her book. She makes a point of mentioning that she studied Tāmihana's original manuscript as well as Graham's translation and the typescript from which Graham made his translation. In her work of over three hundred pages, however, Collins includes thirteen quotes from Tāmihana's manuscript in Māori with an English-language translation, and a further fifteen quotes only in English. Further references attributed to Tāmihana are scattered throughout the work, but given the inconsistent referencing used throughout the book, it is difficult to say with any certainty how extensively Collins made use of Tāmihana's account. For these reasons, it is difficult to assess the impact that Tāmihana's manuscript makes in the work overall.

Collins furthermore brings her own editing skills to bear on Tāmihana's written work. Collins outlines what these alterations are in a note on sources and *te reo* (Māori-language) at the beginning of her book: "Quotes from Tamihana Te Rauparaha's text about his father's life have been adjusted for ease of reading. Tamihana had a number of unusual spelling habits—for example his use of the letter *h*. He consistently wrote 'Wherawera,' who is commonly known as Werawera, and instead of 'whakatauki' he would write 'wakatauki.' . . . Dropping the h is consistent with a dialectal habit in some parts of the North Island, but adding an *h* is rare."[76] Collins highlights a particularly striking feature of Tāmihana's writing in this manuscript, noting his unusual addition or omission of the letter *h* in many names and words where it does not align with modern Māori orthography. While this feature of Tāmihana's writing is certainly noteworthy, particularly in light of te reo Māori revitalization efforts over the past few decades, it is a matter of some regret that Collins felt the need to adjust Tāmihana's writing to fit within a particular contemporary framework.[77] Tāmihana's use of the letter *h* is internally consistent, and I suggest that readers would have no trouble in comprehending Tāmihana's text the way that he himself wrote it. Something of the individuality of the text and the writer is lost when stylistic features such as this are ironed out in the name of contemporary standardization practices, and neither is it clear that standardizing it adds anything of significance to the text. There are also important historical and linguistic issues to consider, not least of which are dialectal, regional, and *iwi* (tribal) differences in pronunciation. This is all the more ironic as an iwi member produced this book. As Rewa Morgan notes in her study of the intersections between oral history and Māori biography, "Collins's narrative is beautifully and thoughtfully illustrated with prints, photographs and whakapapa. However, Collins's history lacked any intimacy that one might expect from whanaungatanga (kinship ties)."[78] Collins might be a tribal member, but there is little in the work itself that defines it as a tribal work. Rather, Collins's book is essentially an updated version of Burns's groundbreaking biographical study of thirty years earlier.

The various ways in which Te Rauparaha's biographers have represented Tāmihana Te Rauparaha's account of the life of his father have undermined and distorted Tāmihana's valuable written contribution. Perhaps not surprisingly, the texts on Te Rauparaha produced by each of the writers profiled in this chapter often reveal more about the writer and their historical context than the man they purport to be about. While all the published works that have dealt with Te Rauparaha have variously borrowed from, drawn on, and, in the case of Butler, reproduced Tāmihana's written work, the original manuscript has in many ways remained hidden in plain view beneath the editorial decisions of subsequent writers. This mirrors the way in which Tāmihana's manuscript also remains hidden in plain view at the Auckland Public Library, where in theory any researcher can access it but first needs to be aware of its existence and then know how to navigate the conventions of the library. As with the Hawaiian-language archive as discussed by Noelani Arista in this volume, the problem of the hidden Māori-language archive is structural and attitudinal, and it is a problem over a century in the making. Although Tāmihana wrote in order to remember his father, "lest it be forgotten," his text, despite having been widely consumed, consulted, and reproduced, albeit most often in English-language translation and through various editorial filters, remains invisible.

READING UP

Tāmihana and his kin were aware of the far-reaching influence, power, and significance of written texts.[79] The manuscript contains, for example, an infamous episode in which a Captain John Blenkinsopp in 1832 attempted to defraud Te Rauparaha of his lands around Karauripē (Cloudy Bay), including the Wairau Plain, some twenty-six thousand hectares of rich, fertile land, for the price of a broken cannon.[80] According to Tāmihana, Captain Blenkinsopp drew up a deed of sale for Wairau and signed Te Rauparaha's and the other chiefs' names to the document, but told Te Rauparaha that it was a document confirming his and the other chiefs' status as rangatira to visiting foreign vessels.[81] When Te Rauparaha returned to Raumati, he asked the local Pākehā trader to explain the meaning of the document: "No te hoatutanga ki tana pakeha hoko muka mana e korero mai nga tikanga o roto o aua pukapuka i tuhia ra e Kapene Piringatapu."[82] The trader explained that it was a deed of sale selling the lands of Wairau to Blenkinsopp in exchange for one big gun. Te Rauparaha reacted to this news by throwing the deed of sale, as well as other documents in the possession of his nephew, Te Rangihaeata, and other chiefs, into the fire and burning them.

Te Rauparaha's immediate and forceful response of throwing not only the deed of sale but also other documents in the possession of the other chiefs into the fire demonstrates the strength of his feelings in regard to both the legitimacy and the worth of the documents. Tāmihana writes that Te Rauparaha burned all of the documents literally to ashes: "tahuna katoatia atu ki te ahi."[83] What we learn of Blenkinsopp following this episode is also very telling. Tāmihana writes that Blenkinsopp continued on his way overseas never to return: "haere tonu atu taua pakeha ki tawhahi kihai i hoki mai ngaro tonu atu."[84] Tāmihana then comments rather ironically, "ko te rironga tenei Whairau i kia nei i hokona atu ki te pakeha" ("these are the terms by which Wairau was said to have been sold to the Pakeha").[85] Tāmihana foreshadows the troubles that would later erupt over the sale of Wairau, when settlers attempted to enforce the fraudulent document, which would ultimately end in bloodshed for both Māori and Pākehā.[86]

The danger inherent in this episode, of unwittingly agreeing to the sale of a vast estate in exchange for what was essentially a trifle, was clearly not lost on Tāmihana. A further example that gives some clues as to Tāmihana's understanding of the potential implications of the written word appears eleven pages later in the manuscript:

> Ka nui haere te pakanga a te Rangihaeata kia te Kawha
> na, Ka nui haere hoki nga korero tito o nga tangata
> me nga pukapuka tuhituhi a nga tangata hei whaka
> pae ia te Rauparaha.[87]

Te Rangihaeata's antagonism toward the governor grew steadily, as did the malicious rumors, spoken and in print, defaming Te Rauparaha.

Following Tāmihana's description of the incident at Wairau in which four Māori and twenty-two Europeans were killed, he describes the troubles that erupted over the sale of land in the Hutt Valley. According to Tāmihana, as the aggravation between Governor Fitzroy and Te Rangihaeata increased in the 1840s, so too did the fabrications, lies, and accusations directed against Te Rauparaha both via word of mouth and, even more important, in print. On 23 December 1843 the *Nelson Examiner and New Zealand Chronicle*, for example, printed the following excerpt from Colonel Wakefield's third dispatch to the New Zealand Company (written in 1839) as part of a long article under the title, "Of Rauparaha and Rangihiaita [*sic*]": "It is impossible for the most charitable to have any feelings towards this old fellow [Te Rauparaha] but those of aversion. It will be a most fortunate thing for any settlement formed hereabouts when he dies; for with his life only will end his mischievous scheming and insatiable cupidity." Tāmihana notes that owing to his being so publicly judged and castigated despite siding with the Pākehā, Te Rauparaha became disillusioned with his Pākehā friends.[88] This example shows that Tāmihana was conscious of the potential for the written word to be manipulated to suit particular agendas and to meet certain ends.

This leads me back again to the beginning of the manuscript where Tāmihana gives his reason for writing the manuscript:

> Na, tana tamaiti tupu ake na Tamihana te
> Rauparaha i tuhituhi kei wareware.[89]

Tāmihana wrote his account against a tide of English-language, Pākehā-authored texts, which at the time received, and today still receive, more public attention than Māori-authored work. It seems reasonable to assume that Tāmihana therefore felt some compulsion to write his own account of Te Rauparaha's life to counter the other narratives, rumors, and lies about Te Rauparaha that were circulating at the time, many of which have persisted well into the present day. As I have discussed elsewhere, historian Angela Ballara notes that Te Rauparaha received a wave of condemnation in print because many of the early visitors to the Kapiti Coast and Cook Strait who published accounts of the area were associates of the New Zealand Company.[90] As Te Rauparaha was the most powerful chief in the southern districts of Te Ika a Māui, the North Island, extending over Raukawa Moana (Cook Strait) into Te Waipounamu, the South Island, he was viewed by the New Zealand Company as the biggest obstacle to their plans of large-scale, organized immigration to New Zealand. According to Ballara, the New Zealand Company "lost no chance to blacken his name in print and ascribe to him all the ills experienced by Company settlers. He was 'cunning,' capable of 'unbound treachery,' and demonstrated the 'savage ferocity of the tiger' and the 'destructive ambition of a selfish despot,' fond of 'slaughter' but at the same time 'cringing' and 'fawning.'"[91] In his 1855 publication *Te Ika a Maui, or New Zealand and Its Inhabitants*, the Anglican missionary Richard Taylor observed:

> The settlers in general viewed him [Te Rauparaha] as everything bad, most treacherous, and deceitful; *but this opinion was not founded on their*

personal acquaintance with him, so much as from report. The whalers and traders who had the best opportunity of being intimately acquainted with him, and that too, at a time when his power to injure was the greatest, invariably speak of him as having ever been the white man's friend; he always placed the best he had before them, and in no instance have I heard of his doing any one of them an injury.[92]

Taylor describes the willingness with which settlers believed and even perpetuated rumor over their own actual lived or personal experience. This view aligned with their own economic interests in New Zealand.

Tāmihana's words, "lest it be forgotten," take on a whole new significance when viewed against the broader historical context. Most important, Tāmihana's account provides an alternative version to the tide of writing in English produced at the time about Te Rauparaha, or in which Te Rauparaha featured, in contemporary periodicals, personal journals and diaries, official dispatches, and more, much of which perpetuated the overwhelmingly negative discourse constructed by the New Zealand Company. Tāmihana's text can thus be understood as an immediate "writing back" to anti–Te Rauparaha narratives and as an insurance against alternative versions of the story of Te Rauparaha being entirely absent from the written record.

Furthermore, Tāmihana's manuscript can itself be viewed as an object of contention. I return full circle here to Grey's note on the front cover of the manuscript book, which reads:

> History of Te Rauparaha written by
> his son Tamehana Te Rauparaha
> at his fathers dictation. Mr Travers
> saw this and published in English
> a summary of it
> Photo of him and wife
> GG

This small note has had far-reaching ramifications whereby generations of historians have taken it for granted that his father dictated this manuscript to Tāmihana Te Rauparaha.[93] Tāmihana was not merely a scribe who recorded Te Rauparaha's story, as this note suggests. As little more than a cursory reading of the manuscript makes plainly obvious, Tāmihana actively shaped the narrative. Even where the account begins with events that preceded both Tāmihana's and his father's lifetimes, it is written entirely from Tāmihana's point of view, and this becomes exponentially more apparent as one reads the manuscript from beginning to end, for its structure mirrors Tāmihana's own development from his childhood to an adult in his early to mid-thirties. The manuscript further includes mention of Te Rauparaha's death in 1849 at Ōtaki.[94]

READING TĀMIHANA TE RAUPARAHA

After relating his father's death, Tāmihana adds a postscript to Te Rauparaha's life toward the end of his manuscript:

> Tenei hoki tetehi kupu he rongo tonu noku ki nga rangatira
> kaumatua ona iwhi ki Kawhia, ki Maungatautari,
> ki Rotorua, ki Tauranga, ki Hauraki, kia Ngapuhi hoki
> kia Whaikato, kia te Atiawha, e ki ana kaore kau
> he kaumatua hei rite mo te Rauparaha te mohio
> ki te whawhai, me te toa hoki, me te tino tangata ki
> te ata whai tangata aha koa mano noa nga rangatira
> o te motu nei, kihai rawha i rite kia te Rauparaha.[95]

Something that I have heard said by the chiefly elders of his tribes of Kāwhia, Maungatautari, Rotorua, Tauranga, Hauraki, and among the Ngāpuhi, Waikato, and Te Āti Awa peoples, is that they have never known a man equal to Rauparaha considering his expertise at warfare and prowess in battle, and his ability to take care of his people. They say that even though there are numerous chiefs in these islands, none is equal to Te Rauparaha.

Tāmihana regarded his father as a singular man to whom no other could be favorably compared; even more important, Tāmihana ends his account as befitting a loving, respectful son of a great chief. This is a history that we ourselves, as Māori, recognize. This is not the history, as Harris reminds us, of "an impersonalised other or even of an amorphous, generic us."[96] We belong to this history, and we are a part of it. In distancing ourselves from this history, that is, in repackaging this history to fit within the conventions of "other" historical traditions and narratives, we effectively "other" ourselves from our own histories and our deep-rooted relationships to our past; we risk "forgetting" that Māori had and have our own writers, our own intellectuals, and our own ways of viewing, understanding, participating in, and thriving in the world. Māori histories, and indeed Māori lives, need not be read through, set against, or defined by colonialism, imperialism, expansionism, or any other frame that works to downplay, ignore, or eliminate Indigenous agency and activism. Rather, I urge that we follow the example set by Tāmihana Te Rauparaha and numerous other nineteenth-century Māori writers and scholars to establish and work through our own frameworks, set our own agendas, and fully reclaim our intellectual sovereignty.[97]

NOTES

This chapter draws on the first section of my doctoral dissertation: Arini Loader, "Tau Mai E Kapiti te Whare Wananga o Ia, o te Nui, o te Wehi, o te Toa: Reclaiming Early Raukawa-Toarangatira Writing from Otaki" (PhD diss., Victoria University of Wellington, 2013), 52–102.

1. Te Rauparaha is the subject of Te Rangihaeata's waiata "Taku Waka Whakairo" and is credited with the composition of a *ngeri* (song with actions) "He Hokioi," a *waiata poroporoaki* (farewell song) "Tērā Ngā Tai O Honipaka," and the *pōkeka* (chant) "Kīkiki Kākaka," the final section of which begins, "Ka Mate, Ka Mate." See Royal, *Kāti Au i Konei*, 102–6, 48–51, 86–87, 82–85. "Ka Mate" is the haka most often performed by the All Blacks, the New Zealand national rugby team, at the beginning of most international test matches. In 1890 Thomas Bracken published his long poem based on Te Rauparaha's career, "March of Te Rauparaha," in his *Musings in Maoriland*. Jessie Mackay and Arthur Adams also published poems about Te Rauparaha in the "Maoriland" vein (Phillips, "Arts and the Nation—Cultural Nationalism, 1890 to 1910"), and in 1963 Alistair Campbell, a New Zealand poet of Cook Island heritage, produced a series of poems entitled *Sanctuary of Spirits* in which a number of Te Rauparaha's contemporaries recall their memories of him. Hamish Clayton's 2010 historical novel *Wulf* presents a view of Te Rauparaha and the infamous fatal episode of the brig *The Elizabeth* from the perspective of a European sailor.

2. Travers, *Some Chapters in the Life and Times of Te Rauparaha, Chief of Ngatitoa*; J. White, *The Ancient History of the Maori, His Mythology and Traditions*, vol. 6; Buick, *An Old New Zealander*; Brewer, *Te Rauparaha*; Burns, *Te Rauparaha*; Butler, *Life and Times of Te Rauparaha by His Son Tamihana Te Rauparaha*; and Collins, *Ka Mate Ka Ora!*

3. Tāmihana Te Rauparaha, "He Pukapuka Tataku Tenei I Nga Mahi a Te Rauparaha Nui," unpublished manuscript, GNZMMSS 27, Sir George Grey Special Collections, Auckland City Libraries (hereafter cited as GNZMMSS 27).

4. Tāmihana Te Rauparaha, GNZMMSS 27, 1.

5. English-language interpretations are by the author. Interpretations should be treated as approximate and as a guide only, for as Claudia Orange reminds us, "translations in any language seldom capture precisely the nuances of meaning and comprehension." Orange, "The Covenant of Kohimarama," 70. A descendant is currently working on a new translation of the manuscript.

6. I follow Ngāi Tahu historian Te Maire Tau in deciding to refer to the *tūpuna* (ancestors) mentioned in this essay by their first name as opposed to following the normal academic convention where the surname is used: Tau, "I-ngā-rā-o-mua," 60. This is done out of respect as well as to avoid confusion between Tāmihana Te Rauparaha and his father, Te Rauparaha.

7. Tāmihana may have foreseen his father's story coming to be "told on the harp strings / Pakeha harp cords / Tuned by the stranger," as Bracken wrote in his poem "March of Te Rauparaha." Bracken, *Musings in Maoriland*, 42.

8. *Great Britain Parliamentary Papers*, 1845, XXXIII, 108, p. 10. Tāwhai's words are taken from a letter written in the English language by W. Shortland to Lord Stanley in 1845 in which Shortland recalls the "speeches" of Māori chiefs at a meeting in Hokianga, in the far north of Te Ika a Māui, the North Island of Aotearoa New Zealand, held for the purpose of obtaining the adherence of the *iwi* (tribes) of that district to the Treaty of Waitangi (signed in 1840). What Tāwhai actually uttered therefore comes to us today via a number of filters: temporal, spatial, and linguistic. See Petrie and Tarau, "Māori Texts and Official Ventriloquism," 129–41, on the importance of challenging English-language translations of Māori-language source material in historical scholarship. On the theme of forgetting, approximately fifty years later New Zealand poet and journalist Jessie Mackay concluded that Te Rauparaha was already "partly forgotten: and doubtless many of the younger generation know scarcely more than the name of this once dreaded and remarkable man." *Otago Witness*, 23 April 1902, 70.

9. All three major research libraries in Aotearoa New Zealand—the Auckland Public Library (APL), Alexander Turnbull Library (ATL), and Hocken Library—date the manuscript to 1845. It is clear, however, as Tāmihana himself states in the manuscript, that this date marks the time at which Tāmihana recorded the whakapapa he includes in the final eight pages of the manuscript from his close relative Te Whatarauihi Nohorua, rather than the date of the manuscript. The manuscript also includes the death of Te Rauparaha in 1849, which does not preclude the possibility that Tāmihana began writing the manuscript earlier than this date, or that he wrote it in several or more sittings over a long period of time.

10. This is the Sir George Grey Special Collections at Central City Library Tāmaki Pātaka Kōrero, part of Auckland City Libraries (formerly Auckland Public Library). Grey likely took the manuscript with him when he left New Zealand in 1853 for England and then when he went to South Africa, where he was governor of the Cape Colony from 1854 to 1861. Tāmihana's manuscript may have lain in South Africa with most of Grey's other Māori material for over forty years before returning to New Zealand. See H. Williams, "Maori Matter at the Cape of Good Hope," 175–80.

11. See Sutherland, "Nineteenth-Century Māori Letters of Emotion." Sutherland notes that Tāmihana Te Rauparaha and his wife, Ruta, along with Mātene Te Whiwhi, Tāmihana's close relative, and his wife, Pipi, interacted with George Grey and his wife, Eliza, in several arenas, not the least of which was reciprocated hospitality (103).

12. S. Oliver, "Te Rauparaha, Tamihana."

13. An early example of a published Māori biography by a Māori writer is Rēweti Kōhere's *The Story of a Maori Chief: Mokena Kohere and His Forbears* about his grandfather, Mōkena Kōhere. This work was published about a century after Tāmihana wrote his manuscript. In an interesting echo of Tāmihana's manuscript, Rēweti Kōhere also wrote a life story of one of his very close senior male relatives. In 1951 Kōhere published *The Autobiography of a Maori*. Both of his books are in English. See Keane, "Māori Non-fiction and Scholarship—ngā tuhinga me te rangahau," page 6, "Writers of Biography."

14. "Matahau," New Zealand History Nga korero a ipurangi o Aotearoa, Ministry for Culture and Heritage, updated 28 June 2016, http://www.nzhistory.net.nz /politics/treaty/signatory/8-110.

15. "Matahau."

16. Published in edited, paraphrased, and translated form in the *Church Missionary Intelligencer* 7, no. 3 (July 1852): 150–57.

17. S. Oliver, "Te Rauparaha, Tamihana."

18. S. Oliver, "Te Rauparaha, Tamihana."

19. S. Oliver, "Te Rauparaha, Tamihana."

20. National Library of New Zealand and Te Rōpu Whakahaere o Rangiātea, *Rangiātea.*

21. Pōmare, "Ngāti Toarangatira," page 3, "19th Century: Rise and Fall."

22. Ngati Toa Rangatira and Trustee of the Toa Rangatira Trust and the Crown, Deed of Settlement of Historical Claims, 2012, 27–28, available at https://www .www.govt.nz/assets/Documents/OTS/Ngati-Toa-Rangatira/Ngati-Toa-Rangatira -Attachments-7-Dec-2012.pdf.

23. S. Oliver, "Te Rauparaha."

24. See Gibbons, "Non-fiction," 31–118; Gibbons, "A Note on Writing, Identity and Colonisation in Aotearoa," 32–38; and Gibbons, "Cultural Colonization and National Identity," 5–17.

25. Aroha Harris, interview, Rangahau, accessed 15 July 2015, http://www .rangahau.co.nz/methodology/58.

26. Cultural clubs, Māori churches, and Māori sports teams were set up, and for issues relating to housing and welfare, tribal councils, the Māori Women's Welfare League, churches, and the Māori Affairs Department of the New Zealand government played important roles. A. Harris, "Ngā tāone nui—Māori and the City," page 5, "Māori Adapt to City Life." See also Anderson, Binney, and Harris, *Tangata Whenua*; A. Harris and McCallum, "'Assaulting the Ears of Government,'" 225–39; and A. Harris, *Hīkoi.*

27. As influential indigenous scholar and leader Linda Tuhiwai Smith writes, "Every issue has been approached by indigenous peoples with a view to rewriting and rerighting our position in history. Indigenous peoples want to tell our own stories, write our own versions, in our own ways, for our own purposes. It is not simply about giving an oral account or a genealogical naming of the land and the events which raged over it, but a very powerful need to give testimony to and restore a spirit, to bring back into existence a world fragmented and dying." Smith, *Decolonizing Methodologies*, 28.

28. Mahuika, "New Zealand History Is Māori History," 5–30.

29. A. Harris, "Theorize This," 83–84.

30. Shepherd, "Travers, William Thomas Locke."

31. Shepherd, "Travers, William Thomas Locke."

32. The *Transactions and Proceedings of the New Zealand Institute* was renamed the *Transactions and Proceedings of the Royal Society of New Zealand* following the society's name change in 1933 to the Royal Society of New Zealand (Transactions and Proceedings of the Royal Society of New Zealand 1868–1961, accessed 10 January 2020, http://rsnz.natlib.govt.nz/volume/rsnz_05/rsnz_05_00_000500 .html).

33. Stack's text was first published under the title *Kaiapohia: The Story of a Siege*.

34. Phillips, "History of Immigration," page 3, "British Immigration and the New Zealand Company."

35. Patricia Burns notes that Travers's and John White's work have been considered basic sources for the life of Te Rauparaha. Burns, *Te Rauparaha*, 12.

36. Travers, *Some Chapters in the Life and Times of Te Rauparaha, Chief of Ngati-toa*, 63.

37. Travers, *Some Chapters in the Life and Times of Te Rauparaha, Chief of Ngati-toa*, 63.

38. Travers, *Some Chapters in the Life and Times of Te Rauparaha, Chief of Ngati-toa*, 75–77.

39. Travers, *Some Chapters in the Life and Times of Te Rauparaha, Chief of Ngati-toa*, 75.

40. George Graham was the son of James Bannatyne Graham, a lawyer and insurance manager, and his wife, Elizabeth Mary Josephine Sheehan. In 1899 George Graham (Junior) married Mary Magdalene Hapi of the Waikato and Ngāti Whanaunga tribes, with whom he had seven children. Graham later formed liaisons with Te Wharetoroa Tiniraupeka (Ngāti Whakaue and Te Arawa) and Mare Potatau (Ngāti Mahuta). Graham and Curnow, "Graham, George Samuel."

41. Quoted in Burns, *Te Rauparaha*, 12.

42. Reilly, "White, John."

43. Reilly, "White, John."

44. Reilly, "White, John."

45. Reilly, "White, John."

46. Reilly, "White, John."

47. J. White, *The Ancient History of the Maori, His Mythology and Traditions*, 6:11.

48. Māui is a famous Polynesian ancestor remembered among other things for his trickster nature and many superhuman feats. Māui is also remembered by the name Māui-Tikitiki-a-Taranga, which commemorates his being thrown into the sea wrapped in the topknot of his father as a stillborn child. The name Māui Pōtiki draws attention to Māui's position in his family as the last-born, the *pōtiki*, of the whānau. Burns notes that Te Rauparaha's also being known as Māui Pōtiki meant that he was lively and mischievous (Burns, *Te Rauparaha*, 12), while Te Rauparaha's position in the whānau as the pōtiki is a further similarity between him and his famous ancestor.

49. Tāmihana Te Rauparaha, GNZMMSS 27, 1–2.

50. J. White, *The Ancient History of the Maori, His Mythology and Traditions*, 6:12.

51. J. White, *The Ancient History of the Maori, His Mythology and Traditions*, 6:11.

52. J. White, *The Ancient History of the Maori, His Mythology and Traditions*, 6:12, 11.

53. Gibbons notes that White "rewrote material in his own style, 'White Maori' it has been called." See Gibbons, "Non-fiction," 59.

54. J. White, *The Ancient History of the Maori, His Mythology and Traditions*, 6:11.

55. See Sparks and Oliver, "Topeora, Rangi Kuini Wikitoria," 546–47.

56. Angela Ballara, in *Taua*, notes that

> many "traditional" accounts were written by Māori in the later nineteenth-century at the request of such Pākehā students of things Māori as John White, S. Percy Smith, T. W. Gudgeon and others. One of the problems with these accounts is that in the published work Smith, White and the rest were not content just to report them as they were given, but rewrote them, changed them, translated them into English and then back into their own "correct" form of Māori. . . . European scholars performed a scissors-and-paste job on Māori accounts, selecting sections, patching them together to create a plausible sequence, and rejecting others that did not agree with their own pet theories. Sometimes they plagiarised Māori authors without acknowledgement, and at others they plagiarised each other. (38)

57. White's *Ancient History* is available via the New Zealand Electronic Text Centre: Te Pūhikotuhi o Aotearoa (http://nzetc.victoria.ac.nz/tm/scholarly/tei -corpus-WhiAnci.html); Travers's material is available online in the *Transactions and Proceedings of the Royal Society of New Zealand 1868–1961* (http://rsnz.natlib .govt.nz/volume/rsnz_05/rsnz_05_00_000500.html); and *Stirring Times* is available at http://babel.hathitrust.org/cgi/pt?id=uc2.ark:/13960/t8gfopvo9;view =1up;seq=1.

58. This trend persists into digital platforms, whereby Travers's *Some Chapters in the Life and Times of Te Rauparaha, Chief of Ngatitoa* and White's *The Ancient History of the Maori* have been digitized and made available online, but Tāmihana's manuscript has not.

59. Linda Tuhiwai Smith notes that much of the Māori material in Sir George Grey's collection "was gathered from his close friendships with chiefs whose names mean little to the non-Maori audience and whose knowledge has been rendered entirely invisible." Smith, *Decolonizing Methodologies*, 83.

60. Meredith and Te Punga Somerville, "Kia Rongo Mai Koutou ki Taku Whakaaro," 97.

61. Traue, "Buick, Thomas Lindsay."

62. Traue, "Buick, Thomas Lindsay."

63. Traue, "Buick, Thomas Lindsay."

64. Traue, "Buick, Thomas Lindsay."

65. Buick, *An Old New Zealander*, viii.

66. Gibbons, "Non-fiction," 66.

67. Gibbons, "Non-fiction," 66.

68. Mundy, *Our Antipodes*, 375. Buick, *An Old New Zealander*, 321. Cited in Burns, *Te Rauparaha*, xix.

69. Burns, "The Foundations of the New Zealand Press"; and Burns, *Te Rauparaha*. Burns won the Goodman Fielder Wattie Book Award in 1981.

70. Āpirana Ngata also noted the poor quality of Graham's translation, writing that it is "free and in places not altogether correct." A. T. Ngata to Mr Barr, Chief Librarian, 24 December 1923, Sir George Grey Special Collections: Ta Hori Kerei—Nga Kohinga Taonga Whakahirahira, Auckland Public Library. The letter is among copies of nine letters and documents relating to the translation of the original manuscript: GNZMMSS 27B.

71. Burns, *Te Rauparaha*, 190.

72. Butler, *Life and Times of Te Rauparaha by His Son Tamihana Te Rauparaha*, 7.

73. See Loader, "Haere Mai Me Tuhituhi He Pukapuka," 35–57; and Biggs, "The Translation and Publishing of Maori Material in the Auckland Public Library," 177–91, for analysis of Grey's editing of Te Rangikāheke's manuscripts.

74. Esther Lauaki, "Descendant of Te Rauparaha Traces the History of Porirua's Haka," *Stuff*, 9 November 2010, http://www.stuff.co.nz/dominion-post/news /local-papers/kapi-mana-news/4320993/Descendant-of-Te-Rauparaha-traces-the -history-of-Poriruas-haka.

75. Quoted in Lauaki, "Descendant of Te Rauparaha Traces the History of Porirua's Haka."

76. Collins, *Ka Mate Ka Ora!*, 9.

77. Collins also adds macrons to indicate long vowels.

78. R. Morgan, "Oral History and Biography," 13.

79. Lachy Paterson notes, for example, that we can deduce from comments made by him at the Kohimarama Conference of 1860 and reported on in the government-sponsored newspaper *Te Karere Maori* that Tāmihana Te Rauparaha "was aware that this conference was an important political event, and that the actions of chiefs were being recorded in history differently from the past" and, further, that Tāmihana knew "that his words were to be fixed in print, to be 'looked at' in different places, and in different times." Paterson, *Colonial Discourses*, 37.

80. Tāmihana Te Rauparaha, GNZMMSS 27, 103–4.

81. John (Jacky) Guard, bought the cannon, known to Māori as "Pūhuriwhenua" (lit. "gun that causes the earth to tremble"), in Sydney, Australia, in 1833. He offered it to Nohorua, Te Rauparaha's half brother, as payment for the right to occupy Kākāpō Bay, where Guard was based in the 1830s. The cannon was subsequently stolen by Blenkinsopp and given to Te Rauparaha in exchange for access to wood and water for his ship. McKinnon, "Puhuriwhenua Cannon."

82. Tāmihana Te Rauparaha, GNZMMSS 27, 103–4.

83. Tāmihana Te Rauparaha, GNZMMSS 27, 104.

84. Tāmihana Te Rauparaha, GNZMMSS 27, 104. Blenkinsopp returned to Sydney and died not long afterward. Stead, *Art Icons of New Zealand*, 28.

85. Tāmihana Te Rauparaha, GNZMMSS 27, 104.

86. Stead notes that around 1839 Colonel William Wakefield paid £300 to Blenkinsopp's widow for another copy of the deed, and "on the basis of this document and another transaction they believed they had negotiated with Te Rauparaha, the Wakefields claimed the Wairau for the New Zealand Company." Stead, *Art Icons of New Zealand*, 28–29. In attempting to enforce its claims and have Te Rauparaha arrested for burning the camps of its contract surveyors, the New Zealand Company instigated what has become known variously as "The Wairau Massacre," "The Wairau Incident," and "The Wairau Affray" of 17 June 1843.

87. Tāmihana Te Rauparaha, GNZMMSS 27, 115–16.

88. Tāmihana Te Rauparaha, GNZMMSS 27, 116.

89. Tāmihana Te Rauparaha, GNZMMSS 27, 1.

90. See Loader, "'Kei Wareware,'" 339–65.

91. Ballara, *Taua*, 34.

92. Taylor, *Te Ika a Maui, or, New Zealand and Its Inhabitants*, 338 (emphasis added).

93. See, for example, McRae, "From Māori Oral Traditions to Print," 32. Also, Chris Maclean writes that Tāmihana's version was based on his father's recollections. See Maclean, *Kapiti*, 112. A notable exception to this is Burns, who clearly considered the manuscript the work of Tāmihana, while Collins rather more ambivalently notes that the manuscript was said to have been dictated to him by his father. Burns, *Te Rauparaha*, 12; and Collins, *Ka Mate Ka Ora!*, 8.

94. This is not evidence on its own that the manuscript was not dictated by Te Rauparaha as it is difficult to tell how long Tāmihana spent writing the manuscript; it is possible that he began writing while Te Rauparaha was still alive and finished it after his death.

95. Tāmihana Te Rauparaha, GNZMMSS 27, 117.

96. Harris, "Theorize This," 83–84.

97. The term *intellectual sovereignty* was coined by Robert Warrior (Osage) in his influential work *Tribal Secrets: Recovering American Indian Intellectual Traditions*. As Craig Womack similarly asserts in his groundbreaking work *Red on Red: Native American Literary Nationalism*, "Native literature, and Native literary criticism, written by Native authors, is part of sovereignty: Indian people exercising the right to present images of themselves and to discuss those images" (14).

CHAPTER TWELVE

Writing and Beyond in Indigenous North America:
The Occom Network

IVY SCHWEITZER

ON 25 AUGUST 1773, four years after the founding of Dartmouth College in the wilderness of northern New England, the trustees voted to create an official seal (figure 12.1). The minutes for that meeting describe the design as "an Oval . . . within projecting a Pine Grove on the Right, whence proceed Natives towards an Edifice two Storey on the left; which bears in a Label over the Grove these Words 'vox clamantis in deserto' the whole supported by Religion on the Right and Justice on the Left, and bearing in a Triangle irradiate, with the Hebrew Words ydv la."[1] This overly complex design, authorized, if not created, by Eleazar Wheelock (1711–79), the Congregational minister who founded Dartmouth College, was eventually simplified in 1926 and became the college's emblem for general use (figure 12.2).

The trustees' description, however, omits an important visual element, prominent in both the original and streamlined designs, that the Natives approaching Dartmouth Hall (still the iconic building on campus) are carrying—a book. Since we have no record of what Wheelock intended by his design and must identify this book by hints, I invoke poetic license to read it as a representation of the existence and recognition of Indigenous textuality and

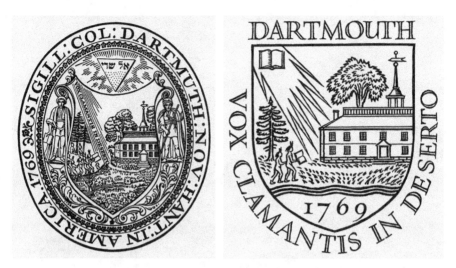

FIGURE 12.1 (LEFT) The seal of Dartmouth College, 1773. Courtesy of Dartmouth College Library. FIGURE 12.2 (RIGHT) The Dartmouth emblem, 1926. Courtesy of Dartmouth College Library.

publication, which, I argue, are best understood in terms quite different from early or contemporary European meanings. Native textuality in the North American colonial period was inextricably bound up with orality and collectivity as well as with specific places and notions of space. Likewise, recent theorists argue for understanding Native writing not in European terms as semiotic evidence of the teleological progress toward civilization but as a "publication event" that involves networks of relations existing within time and space.[2] After outlining the orality-literacy debate that has shaped—and distorted—Eurocentric views of Indigenous textuality, I discuss in more detail some of this recent theory that calls for shifting away from the category of "writing," as a largely linguistic form, toward the concept of "media," which encompasses discourse, performance, and "scenes of communication . . . as events that not only shaped settlement history but also conditioned access to the past."[3] Finally, as illustration, I apply these methods to the journals of Samson Occom (1723–92), a Mohegan Indian, Presbyterian minister, public intellectual, and tribal activist, accessed from my digital archive, The Occom Circle.[4] Occom was Wheelock's star student and possibly the prototype for the book-carrying Native of the Dartmouth seal.

One commentary notes that Wheelock's original design resembles the seal of the Society for the Propagation of the Gospel in Foreign Parts (figure 12.3), an Anglican missionary organization founded in 1701 with which

FIGURE 12.3 Seal of the Society for the Propagation of the Gospel in Foreign Parts, 1701. Reproduced in Anderson and Eastman, *Saint Philip's Church of Charleston*.

Wheelock clashed over access to the Six Nations of the Haudenosaunee (Iroquois) Confederation in the 1760s.[5] In the society's seal, an oversized minister placed at the center of the scene holds out the iconic book of the missionary—the Bible—to eager Natives who gather with outstretched arms at the edge of a steep headland. The speech ribbon above them, in a language—Latin—indelibly tied to elite European textual education, adapts Paul's vision of the missionary calling from Acts 16:9 and puts it in the mouths of American "savages": "Come over and help us."[6] The motto beneath the oval further clarifies the scene, labeling knowledge of the Bible as "the Gift of the Society."

This seal epitomizes patriarchal Eurocentric attitudes that regarded Indigenous peoples of the Americas as primarily oral, illiterate, and heathenish cultures not only desperately in need of the superior alphabetic literacy and Christianity of the West but painfully aware of that lack. It advances the imperial teleology that orality is primitive and necessarily evolves into writing, which allows for the abstract thinking and historical reckoning of advanced societies.[7] By contrast, in the Dartmouth seal, an Indian holding an oversized book leads a group of Natives toward the imposing edifice of the college, while speech from the heavens irradiates this book with Latin words that translate as "the voice of one crying in the wilderness." The other book in this busy design, held by the figure of Religion on the left, migrates to the upper left corner of the simplified emblem of 1926 and becomes the source of the voice.

While it seems logical to identify the book held by the Native figure as the Bible, other elements in the design suggest an unsettling of the imperial hierarchy of speaking and writing. By alluding to the seal of a rival missionary organization, Wheelock associated his new college with the conversion and education of Indians. This was a strategic, even mercenary move on Wheelock's part, because by 1773 he had all but given up on educating Indians and had turned his attentions to Anglo-American men. Yet he wanted access to the considerable funds Occom had raised on a fundraising trip in England and Scotland four years earlier, which were specifically earmarked for Indian education. To gain that access, Wheelock would have to maintain the illusion of advancing Indian education for the English trustees who zealously guarded the funds. His ambivalence, or ruse, shaped a design in which the Indians are the sole actors, holding a book that they seem to offer, or that leads them to the college. White ministers or educators are conspicuously absent, subsumed perhaps by the heavenly voice issuing from the book in the upper left corner and speaking words from Isaiah 40:3 that refer to John the Baptist. Although these words are often taken as an allusion to Dartmouth's rural setting, they associate the Native figures with prophets and precursors of Christ—that is, with spiritually and culturally powerful voices. The voice crying in the wilderness could also represent the pleas of Indians for supposedly more advanced textual literacy and religious conversion, as in the speech ribbon in the seal of the Society for the Propagation of the Gospel in Foreign Parts. But these Indians already *have* a book, and one whose textuality is inextricably bound up with representations of orality and place.

We do know that Wheelock enthusiastically participated in the British imperial design of subduing the Native peoples of North America, regarding this as a sacred calling and dedicating most of his life and a good deal of his personal fortune to what he called his "great design." This would occur, first, through education and alphabetic literacy, which was meant to assimilate Natives to European habits and would, second, prepare them for religious conversion and the "purging" of their "savage" identities.[8] Wheelock saw himself walking in the footsteps of John Eliot (ca. 1604–90), the first colonial Puritan "Apostle to the Indians," who described his mission with the Massachusetts Tribe as a similar purging and then a literal and violent inscription of holy words on their minds and bodies: "My scope is to write and imprint no nother but Scripture principles in the *abrasa tabula scraped board* of these naked people."[9] Wheelock also embraced the educational plan of fellow missionary John Sergeant (1710–49), whose methods combined academic and practical learning for Indians of both sexes "as shall in the most effectual manner change their whole habit of thinking and acting."[10]

Two facts distinguish Wheelock from these earlier missionaries and may account for his eccentric design. First, he was a New Light Congregationalist, which meant that he subscribed to the ideas of the Great Awakening, which disparaged strict adherence to formal modes of preaching and privileged the inspired voice of preachers who allowed God to speak through them, what

New Lights described as the dead letter versus the living word. This does not mean Wheelock disparaged book learning or textuality; far from it. In the face of much opposition from his fellow clergy, who thought he was wasting his time, Wheelock insisted on teaching his Native students the classical languages, thereby giving them the education of European gentlemen. But he was fully aware of and open to the power of the voice through his adherence to the revivalists' insistence on inspiration and extemporary preaching. This performative orality accorded well with Native communication preferences and created a separatist movement in mainstream Congregational churches and a wave of conversions and revivals among the northeastern tribes that offered them autonomy from Anglo-American oversight and authority.[11]

Second, Wheelock was Occom's mentor and missionary sponsor, but there is no reason to believe the influence went only one way. When nineteen-year-old Occom arrived at Wheelock's home in Lebanon, Connecticut, in December 1742 desiring an English education, he had already been converted by the New Light enthusiast James Davenport, Wheelock's brother-in-law, who was infamous for organizing public "Bonfires of the Vanities" that included burning books by Puritan authors he considered erroneous.[12] According to Occom's short autobiographical account, by this time he had taught himself to read with the help of a primer and English neighbors.[13] Furthermore, after the recent death of his father, Occom took over his seat on the tribal council and served as counselor to the Mohegan sachem Ben Uncas II, who was controversial for embracing English religion and cultural practices at the expense of Mohegan traditions and survival. Also formative was Occom's attendance, during the summer of 1742, at hearings on the Mohegan Land Case held in nearby Norwich, Connecticut, a century-old dispute between the colony of Connecticut and the Mohegan Tribe over possession of ancestral lands. There Occom witnessed firsthand the vulnerability of his people because of their lack of Western literacy.[14] Thus, when Occom arrived on Wheelock's doorstep, he already had the book, in the sense of a preliminary skill set of the white man's letters, as well as a palpable sense of its spiritual and secular power, and he also had the "books" of his Native Mohegan culture: an intimate knowledge of the landscape (he inherited his father's famous hunting skills), collective oral traditions of rhetoric and memory, and communal and intertribal networks of communication and support.

After living for three years at Wheelock's home and becoming fluent in English, Latin, and Greek, with some Hebrew and French, Occom started to prepare for university, but severe eyestrain prevented his matriculation, and he began to keep school and missionize in various Native communities. He was ordained a Presbyterian minister in 1759. Based on his success with Occom, in the early 1750s Wheelock began soliciting educating other northeastern Native children, and in 1754 founded an Indian Charity School whose goal was the education of Indian boys to become missionaries to their own people, and Indian girls to become their wives and helpmates. This school, which also included some Anglo-American boys, became the heart of his "great design" of Indian redemption and produced "perhaps the single most significant collection of letters by and about Native students and teachers in the eighteenth century."[15] At the end of 1765, desperate for funds for his design, Wheelock sent Occom on a fundraising tour of England and Scotland that lasted two and a half years and produced £12,000, an enormous sum for the school, and brought Occom international renown as that seeming oxymoron: an "Indian preacher." But by the late 1760s, Wheelock regarded his scheme as a failure because most of his Native graduates had not assimilated into white culture but had either disappeared or rejoined their Native communities. Occom was the exception that seemed to prove the rule.

Despite Occom's success, Wheelock feared that he was using his celebrity and literacy skills to argue the Mohegan Tribe's side in the infamous Land Case, which in 1769 was being heard in the royal courts in London. Finally, Wheelock lost the confidence and friendship of the Haudenosaunee Tribes when he sent his son and heir apparent, Ralph, to negotiate with them about receiving missionaries and schoolteachers. Ralph's haughtiness and lack of attention to diplomatic protocols so infuriated the Indians that in 1769 they withdrew all their students from Wheelock's school. After this debacle, although Wheelock began recruiting Indian scholars from among the Canadian tribes, he made his primary goal the education of white men. He moved the Indian Charity School to Hanover, New Hampshire, and merged it with the newly established Dartmouth College, in order to access the large sums Occom had raised, which were controlled by an English trust committed to the original design of Indian education. In the 1770s Occom eventually broke with Wheelock over this shift in focus and turned his attention to the establishment of Brothertown, a pan-Indian Christian settlement on lands of the Oneida Nation in central New York.

Despite its checkered history, Wheelock's Indian Charity School produced a large cohort of educated Christian Indians from several northeastern tribes who were instrumental in creating an Indian form of Christianity and an Indian form of English that adapted the imperial literacy technologies of their English mentors to their own purposes of communal resistance, response, and survival. In effect, these Native men and women not only inhabited the English book with their own voices but radically trans-formed its textuality by infusing it with Native modes of communication. Although many of them were effective and prolific writers, Occom is now the best known of this group and has become a staple of American literature anthologies. He produced a large body of written work and published one of the first books in North America authored by an American Indian. Still, his reputation rests on an insufficient understanding of his role in the cultural and political life of his people, and on an incomplete reading of his writings, the full range of which only appeared in print in 2006.[16]

One reason for this failure is the imposition of Western definitions of literacy on Native expression. Since the 1980s scholars have been working to dismantle the binary between orality and writing popularized by Walter Ong and others that characterizes oral cultures as static and primitive and scribal cultures as dynamic and advanced. This value-laden distinction took par-ticularly strenuous hold through the work of French anthropologist Claude Lévi-Strauss, whose four-volume study of Indigenous American cultures, entitled *Mythologiques*, began appearing in 1964 and was first translated into English in 1969. Although Lévi-Strauss brought needed attention to Amerin-dian cultures, he gave preference to verbal over visual languages in his study and thus promoted a view of scriptless Native societies as utopian but also illiterate in Western terms. In response, the poststructuralist philosopher Jacques Derrida in his foundational text, *Of Grammatology* (1967), set out to demonstrate and dismantle Western culture's preference for speech over writing, in the process arguing that Lévi-Strauss's implicit privileging of pho-netic writing over Indigenous orality or nonphonetic writing was another version of ethnocentric, logocentric imperialism. "The concept of writing," Derrida insisted, "exceeds and comprehends that of language."[17]

In the 1990s scholars began to rethink the category of writing in terms of Indigenous cultures. In his extensive work on Native American litera-ture, for example, Gordon Brotherston rejects the "crass evolutionism that celebrates the Semitic-Greek alphabet, like the wheel, as a turning point in human achievement to which America was unfortunately not party." Apply-ing Derridean theories, he demonstrates that "the Fourth World," his term for Indigenous America, "has its own complex grammatology" embodied in "texts," which he defines in Derridean terms as "the space in which meaning happens."[18] Indigenous American textuality had a wide variety of forms that adapted and evolved as Europeans imposed alphabetic literacy on Native populations, which many embraced with alacrity. There were nonverbal textual forms, such as the screenfold books of Mesoamerica and the quipu (knotted strings) of Tahuantinsuya; combined textual and verbal forms, such as the chants and dry paintings of the Navajo and the songs and incised birch-bark scrolls of the Mideiwin; and hybrid forms that adapted Western alphabets to Indigenous thinking and writing systems, such as the great codices like the *Popol Vuh*. Much of this textuality was destroyed by conquering Europeans to erase evidence of Indigenous civilizations, while some of it was hidden from the conquerors to protect it and subsequently lost.[19] Because most of the preconquest forms of "text" do not involve alphabetic notation—the representation of speech—but use pictures, shapes, patterns, or knots in string, Westerners did not recognize them as forms of writing or literacy. But Brotherston also notes that "the impoverishment implicit in the phonetic alphabet was well understood in the Fourth World."[20]

A different and important response to Derrida's project appears in Walter D. Mignolo's remarks concluding a collection he coedited, entitled *Writing without Words: Alternative Literacies in Mesoamerica and the Andes*. Mignolo wants to "circumvent" Derrida's ideas and "explore the possibility of rereading Derrida's grammatology *from* the experience of the Americas."[21] Specifically, he argues that Derrida's project rests on the assumption that Western culture conceptualizes speech as more fundamental than writing, and writing as merely the representative of speech, using examples from Plato to Jean-Jacques Rousseau. But there is no evidence, Mignolo argues, even after the adaption of alphabetic writing to their own signification systems, that Indigenous cultures conceptualized writing in Western terms, as the representation of speech. Furthermore, he points out, Derrida ignores the global effects of the European Renaissance and remains within a Western frame of analysis. It was during the Renaissance, Mignolo observes, "at the fringes of Occidentalization and colonial expansion, that writing was first theorized and conceptualized as an instrument for taming (not representing) the voice, conceived in conjunction with territorial control."[22] For him, the central issue is not the development of "a grammatology of the Americas," as Brotherston has done, but the recognition of "alternative literacies in non-Western societies and the conflict of literacies in colonial situations" and, furthermore, the imagination of "*alternative politics of intellectual inquiry* and *alternative loci of enunciation*" that take into account the colonization of language. To shift our frame of analysis, Mignolo advises that we start not with Western notions of writing but with American examples that "allow[ ] for a rethinking of the relationship between speech and writing which does not make the second subservient to the first."[23]

The American colonial period is a particularly rich moment in this history, showing the development of different writing systems, the clash of

FIGURE 12.4 1794 Canandaigua Treaty Belt or "George Washington Belt," the longest belt at six feet, presented by President Washington to the Haudenosaunee to signify the end of their quarrels after the Revolution. The thirteen figures represent the thirteen states of the newly formed United States of America, and the house is the longhouse of the Haudenosaunee with a Mohawk and Seneca on either side, symbolizing the Keepers of the Eastern and Western Doors, respectively. The white background and linked hands symbolize friendship. This is a reproduction created by Dr. Richard Hamell, professor emeritus, Monroe Community College. Macedon Public Library, Monroe, New York.

consciousness this entailed, and the complex materiality of reading and writing. While Hispanists like Mignolo redefined the earlier question of writing as the signifier of higher consciousness and what it means to be "human" to instead ask how writing produces domination and subordination, a new set of questions arise when we reconceive writing altogether, not as based in linguistics but as media and event. Recent theorists who embrace the post-semiotic understanding of literacy "suggest tweaking the question in order to produce methodological leverage and new questions: How do different media become political and social facts?" and, perhaps more provocatively, "What would literary studies look like—more precisely, what new question and problems could be identified—if we embrace nontextual media and move beyond the oral-literate dynamic?"[24]

An American example close to my focus on Occom is wampum—woven belts, strings, or collars of white ("Wòmpi") and purple-black ("Súki") beads (figure 12.4). The beads were handcrafted by women from whelk

("Meteaûhock") and quahog ("Suckauanaûsuck") shells native only to the waters of southern New England at the mouth of the Connecticut (Kwini-tekw) River. Patterns created from the two colors were "read" by shamans or ambassadors charged with delivering and exchanging wampum, in order to secure and record agreements between nations and bind leaders to their promises. After European contact and the introduction of the metal drill bit, the Narragansett and Pequot Tribes of coastal New England mass-produced wampum and monopolized its distribution, up the Connecticut River into Haudenosaunee territory, where it was in high demand for ceremonies of condolence and adoption. But because of the scarcity of coins in early New England, wampum quickly became a form of currency and remained so, even among the English, up to the American Revolution.[25]

In a 1999 essay entitled "In Search of 'The Word of the Other,'" Germaine Warkentin, a Canadian book historian, offers wampum as a form of *semasio-graphic* (that is, nonphonetic or pictographic) writing that challenges narrow ethnocentric definitions of literacy. Warkentin begins with the story of a captive exchange between the French colonists and Mohawks that occurred on 5 July 1645 at Trois-Rivières in New France. A Mohawk emissary named Kiotsaeton ("the Hook") arrived covered from head to foot with wampum and addressed the assembled Europeans, who, according to several accounts, were fully prepared to comprehend him based on their knowledge of Native customs as well as their familiarity with the "Renaissance symbolic gestural repertoire (literary, rhetorical, ecclesiastical, diplomatic)."[26] Historians of the period record many such spectacles in intertribal and intercultural encounters in the Northeast. From this example, Warkentin argues that wampum represents a form of Indigenous writing that is not merely an object (that is, the equivalent of a book) but a behavior, one that requires the mediation of human speech, gesture, and performance and solicits a response from its audience. Not just words but tones, gestures, and the impressive bodily presence of Kiotsaeton are as necessary to the creation, "reading," and reception of the text as are the wampum belts that contain the "written" message. In this kind of writing, the oral and scribal registers are not in a hierarchical relation but a complementary one.[27] From this complex event, Warkentin argues for understanding Indigenous semasiographic writing as "relational," that is, as a dynamic social process rather than a linguistic representation, occurring, furthermore, in cultures that welcome change and embrace transience.[28]

Precolonial Native signification systems, of which wampum is only one example, persisted in the early colonial period and existed alongside several other textual cultures, like the alphabetic syllabaries of spoken Indigenous languages, which also show relational and bicultural tendencies. For example, because Puritan religious culture was grounded in the book, it advocated reading literacy for all people. Thus, in the 1660s John Eliot and his Native converts and translators John Sassamon (Wampanoag), Job Nesuton (Massachusetts), and James Printer (Nipmuck) created an alphabetic syllabary of the Massachusetts dialect of Algonquian and produced what scholars call "the Indian Library," a series of religious works printed in an Indian vernacular and used by "praying" or Christianized Indians. Its crowning achievement was the *Mamusse wunneetupanatamwe up biblum God*, an Old and New Testament in Massachusetts, which was in fact the first Bible printed in North America. Recent scholarship shows that this so-called Eliot Bible (its usual appellation, which essentially erases Native participation in its production and Native agency) and the entire Indian Library depended on the knowledge and skills of Indian converts as translators and printers.

For Philip Round, who has done groundbreaking work on the understudied existence and importance of Indigenous books, the Indian Library reveals "the collaborative bicultural social horizon from which the Native print vernacular emerged . . . that would shape the history of the book in Indian country down through the nineteenth century."[29] Eliot favored gathering converted Natives into praying towns where they could practice a unique form of Indian Christianity through an emerging Native vernacular literacy. Incensed English colonists destroyed these towns, and the collections of books, tracts, and primers that supported them, after King Philip's (Pumetacom's) War of 1675–76, accusing praying Indians of spying and betrayal. This represented a huge setback to the Native vernacular movement, which did not reemerge with any force until 1821, when Sequoyah (ca. 1767–1843), previously unlettered, developed the Cherokee syllabary, a system of eighty-five characters that represent syllables of the spoken language, rather than phonemes. Within a span of five years, the Cherokees and related tribes achieved near-total literacy and produced the first national Indigenous newspaper in North America, the *Cherokee Phoenix*.[30] This bilingual paper (in Cherokee and English) was published from 1828 to 1834 and was revived in the twentieth century.[31]

At the same time, a transatlantic European epistolary and manuscript culture flourished, and when English literacy expanded in the eighteenth century, the printing and publishing spheres exploded in the American colonies. But even as late as Occom's first mission to the Oneida Indians in 1761 and later still on a return trip in 1773, he records receiving wampum belts from the Haudenosaunee Tribes he visited as potential sites of missions, accompanied by lists of promises and requests from his hosts, both to be passed on to the colonial powers he represented in order to record, bind, and seal any agreements they reached.[32]

Given this history, and in the spirit of Mignolo's challenge, we must shift our frame of analysis to consider forms of literacy from a Native perspective. Wheelock's white missionaries, such as Samuel Kirkland (1741–1808), who first lived with the Senecas, the westernmost nation of the Haudenosaunee Confederacy, and spent the next forty years, from 1766 to his death, with the Oneidas in central New York, had to learn the discourse and rhetoric of wampum exchange on the fly, though such skills might have served him better than his knowledge of Latin and Greek. To the Haudenosaunee chiefs and people he desired to both serve and "save," Kirkland probably appeared, at first, at least partially illiterate.[33]

By contrast, Native missionaries like Occom, whose Mohegan people descended from the Pequots, who originated and controlled the wampum trade, were literate in both—indeed, in several forms of—textuality. Occom understood the uses of wampum and Native protocols of exchange. But he also wrote letters to influential people in transatlantic revivalist/ missionary circles that reveal his mastery of those genteel discourses, and he delivered eloquent and effective sermons. The most famous, *A Sermon Preached at the Execution of Moses Paul, an Indian* (1772), was one of the first published works by a Native American, as well as a colonial best seller that went through twenty-one editions, by the latest count, and was translated into Welsh. Occom also kept extensive journals, which Wheelock required of all his missionaries, and from which Wheelock quoted in the many letters and narratives he sent across the colonies and the ocean to donors and supporters like the influential English evangelical George Whitefield. Scholars are beginning to reread this complex archive not solely from a European framework but as situated in the Native spaces of North America and thus as shaped by, and embedded in, various Native systems of communication.

One of these important systems is performance. In 2000 Sandra Gustafson published *Eloquence Is Power: Oratory and Performance in Early America*, which responded to accounts of early republican culture that argue for the centrality of textuality and literacy in the founding of the United States.[34] Adroitly shifting the discussion by placing oratory in a much broader, multicultural, and gendered historical context, Gustafson traces European colonists' increasing dependence on text and the collisions with seemingly illiterate Africans and Native Americans, revealing the hierarchies that structured gender and class relations among settler colonies. To unsettle these structures,

Gustafson adopted a performance studies approach: "Viewing speech and text as symbolic and performative forms of language rather than as discrete and hierarchical," she argues, "opens understanding of the ways that the bodies of language figure constructions of the social body in oratorical performance." Two historical moments bookend her argument, both involving Native actors: the first was the Salem witchcraft crisis of the 1690s, where young Anglo-American girls, ostensibly "enticed" by an Arawak slave woman named Tituba who was brought over from Barbados, staged a parodic reversal of the Puritan patriarchal and logocentric social order that raised fears of undisciplined female and savage orality. This crisis achieved "full theorization" in her second iconic moment, the Great Awakening revivals of the 1740s, from which emerged an understanding of "the oral and textual bodies of language, not as fixed categories, but as figures for competing constructions of the social body." Gustafson calls this development "the performance semiotic of speech and text," a form of situated orality through which actors negotiate and gain authenticity and power.[35]

Not only an important corrective to the binary of orality and literacy, this semiotic draws attention to the creativity of oral genres and their dominance in the American colonial period as major political and religious media. A persistent figure in this semiotic is the "savage speaker," as evidenced by modern Native writers' emphasis on oral traditions and the voice in Native American writing.[36] In fact, some contemporary Native American scholars argue that adoption of alphabetic writing signaled a move away from "pure" Native traditions, a position based on a temporal model of culture and authenticity that obscures the creative ways Native communities have embraced and modified alien tools, like alphabetic writing and printing, for their own purposes.[37]

While Gustafson cites several female and Indian figures to illustrate her semiotic, Occom gets special notice for the way he rescued the "savage speaker" from debasement and mere spectacle by employing "Indian English as a kind of Pentecostal speech" to forge "a hybridized, evangelical savage persona, whose liminal position between cultures permitted a range of identifications across cultures."[38] As evidence, Gustafson cites the way Occom positioned himself in the "preface" of his most famous sermon, delivered to a large mixed crowd at the invitation of Moses Paul, a Wampanoag Christian Indian who was convicted for murdering a white tavern patron while intoxicated. In his sermon Occom invokes the Pauline paradox of personal weakness transformed into public power and combines it with the contemporary stereotype of the savage orator, capable only, as he says, of "broken" and "common" speech, who derives spiritual authority from his cultural debasement: "God works where and when he pleases," Occom concludes, "and by what instruments he sees fit, and he can and has used weak and unlikely instruments to bring about his great work."[39]

But this highly performative and effective self-portrait was a strategic achievement, and a costly one as well. Just a year earlier, Occom betrayed his painful awareness of the costs when he confided to Wheelock in what I call their "breakup" letter, written 24 July 1771, in which Occom angrily accuses his mentor of betraying the cause of Indian education: "I was quite Willing to become a Gazing Stock, Yea Even a Laughing Stock, in Strange Countries to Promote your Cause."[40] While the "performance semiotic of speech and text" is an innovative critical tool, it does not quite capture the stinging humiliation that often accompanied it.

A more effective approach is explored by Lisa Brooks (Wabanaki) in *The Common Pot: The Recovery of Native Space in the Northeast* (2008). As her title indicates, Brooks grounds her approach to Native literature not just in Native language and a detailed history of the Native Northeast but in the geography of this area, a vast network of interconnected waterways that were the physical basis for, and that stand as a symbol of, Native systems of communication. To do this, Brooks first recovers the origins of Native writing in mapping. She points out that in the Abenaki language, the root word *awigha-* means "to draw, to write, to map," and its derivative, *awikhigan*, which originally referred to birch-bark messages, maps, and scrolls, eventually came to designate books and letters. But the other root of the word for book, *-igan*, signifies an instrument, so that a book of writing "is at once an activity in which we participate, an instrument, and a map. It is a map of a network of writers and texts, as well as a process of mapping the historical space they inhabit. It is a mapping of how Native people in the northeast used writing as an instrument to reclaim lands and reconstruct communities, but also a mapping of the *instrumental* activity of writing, its role in the remembrement of a fragmented world."[41] The important element here, missing in Gustafson, is Brooks's emphasis on the communal aspect of Native writing and performance, grounded in the materiality of and human interaction with place through mapping and through the experience, almost pervasive in the colonial period, of what historian Jean O'Brien calls "dispossession by degrees" of ancestral tribal lands and Indigenous languages.[42] Wampum, Brooks observes, was one of several forms of "spatialized" Indigenous writing that combined graphic and oral/social elements, moved across spaces and among communities, and was used to "bind words to deeds."[43]

Through such relationships and activities, place becomes space: Brooks recovers the central aspects of Native space through an exploration of a "prominent trope" in early Native speeches and writings, the metaphor of "the common pot" (*Wlôgan*). This is the foundational notion shared by all the Algonquian-speaking peoples that everyone and everything in communities is related and interdependent for survival and flourishing. When Europeans arrived in North America, Brooks argues, they entered what was already Native space and thus were party to the common pot and could materially affect it, whether they were aware of its existence or not. In one of the earliest accounts of Algonquian, *A Key into the Language of America* (1643), Roger Williams recounts that upon encountering English writing, the Narragansetts said "*Manittowoc*," which he translated as "They are Gods."[44] From this and other misconstrued instances arose the English belief that Indians instantly recognized the superior spiritual character of European script and books. But Brooks notes that a more accurate translation suggests that the Narragansetts thought writing "held *Manitou*," which she defines as "the power of transformation." Because this power could be used for good or ill, Native peoples regarded the alphabetic writing of Europeans as a powerful being that could materially affect the common pot. How to maintain the integrity of the common pot, the network of relations it represented and held in delicate balance, would occupy Native peoples for centuries.[45]

Brooks's study reverses the usual approach of literary history. After first demonstrating that Native peoples had sophisticated spatialized systems of communication, including *awikhigawogan* ("writing," understood as an activity that has manitou, that can transform), before the arrival of Europeans, she goes on to explore how Native people adapted and incorporated European writing: "Birchbark messages became letters and petitions, wampum records became treaties and journey pictographs became written 'journals' that contained similar geographic and relational markers, while histories recorded on birchbark and wampum became written communal narratives." Emerging from Native space, and adapted to Western writing, these various genres helped Indians resist the dispossessions of colonization and "represent an indigenous American literary tradition."[46]

From this perspective, Occom is no longer merely Eleazar Wheelock's star student who inspired him to establish his Indian Charity School but a young, newly appointed tribal leader who, realizing the vital necessity, even ethical responsibility, of attaining European knowledge in order to play an informed role in the Mohegan land controversy, seeks out Wheelock to get the schooling he needs. In accounts written from the Anglo-American perspective, Occom's history ends with his break with Wheelock, but Brooks insists that we view Occom in terms of the international legal case, whose failure drives Occom to become a Mohegan leader and visionary, working with other Native graduates of Wheelock's school like David Fowler, his brother-in-law, and Joseph Johnson, his son-in-law, to establish the pan-Indian Brothertown project. As Brooks observes, Wheelock's school was only one location within Occom's extensive sphere of activities, and while it functioned as a colonializing project, it also served as a site within Native space that produced graduates who used their education to reconstruct and replenish the common pot.[47]

Brooks's spatialized concept of Native writing is bolstered by Matt Cohen's *The Networked Wilderness: Communicating in Early New England* (2009). Although Cohen confines his study to seventeenth-century New England, ending with the Pequot War in 1675, its implications reverberate much more widely. Reviewing the debates about the oral-literate divide in considerations of precontact Native cultures across the Americas, Cohen suggests "that something like multimedia literacy might be a better characterization of American communication norms." Such a conception of literacy factors in the "full material contexts of production" and recognizes Native and English as "both oral and inscribing people," who then "constituted each other's audiences in ways scholars have only begun to consider." In a nod to Gustafson, he explains that he prefers the term *communication* to *semiotic*, because he takes his cue not from poststructuralist theories but from the history of the book, which defines communication as "a relative and emergent process" that is deliberately indeterminate and encompasses interpretation, audience, the fluidity of language and performance, and—what is important in the colonial period of intercultural contact—deception as well as sincerity.[48]

The basic unit of this multimedia literacy is what Cohen calls "a publication event," which he defines broadly as "an embodied act of information exchange . . . also constituted by its retransmission . . . some anticipated by the participants and some beyond their control." In Native American terms, publication "involved language, narrative form, music, rhythm, intonation, gesture, choreography, costume, painting, and a range of inscriptive techniques"; had historically and regionally specific rules; recognized its context (what came before it and other forms of communication); and "engaged with colonial discourses in a complex interplay involving emulation, appropriation, subversion, signifying, and outright contest."[49] Most significantly, what becomes important in the publication event is not just the result or end product but the set of interactions that produce it, so that literature can be reconceived not as an object or end but an evolving process and, as Gustafson argues, a site of struggles over power.

Cohen emphasizes the need to acknowledge cultural differences and their effects, without identifying a single, apprehensible source of difference. Thus, he argues for dissolving the orality-literacy divide into "a continuous topography or spectrum rather than a series of overlapping but always distinct cognitive categories or habits," "approaching the analysis of moments on a spectrum of publication in space and through performance," and cultivating a more patient and provisional, less linear mode of historical and critical analysis.[50] To this end, he does not begin his study with the signal moments scholars often use to illustrate Native Americans' worshipful responses to Western technologies of the book, such as Williams's description of the Narragansetts hailing books as "Manitou" or Thomas Hariot's account of the Roanoke Indians' reverence for the physical form of the Bible and their belief in the Englishmen's use of "invisible bullets."[51] Rather, he begins with "techniques of signification" Native Americans employed. The example he gives is a brilliant rereading of Thomas Morton's "maypole," erected in 1628 to the horror of the neighboring Puritan colonists at Plymouth, as a publication event adeptly shaped to Native understanding, with its use of orality, rhetoric, feasts, dancing, and the totemic pole itself topped with deer antlers.[52] Cohen goes on to show how the performative elements of Morton's text, not just its apparatuses but its layout, fonts, and paper size, "overlap in provocative ways with the spatial approach to oral performance" and how this reading of "negative space, both in discourse and in physical bodies or places, can bridge the gap in our discussions of material and oral communications techniques and the construction and reproduction of social hierarchies and social justice."[53]

My own work on Occom pursues a networked reading and presentation of his "writing." In 2010 I received a three-year National Endowment for the Humanities grant to produce The Occom Circle (https://www.dartmouth.edu/occom/), a freely accessible scholarly digital edition of primary documents in Dartmouth's libraries by and about Occom. This project began in 2006 as a way to bring Occom's then-unpublished materials into my classroom. Rather than replicating Joanna Brooks's edition of *The Collected Writings of Samson Occom, Mohegan: Leadership and Literature in Eighteenth-Century Native America* (2006), The Occom Circle places a Native figure at the center of a network of interethnic and transatlantic relations, illuminating what Lisa Brooks labels "Native space" and the power negotiations that reshaped and almost destroyed it. By including the voices of other Native students at Wheelock's school, including rare examples of the alphabetic literacy of Native women, as well as Wheelock and his wide network of associates and correspondents, this digital archive attempts to illustrate one aspect of the common pot in New England in the second half of the eighteenth century.[54]

Furthermore, in the course of my work on Occom and early Native America, I began to realize that the usual form of author canonization in the West, through an edited collection of their works, replicates a Romantic ideal of individual genius and writers working in isolation. Although in the case of minority writers such canonization is strategic, it also displaces figures like Occom out of the communal and collective contexts he deliberately embraced as a tribal spokesman and pan-tribal leader. A digital archive offers users the opportunity to re-create a complex network of relations from a wide range of writers and locations, and to access them in a variety of ways, amplifying the limited linear presentation of print media.

Out of the rich field of Indigenous colonial literacy, I focus here on the underexamined genre of the journal, at which Occom excelled. From the moment he arrived in Lebanon, Connecticut, to study with Wheelock, until two years before his death in New Stockbridge near the Brothertown settlement in New York, Occom kept journals, twenty-four in all. In her introduction to Occom's journals in *The Collected Writings*, Joanna Brooks positions them within the tradition of early American life writing, the requirement of missionary journal keeping, and examples of Indian life writing. She concludes that Occom's "patterns of self-accounting remind us that identity can be understood as an exercise of responsibility, rather than primarily as the product of self-expression, performance, or affective manifestation."[55] Indeed, readers are usually disappointed in these journals because they do not illuminate Occom's inner thoughts and offer only the briefest glimpses of the important events that marked his professional life, such as his experiences of cosmopolitan London or the momentous founding of the Brothertown settlement. But if we think of these journals as publication events, they become infinitely more revealing.

First, as material objects: the journals are small booklets of varying numbers of pages made from folded and now-yellowed paper. They are often sewn together or tacked with small nails that are still clearly visible. This reminds us of one of Occom's earliest handicrafts and the discrimination he continually faced. During his very first mission to the Montauketts on eastern Long Island, he was so poorly paid by the missionary society that he had to supplement his salary by various means; one of those was bookbinding. Although Occom did not explicitly express an intention of publishing his journals in print, these booklets, like Emily Dickinson's fascicles, can be regarded as a form of self-publication.[56] We know Occom circulated them to Wheelock, who trained and required his missionaries to keep records of where they preached, what texts they used, and how much money they collected, in order to have records for the sponsoring missionary organizations. Wheelock also retransmitted parts of these journals in his letters to donors and in his annual narratives of the progress of the Indian Charity School, probably in ways Occom anticipated and in some he did not. We do not know how far this circulation went, or precisely how these journals, especially the ones written after their break in 1772, came into Wheelock's possession.

Second, the genre: journal writing for Occom required engaging in a variety of colonial discourses—a knowledge of writing, narrative, the Bible and preaching techniques, and the use of numbers and accounts, all of which Occom employed. But as Joanna Brooks points out, Occom continues this writing discipline long after he breaks with Wheelock and all other missionary societies that supported him. His most fulsome journals are from 1785 to 1790, when he finally moved to Brothertown, was free from missionary surveillance, and engaged in tireless itinerant preaching throughout the surrounding area. I recall transcribing Occom's journals in preparation for their markup in HTML and thinking how formulaic and sparse they were. For example, on his second experience of preaching at George Whitefield's famous Tabernacle at Moorfields in London in 1765, he recorded this entry: "~~Wednesday~~ Tuesday April 22: Preach'd in the Evening at Mr Whitefield's Tottenham Court Capel, to a great Multi~~d~~tude, ~~and~~ the Ld was present with us I hope—."[57] Or, traversing rural central New York on horseback, by wagon, by "slay," or on foot, Occom records setting out early from one place, getting to another place, having a meeting or preaching from a certain text to an audience of a certain size, lodging and dining with friends, being entertained, and resting. These repetitive and seemingly formulaic professional records left me eager for the rare moments of digression and personal amplification.

Third, the network: what I could not see through the repetition was that each journal depicts a network of social and political relations that continually reconstitutes Occom's Native space, which came to encompass greater London, large areas of England, and Scotland, where he went to raise funds for Wheelock's Indian Charity School, as well as the American Northeast and as far south as Philadelphia. In this way Occom enacted a decolonizing form of reverse colonialism, encompassing large areas of imperial Europe in his own Native space.[58] Each journal traverses a specific physical geography and lays out an accompanying neighborhood of social and political bonding that includes "interdependence, disparities in power, and vulnerability."[59] In these self- and community-constituted/ing neighborhoods, Occom visits, dines, drinks tea, uses his "Christian cards" (professionally printed teaching aids that contained biblical excerpts), sings hymns, and goes fishing with friends, acquaintances, and strangers, at the same time giving his spiritual performances and doing the pastoral work of baptizing, marrying, comforting, and putting the dead to rest.[60] Each terse journal entry is one of many "moments on a spectrum of publication in space and through performance," a node in a wider, rhizomatic set of connections that expands and deepens each time Occom returns, renews his friendships, meets new people, and draws old and new audiences.[61]

Fourth, the common pot: we can read Occom's entry on his preaching at Whitefield's Tabernacle as an example of how place becomes space in the spatialized form of "writing" that Lisa Brooks proposes. The terseness of Occom's entry (figure 12.5) belies the weightiness of the event. Whitefield was at the height of his influence at this point in both England and America. His Tabernacle held around four thousand people, and while we have no record of how filled it was on 22 April, Occom's use of the term *multitude* is telling from a man not prone to exaggerations; it is likely that many Londoners came out to see the strange "Indian preacher," who, the following year, would be mimicked on the London stage.[62] In very few words, Occom records his profound hopes for the spiritual efficacy of his performance, on which much was riding: "the Ld was with us I hope." The abbreviation of "Ld" for "Lord" further sublimates a linguistic signifier whose meaning already exceeds its form. It is significant that Occom does not write, "with me," although this would have been personally appropriate as he stood before an enormous sea of strangers on a mission he regarded as sacred, negotiating what he would later identify to Wheelock as the dangerous waters between being a "Gazing stock" and a "Laughing stock." Rather, Occom enacts a Native adaptation when he says, "with us," a tiny change through which he performatively and provisionally constitutes the body of curious (and perhaps skeptical or even hostile) people as a spiritual collective, as part of the common pot.

Ardently, Occom records his hopes in retrospect that he spoke with "freedom," a term he uses in other journal entries to characterize his preaching. By this he means speaking with the self-abandonment that makes him a vessel or mouthpiece of divinity, so that his hearers can be truly touched and elevated. In this short entry, Occom uses an English form, structured by missionary expectations, to embody a Native mode of spatializing: marking out a community and a set of spiritual and political affiliative connections. He also, quietly, reverses the usual missionary scenario: in a highly visible,

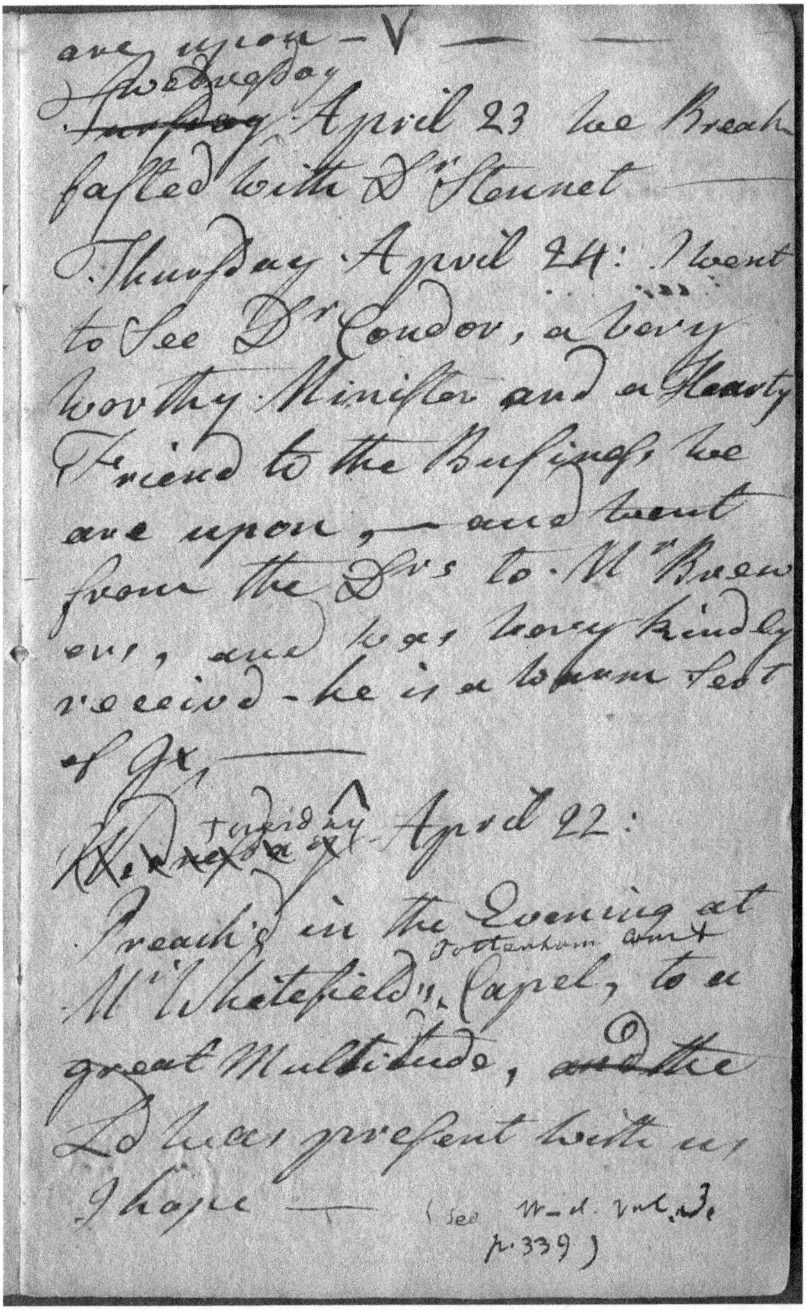

are upon — V — — —

Wednesday

~~Tuesday~~ April 23 we Break
fasted with D.ʳ Stennet

Thursday April 24: I went
to See D.ʳ Condor, a very
worthy Minister and a Hearty
Friend to the Busines we
are upon, — and went
from the D.ʳs to Mʳ Brew
ers, and was very kindly
receivd — he is a whom fest
of g x,

X ~~Drexel x~~ ^torsion^ April 22:
Preach'g in the Evening at
Mʳ Whitefield'ʳ Capel, to a
great Multitude, ~~and the~~
Lᵈ was present with us
I hope — (see W-d. vol. 3,
p. 339)

FIGURE 12.5 Page of Occom's journal for 22 April 1765. The entry is on the lower half of the
page. Courtesy of Dartmouth College Library (MS 765621.6, p. 12r).

English evangelical venue, Occom, an American Indian, preaches to a vast sea of English people, attempting to convince them of (convert them to a belief in) his ability to be Christian and literate, so that they will open their pockets and give generously to the cause of Indian education. In this spare utterance, Occom traverses the continuous topography of the oral and literate as he enacts the paradox of the savage speaker as Pentecostal mouthpiece and records a moment in the evolving process of his spiritual and professional journey.

Reading Occom's journals in light of these new methodologies, we recognize the radical, resistant, and culture-sustaining uses to which he put the range of writing technologies he mastered. We also see the many forms that literacy takes in this early period, and how these situated forms operate within Native spaces to create connection and community in ways that become startlingly legible when read from a Native perspective. To return to the beginning of the essay, though it might be too fanciful to think that in his design for Dartmouth's seal, Wheelock depicted Native space populated by Native people bringing the various and flexible "books" of their Indigenous knowledge to the fledgling college, it is now our task to rewrite this history.

NOTES

1. Dartmouth College, Trustee's Records, 1:26, DA-1, Special Collections, Dartmouth College Library, Hanover, New Hampshire. Jonathan Good notes that "as traditional heraldry requires, directions on the shield are described by the bearer's position behind it," so that the description in the trustees' minutes locates the elements in reverse. Good, "Notes from the Special Collections," n.p.

2. Cohen, *The Networked Wilderness*, 7.

3. Cohen and Glover, "Introduction," 4.

4. A good introduction to Occom's life, context, and work is J. Brooks, "'This Indian World,'" 3–39. My digital archive can be accessed at https://www.dartmouth .edu/occom/.

5. Good, "Notes from the Special Collections," n.p.

6. Pascoe, *Two Hundred Years of the s.p.g.*, 6. Good, "Notes from the Special Collections," note 12, observes that the first seal of the Massachusetts Bay Colony featured an Indian saying, "Come over and help us," a version of Acts 16:9: "And a vision appeared to Paul in the night; There stood a man of Macedonia, and prayed to him, saying, Come over into Macedonia, and help us."

7. The most influential formulation of this divide is Ong, *Orality and Literacy*.

8. Wheelock's exact phrase is "purging the Indian." See his letter to Ebenezer Pemberton, 10 October 1764, Dartmouth College Archives, Rauner Library, Hanover, New Hampshire.

9. Eliot, "The Learned Conjectures of Reverend Mr. Eliot," 409–28. For a reading of this passage, see Matthew Brown, *The Pilgrim and the Bee*, 183–88.

10. Sergeant, *A Letter from the Revd Mr. Sergeant of Stockbridge, to Dr. Colman of Boston*, 3. For an analysis of Sergeant's methods, and his failure, see Wyss, *English Letters and Indian Literacies*, 9–11, 42–48.

11. For an account of Native separatism, see Fisher, *The Indian Great Awakening*.

12. Fisher includes a history of Davenport, his activities, and his relations with Indians in *The Indian Great Awakening* (65ff.).

13. Occom, "Autobiographical Narrative, Second Draft (September 17, 1768)," 53. All references to Occom's works are from *The Collected Writings* and *The Occom Circle*, https://www.dartmouth.edu/occom/, where available.

14. Lisa Brooks gives a thorough treatment of this legal case from the Mohegans' perspective, situating it in a regional history of land rights and tying it directly to issues of literacy and Occom's studying with Wheelock. See L. Brooks, *The Common Pot*, 64–105.

15. Wyss, *English Letters and Indian Literacies*, 22. Hilary E. Wyss goes on to say that this archive must be approached with caution and understood within the context of English literacy as an attempt to dominate Native space.

16. See Occom, *The Collected Writings of Samson Occom, Mohegan*.

17. Derrida, *Of Grammatology*, 8.

18. Brotherston, *Book of the Fourth World*, 44–45.

19. For an excellent account of this process, see Boone and Mignolo, *Writing without Words*.

20. Brotherston, *Book of the Fourth World*, 45.

21. Mignolo, "Afterword," 302–3 (emphasis in the original). The essays in Boone and Mignolo's collection represent a post-Derridean strand. For recent scholarship on Native signification that uses and extends Derrida, see Teuton, *Deep Waters*, 28–36.

22. Mignolo, "Afterword," 294.

23. Mignolo, "Afterword," 303–5 (emphasis in the original).

24. Cohen and Glover, "Introduction," 16, 30.

25. "Wampum History and Background," NativeTech: Native American Technology and Art, 2019, http://www.nativetech.org/wampum/wamphist.htm.

26. Warkentin, "In Search of 'The Word of the Other,'" 2.

27. For a discussion of the complementarity of "oral and graphic impulses" in wampum and other precontact Native sign systems, see Teuton, *Deep Waters*, ch. 1. See also Haas, "Wampum as Hypertext," 77–100; Haas argues, as does Matt Cohen (see later in this chapter), that wampum is a "multimedia" Indigenous mode. In *On Records: Delaware Indians, Colonists, and the Media of History and Memory*, Andrew Newman considers wampum and other material forms and asks, "Is alphabetic writing a reliable repository for memory, or does it distort memory by alienating it from necessary interpretive context?" (2–3).

28. Warkentin, "In Search of 'The Word of the Other,'" 12, 17. For the term *relational*, she draws on the work of linguist Roy Harris in *Signs of Writing*, pt. 1, ch. 2.

29. Round, *Removable Type*, 27.

30. For more on Sequoyah, his syllabary, and the creation of an Indian public sphere, see Round, *Removable Type*, 123–49.

31. It now publishes on the web at www.cherokeephoenix.org.

32. Occom's journal, 20 September 1761, in *The Collected Writings*, 263 (MS 761515.1 in The Occom Circle); and his letter to Wheelock, 27 January 1773, in *The Collected Writings*, 102 (MS 772127.1 in The Occom Circle); see also Wheelock's letter to George Whitefield (MS 761625.1 in The Occom Circle), which suggests how the significance of wampum circulated in transatlantic evangelical circuits.

33. For a detailed account of the role of wampum in the missionary efforts of Wheelock's students and in the literary archive they produced, including an account of the complex history of one ill-fated wampum belt, see Calcaterra, "Haudenosaunee Eloquence and the Forms of Early American Alliance."

34. See, for example, Warner, *The Letters of the Republic*.

35. Gustafson, *Eloquence Is Power*, xvi.

36. Gustafson, *Eloquence Is Power*, xxii, cites Leslie Marmon Silko's *Yellow Woman and a Beauty of the Spirit: Essays on Native American Life Today*, 48–59, and N. Scott Momaday's "The Native Voice," 5–15.

37. L. Brooks, *The Common Pot*, xxxi. See Maureen Konkle's critique of Arnold Krupat's position on authenticity; Konkle, *Writing Indian Nations*, 28–29. Also, Craig Womack points out the "vast, and vastly understudied, written tradition"; Womack, *Red on Red*, 2.

38. Gustafson, *Eloquence Is Power*, 91.

39. Occom, *The Collected Writings*, 177.

40. Occom, letter to Wheelock, 24 July 1771, *The Collected Writings*, 99 (MS 771424 in The Occom Circle).

41. L. Brooks, *The Common Pot*, xxi–xxii.

42. O'Brien, *Dispossession by Degrees*.

43. L. Brooks, *The Common Pot*, 13.

44. R. Williams, *A Key into the Language of America*, 118.

45. L. Brooks, *The Common Pot*, 3–8.

46. L. Brooks, *The Common Pot*, 13. See also Bross and Wyss, *Early Native Literacies in New England*, whose goal is to recognize and make space for "the fluid intersection of various ways of writing," including "new uses of Western modes of writing" (5).

47. L. Brooks, *The Common Pot*, xii, 87.

48. Cohen, *The Networked Wilderness*, 2, 8. Both Cohen and Round draw on the work of bibliographic theorist D. F. McKenzie to argue for attending to the social contexts of texts, but Cohen (14–15) offers a strong critique of "the surprisingly restrictive conclusions [McKenzie] draws from his analysis of indigenous communications spheres" in his important essay "The Sociology of a Text: Oral Culture, Literacy and Print in Early New Zealand," which analyzes misunderstandings over the Treaty of Waitangi in 1840. McKenzie's essay was published in *The Library*.

49. Cohen, *The Networked Wilderness*, 7. Cohen borrows the concept of multimedia from Martin Lienhard, "Las prácticas textuales indígenas," 77–88. See also the work of Teuton and Haas.

50. Cohen, *The Networked Wilderness*, 21, 25.

51. See Hariot, *A Brief and True Report of the New Found Land of Virginia* (1588), 39–40, 43.

52. See Cohen, *The Networked Wilderness*, 29–64.

53. Cohen, *The Networked Wilderness*, 25.

54. Wyss argues, rightly, that because the archive at Dartmouth was preserved by Wheelock, many of the letters "to him are carefully crafted by Native students to manage his desires and expectations," while the other main source of papers, the collection at the Connecticut Historical Society, "is dominated by what seems to have been Samson Occom's own private records." Thus, they must be taken together. Wyss, *English Letters and Indian Literacies*, 29.

55. J. Brooks, "'This Indian World,'" 3–39.

56. Dickinson's fascicles as forms of self-publication have gotten a good deal of attention in recent years. An introduction to her practice is Oberhaus, *Emily Dickinson's Fascicles*; and, more recently, Crumbley and Heginbotham, *Dickinson's Fascicles*.

57. Occom, *The Collected Writings*, 270 (MS 765621.6 in The Occom Circle).

58. I am indebted to Hilary Wyss for this idea and several others in the section, taken from her cogent reading of an earlier draft of this essay.

59. Wigginton, *In the Neighborhood*, 16. This study represents an insightful application and extension of Cohen's approach.

60. Round finds an example of the type of card Occom probably used for his instructional games in the archives of the American Philosophical Society; for an illustration, see Round, *Removable Type*, 71.

61. Cohen, *The Networked Wilderness*, 21.

62. Occom mentions this in his entry for 23 June 1766 (MS 765621.6 in The Occom Circle).

Achebe, Chinua. "English and the African Writer." *Transition* 18 (1965): 342–49.

Allen, Bryant. "The Development of Commercial Agriculture on Mangaia: Social and Economic Change in a Polynesian Community." Master's thesis, Massey University, 1969.

Althaus, Gerhart. *Mamba—Anfang in Afrika*. Erlangen, Germany: Verl. der Ev.-Luth. Mission, 1992.

Ammann, Raymond. *Kanak Dance and Music: Ceremonial and Intimate Performance of the Melanesians of New Caledonia, Historical and Actual*. Noumea, New Caledonia: Kegan Paul International, 1997.

Anderson, Atholl, Judith Binney, and Aroha Harris. *Tangata Whenua: An Illustrated History*. Wellington: Bridget Williams Books, 2014.

Anderson, Dorothy Middleton, and Margaret Middleton Rivers Eastman. *Saint Philip's Church of Charleston: An Early History of the Oldest Parish in South Carolina*. Cheltenham, UK: The History Press, 2014.

Angas, G. F. *Savage Life and Scenes in Australia and New Zealand*. Vol. 2. London: Smith, Elder, 1847.

Aratangi, Papa. "The Entry of Christianity into Mangaian Society in the 1820s." Bachelor's thesis, Pacific Theological College, 1986.

Aratangi, Papa. "The Transformation of the Mangaian Religion." Master's thesis, Pacific Theological College, 1988.

Ariss, Robert. "Writing Black: The Construction of an Aboriginal Discourse." In *Past and Present: The Construction of Aboriginality*, edited by Jeremy R. Beckett, 131–46. Canberra: Aboriginal Studies Press, 1988.

Arista, Noelani. *The Kingdom and the Republic: Sovereign Hawaiʻi and the Early United States*. Philadelphia: University of Pennsylvania Press, 2019.

Arutangai, Selwyn, and Ronald G. Crocombe. *Land Tenure in the Pacific*. Suva, Fiji: University of the South Pacific, 1987.

Ashton, Bishop Jeremy. "Some Thoughts on Community Education." *Catalyst* 7, no. 2 (1977): 139–46.

Askew, Kelly. "Everyday Poetry from Tanzania: Microcosm of the Newspaper Genre." In *African Print Cultures: Newspapers and Their Publics in the Twentieth*

Century, edited by Derek R. Peterson, Emma Hunter, and Stephanie Newell, 179–223. Ann Arbor: University of Michigan Press, 2016.

Atkinson, Alan. *The Commonwealth of Speech: An Argument about Australia's Past, Present and Future*. Melbourne: Australian Scholarly Publishing, 2002.

Atkinson, Alan. *The Europeans in Australia*. Vol. 2, *Democracy*. South Melbourne: Oxford University Press, 2004.

Atkinson, Alan. *The Europeans in Australia*. Vol. 3, *Nation*. Kensington, Australia: University of New South Wales Press, 2014.

Attwood, Bain, and Andrew Markus. *The Struggle for Aboriginal Rights: A Documentary History*. St Leonards, Australia: Allen and Unwin, 1998.

Austin-Broos, Diane. "The Meaning of Pepe: God's Law and the Western Arrernte." *Journal of Religious History* 27, no. 3 (2003): 311–28.

Baker, Gwenda. "Indigenous Workers on Methodist Missions in Arnhem Land: A Skilled Labour Force Lost." In *Indigenous Participation in Australian Economies*, vol. 2, *Historical Engagements and Current Enterprises*, edited by Natasha Fijn, Ian Keen, Christopher Lloyd, and Michael Pickering, 135–52. Canberra: Australia National University Press, 2012.

Balaton-Chrimes, Samantha. *Ethnicity, Democracy and Citizenship in Africa: Political Marginalisation of Kenya's Nubians*. Farnham, UK: Ashgate, 2015.

Ballantyne, Tony. "Christianity, Colonialism and Cross-Cultural Communication." In *Christianity, Modernity and Culture*, edited by John Stenhouse and G. A. Wood, 23–57. Hindmarsh, Australia: Australian Theological Forum Press/ Australian Theological Forum, 2005.

Ballantyne, Tony. "Contesting the Empire of Paper: Cultures of Print and Anti-colonialism in the Modern British Empire." In *Indigenous Networks: Mobility, Connections, and Exchange*, edited by Jane Carey and Jane Lydon, 219–40. New York: Routledge, 2014.

Ballantyne, Tony. "Culture and Colonization: Revisiting the Place of Writing in Colonial New Zealand." *Journal of New Zealand Studies* 9 (2010): 1–22.

Ballantyne, Tony. *Orientalism and Race: Aryanism in the British Empire*. Houndmills, UK: Palgrave Macmillan, 2002.

Ballantyne, Tony. "Paper, Pen, and Print: The Transformation of the Kai Tahu Knowledge Order." *Comparative Studies in Society and History* 53, no. 2 (2011): 232–60.

Ballantyne, Tony. "Placing Literary Culture: Books and Civic Culture in Milton." *Journal of New Zealand Literature* 28, no. 2 (2010): 82–104.

Ballantyne, Tony. "Print, Politics and Protestantism in an Imperial Context: New Zealand c. 1769–1870." In *Information, Media and Power through the Ages*, edited by Hiram Morgan, 152–78. Dublin: University College Dublin Press, 2001.

Ballantyne, Tony. "Reading the Newspaper in Colonial Otago." *Journal of New Zealand Studies* 12 (2011): 47–63.

Ballantyne, Tony. *Talking, Listening, Writing, Reading: Communication and Colonisation*. Canberra: History Program, Research School of Social Sciences, Australian National University, 2009.

Ballantyne, Tony. "What Difference Does Colonialism Make? Reassessing Print and Social Change in an Age of Global Imperialism." In *Agents of Change: Print Culture Studies after Elizabeth L. Eisenstein*, edited by Sabrina Baron, Eric N. Lindquist, and Eleanor F. Shevlin, 342–52. Amherst: University of Massachusetts Press, 2007.

Ballantyne, Tony, and Antoinette Burton. *Empires and the Reach of the Global*. Cambridge, MA: Harvard University Press, 2014.

Ballara, Angela. *Taua: "Musket Wars," "Land Wars" or Tikanga? Warfare in Māori Society in the Early Nineteenth Century*. Auckland: Penguin, 2003.

Banerjee, Sukanya. *Becoming Imperial Citizens: Indians in the Late-Victorian Empire*. Durham, NC: Duke University Press, 2010.

Bang, Anne K. *Sufis and Scholars of the Sea: Family Networks in East Africa, 1860–1925*. London: Routledge Curzon, 2003.

Barber, Karin. "Acknowledgements." In *Africa's Hidden Histories: Everyday Literacy and Making the Self*, edited by Karin Barber, ix–x. Bloomington: Indiana University Press, 2006.

Barber, Karin. "Audiences and the Book in Africa." *Current Writing: Text and Reception in Southern Africa* 13, no. 2 (2001): 9–19.

Barber, Karin. "Authorship, Copyright and Quotation in Oral and Print Spheres in Early Colonial Yorubaland." In *Copyright Africa: How Intellectual Property, Media and Markets Transform Immaterial Cultural Goods*, edited by Ute Röschenthaler and Mamadou Diawara, 105–27. Oxford: Sean Kingston, 2016.

Barber, Karin. "Introduction: Hidden Innovators in Africa." In *Africa's Hidden Histories: Everyday Literacy and Making the Self*, edited by Karin Barber, 1–24. Bloomington: Indiana University Press, 2006.

Barber, Karin. *Print Culture and the First Yoruba Novel: I. B. Thomas's "Life Story of Me, Segilola" and Other Texts*. Leiden: Brill, 2012.

Baré, Jean-François. *Tahiti, les temps et les pouvoirs: Pour une anthropologie historique du Tahiti post-européen*. Paris: ORSTOM, 1987.

Barton, David, and Mary Hamilton. "Literacy Practices." In *Situated Literacies: Reading and Writing in Context*, edited by David Barton, Mary Hamilton, and Roz Ivanič, 7–15. London: Routledge, 2000.

Bayly, C. A. *Empire and Information: Intelligence Gathering and Social Information in India, 1780–1870*. Cambridge: Cambridge University Press, 1999.

Bays, Glen. "Creative Writing: The Road to New Life." *Precept* 1 (1972): 1–4.

Bebbington, David. *Evangelicalism in Modern Britain: A History from the 1730s to the 1980s*. London: Unwin Hyman, 1989.

Becker, C. L. *Progress and Power*. Stanford, CA: Stanford University Press, 1936.

Belich, James. *Making Peoples: A History of the New Zealanders from Polynesian Settlement to the End of the Nineteenth Century*. Auckland: Penguin, 2007.

Belmessous, Saliha. "Introduction: The Problem of Indigenous Claim Making in Colonial History." In *Native Claims: Indigenous Law against Empire, 1500–1920*, edited by Saliha Belmessous, 3–18. Oxford: Oxford University Press, 2011.

Bensa, Alban. "La tradition écrite kanak: Un engagement mémoriel et politique essentiel en Nouvelle-Calédonie." In *Destins des collectivités politiques* d'Océanie, edited by J.-Y. Faberon and J. Regnault, 647–53. Aix-en-Provence: Presses Universitaires d'Aix-Marseille, 2011.

Bensa, Alban, Kacué Yvon Goromoedo, and Adrian Muckle. *Les Sanglots de l'aigle pêcheur: Nouvelle-Calédonie; La Guerre kanak de 1917.* Toulouse: Anacharsis, 2015.

Bently, Lionel. "Copyright, Translations, and Relations between Britain and India in the Nineteenth and Early Twentieth Centuries." *Chicago-Kent Law Review* 82, no. 1181 (2007): 1181–240.

Bhabha, Homi. *The Location of Culture.* New York: Routledge, 1994.

Biggs, Bruce. "Maori Affairs and the Hunn Report." *Journal of the Polynesian Society* 70, no. 3 (1961): 361–64.

Biggs, Bruce. "The Translation and Publishing of Maori Material in the Auckland Public Library." *Journal of the Polynesian Society* 61 (1952): 177–91.

Binney, Judith. "History and Memory: The Wood of the Whau Tree, 1766–2005." In *The New Oxford History of New Zealand,* edited by Giselle Byrnes, 73–98. South Melbourne: Oxford University Press, 2009.

Binney, Judith. *The Legacy of Guilt: A Life of Thomas Kendall.* 2nd ed. Wellington: Bridget Williams Books, 2005.

Binney, Judith. *Stories without End: Essays, 1975–2010.* Wellington: Bridget Williams Books, 2010.

Binney, Judith, Judith Bassett, and Erik Olssen. *The People and the Land/Te Tangata me te Whenua: An Illustrated History of New Zealand, 1820–1920.* Wellington: Allen and Unwin, 1990.

Birnhack, Michael D. *Colonial Copyright: Intellectual Property in Mandate Palestine.* Oxford: Oxford University Press, 2012.

Blackwell, Thomas. *An Enquiry into the Life and Writings of Homer.* London, 1735.

Bollen, J. D. "English Missionary Societies and the Australian Aborigine." *Journal of Religious History* 9, no. 3 (1977): 263–90.

Boone, Elizabeth Hill, and Walter D. Mignolo, eds. *Writing without Words: Alternative Literacies in Mesoamerica and the Andes.* Durham, NC: Duke University Press, 1994.

Boubin-Boyer, Sylvette. *De la Première Guerre Mondiale en Océanie: Les guerres de tous les calédoniens.* Villeneuve d'Ascq, France: Presses Universitaires du Septentrion, 2003.

Bracken, Thomas. *Musings in Maoriland.* Dunedin: Keirle, 1890.

Brandt, Deborah. "Sponsors of Literacy." *College Composition and Communication* 49, no. 2 (1998): 165–85.

Brash, Elton. "Tok Pisin!" *Meanjin* 34, no. 3 (1975): 320–27.

Brewer, Ian H. *Te Rauparaha.* Wellington: School Publications Branch, Department of Education, 1966.

British Columbia Legislative Assembly. *Papers Connected with the Indian Land Question, 1850–1875.* Victoria, BC: Government Printer, 1875.

Brodie, Walter. *Remarks on the Past and Present State of New Zealand.* London: Whittaker, 1845.

Brooks, Joanna. "'This Indian World': An Introduction to the Writings of Samson Occom." In *The Collected Writings of Samson Occom, Mohegan: Leadership and Literature in Eighteenth-Century Native America,* edited by Joanna Brooks, 3–39. Oxford: Oxford University Press, 2006.

Brooks, Lisa. *The Common Pot: The Recovery of Space in the Northeast.* Minneapolis: University of Minnesota Press, 2008.

Broomfield, G. W. "The Re-Bantuization of the Swahili Language." *Africa* 4 (1931): 77–85.

Bross, Kristina, and Hilary E. Wyss, eds. *Early Native Literacies in New England: A Documentary and Critical Anthology.* Amherst: University of Massachusetts Press, 2008.

Brotherston, Gordon. *Book of the Fourth World: Reading the Native Americas through Their Literature.* Cambridge: Cambridge University Press, 1992.

Brown, Matthew P. *The Pilgrim and the Bee: Reading Rituals and Book Culture in Early New England.* Philadelphia: University of Pennsylvania Press, 2007.

Brown, Michael F. *Who Owns Native Culture?* Cambridge, MA: Harvard University Press, 2004.

Brown, William. *New Zealand and Its Aborigines.* London: J. and D. A. Darling, 1851.

Brumfit, Ann. "The Rise and Development of a Language Policy in German East Africa." *Sprache und Geschichte in Afrika* 2 (1980): 219–331.

Buck, Peter H. (Te Rangi Hiroa). *Mangaia and the Mission.* Edited by Rod Dixon and Teaea Parima. Suva, Fiji: Institute of Pacific Studies, University of the South Pacific, in association with B. P. Bishop Museum, 1993.

Buick, T. Lindsay. *An Old New Zealander, or Te Rauparaha, the Napoleon of the South.* London: Whitcombe and Tombs, 1911.

Bullock, Marita. *Memory Fragments: Visualising Difference in Australian History.* Bristol: Intellect, 2012.

Burns, Patricia. "The Foundations of the New Zealand Press." PhD diss., Victoria University College, 1957.

Burns, Patricia. *Te Rauparaha: A New Perspective.* Auckland: Penguin, 1983.

Burton, Antoinette, and Tony Ballantyne, eds. *World History from Below: Disruption and Dissent, 1750 to the Present.* London: Bloomsbury, 2016.

Burton, Antoinette, and Isabel Hofmeyr. "Introduction: The Spine of Empire? Books and the Making of an Imperial Commons." In *Ten Books That Shaped the British Empire: Creating an Imperial Commons,* edited by Antoinette Burton and Isabel Hofmeyr, 1–28. Durham, NC: Duke University Press, 2014.

Buse, Jasper. *Cook Islands Maori Dictionary.* With Raututi Taringa. Edited by Bruce Biggs and Rangi Moekaʻa. Rarotonga: Ministry of Education, Government of the Cook Islands, 1995.

Butler, Peter. *Life and Times of Te Rauparaha by His Son Tamihana Te Rauparaha.* Martinborough, New Zealand: Alister Taylor, 1980.

Byrnes, Giselle. "Introduction: Reframing New Zealand History." In *The New Oxford History of New Zealand,* edited by Giselle Byrnes, 1–18. South Melbourne: Oxford University Press, 2009.

Cairns, Alan. *Citizens Plus: Aboriginal Peoples and the Canadian State.* Vancouver: University of British Columbia Press, 2001.

Calcaterra, Angela. "Haudenosaunee Eloquence and the Forms of Early American Alliance." In *Literary Indians: Aesthetics and Encounter in Early American Literature*, edited by Mark Simpson-Vox and Lucas Church. Chapel Hill: University of North Carolina Press, forthcoming.

Campbell, Alistair. *Sanctuary of Spirits*. Wellington: Wai-te-Ata Press, 1963.

Carey, James W. *Communication as Culture: Essays on Media and Society*. Rev. ed. Hoboken, NJ: Taylor and Francis, 2008.

Carey, Jane, and Jane Lydon, eds. *Indigenous Networks: Mobility, Connections and Exchange*. New York: Routledge, 2014.

Carlson, Keith Thor. "Orality about Literacy: The 'Black and White' of Salish History." In *Orality and Literacy: Reflections across Disciplines*, edited by Keith Thor Carlson, Kristina Fagan, and Natalia Khanenko-Friesen, 43–69. Toronto: University of Toronto Press, 2011.

Carlson, Keith Thor. *The Power of Place, the Problem of Time: Aboriginal Identity and Historical Consciousness in the Cauldron of Colonialism*. Toronto: University of Toronto Press, 2010.

Carlson, Keith Thor. "Reflections on Indigenous History and Memory: Reconstructing and Reconsidering Contact." In *Myth and Memory: Stories of Indigenous-European Contact*, edited by John Lutz, 46–68. Vancouver: University of British Columbia Press, 2007.

Carlson, Keith Thor, ed. *A Sto:lo-Coast Salish Historical Atlas*. Vancouver: Douglas and McIntyre, 2001.

Carlson, Keith Thor. *The Twisted Road to Freedom: America's Granting of Independence to the Philippines in 1946*. Manila: University of the Philippines; Honolulu: University of Hawai'i Press, 1996.

Carlson, Keith Thor, John Sutton Lutz, David M. Schaepe, and Naxaxalhts-Albert "Sonny" McHalsie. *Towards a New Ethnohistory: Community Engaged Scholarship among People of the River*. Winnepeg: University of Manitoba Press, 2018.

Cass, Philip. *Press, Politics and People in Papua New Guinea, 1950–1975*. Auckland: Unitec ePress, 2014.

Cates, Ann F. "Why Teach First in the Vernacular?" READ: *The Adult Literacy and Literature Magazine* 10, no. 1 (1975): 2.

Chapin, Helen Geracimos. *Shaping History: The Role of Newspapers in Hawai'i*. Honolulu: University of Hawai'i Press, 1996.

Charlot, John. *Classical Hawaiian Education: Generations of Hawaiian Culture*. Laie, HI: Pacific Institute, Brigham Young University, 2005.

Clark, Michael, ed. *The Eliot Tracts: With Letters from John Eliot to Thomas Thorowgood and Richard Baxter*. Westport, CT: Praeger, 2003.

Clayton, Hamish. *Wulf*. Auckland: Penguin, 2010.

Clerk, Christian. "The Animal World of the Mangaians." PhD diss., University College, London, 1981.

Clifford, James. *Person and Myth: Maurice Leenhardt in the Melanesian World*. Berkeley: University of California Press, 1982.

Cohen, Matt. *The Networked Wilderness: Communicating in Early New England*. Minneapolis: University of Minnesota Press, 2009.

Cohen, Matt, and Jeffrey Glover. "Introduction." In *Colonial Mediascapes: Sensory Worlds of the Early Americas,* edited by Matt Cohen and Jeffrey Glover, 1–47. Lincoln: University of Nebraska Press, 2014.

Cohn, Bernard S. *Colonialism and Its Forms of Knowledge.* Princeton, NJ: Princeton University Press, 1996.

Cole, Douglas, and Ira Chaikin. *An Iron Hand upon the People: The Law against the Potlatch on the Northwest Coast.* Vancouver: Douglas and McIntyre; Seattle: University of Washington Press, 1990.

Cole, Juan R. I. "Printing and Urban Islam in the Mediterranean World, 1890–1920." In *Modernity and Culture: From the Mediterranean to the Indian Ocean,* edited by Leila Tarazi Fawaz and C. A. Bayly, 344–64. New York: Columbia University Press, 2002.

Collins, C. "Teaching the Vernacular in Government Primary Schools." Special issue, READ: *The Adult Literacy and Literature Magazine* 2 (June 1976): 42–44.

Collins, Hēni. *Ka Mate, Ka Ora! The Spirit of Te Rauparaha.* Wellington: Steele Roberts, 2010.

"Colloque: Être kanak aujourd'hui." *Mwà Véé* 9 (1995): 17–19.

Comaroff, Jean, and John L. Comaroff. *Ethnicity Inc.* Chicago: University of Chicago Press, 2009.

Cook, James. *Captain Cook's Journal during His First Voyage Round the World in H.M. Bark "Endeavour" 1768–71.* Adelaide: eBooks@Adelaide, University of Adelaide, updated 2015. https://ebooks.adelaide.edu.au/c/cook/james/c77j/index.html.

Coombe, Rosemary. *The Cultural Life of Intellectual Properties: Authorship, Appropriation, and the Law.* Durham, NC: Duke University Press, 1998.

Cooper, Frederick. *Colonialism in Question: Theory, Knowledge, History.* Berkeley: University of California Press, 2005.

Crawford, J. C. *Recollections of Travel in New Zealand and Australia.* Edinburgh: Ballantyne, Hanson, 1880.

Crocombe, M. "Papua New Guinea." Special issue of "Mana" section, *Pacific Islands Monthly* 44, no. 12 (1973): 61–67.

Crocombe, R. G. *Land Tenure in the Cook Islands.* Melbourne: Oxford University Press, 1964.

Crumbley, Paul, and Eleanor Elson Heginbotham, eds. *Dickinson's Fascicles: A Spectrum of Possibilities.* Columbus: Ohio State University Press, 2014.

Curnow, Allen. *Four Plays.* Wellington: A. H. and A. W. Reed, 1972.

Curnow, Jenifer. "Te Rangikaheke, Wiremu Maihi." In *Dictionary of New Zealand Biography.* Ministry of Culture and Heritage. Article published 1990. Online in *Te Ara—the Encyclopedia of New Zealand.* http://www.TeAra.govt.nz/en/biographies/1t66/te-rangikaheke-wiremu-maihi.

Curnow, Jenifer, Ngapare Hopa, and Jane McRae, eds. *Rere Atu, Taku Manu! Discovering History, Language, and Politics in the Maori-Language Newspapers, 1842–1933.* Auckland: Auckland University Press, 2002.

Curthoys, Ann. "Genocide in Tasmania: The History of an Idea." In *Genocide and Colonialism,* edited by A. Dirk Moses and Dan Stone, 229–52. New York: Berghahn Books, 2008.

Curthoys, Ann, and Jessie Mitchell. "'Bring This Paper to the Good Governor': Aboriginal Petitioning in Britain's Australian Colonies." In *Native Claims: Indigenous Law against Empire, 1500–1920*, edited by Saliha Belmessous, 182–203. Oxford: Oxford University Press, 2011.

Cushman, Ellen. *The Cherokee Syllabary: Writing the People's Perseverance*. Norman: University of Oklahoma Press, 2012.

Damousi, Joy. *Colonial Voices: A Cultural History of English in Australia, 1840–1940*. New York: Cambridge University Press, 2010.

Davis, Caroline, and David Johnson. "Introduction." In *The Book in Africa: Critical Debates*, edited by Caroline Davis and David Johnson, 1–17. Basingstoke, UK: Palgrave, 2015.

Davis, Jack, and Bob Hodge, eds. *Aboriginal Writing Today*. Canberra: Australian Institute of Aboriginal Studies, 1985.

de Certeau, Michel. *The Writing of History*. Translated by Tom Conley. New York: Columbia University Press, 1988.

de Costa, Ravi. "Identity, Authority, and the Moral Worlds of Indigenous Petitions." *Comparative Studies in Society and History* 48, no. 3 (2006): 669–98.

Deloria, Philip J. *Indians in Unexpected Places*. Lawrence: University Press of Kansas, 2004.

Demos, John. *The Unredeemed Captive: A Family Story from Early America*. New York: Vintage, 1995.

Dening, Greg. *History's Anthropology: The Death of William Gooch*. Melbourne: Melbourne University Publishing, 1995.

Derby, Mark. "Māori–Pākehā Relations." Page 2, "Missions and Māori." In *Te Ara—the Encyclopedia of New Zealand*. Ministry of Culture and Heritage. Article published 5 May 2011. http://www.TeAra.govt.nz/en/maori-pakeha-relations/page-2.

Derrida, Jacques. *L'écriture et la différence*. Paris: Le Seuil, 1967.

Derrida, Jacques. *Of Grammatology*. Translated by Gayatri Spivak. Baltimore: John Hopkins University Press, 1976.

Dhupelia-Mesthrie, Uma. "Betwixt the Oceans: The Chief Immigration Officer in Cape Town, Clarence Wilfred Cousins (1905–1915)." *Journal of Southern African Studies* 42, no. 3 (2016): 463–81.

Dick, Archie L. *The Hidden History of South Africa's Book and Reading Cultures*. Toronto: University of Toronto Press, 2012.

Drahos, Peter, and John Braithwaite. *Information Feudalism: Who Owns the Knowledge Economy?* London: Earthscan, 2002.

Driessen, H. A. H. "Outriggerless Canoes and Glorious Beings: Pre-contact Prophecies in the Society Islands." *Journal of Pacific History* 17, no. 1 (1982): 3–26.

Duff, Wilson. *The Upper Stalo Indians of the Fraser Valley, British Columbia*. Anthropology in BC, Memoir No. 1. Victoria: BC Provincial Museum, Department of Education, 1952.

East, Rodney V. "The Development of a Papua New Guinea National Information System: Pangis." Master's thesis, University of Aberstwyth, Wales, 1977.

Edgar, Andrew. "Cultural Anthropology." In *Key Concepts in Cultural Theory*, edited by Andrew Edgar and Peter R. Sedgwick, 64–66. New York: Routledge, 1999.

"Editorial." *Precept* 1 (1974): 2–5.

Eliot, John. "The Learned Conjectures of Reverend Mr. Eliot." In *The Eliot Tracts: With Letters from John Eliot to Thomas Thorowgood and Richard Baxter*, edited by Michael Clark, 409–28. Westport, CT: Praeger, 2003.

Ellemor, Arthur F. *Can the Aboriginal Be Assimilated?* Sydney: Methodist Overseas Mission, 1956.

Epling, P. J. "O le Gafa o Talo'olema'aga o Satalo: A Traditional Samoan Family History." *Journal of Pacific History* 5 (1970): 164–75.

Evans, Nicholas, and Monica Seeber, eds. *The Politics of Publishing in South Africa*. New York: Transaction, 2000.

Fairburn, Miles. *The Ideal Society and Its Enemies: The Foundations of Modern New Zealand Society, 1850–1900*. Auckland: Auckland University Press, 1989.

Faraclas, Nicholas. "Literacy, Awareness, Development and Communication in Papua New Guinea." *Catalyst* 20, no. 1 (1990): 52–61.

Finnegan, Ruth. *Literacy and Orality: Studies on the Technology of Communication*. Oxford: Oxford University Press, 1988.

Finnegan, Ruth. *Oral Poetry*. Cambridge: Cambridge University Press, 1977.

Fisher, Linford D. *The Indian Great Awakening: Religion and the Shaping of Native Cultures in Early America*. Oxford: Oxford University Press, 2012.

Franklin, Joice. "Towards a Language and Literature Directory of Papua New Guinea." In *Studies on Literacy and Education: Workpapers in Papua New Guinea Languages*, edited by Richard Loving, 2:5–36. Ukarumpa, PNG: Summer Institute of Linguistics, 1975.

Fraser, Robert. *Book History through Postcolonial Eyes: Rewriting the Script*. London: Routledge, 2008.

Fraser, Simon. *Letters and Journals, 1806–1808*. Edited with an introduction by W. Kaye Lamb. Toronto: Macmillan, 1966.

Frazer, Thomas L. "A Study of the Development, Format and Content of the *Niugini Toktok*, Neo-Melanesian Newspaper of New Guinea to April 13, 1966." Master's thesis, Louisiana State University, 1969.

Gallagher, Sarah K. J. "'A Curious Document': Ta Moko as Evidence of Pre-European Textual Culture in New Zealand." BSANZ *Bulletin* 27, no. 3/4 (2003): 39–47.

Garvey, Ellen Gruber. *Writing with Scissors: American Scrapbooks from the Civil War to the Harlem Renaissance*. New York: Oxford University Press, 2013.

Gee, James Paul. "Orality and Literacy: From *The Savage Mind* to *Ways with Words*." TESOL *Quarterly* 20, no. 4 (1986): 719–46.

Gendre, R. P. *Oblats de Marie Imaculée, Missions de la Congrégation des Missionnaires Oblats de Marie Immaculée*. Rome: Maison Generale OMI; Marseille: Typographie Veuve, Marius Olive, 1865.

George, Kenneth. "Felling a Story with a New Ax: Writing and Reshaping of Ritual Song Performance in Upland Sulawesi." *Journal of American Folklore* 103 (1990): 3–24.

Ghazal, Amal N. *Islamic Reform and Arab Nationalism: Expanding the Crescent from the Mediterranean to the Indian Ocean (1880s–1930s)*. London: Routledge, 2010.

Gibbons, Peter. "Cultural Colonization and National Identity." *New Zealand Journal of History* 36, no. 1 (2002): 5–17.

Gibbons, Peter. "Non-fiction." In *The Oxford Dictionary of New Zealand Literature in English*, edited by Terry Sturm, 31–118. Oxford: Oxford University Press, 1998.

Gibbons, Peter. "A Note on Writing, Identity and Colonisation in Aotearoa." *Sites* 13 (1986): 32–38.

Gill, William. *Gems from the Coral Islands*. Reprint, Rarotonga: Cook Islands Library and Museum Society, 2001.

Gill, William Wyatt. *From Darkness to Light in Polynesia*. Reprint, Suva, Fiji: Institute of Pacific Studies, University of the South Pacific, 1984.

Gill, William Wyatt. *Life in the Southern Isles*. London: Religious Tract Society, 1876.

Gill, William Wyatt. *Myths and Songs from the South Pacific*. London: Henry S. King, 1876.

Gilson, Richard. *The Cook Islands, 1820–1950*. Edited by Ron Crocombe. Wellington: Victoria University Press; Suva, Fiji: Institute of Pacific Studies, University of the South Pacific, 1980.

Good, Jonathan. "Notes from the Special Collections: The Dartmouth College Seal." *Dartmouth College Library Bulletin* 37, no. 2 (April 1997): n.p. https://www.dartmouth.edu/~library/Library_Bulletin/Apr1997/Good.html.

Goody, Jack. *The Domestication of the Savage Mind*. Cambridge: Cambridge University Press, 1977.

Goody, Jack. *The Interface between the Written and the Oral*. Cambridge: Cambridge University Press, 1987.

Goody, Jack. *The Power of the Written Tradition*. Washington, DC: Smithsonian Institution Press, 2000.

Goody, Jack. *Restricted Literacy in Northern Ghana*. Cambridge: Cambridge University Press, 1968.

Goody, Jack, and Ian Watt. "The Consequences of Literacy." In *Literacy in Traditional Societies*, edited by Jack Goody, 27–68. Cambridge: Cambridge University Press, 1968.

Grace, T. S. *A Pioneer Missionary among the Maoris, 1850–1879: Being the Letters and Journal of Thomas Samuel Grace*. Edited by S. J. Brittan, G. F. Grace, C. W. Grace, and A. V. Grace. Palmerston North, New Zealand: G. H. Bennett, 1928.

Graham, Edward Rahiri, and Jenifer Curnow. "Graham, George Samuel." In *Dictionary of New Zealand Biography*. Ministry of Culture and Heritage. Article published 1998. Online in *Te Ara—the Encyclopedia of New Zealand*. http://www.TeAra.govt.nz/en/biographies/4g17/graham-george-samuel.

Greenblatt, Stephen. *Marvellous Possessions: The Wonder of the New World*. Oxford: Oxford University Press, 1992.

Grimshaw, Patricia, Elizabeth Nelson, and Sandra Smith. *Letters from Aboriginal Women in Victoria, 1867–1926*. Melbourne: History Department, University of Melbourne, 2002.

Gustafson, Sandra. *Eloquence Is Power: Oratory and Performance in Early America*. Chapel Hill: University of North Carolina Press, 2000.

Gwyther-Jones, Roy. "How to Get Writers Writing." READ: *The Adult Literacy and Literature Magazine* 8, no. 1 (1973): 12–15.

Gwyther-Jones, Roy. "Pasina Ätre'amofo näneke." In *Literature for a New Nation (Ol Buk Bilong Papua Nu Gini)*, 10. Ukarumpa: Summer Institute of Linguistics and Dept. of Posts and Telegraphs, 1972.

Haami, Bradford. *Pūtea Whakairo: Māori and the Written Word*. Wellington: Huia, 2007.

Haami, Bradford. "Tā Te Ao Māori: Writing the Māori World." In *Huia Histories of Māori: Ngā Tāhuhu Kōrero*, edited by Danny Keenan, 164–95. Wellington: Huia, 2012.

Haas, Angela. "Wampum as Hypertext: An American Indian Intellectual Tradition of Multimedia Theory and Practice." *Studies in American Indian Literature* 19, no. 4 (2007): 77–100.

Haig-Brown, Celia. *Resistance and Renewal: Surviving the Indian Residential School*. Vancouver, BC: Arsenal Pulp, 1988.

Hākopa, Hauiti. "The *Paepae*: Spatial Information Technologies and the Geography of Narratives." PhD diss., University of Otago, 2011.

Hamilton, Alexander. "Wilkins's *Sanscrit Grammar*." *Edinburgh Review* 13 (January 1809): 372.

Hariot, Thomas. *A Brief and True Report of the New Found Land of Virginia*. 1588. Edited by Paul Royster. Electronic Texts in American Studies 20. DigitalCommons@University of Nebraska-Lincoln, Libraries at University of Nebraska-Lincoln. https://digitalcommons.unl.edu/etas/20.

Harper, Tim. "Globalism and the Pursuit of Authenticity: The Making of a Diasporic Public Sphere in Singapore." *Sojourn* 12, no. 2 (1997): 261–92.

Harris, Aroha. *Hīkoi: Forty Years of Māori Protest*. Wellington: Huia, 2004.

Harris, Aroha. "Ngā tāone nui—Māori and the City." Page 5, "Māori Adapt to City Life." In *Te Ara—the Encyclopedia of New Zealand*. Ministry of Culture and Heritage. Article published 11 March 2010. http://www.TeAra.govt.nz/en/nga-taone-nui-maori-and-the-city/page-5.

Harris, Aroha. "Theorize This: We Are What We Write." *Te Pouhere Kōrero* 3 (2009): 83–90.

Harris, Aroha, and M. J. McCallum. "'Assaulting the Ears of Government': The Indian Homemakers' Clubs and the Maori Women's Welfare League in the Formative Years." In *Indigenous Women and Work: From Labor to Activism*, edited by Carol Williams, 225–39. Urbana: University of Illinois Press, 2012.

Harris, Roy. *Signs of Writing*. London: Routledge, 1995.

Harvey, Megan. "Story People: Stó:lō-State Relations and Indigenous Literacies in British Columbia, 1864–1874." *Journal of the Canadian Historical Association/Revue de la Société historique du Canada* 24, no. 1 (2013): 51–88.

Havelock, Eric A. *The Muse Learns to Write: Reflections on Orality and Literacy from Antiquity to the Present*. New Haven, CT: Yale University Press, 1986.

Havelock, Eric A. *Preface to Plato*. Cambridge, MA: Belknap Press of Harvard University Press, 1963.

Head, Lyndsay. "Land, Authority and the Forgetting of Being in Early Colonial Maori History." PhD diss., University of Canterbury, 2006.

Head, Lyndsay, and Buddy Mikaere. "Was 19th Century Maori Society Literate?" *Archifacts* 2 (1988): 17–20.

Henry, Teuira. *Ancient Tahiti*. Honolulu: Bishop Museum, 1928.

Heyum, Renée. "Publishing in the Islands." *Written Word* 14, no. 2 (1985): 18–22.

Hofmeyr, Isabel. *Gandhi's Printing Press: Experiments in Slow Reading*. Cambridge, MA: Harvard University Press, 2013.

Hofmeyr, Isabel. *The Portable Bunyan: A Transnational History of "The Pilgrim's Progress."* Princeton, NJ: Princeton University Press, 2004.

Hofmeyr, Isabel, and Lize Kriel. "Book History in Southern Africa: What Is It and Why Should It Interest Historians?" *South African Historical Journal* 55, no. 1 (2006): 1–19.

Hogan, Helen. *Renata's Journey: Ko te Haerenga o Renata*. Christchurch: Canterbury University Press, 1994.

Hohepa, Pat. "Current Issues in Promoting Maori Language Use." *Language Planning Newsletter* 10, no. 3 (1984): 1–4.

Hokari, Minoru. "Cross-Culturalizing History: Journey to the Gurindji Way of Historical Practice." PhD diss., Australian National University, 2001.

Hoogestraat, Jane Susan. "'Discoverers of Something New': Ong, Derrida, and Postcolonial Theory." In *Time, Memory, and the Verbal Arts: Essays on the Thought of Walter Ong*, edited by Dennis L. Weeks, 51–61. Selinsgrove, PA: Susquehanna University Press, 1998.

Hooley, Bruce. "SIL Research in New Guinea." *Kivung* 1, no. 2 (1968): 63–70.

Ho'omanawanui, Ku'ualoha. *Voices of Fire: Reweaving the Literary Lei of Pele and Hi'iaka*. Minneapolis: University of Minnesota Press, 2014.

Hooper, Antony. "Orality, Literacy, Tradition, History." *New Pacific Review*, Proceedings of the 16th Pacific History Association Conference, 3, no. 1 (2006): 6–17.

Hooper, Antony. Review of *Tahitians: Mind and Experience in the Society Islands*, by Robert Levy. *Journal of the Polynesian Society* 84, no. 3 (1975): 369–77.

Hooper, Antony, and Judith Huntsman, eds. and trans. *Matagi Tokelau: History and Traditions of Tokelau*. English ed. Apia, Samoa: Office of Tokelau Affairs; Suva, Fiji: Institute of Pacific Studies, University of the South Pacific, 1991.

Horton, Jessica. "Rewriting Political History: Letters from Aboriginal People in Victoria, 1886–1919." *History Australia* 9, no. 2 (2012): 157–81.

Hunter, Emma. "Dutiful Subjects, Patriotic Citizens, and the Concept of 'Good Citizenship' in Twentieth-Century Tanzania." *Historical Journal* 56, no. 1 (2013): 257–77.

Hunter, Emma. "Languages of Politics in Twentieth-Century Kilimanjaro." PhD diss., University of Cambridge, 2008.

Huntsman, Judith. "Just Marginally Possible: The Making of *Matagi Tokelau*." *Journal of Pacific Studies* 28 (1996): 138–54.

Innis, Harold. *Empire and Communications*. Oxford: Clarendon, 1950.

Jeppie, Shamil. "Writing, Books, and Africa." *History and Theory* 53 (2014): 94–104.

Johns, Adrian. *The Nature of the Book and the Book of Nature: Print and Knowledge in the Making.* Chicago: University of Chicago Press, 1998.

Johnson, David, and Caroline Davis. "Introduction." In *The Book in Africa: Critical Debates,* edited by Caroline Davis and David Johnson, 1–17. Basingstoke, UK: Palgrave Macmillan, 2015.

Johnson, R. K. "Bilingual Education and Teacher Training in Papua New Guinea." Research Report 3. Port Moresby, New Guinea: Faculty of Education, University of Papua New Guinea, 1975.

Johnston, Anna. *The Paper War: Morality, Print Culture and Power in Colonial New South Wales.* Perth: University of Western Australia Publishing, 2011.

Johnston, Ray. "Devising a Written Style in an Unwritten Language." READ: *The Adult Literacy and Literature Magazine* 11, no. 3 (1976): 66–70.

Jones, Alison, and Kuni Jenkins. *He Kōrero: Words between Us; First Māori-Pākehā Conversations on Paper.* Wellington: Huia, 2011.

Kaa, Wiremu, and Te Ohorere Kaa, eds. *Apirana Turupa Ngata, Kt., M.A., LLB., D. LIT., M.P.: Āna Tuhinga i Roto i te Reo Māori.* Wellington: Victoria University Press, 1996.

Kaa, Wiremu, and Te Ohorere Kaa, eds. *Nga Korero a Reweti Kohere ma.* Wellington: Victoria University Press, 1994.

Kaestle, Carl F. "The History of Literacy and the History of Readers." *Review of Research in Education* 12 (1985): 11–53.

Kamakau, S. M. "Huikau, Pohihihi Ke Kuikahi Panai Like me Ka Uku Kaulele o Puuloa." *Ko Hawaii Ponoi,* 20 August 1873.

Kamensky, Jane. *Governing the Tongue: The Politics of Speech in Early New England.* Oxford: Oxford University Press, 1997.

Kasarhérou, Emmanuel. "Traces littéraires et poétiques: Le patrimoine écrit kanak." *Mwà Véé* 33 (2001): 19.

Kauraka, Kauraka. *Manihikian Traditional Narratives in English and M[a]nihikian.* Papatoetoe, New Zealand: Te Ropu Kahurangi, 1988.

Kauraka, Kauraka, ed. *Oral Traditions of Manihiki.* Suva: Institute of Pacific Studies, University of the South Pacific; Rarotonga: Cook Islands Extension Centre of the University of the South Pacific, 1987.

Keane, Basil. "Māori Non-fiction and Scholarship—ngā Tuhinga me te Rangahau." Page 6, "Writers of Biography." In *Te Ara—the Encyclopedia of New Zealand.* Ministry of Culture and Heritage. Article published 22 October 2014. http://www.TeAra.govt.nz/en/maori-non-fiction-and-scholarship-nga-tuhinga-me-te-rangahau/page-6.

Keenan, Danny. "'Separating Them from That Common Influence': The Dissolution of Customary Authority, 1840–1890." In *Huia Histories of Māori: Ngā Tāhuhu Kōrero,* edited by Danny Keenan, 131–62. Wellington: Huia, 2012.

Kirch, Patrick Vinton. *How Chiefs Became Kings: Divine Kingship and the Rise of Archaic States in Ancient Hawai'i.* Berkeley: University of California Press, 2010.

Kirch, Patrick Vinton. *A Shark Going Inland Is My Chief: The Island Civilization of Ancient Hawaii.* Berkeley: University of California Press, 2012.

Klenke, Karin. "Whose *Adat* Is It? *Adat*, Indigeneity and Social Stratification in Toraja." In *Adat and Indigeneity in Indonesia: Culture and Entitlements between Heteronomy and Self-Ascription*, edited by Brigitta Hauser-Schäublin, 149–65. Göttingen, Germany: Universitätsverlag Göttingen, 2013.

Kohere, Reweti. *The Autobiography of a Maori*. Wellington: A. H. and A. W. Reed, 1951.

Kohere, Reweti. *The Story of a Maori Chief: Mokena Kohere and His Forbears*. Wellington: A. H. and A. W. Reed, 1949.

Komedja, Holiday. *Writing the New Nation in a West African Borderland: Ablɔɖe Safui (the Key to Freedom)*. Edited and translated by Kate Skinner and Wilson Yayoh. New York: Oxford University Press, 2020.

Konkle, Maureen. *Writing Indian Nations: Native Intellectuals and the Politics of Historiography*. Chapel Hill: University of North Carolina Press, 2004.

Kulick, Don, and Christopher Stroud. "Conceptions and Uses of Literacy in a Papua New Guinean Village." In *Cross-Cultural Approaches to Literacy*, edited by Brian V. Street, 30–61. Cambridge: Cambridge University Press, 1993.

Kuykendall, Ralph. *The Hawaiian Kingdom*. 3 vols. Honolulu: University of Hawai'i Press, 1938.

Lamont, E. H. *Wild Life among the Pacific Islanders*. Reprint, Rarotonga: Institute of Pacific Studies, University of the South Pacific, 1994.

Lange, Raeburn. "Indigenous Agents of Religious Change in New Zealand, 1830–1860." *Journal of Religious History* 24, no. 3 (2000): 279–95.

Larkin, Brian. "Degraded Images, Distorted Sounds: Nigerian Video and the Infrastructure of Piracy." *Public Culture* 16, no. 2 (2004): 289–314.

Laws of the Republic of Hawaii Passed by the Legislature at Its Session, 1896. Honolulu: Hawaiian Gazette Company's Print, 1896.

Leadley, Alan. "Emancipating Relevant Education." *Catalyst* 5, no. 1 (1975): 4–15.

Lemke, Hilda. "Die Suaheli-Zeitungen und Zeitschriften in Deutsch-Ostafrika." PhD diss., Leipzig University, 1929.

Lepore, Jill. *In the Name of War: King Philip's War and the Origins of American Identity*. New York: Knopf, 1998.

Leslie, John. *The Historical Development of the Indian Act*. 2nd ed. Ottawa: Department of Indian Affairs and Northern Development, Treaties and Historical Research Branch, 1978.

Lessig, Lawrence. *The Future of Ideas: The Fate of the Commons*. New York: Random House, 2001.

Lévi-Strauss, Claude. *Family and Social Life of the Nambikwara Indians*. Translated by Eileen Sittler. New Haven, CT: Human Relations Area Files, 1958.

Lévi-Strauss, Claude. *Mythologiques*. 4 vols. Chicago: University of Chicago Press, 1983.

Lévi-Strauss, Claude. *The Savage Mind*. Chicago: University of Chicago Press, 1966.

Lévi-Strauss, Claude. *Structural Anthropology*. New York: Doubleday, 1967.

Levy, Robert. *Tahitians: Mind and Experience in the Society Islands*. Chicago: University of Chicago Press, 1973.

Lienhard, Martin. "Las prácticas textuales indigenas: Aproximaciones a un nuevo objeto de investigacíon." *Nuevo Texto Crítico* 7, no. 14–15 (July 1994–June 1995): 77–88.

Lineham, Peter J. "Missions and Missionaries." Page 5, "Māori Converts." In *Te Ara—the Encyclopedia of New Zealand*. Ministry of Heritage and Culture. Article published 5 May 2011, updated 8 August 2018. http://www.TeAra.govt.nz/en/missions-and-missionaries/page-5.

Loader, Arini. "Haere Mai Me Tuhituhi He Pukapuka: Muri Iho Ka Whawhai Ai Tātou; Reading Te Rangikāheke." Master's thesis, Victoria University of Wellington, 2008.

Loader, Arini. "'Kei Wareware': Remembering Te Rauparaha." *Biography* 39, no. 3 (2016): 339–65.

Loader, Arini. "Tau Mai E Kapiti te Whare Wananga o Ia, o te Nui, o te Wehi, o te Toa: Reclaiming Early Raukawa-Toarangatira Writing from Otaki." PhD diss., Victoria University of Wellington, 2013.

Locke, John. *Second Treatise of Government*. 1690. Edited by C. B. Macpherson. Indianapolis, IN: Hackett, 1980.

Loomba, Ania. *Colonialism/Postcolonialism*. London: Routledge, 1998.

Luria, Aleksandr Romanovich. *Cognitive Development: Its Cultural and Social Foundations*. Edited by Michael Cole. Translated by Martin Lopez-Morillas and Lynn Solotaroff. Cambridge, MA: Harvard University Press, 1976.

Lynch, Charles Dominic. *Church, State and Language in Melanesia: An Inaugural Lecture*. Port Moresby: University of Papua New Guinea, 1979.

Lyons, Martyn, and Lucy Taksa. *Australian Readers Remember: An Oral History of Reading, 1890–1930*. Oxford: Oxford University Press, 1992.

MacDonald, Andrew. "Colonial Trespassers in the Making of South Africa's International Borders, 1900 to c. 1950." PhD diss., University of Cambridge, 2012.

MacDonald, Andrew. "Strangers in a Strange Land: Undesirables and Border-Controls in Colonial Durban, 1897–c.1910." Master's thesis, University of KwaZulu-Natal, 2007.

Mack, Beverley B., and Jean Boyd. *One Woman's Jihad: Nana Asma'u, Scholar and Scribe*. Bloomington: Indiana University Press, 2009.

Mackay, Ian. *Broadcasting in Papua New Guinea*. Melbourne: Melbourne University Press, 1976.

MacLachlan, Morag, ed. *The Fort Langley Journals, 1827–30*. Vancouver: University of British Columbia Press, 1998.

Maclean, Chris. *Kapiti*. Wellington: Whitcombe Press with the Assistance of the Historical Branch, Department of Internal Affairs, 1999.

Mahuika, Nēpia. "New Zealand History Is Māori History: Tikanga as the Ethical Foundation of Historical Scholarship in Aotearoa New Zealand." *New Zealand Journal of History* 49, no. 1 (2015): 5–30.

Malone, Dennis. "International Literacy Year—1990: What Does It Mean for Papua New Guinea?" *READ: The Adult Literacy and Literature Magazine* 25, no. 1 (1990): 2–12.

Mamdani, Mahmood. "Beyond Settler and Native as Political Identities: Overcoming the Political Legacy of Colonialism." *Comparative Studies in Society and History* 43, no. 4 (2001): 651–64.

Mamdani, Mahmood. "The Invention of the Indigène." *London Review of Books* 33, no. 2 (20 January 2011): 31–33.

Mandler, Peter. "The Problem with Cultural History." *Cultural and Social History* 1, no. 1 (2004): 94–117.

Marshall, P. *Geology of Mangaia*. Bernice P. Bishop Museum Bulletin 36. Honolulu: The Bernice Pauahi Museum, 1927.

Marten, Helen. "Keeping Literates Literate." READ: *The Adult Literacy and Literature Magazine* 9, no. 4 (1974): 111–16.

Marten, Helen. "Literacy for Those Who Don't Want It." READ: *The Adult Literacy and Literature Magazine* 4, no. 2 (1969): 13–14.

Martin, Lady Ann. *Our Maoris*. London: Society for Promoting Christian Knowledge, 1884. Facsimile ed., Auckland: Wilson and Horton, n.d.

Mathews, R. H. "Message-Sticks Used by the Aborigines of Australia." *American Anthropologist* A10, no. 9 (1897): 288–98.

Maybury-Lewis, David. *Indigenous Peoples, Ethnic Groups, and the State*. Boston: Allyn and Bacon, 1997.

McGregor, Russell. "Protest and Progress: Aboriginal Activism in the 1930s." *Australian Historical Studies* 25, no. 101 (1993): 555–68.

McKenzie, D. F. *Oral Culture, Literacy and Print in Early New Zealand: The Treaty of Waitangi*. Wellington: Victoria University Press, 1985.

McKenzie, Don F. "The Sociology of a Text: Oral Culture, Literacy and Print in Early New Zealand." In *The Social History of Language*, edited by Peter Burke and Roy Porter, 161–97. Cambridge: Cambridge University Press, 1987.

McKenzie, D. F. "The Sociology of a Text: Orality, Literacy, and Print in Early New Zealand." *The Library* 6, no. 4 (December 1984): 333–65.

McKinnon, Malcolm. "Puhuriwhenua Cannon." In *Te Ara—the Encyclopedia of New Zealand*. Ministry of Culture and Heritage. Article published 12 May 2012, updated 1 November 2016. http://www.TeAra.govt.nz/en/photograph/31761/puhuriwhenua-cannon.

McLuhan, Marshall. *The Gutenberg Galaxy: The Making of Typographic Man*. Toronto: University of Toronto Press; London: Routledge and Kegan Paul, 1962.

McLuhan, Marshall. *War and Peace in the Global Village*. New York: Bantam, 1968. Reprint, Hamburg, Germany: Ginko, 2011.

McMath, Marivee, and Teaea Parima. "Winged Tangi'ia: A Mangaian Dramatic Performance." In *South Pacific Oral Traditions*, edited by Ruth Finnegan and Margaret Orbell, 376–413. Bloomington: Indiana University Press, 1995.

McRae, Jane. "'E manu, tena koe!' 'O Bird, Greetings to You': The Oral Tradition in Newspaper Writing." In *Rere Atu, Taku Manu! Discovering History, Language and Politics in the Maori-Language Newspapers*, edited by Jenifer Curnow, Ngapare Hopa, and Jane McRae, 42–59. Auckland: University of Auckland Press, 2002.

McRae, Jane. "From Māori Oral Traditions to Print." In *Book and Print in New Zealand: A Guide to Print Culture in Aotearoa*, edited by Penny Griffith, Ross Harvey, and Keith Maslen, 17–40. Wellington: Victoria University Press, 1997.

McRae, Jane. "Māori Oral Tradition Meets the Book." In *A Book in the Hand: Essays on the History of the Book in New Zealand*, edited by Penny Griffith, Peter Hughes, and Alan Loney, 1–16. Auckland: Auckland University Press, 2000.

Mead, Hirini Moko. *Tikanga Māori: Living by Māori Values*. Wellington: Huia, 2003.

Megarrity, Lyndon. "Indigenous Education in Colonial Papua New Guinea: Australian Government Policy (1945–1975)." *History of Education Review* 34, no. 2 (2005): 41–58.

Meredith, Paul, and Alice Te Punga Somerville. "'Kia Rongo Mai Koutou ki Taku Whakaaro': Maori Voices in the Alexander Turnbull Library." *Turnbull Library Record* 43 (2010/11): 96–105.

Merlan, Francesca. "Indigeneity: Global and Local." *Current Anthropology* 50, no. 3 (2009): 303–33.

Messick, Brinkley. "Legal Documents and the Concept of 'Restricted Literacy' in a Traditional Society." *International Journal of the Sociology of Language* 42 (1983): 41–52.

Mignolo, Walter D. "Afterword: Writing and Recorded Knowledge in Colonial and Postcolonial Situations." In *Writing without Words: Alternative Literacies in Mesoamerica and the Andes*, edited by Elizabeth Hill Boone and Walter D. Mignolo, 292–312. Durham, NC: Duke University Press, 1994.

Mihalic, Frank. "Tok Pisin: Yesterday, Today, and Tomorrow." *Catalyst* 16, no. 2 (1986): 89–99.

Miller, J. R. *Shingwauk's Vision: A History of Native Residential School*. Toronto: University of Toronto Press, 1996.

Miller, Stuart Creighton. *Benevolent Assimilation: The American Conquest of the Philippines, 1899–1903*. New Haven, CT: Yale University Press, 1982.

Milloy, John. *A National Crime: The Canadian Government and the Residential School System, 1879–1986*. Winnipeg: University of Manitoba Press, 1999.

Momaday, N. Scott. "The Native Voice." In *The Columbia Literary History of the United States*, edited by Emory Elliott, Martha Banta, and Houston A. Baker, 5–15. New York: Columbia University Press, 1988.

Moorfield, John C. *Te Aka: Māori-English, English-Māori Dictionary*. Accessed 9 January 2020. https://maoridictionary.co.nz/.

Morgan, Mindy J. *The Bearer of This Letter: Language Ideologies, Literacy Practices, and the Fort Belknap Indian Community*. Lincoln: University of Nebraska Press, 2009.

Morgan, Rewa. "Oral History and Biography: The Oral Accounts of Te Rauparaha." Honours diss., University of Auckland, 2010.

Morphy, Howard. "The Art of Northern Australia." In *Traditional Aboriginal Society*, edited by William Howell Edwards, 2nd ed., 1–33. South Melbourne, Macmillan Education Australia, 1998.

Morphy, Howard. "Too Many Meanings: An Analysis of the Artistic System of the Yolngu of Northeast Arnhem Land." PhD diss., Australian National University, 1977.

Morris, Katherine. *Nari and Minala Go to School.* Bush Books, book 4. Canberra: Commonwealth Office of Education, 1950.

Morris, Katherine. *Nari and Minala Go to Work.* Bush Books, book 6. Canberra: Commonwealth Office of Education, 1955.

Morshead, L. F., comp. *The Merchandise Marks Manual.* Calcutta: n.p., 1908.

Muckle, Adrian. *Specters of Violence in a Colonial Context: New Caledonia, 1917.* Honolulu: University of Hawai'i Press, 2012.

Nahe, Hoani. "Maori, Tangata Maori." *Journal of the Polynesian Society* 3, no. 1 (1894): 27–35.

Narogin, Mudrooroo. *Writing from the Fringe: A Study of Modern Aboriginal Literature.* South Yarra, Australia: Hyland House, 1990.

National Library of New Zealand and Te Rōpu Whakahaere o Rangiātea. *Rangiātea: Ko Ahau Te Huarahi Te Pono Me Te Ora.* Wellington: National Library of New Zealand and Te Rōpu Whakahaere o Rangiātea, 1997.

Newell, Stephanie. "Articulating Empire: Newspaper Readerships in Colonial West Africa." *New Formations* 73 (2011): 26–42.

Newell, Stephanie. *Ghanaian Popular Fiction: "Thrilling Discoveries in Conjugal Life" and Other Tales.* Oxford: James Currey, 2000.

Newell, Stephanie. *Literary Culture in Colonial Ghana: "How to Play the Game of Life."* Manchester: Manchester University Press, 2002.

Newell, Stephanie. *The Power to Name: A History of Anonymity in Colonial West Africa.* Athens: Ohio University Press, 2013.

Newman, Andrew. *On Records: Delaware Indians, Colonists, and the Media of History and Memory.* Lincoln: University of Nebraska Press, 2012.

Ngũgĩ wa Thiong'o. *Decolonising the Mind: The Politics of Language in African Literature.* London: James Currey, 1986.

Nicole, Jacques. *Au pied de l'écriture: Histoire de la traduction de la Bible en tahitien.* Papeete, Tahiti: Haere po no Tahiti, 1988.

Niezen, Ronald W. "Hot Literacy in Cold Societies: A Comparative Study of the Sacred Value of Writing." *Comparative Studies in Society and History* 33, no. 2 (1991): 225–54.

Niezen, Ronald W. *The Origins of Indigenism: Human Rights and the Politics of Identity.* Berkeley: University of California Press, 2003.

Niezen, Ronald W. *A World beyond Difference: Cultural Identity in the Age of Globalization.* Malden, MA: Blackwell, 2005.

Nogelmeier, Puakea. *Mai Pa'a i ka Leo: Historical Voice in Hawaiian Primary Materials, Looking Forward and Listening Back.* Honolulu: Bishop Museum Press, 2010.

"Notes and News: Vernacular Periodicals." *Africa* 4 (1931): 498–500.

Nouvelle-Calédonie et Dépendances. *Procès-Verbaux du Conseil Général, Session ordinaire de Mai 1903.* Nouméa: Imprimerie Calédonienne, 1903.

Nyamnjoh, Francis Beng. "Ever-Diminishing Circles: The Paradoxes of Belonging in Botswana." In *Indigenous Experience Today*, edited by Marisol de la Cadena and Orin Starn, 305–32. Oxford: Berg, 2007.

Oberhaus, Dorothy. *Emily Dickinson's Fascicles: Method and Meaning.* Philadelphia: Penn State University Press, 1995.

O'Brien, Jean. *Dispossession by Degrees: Indian Land and Identity in Natick, Massachusetts, 1650–1790*. Lincoln: University of Nebraska Press, 2003.

Occom, Samson. *The Collected Writings of Samson Occom, Mohegan: Leadership and Literature in Eighteenth-Century Native America*. Edited by Joanna Brooks. Oxford: Oxford University Press, 2006.

O'Donnell, Rosemary S. "The Value of Autonomy: Christianity, Organisation and Performance in an Aboriginal Community." PhD diss., University of Sydney, 2007.

Oliver, Douglas. *Ancient Tahitian Society*. 3 vols. Honolulu: University of Hawai'i Press, 1974.

Oliver, Steven. "Te Rauparaha." In *Dictionary of New Zealand Biography*. Online in *Te Ara—the Encyclopedia of New Zealand*. Ministry of Culture and Heritage. Article published 1990. http://www.TeAra.govt.nz/en/biographies/1t74/te -rauparaha.

Oliver, Steven. "Te Rauparaha, Tamihana." In *Dictionary of New Zealand Biography*. Online in *Te Ara—the Encyclopedia of New Zealand*. Ministry of Culture and Heritage. Article published 1990. http://www.TeAra.govt.nz/en/biographies /1t75/te-rauparaha-tamihana.

Ong, Walter J. *Orality and Literacy: The Technologizing of the Word*. New York: Methuen, 1982. Reprint, London: Routledge, 1993, 2002.

Ong, Walter J. "Writing Is a Technology That Restructures Thought." In *The Written Word: Literacy in Transition*, edited by Gerd Baumann, 23–50. Oxford: Clarendon, 1986.

Openshaw, Roger, Greg Lee, and Howard Lee. *Challenging the Myths: Rethinking New Zealand's Educational History*. Palmerston North, New Zealand: Dunmore, 1993.

Opland, Jeff. *The Greater Dictionary of isiXhosa*. Alice, South Africa: University of Fort Hare, 2006.

Opland, Jeff. *Xhosa Poets and Poetry*. Cape Town: David Philip, 1998.

Opland, Jeff, Wandile Kuse, and Pamela Maseko, eds. and trans. *William Wellington Gqoba: Isizwe Esinembali: Xhosa Histories and Poetry (1873–1888)*. Pietermaritzburg: University of KwaZulu-Natal Press, 2015.

Orange, Claudia. "The Covenant of Kohimarama: A Ratification of the Treaty of Waitangi." *New Zealand Journal of History* 14, no. 1 (1980): 61–82.

Orange, Claudia. "The Māori People and the British Crown (1769–1840)." In *The Oxford Illustrated History of New Zealand*, edited by Keith Sinclair, 21–48. Oxford: Oxford University Press, 1990.

Orbell, Margaret. *Hawaiki: A New Approach to Maori Tradition*. Christchurch: Canterbury University Press, 1991.

O'Regan, Hana. "The Fate of Customary Language: Te reo Māori 1900 to the Present." In *Huia Histories of Māori: Ngā Tāhuhu Kōrero*, edited by Danny Keenan, 297–324. Wellington: Huia, 2012.

Osterhammel, Jürgen. *Colonialism: A Theoretical Overview*. Translated by Shelley I. Frisch. Princeton, NJ: Markus Wiener; Kingston, Jamaica: Ian Randle, 1999.

Panoff, Michel. *La terre et l'organisation sociale en Polynésie*. Paris: Payot, 1970.

Parr, C. J. "Maori Literacy, 1843–1867." *Journal of the Polynesian Society* 72, no. 3 (1963): 211–34.

Parr, C. J. "A Missionary Library: Printed Attempts to Instruct the Maori, 1815–1845." *Journal of the Polynesian Society* 70, no. 4 (1961): 429–50.

Parsonson, G. S. *The Conversion of Polynesia.* Dunedin: Hocken Library, 1984.

Parsonson, G. S. "The Literate Revolution." *Journal of Pacific History* 2 (1967): 39–57.

Pascoe, Charles Frederick. *Two Hundred Years of the s.p.g.: An Historical Account of the Society for the Propagation of the Gospel in Foreign Parts, 1701–1900.* Rev. ed. London: SPG Office, 1901.

Paterson, Lachy. *Colonial Discourses: Niupepa Māori, 1855–1863.* Dunedin: Otago University Press, 2006.

Paterson, Lachy. "Identity and Discourse: *Te Pipiwharauroa* and the South African War, 1899–1902." *South African Historical Journal* 65, no. 3 (2013): 444–62.

Paterson, Lachy. "Kiri Ma, Kiri Mangu: The Terminology of Race and Civilisation in the Mid-Nineteenth-Century Maori-Language Newspapers." In *Rere Atu, Taku Manu! Discovering History, Language and Politics in the Maori-Language Newspapers,* edited by Jenifer Curnow, Ngapare Hopa, and Jane McRae, 60–77. Auckland: Auckland University Press, 2002.

Paterson, Lachy. "Print Culture and the Collective Māori Consciousness." *Journal of New Zealand Literature* 28, no. 2 (2010): 105–29.

Paterson, Lachy. "*Te Hokioi* and the Legitimization of the Māori Nation." In *The Fourth Eye: Māori Media in Aotearoa New Zealand,* edited by Brendan Hokowhitu and Vijay Devidas, 124–42. Minneapolis: University of Minnesota Press, 2013.

Paterson, Lachy. "The *Te Waka Maori* Libel Case of 1877." *Law & History* 4, no. 1 (2017): 88–112.

Paterson, Lachy, and Angela Wanhalla. *He Reo Wāhine: Māori Women's Voices from the Nineteenth Century.* Auckland: Auckland University Press, 2017.

Payn, Howard. *The Merchandise Marks Act of 1887: With Special Reference to the Importation Sections and the Customs Regulations and Orders Made Thereunder Together with the Conventions with Foreign States for Protection of Trade Marks and Orders in Council under the Patents, Designs and Trade Marks Act, 1883, etc.* London: Stevens and Sons, 1888.

Peires, Jeffrey B. *The House of Phalo: A History of the Xhosa People in the Days of Their Independence.* Johannesburg: Ravan, 1981.

Peires, Jeffrey. "Lovedale Press: Literature for the Bantu Revisited." *English in Africa* 71, no. 1 (1980): 71–85.

Peters, Julie Stone. "Orality, Literacy and Print Revisited." In *Time, Memory, and the Verbal Arts: Essays on the Thought of Walter Ong,* edited by Dennis L. Weeks, 27–50. Selinsgrove, PA: Susquehanna University Press, 1998.

Peterson, Derek R. *Creative Writing: Translation, Bookkeeping, and the Work of Imagination in Colonial Kenya.* Portsmouth, NH: Heinemann, 2004.

Peterson, Derek R. "Language Work and Colonial Politics in Eastern Africa: The Making of Standard Swahili and 'School Kikuyu.'" In *The Study of Language and the Politics of Community in Global Context,* edited by David L. Hoyt and Karen Oslund, 185–214. Lanham, MD: Rowman and Littlefield, 2006.

Peterson, Derek R., and Emma Hunter. "Print Cultures in Colonial Africa." In *African Print Cultures: Newspapers and Their Publics in the Twentieth Century*, edited by Derek R. Peterson, Emma Hunter, and Stephanie Newell, 1–48. Ann Arbor: University of Michigan Press, 2016.

Peterson, Derek R., and Giacomo Macola. "Introduction: Homespun Historiography and the Academic Profession." In *Recasting the Past: History Writing and Political Work in Modern Africa*, edited by Derek R. Peterson and Giacomo Macola, 1–30. Athens: Ohio University Press, 2009.

Petrie, Hazel, and Hohipere Tarau. "Māori Texts and Official Ventriloquism." *New Zealand Journal of History* 46, no. 2 (2012): 129–41.

Peukert, Alexander. "The Colonial Legacy of the International Copyright System." In *Copyright Africa: How Intellectual Property, Media and Markets Transform Immaterial Cultural Goods*, edited by Ute Röschenthaler and Mamadou Diawara, 37–68. Oxford: Sean Kingston, 2016.

Phillips, Jock. "Arts and the Nation—Cultural Nationalism, 1890 to 1910." In *Te Ara—the Encyclopedia of New Zealand*. Ministry of Culture and Heritage. Article published 22 October 2014. http://www.teara.govt.nz/en/arts-and -the-nation/page-2.

Phillips, Jock. "History of Immigration." Page 3, "British Immigration and the New Zealand Company." In *Te Ara—the Encyclopedia of New Zealand*. Ministry of Culture and Heritage. Article published 8 February 2005, updated 1 August 2015. http://www.TeAra.govt.nz/en/history-of-immigration/page-3.

Plaatje, Sol T. "Preface to the Original Edition." In *Mhudi*, 21–22. 1930. London: Heinemann, 1978.

PNG Central Planning Office. *Programmes and Performance, 1975–76*. Port Moresby, Papua New Guinea: Government Printer, 1976.

Pōmare, Mīria. "Ngāti Toarangatira." Page 3, "19th Century: Rise and Fall." In *Te Ara—the Encyclopedia of New Zealand*. Ministry of Culture and Heritage. Article published 8 February 2005, updated 3 March 2017. http://www.TeAra .govt.nz/en/ngati-toarangatira/page-3.

Poovey, Mary. *A History of the Modern Fact: Problems of Knowledge in the Sciences of Wealth and Society*. Chicago: University of Chicago Press, 2009.

Poovey, Mary. *Making a Social Body: British Cultural Formation, 1830–1864*. Chicago: University of Chicago Press, 1995.

Potiki, Megan. "Me Ta Taua Mokopuna: The Te Reo Māori Writings of H. K. Taiaroa and Tame Parata." *New Zealand Journal of History* 49, no. 1 (2015): 31–53.

Pouwels, Randall L. *Horn and Crescent: Cultural Change and Traditional Islam on the East African Coast, 800–1900*. Cambridge: Cambridge University Press, 1987.

Pouwels, Randall L. "Sh. al-Amin b. Ali Mazrui and Islamic Modernism in East Africa, 1875–1947." *International Journal of Middle Eastern Studies* 13 (1981): 329–45.

Powell, Kirsty. *The First Papua New Guinea Playwrights and Their Plays*. Boroko: Institute of Papua New Guinea Studies, 1979.

"Providing Literature for New Literates." Special issue, READ: *The Adult Literacy and Literature Magazine* 2 (1976).

Purchas, Samuel. *Hakluytus Posthumus, or Purchas His Pilgrimes: Contayning a History of the World in Sea Voyages and Lande Travells by Englishmen and Others.* Vol. 1. 1625. Cambridge: Cambridge University Press, 1905.

Rademaker, Laura. *Found in Translation: Many Meanings on a North Australian Mission.* Honolulu: University of Hawai'i Press, 2018.

Rademaker, Laura. "'Only Cuppa Tea Christians': Colonisation, Authentic Indigeneity and the Missionary Linguist." *History Australia* 13, no. 2 (2016): 228–42.

Rasmussen, Birgit Brander. *Queequeg's Coffin: Indigenous Literacies and Early American Literature.* Durham, NC: Duke University Press, 2012.

READ. Editorial. READ: *The Adult Literacy and Literature Magazine* 11, no. 3 (1976): 65.

Reese, Scott S. *The Transmission of Learning in Islamic Africa.* Leiden: Brill, 2004.

Reilly, Michael P. J. *Ancestral Voices from Mangaia: A History of the Ancient Gods and Chiefs.* Memoir No. 54. Auckland: Polynesian Society, 2009.

Reilly, Michael P. J. "Leadership in Ancient Polynesia." In *Disputed Histories: Imagining New Zealand's Pasts,* edited by Tony Ballantyne and Brian Moloughney, 43–63. Dunedin: Otago University Press, 2006.

Reilly, Michael P. J. "Mangaia in the Colonial World, 1863–1899." *Pacific Studies* 31, no. 1 (2008): 1–30.

Reilly, Michael P. J. *War and Succession in Mangaia from Mamae's Texts.* Memoir No. 52. Auckland: Polynesian Society, 2003.

Reilly, Michael P. J. "White, John." In *Dictionary of New Zealand Biography.* Online in *Te Ara—the Encyclopedia of New Zealand.* Ministry of Culture and Heritage. Article published 1990. http://www.TeAra.govt.nz/en/biographies/1w18/white-john.

Rendall, Jane. "Scottish Orientalism: From Robertson to James Mill." *Historical Journal* 25, no. 1 (1982): 43–69.

Rewi, Poia. *Whaikōrero: The World of Māori Oratory.* Auckland: Auckland University Press, 2010.

Reynolds, Henry. *Fate of a Free People.* Ringwood, Australia: Penguin, 1995.

Richter, Daniel K. *Facing East from Indian Country: A Native History of Early America.* Cambridge, MA: Harvard University Press, 2003.

Riseman, Noah. "Disrupting Assimilation: Soldiers, Missionaries and Aboriginal People in Arnhem Land during World War II." In *Evangelists of Empire? Missionaries in Colonial History,* edited by Amanda Barry, Joanna Cruikshank, and Andrew Brown-May, 245–62. Melbourne: eScholarship Research Centre, 2008. http://msp.esrc.unimelb.edu.ac/shs/missions.

Roa, Te Raukura o Te Rangimarie. "Formulaic Discourse Patterning in Mōteatea." PhD diss., University of Waikato, 2008.

Robertson, David. "Kamloops Chinúk Wawa, Chinuk Pipa, and the Vitality of Pidgins." PhD diss., University of Victoria, British Columbia, Canada, 2011.

Rogers, Everett M. *Diffusion of Innovations.* New York: Free Press, 1962. 5th ed., New York: Simon and Schuster, 2003.

Röschenthaler, Ute, and Mamadou Diawara. "African Intellectual Worlds in the Making." In *Copyright Africa: How Intellectual Property, Media and Markets*

Transform Immaterial Cultural Goods, edited by Ute Röschenthaler and Mamadou Diawara, 1–34. Oxford: Sean Kingston, 2016.

Rose, Mark. Authors and Owners: The Invention of Copyright. Cambridge, MA: Harvard University Press, 1995.

Round, Philip. Removable Type: Histories of the Book in Indian Country, 1663–1880. Chapel Hill: University of North Carolina Press, 2010.

Rowse, Tim. "Indigenous Heterogeneity." Australian Historical Studies 45, no. 3 (2014): 297–310.

Royal, Te Ahukaramū Charles. Kāti Au i Konei: He Kohikohinga i ngā Waiata a Ngāti Toarangatira, a Ngāti Raukawa. Wellington: Huia, 1994.

The Royal Copyright Commission. Minutes of Evidence. London: House of Commons, 1878.

Rubusana, W. B. Zemk'inkomo Magwalandini. 1906. Frome, UK: Burton and Tanner, 1911.

Ryan, Lyndall. "'Hard Evidence': The Debate about Massacre in the Black War in Tasmania." In Passionate Histories: Myth, Memory and Indigenous Australia, edited by Frances Peters-Little, Ann Curthoys, and John Docker, 39–50. Canberra: Australia National University Press, 2010.

Sahlins, Marshall. How "Natives" Think: About Captain Cook, for Example. Chicago: University of Chicago Press, 1996.

Salaün, Marie. L'école indigène: Nouvelle-Calédonie, 1885–1945. Rennes: Presses universitaires de Rennes, 2005.

Salesa, Damon I. "Opposite-Footers: Afterword." In The Atlantic World in the Antipodes: Effects and Transformations since the Eighteenth Century, edited by Kate Fullagar, 285–302. Newcastle upon Tyne, UK: Cambridge Scholars Press, 2012.

Saura, Bruno. "Des Incas en Polynésie? Spéculations occidentales et traditions autochtones de Rurutu 'd'hommes rouges venus de l'Est.'" In L'Amérique hispanique et le Pacifique: Hommage à Hugo Neira, edited by Pierre Verin and Robert Veccella, 45–68. Paris: Karthala, 2005.

Saura, Bruno. "Est-ce que dire, c'est penser? A propos de la logique des discours protestants polynésiens et de l'ouvrage de Yannick et Gwendoline Fer, Tuaro'i, réflexions bibliques à Rapa." Bulletin de la Société des Etudes Océaniennes 294 (2002): 150–60.

Saura, Bruno. "Les généalogies de Rurutu sont-elles vraies? Ou comment on écrit l'histoire en Polynésie." Bulletin de la Société des Études Océaniennes 312 (2008): 32–52.

Saura, Bruno. "Quand la voix devient la lettre: Les manuscrits autochtones de Polynésie française." Journal de la Société des Océanistes 126–27 (2008): 293–309.

Saura, Bruno, Daubard Matari'i, and Hiriata Millaud. Histoire et traditions de Huahine et Pora Pora. Edited by Bruno Saura. Translated by Patrick Matarii Daubard. Orthography standardized by Hiriata Millaud. Cahier du Patrimoine 1. Papeete: Ministère de la Culture et de l'enseignement supérieur de la Polynésie française, 2000.

Saura, Bruno, and Hiriata Millaud. *La dynastie des Tama-toa de Ra'iātea (îles-sous-le-Vent): Puta 'ā'amu nō te 'ōpū ari'i Tama-toa nō Ra'iātea*. Edited and translated by Bruno Saura. Orthography standardized by Hiriata Millaud. Cahier du Patrimoine 6. Papeete: Ministère de la Culture et de l'enseignement supérieur de la Polynésie française, 2003.

Savage, Stephen. *A Dictionary of the Maori Language of Rarotonga*. Reprint, Suva, Fiji: Institute of Pacific Studies, University of the South Pacific; Rarotonga: Ministry of Education, Government of the Cook Islands, 1980.

Schild, Ulla. *Literaturen in Papua-neuguinea*. Berlin: Dieter Reimer, 1981.

Schutz, Albert J. *Voices of Eden: A History of Hawaiian Language Studies*. Honolulu: University of Hawai'i Press, 1995.

Scollon, R., and S. W. Scollon. *Intercultural Communication*. Oxford: Blackwell, 1995.

Scott, Dick. *Years of the Pooh-Bah: A Cook Islands History*. Rarotonga: Cook Islands Trading Corporation; Auckland: Hodder and Stoughton, 1991.

Scribner, Sylvia. "Literacy in Three Metaphors." *American Journal of Education* 93, no. 1 (1984): 6–21.

Scribner, Sylvia. "The Practice of Literacy: Where Mind and Society Meet." *Annals of the New York Academy of Sciences* 433 (December 1984): 5–19.

Scribner, Sylvia, and Michael Cole. *The Psychology of Literacy*. Cambridge, MA: Harvard University Press, 1981.

Sergeant, John. *A Letter from the Revd Mr. Sergeant of Stockbridge, to Dr. Colman of Boston; Containing Mr. Sergeant's Proposal of a More Effectual Method for the Education of Indian Children*. Boston: Rogers and Fowle, for D. Henchman in Cornhill, 1743.

Seville, Catherine. *The Internationalisation of Copyright Law: Books, Buccaneers and the Black Flag in the Nineteenth Century*. Cambridge: Cambridge University Press, 2006.

Sewell, William H., Jr. "The Concept(s) of Culture." In *Beyond the Cultural Turn: New Directions in the Study of Society and Culture*, edited by Victoria E. Bonnell and Lynn Hunt, 35–61. Berkeley: University of California Press, 1999.

Sewell, William H., Jr. *Logics of History: Social Theory and Social Transformation*. Chicago: University of Chicago Press, 2005.

Shankman, Paul. "The Thick and the Thin: On the Interpretive Theoretical Program of Clifford Geertz." *Current Anthropology* 25, no. 3 (1984): 261–80.

Shepherd, R. Winsome. "Travers, William Thomas Locke." In *Dictionary of New Zealand Biography*. Online in *Te Ara—the Encyclopaedia of New Zealand*, Ministry of Culture and Heritage. Article published 1990, updated 18 March 2014. http://www.TeAra.govt.nz/en/biographies/1t105/travers-william-thomas-locke.

Shibata, Norio. *Mangaian-English Dictionary*. Part 2 of *Prehistoric Cook Islands: People, Life and Language, An Official Report for Kyoto University Cook Islands Scientific Research Programme (KUCIP) in 1989–1998*, edited by Kazumichi Katayama and Norio Shibata. Inuyama City, Japan: Department of Evolution and Phylogeny, Primate Research Institute, Kyoto University; Rarotonga: Cook Islands Library and Museum Society, 1999.

Shoemaker, Adam. *Black Words, White Page: Aboriginal Literature, 1929–1988*. St Lucia: University of Queensland Press, 1992.

Siikala, Anna-Leena, and Jukka Siikala. *Return to Culture: Oral Tradition and Society in the Southern Cook Islands*. Helsinki: Suomalainen Tiedeakatemia, 2005.

Siikala, Jukka. *'Akatokamanāva: Myth, History and Society in the Southern Cook Islands*. Auckland: Polynesian Society, 1991.

Silko, Leslie Marmon. *Yellow Woman and a Beauty of the Spirit: Essays on Native American Life Today*. New York: Simon and Schuster, 1996.

Silva, Noenoe K. *Aloha Betrayed: Native Hawaiian Resistance to American Colonialism*. Durham, NC: Duke University Press, 2004.

Simiona, Tangata, ed. "Akamārama'anga." In *E Au Tua Ta'ito nō te Kūki 'Airani*, iv. Suva, Fiji: Institute of Pacific Studies, University of the South Pacific; Rarotonga: South Pacific Creative Arts Society and the Cook Islands Ministry of Education (Tumu Kōrero Division), n.d.

Simon, Judith, and Linda Tuhiwai Smith. *A Civilising Mission? Perceptions and Representations of the New Zealand Native Schools System*. Auckland: Auckland University Press, 2001.

Sissons, Jeffrey. *Nation and Destination: Creating Cook Islands Identity*. Suva, Fiji: Institute of Pacific Studies, University of the South Pacific; Rarotonga: University of the South Pacific Centre in the Cook Islands, 1999.

Smith, Linda Tuhiwai. *Decolonizing Methodologies: Research and Indigenous Peoples*. London: Zed Books; Dunedin: Otago University Press, 1999.

Société d'Études historiques de la Nouvelle-Calédonie, ed. *Centenaire Maurice Leenhardt (1878–1954): Pasteur et ethnologue*. 1978. Reprint, Nouméa: Société d'Études historiques de la Nouvelle-Calédonie, 1994.

South African Railways and Harbours. *Official Railway Tariff Handbook*. Johannesburg: Office of the General Manager of Railways, 1911.

Sparks, Teremoana, and W. H. Oliver. "Topeora, Rangi Kuini Wikitoria." In *The Dictionary of New Zealand Biography*, vol. 1, *1769–1869*, edited by W. H. Oliver, 546–47. Wellington: Allen and Unwin and the Department of Internal Affairs, 1990.

Spitulnik, Debra. "Documenting Radio Culture as Lived Experience: Reception Studies and the Mobile Machine in Zambia." In *African Broadcast Cultures: Radio in Transition*, edited by R. Fardon and G. Furniss, 144–63. Oxford: James Currey, 2000.

Stack, J. W. *Kaiapohia: The Story of a Siege*. Christchurch: Whitcombe and Tombs, 1893.

Stead, Oliver. *Art Icons of New Zealand*. Auckland: David Bateman, 2008.

Stevens, Leonie. "'Me Write Myself': A Counter-narrative of the Exile of the First Nations People of Van Diemen's Land to Flinders Island, 1832–47." PhD diss., Monash University, 2014.

Stevens, Michael J. "Kāi Tahu Writing and Cross-Cultural Communication." *Journal of New Zealand Literature* 28, no. 2 (2010): 130–57.

Stevens, Michael J. "A 'Useful' Approach to Maori History." *New Zealand Journal of History* 49, no. 1 (2015): 54–77.

Stevens, Michael J. "'What's in a Name?' Murihiku, Colonial Knowledge-Making, and 'Thin-Culture.'" *Journal of the Polynesian Society* 120, no. 4 (2011): 333–47.

Storey, Kenton. "Anxiety, Humanitarianism, and the Press: New Zealand and Vancouver Island in the British Empire." PhD diss., University of Otago, 2011.

Street, Brian V. *Critical Approaches to Literacy in Development, Ethnography and Education.* London: Longman, 1995.

Street, Brian V. *Cross-Cultural Approaches to Literacy.* Cambridge: Cambridge University Press, 1993.

Street, Brian V. *Literacy in Theory and Practice.* Cambridge: Cambridge University Press, 1984.

Summer Institute of Linguistics. *Annual Report 1988.* Ukarumpa: Summer Institute of Linguistics, 1988.

Summer Institute of Linguistics. *Bibliography of the Summer Institute Linguistics, Papua New Guinea Branch, 1956–90.* Ukarumpa: Summer Institute of Linguistics, 1992.

Sunder, Madhavi. *From Goods to a Good Life: Intellectual Property and Global Justice.* New Haven, CT: Yale University Press, 2012.

Sutherland, Yvonne. "Nineteenth-Century Māori Letters of Emotion: Orality, Literacy, and Context." PhD diss., University of Auckland, 2007.

Sutton, Peter. *Dreamings: The Art of Aboriginal Australia.* Ringwood, Australia: Viking, 1989.

Sweeney, G. "An Experiment in a Mission Trading Outpost." *Missionary Review* 59, no. 7 (1951).

Tau, Te Maire. "I-ngā-rā-o-mua." *Journal of New Zealand Studies* 10 (2011): 45–62.

Taylor, Anthea. "Education for Democracy: Assimilation or Emancipation for Aboriginal Australians?" *Comparative Education Review* 40, no. 4 (1996): 426–38.

Taylor, Richard. *Te Ika a Maui, or New Zealand and Its Inhabitants: Illustrating the Origin, Manners, Customs, Mythology, Religion, Rites, Songs, Proverbs, Fables, and Language of the Natives; Together with the Geology, Natural History, Productions, and Climate of the Country, Its State as Regards Christianity, Sketches of the Principal Chiefs, and Their Present Position.* London: Wertheim and Macintosh, 1855.

Taylor, Robert. "The Summer Institute of Linguistics/Wycliffe Bible Translators in Anthropological Perspective." In *Missionaries and Anthropologists,*, edited by Frank Salamone, 93–116. Williamsburg, VA: Department of Anthropology, College of William and Mary, 1985.

Te Are Korero o Aitutaki. *Te Korero o Aitutaki.* Rarotonga, Cook Islands: Ministry of Cultural Development, 1992.

Te Punga Somerville, Alice. "Living on New Zealand Street: Maori Presence in Parramatta." *Ethnohistory* 61, no. 4 (2014): 665–69.

Te Rangi Hiroa (P. H. Buck). *Mangaian Society.* Bernice P. Bishop Museum Bulletin 122. Reprint, New York: Kraus, 1971.

Terooatea, Daniel. *Te va'a ta'ata mātāmua i tapae i Rurutu.* Papeete: author, 1997.

Teuton, Christopher. *Deep Waters: The Textual Continuum in American Indian Literature.* Lincoln: University of Nebraska Press, 2010.

Thomas, Nicholas. *Entangled Objects: Exchange, Material Culture, and Colonialism in the Pacific*. Cambridge, MA: Harvard University Press, 1991.

Traue, J. E. "Buick, Thomas Lindsay." In *Dictionary of New Zealand Biography*. Online in *Te Ara—the Encyclopaedia of New Zealand*. Ministry of Culture and Heritage. Article published 1996. http://www.TeAra.govt.nz/en/biographies/3b57/1.

Travers, W. T. L. "On the Life and Times of Te Rauparaha." *Transactions and Proceedings of the New Zealand Institute* 5 (1872): 19–93.

Travers, W. T. L. *Some Chapters in the Life and Times of Te Rauparaha, Chief of Ngatitoa*. Wellington: James Hughes, 1872.

Tremewan, Christine. "Poetry in Te Waka Maori." In *Rere Atu, Taku Manu! Discovering History, Language and Politics in the Maori-Language Newspapers*, edited by Jenifer Curnow, Ngapare Hopa, and Jane McRae, 134–52. Auckland: University of Auckland Press, 2002.

Trépied, Benoît. "Langues et pouvoir en Nouvelle-Calédonie coloniale: Les Kanak locuteurs du français dans la région de Koné." In *Cultures d'Empire: Echanges et affrontements culturels en situation coloniale*, edited by Romain Bertrand, Hélène Blais, and Emmanuelle Sibeud, 145–70. Paris: Karthala, 2015.

Treur, Anton. *The Assassination of Hole in the Day*. St. Paul: Borealis Books, 2011.

Turnbull, Clive, *Black War: The Extermination of the Tasmanian Aborigines*. Melbourne: Cheshire, 1948.

Turner, David H. *Genesis Regained: Aboriginal Forms of Renunciation in Judeo-Christian Scriptures and Other Major Traditions*. New York: Peter Lang, 1999.

Turner, David H. *Return to Eden: A Journey through the Promised Landscape of Amagalyuagba*. New York: Peter Lang, 1989.

Turner, James. *Philology: The Forgotten Origins of the Modern Humanities*. Princeton, NJ: Princeton University Press, 2014.

United Nations. *The International Year for the World's Indigenous People: Who Are the World's Indigenous Peoples?* New York: UN Department of Public Information, 1992. http://www.ciesin.org/docs/010-000a/Year_Worlds_Indig.html.

van Loon Apeldoorn, Jeanne, and Ngametua Kareroa. "The Last Peacemakers?" [1980?] Unpublished manuscript.

Vansina, Jan. *Oral Tradition as History*. London: James Currey, 1985.

van Toorn, Penny. *Writing Never Arrives Naked: Early Aboriginal Cultures of Writing in Australia*. Canberra: Aboriginal Studies Press, 2006.

Veracini, Lorenzo. *Settler Colonialism: A Theoretical Overview*. Basingstoke, UK: Palgrave Macmillan, 2010.

Wachtel, Nathan. *The Vision of the Vanquished: The Spanish Conquest of Peru through Indian Eyes, 1530–1570*. New York: Barnes and Noble, 1971.

Wade, William. *A Journey in the Northern Island of New Zealand*. Hobart, Australia: George Rolwegan, 1842.

Wakefield, Roberta P., and U.S. Department of Commerce/Bureau of Foreign and Domestic Commerce. *Foreign Marks of Origin Regulations*. Washington, DC: U.S. Government Printing Office, n.d.

Walcot, Kevin. "Perspectives on Publishing, Literacy and Development." In *Publishing in the Pacific Islands: A Symposium*, edited by Jim Richstad and

Miles M. Jackson, 11–40. Honolulu: Graduate School of Library Studies, University of Hawai'i, 1984.

Walker, Ranginui. *Ka Whawhai Tonu Matou: Struggle without End.* Auckland: Penguin, 2004.

Walter, Richard, and Michael P. J. Reilly. "A Prehistory of the Mangaian Chiefdom." *Journal of the Polynesian Society* 119, no. 4 (December 2010): 335–75.

Warkentin, Germaine. "In Search of 'The Word of the Other': Aboriginal Sign Systems and the History of the Book in Canada." *Book History* 2 (1999): 1–27.

Warner, Michael. *The Letters of the Republic: Publication and the Public Sphere in Eighteenth-Century America.* Cambridge, MA: Harvard University Press, 1992.

Warrior, Robert. *The People and the Word: Reading Native Nonfiction.* Minneapolis: University of Minnesota Press, 2005.

Warrior, Robert. *Tribal Secrets: Recovering American Indian Intellectual Traditions.* Minneapolis: University of Minnesota Press, 1995.

Weaver, Jace. *That the People Might Live: Native American Literatures and Native American Community.* Oxford: Oxford University Press, 1997.

"What Is CWAMEL?" *Papua New Guinea Writing* 8 (1972): 19.

White, John. *The Ancient History of the Maori, His Mythology and Traditions.* 6 vols. Wellington: Government Printer, 1887–90. http://nzetc.victoria.ac.nz/tm/scholarly/tei-corpus-WhiAnci.html.

White, Tim. "The Lovedale Press during the Directorship of R. H. W. Shepherd, 1930–1955." *English in Africa* 19, no. 2 (1992): 69–84.

Whiteley, William. *Swahili: The Rise of a National Language.* Aldershot, UK: Gregg Revivals, 1993.

Wickens, Corinne M., and Jennifer Sandlin. "Literacy for What? Literacy for Whom? The Policies of Literacy Education and Neocolonialism in UNESCO- and World Bank-Sponsored Literacy Programs." *Adult Education Quarterly* 57, no. 4 (2007): 275–92.

Wickwire, Wendy. "To See Ourselves as the Other's Other: Nlaka'pamux Contact Narratives." *Canadian Historical Review* 75, no. 1 (1994): 1–20.

Wigginton, Caroline. *In the Neighborhood: Women's Publication in Early America.* Amherst: University of Massachusetts Press, 2016.

Willan, Brian. *Sol Plaatje: A Biography—Solomon Tshekisho Plaatje, 1876–1932.* Johannesburg: Ravan, 1984.

Williams, H. W. "Maori Matter at the Cape of Good Hope." *Journal of the Polynesian Society* 15 (1906): 175–80.

Williams, Melissa Matutina. *Panguru and the City: Kāinga Tahi, Kāinga Rua: An Urban Migration History.* Wellington: Bridget Williams Books, 2014.

Williams, Roger. *A Key into the Language of America.* London: Gregory Dexter, 1643.

Wimmelbücker, Ludger. *Kilimanjaro—a Regional History.* Munster: Lit, 2002.

Wirtén, Eva Hemmungs. *Terms of Use: Negotiating the Jungle of the Intellectual Commons.* Toronto: University of Toronto Press, 2008.

Wolfe, Patrick. "Settler Colonialism and the Elimination of the Native." *Journal of Genocide Research* 8, no. 4 (2006): 387–409.

Wolfe, Patrick. *Settler Colonialism and the Transformation of Anthropology: The Politics and Poetics of an Ethnographic Event.* London: Cassell, 1999.

Womack, Craig. *Red on Red: Native American Literary Separatism.* Minneapolis: University of Minnesota Press, 1999.

Woodmansee, Martha, and Peter Jaszi, eds. *The Construction of Authorship: Textual Appropriation in Law and Literature.* Durham, NC: Duke University Press, 1994.

Wyss, Hilary E. *English Letters and Indian Literacies: Reading, Writing, and New England Missionary Schools, 1750–1830.* Philadelphia: University of Pennsylvania Press, 2012.

Yate, William. *An Account of New Zealand and of the Church Missionary Society's Mission in the Northern Island.* London: Seeley and Burnside, 1835.

Yates, Barbara. "Knowledge Brokers: Books and Publishers in Early Colonial Zaire." *History in Africa* 14 (1987): 311–40.

Zumthor, Paul. *La lettre et la voix: De la "literature" médiévale.* Paris: Éditions du Seuil, 1987.

CONTRIBUTORS

NOELANI ARISTA (KANAKA MAOLI) is an associate professor of Hawaiian and American history at the University of Hawai'i at Mānoa. Her areas of interest include Hawaiian legal and intellectual history, nineteenth-century Hawaiian and U.S. religious history, Hawaiian historical methods, and historiography. Her current project considers the preservation of Hawaiian historical knowledge in digital mediums, including gaming. Her recent book is entitled *The Kingdom and the Republic: Sovereign Hawai'i and the Early United States* (2018).

TONY BALLANTYNE is a professor of history and pro-vice-chancellor humanities at the University of Otago, where he is also the codirector of the Centre for Research on Colonial Culture. He has published widely on the cultural history of the British Empire, and his most recent sole-authored book is the award-winning *Entanglements of Empire: Missionaries, Maori, and the Question of the Body* (Duke University Press, 2014).

ALBAN BENSA is an anthropologist specializing in the Kanak people of New Caledonia and is director of studies at the Advanced School for Social Sciences in Paris. With Kacué Yvon Goromoedo and Adrian Muckle he coauthored *Les Sanglots de l'aigle pêcheur: Nouvelle-Calédonie; La Guerre kanak de 1917* (2015), which presents and explores the written and oral texts of New Caledonia's 1917 war.

KEITH THOR CARLSON is a professor of history at the University of the Fraser Valley in British Columbia where he holds the Canada research chair in Indigenous and community-engaged history. Prior to this he spent eighteen years as a faculty member at the University of Saskatchewan, and before that served for a decade as staff historian and research coordinator for the Stó:lō Nation (representing eighteen Fraser River First Nations). Keith has authored five books, including the multi-award-winning *The Power of Place, the Problem of Time: Aboriginal Identity and Historical Consciousness in the Cauldron of Colonialism* (2010) and has edited or coedited six additional books, including *A Stó:lō-Coast Salish Historical Atlas* (2001), *Orality and Literacy: Reflections across Disciplines* (2011), and *Towards a New Ethnohistory* (2018). His research focuses on Coast Salish history, the history of settler colonialism, and Indigenous historical consciousness.

EVELYN ELLERMAN founded the communication studies program at Athabasca University, where she also initiated and directed the university's e-Lab. Her doctoral thesis explored how individuals and institutions worked during decolonization to establish literary systems in Papua New Guinea, a subject about which she has published and presented many times over the past two decades. These endeavors developed her interest in the intellectual currents of the colonial world. Her more recent research explores the intersection of communication technologies and colonial history, especially as it applies to colonial print cultures and other media. She is currently completing a typology of print-culture sponsorship in late-colonial states that uses Papua New Guinea as a case study.

ISABEL HOFMEYR is a professor of African literature at the University of the Witwatersrand in Johannesburg and global distinguished professor in the English Department of New York University. Her most recent book is *Gandhi's Printing Press: Experiments in Slow Reading* (2013). Along with Antoinette Burton, she edited *Ten Books That Shaped the British Empire: Creating an Imperial Commons* (Duke University Press, 2014). Hofmeyr currently heads up a Mellon-funded research project entitled "Oceanic Humanities for the Global South."

EMMA HUNTER is a professor of global and African history at the University of Edinburgh. She is the author of *Political Thought and the Public Sphere in Tanzania: Freedom, Democracy and Citizenship in the Era of Decolonization* (2015) and a coeditor of *African Print Cultures: Newspapers and Their Publics in the Twentieth Century* (2016).

ARINI LOADER (NGĀTI RAUKAWA) is a lecturer in history at Victoria University of Wellington. Her research interests include early Māori literacies, *mōteatea* (sung poetry), and the Māori language. She also suffers the occasional bout of cacoëthes scribendi.

ADRIAN MUCKLE is a senior lecturer in history at Victoria University of Wellington. His specialist research interest is the history of New Caledonia. With Kacué Yvon Goromoedo and Alban Bensa he coauthored *Les Sanglots de l'aigle pêcheur: Nouvelle-Calédonie; La Guerre kanak de 1917* (2015), which presents and explores the written and oral texts of New Caledonia's 1917 war.

LACHY PATERSON is a professor in Te Tumu: School of Māori, Pacific and Indigenous Studies at the University of Otago. His primary research has involved *niupepa* (Māori-language newspapers) of the mid-nineteenth and early twentieth centuries, from which he explores the social, political, and religious discourses promulgated within these publications. His publications include a monograph on mid-nineteenth-century Māori-language newspapers, *Colonial Discourses: Niupepa Māori, 1855–1863* (2006), and *He Reo Wāhine: Māori Women's Voices from the Nineteenth Century* (2017), coauthored with Angela Wanhalla.

LAURA RADEMAKER is a senior lecturer at the Australian National University. Her research covers themes of histories of race, religion, language, and gender, particularly at Christian missions. She received her PhD from the Australian National University in 2015. Her doctoral thesis on language at Aboriginal missions was awarded the Australian Historical Association's Serle Award as well as the Australian National University's J. G. Crawford Prize. She is the author of *Found in Translation: Many Meanings on a North Australian Mission* (2018).

MICHAEL P. J. REILLY is a professor in Te Tumu: School of Māori, Pacific and Indigenous Studies at the University of Otago. He has taught aspects of Māori and Pacific historical knowledge in the school since 1991 following his completion of his PhD from the Australian National University. He is interested in understanding deeper cultural motifs and concepts located in indigenous historical narratives, with much of his research concerning the study of such narratives from Mangaia in the Cook Islands as well as from Aotearoa New Zealand. Michael has published extensively, including five coedited collections and two monographs, *Ancestral Voices from Mangaia: A History of the Ancient Gods and Chiefs* (2009) and *War and Succession in Mangaia from Mamae's Texts* (2003). His interests were sparked by a lifelong fascination with history and, in particular, by the study of *te reo Māori* and Māori culture both at high school in Auckland and later on at Victoria University of Wellington.

BRUNO SAURA is a professor of Polynesian civilization at the Université de la Polynésie française (Tahiti). He has a background in anthropology and political science. He is now director of a multidisciplinary research group—EASTCO (Equipe d'Accueil Sociétés Traditionnelles et Contemporaines en Océanie)—working on Pacific societies of the past and the present. Bruno has written extensively on ethnic, linguistic, and religious issues in today's Polynesia, authoring several books (*Les bûchers de Faaite* [1990]; *La société tahitienne au miroir d'Israël* [2004]; *Tahiti ma'ohi* [2008]; *Mythes et usages des mythes: Autochtonie et idéologie de la Terre Mère en Polynésie* [2013]), and has contributed articles to scholarly journals (*The Contemporary Pacific, Pacific Studies, Journal of Pacific History, Journal of the Polynesian Society, Journal of Pacific Studies, International Journal of Research into Island Cultures*). He is now working on Polynesian oral tradition and mythology in a comparative and diachronic perspective, as can be seen in his most recent book, *Un poisson nommé Tahiti: Mythes et pouvoirs aux temps anciens polynésiens* (*Tahiti, Ra'iātea, Hawaii, Nouvelle-Zélande*) (2019).

IVY SCHWEITZER is a professor of English and past chair of women's, gender, and sexuality studies at Dartmouth College, Hanover, New Hampshire. Her fields are early American literature, digital humanities, and gender and cultural studies. She is the author of *The Work of Self-Representation: Lyric Poetry in Colonial New England* (1991) and *Perfecting Friendship: Politics and Affiliation in Early American Literature* (2006);

coeditor of *The Literatures of Colonial America: An Anthology* (2001) and *Companion to "The Literatures of Colonial America"* (2005); and a member of the editorial board of the *Heath Anthology of American Literature*. She is the editor of The Occom Circle (https://www.dartmouth.edu/occom) and White Heat: Emily Dickinson in 1862: A Weekly Blog (https://journeys.dartmouth.edu/whiteheat/), and coeditor of *Afterlives of Indigenous Archives: Essays in Honor of the Occom Circle* (2019).

ANGELA WANHALLA (KĀI TAHU) is an associate professor in the History Programme at the University of Otago. She is a historian of race, gender, and colonialism. Her most recent books include *He Reo Wāhine: Māori Women's Voices from the Nineteenth Century* (2017), cowritten with Lachy Paterson, and *Mothers' Darlings of the South Pacific: The Children of Indigenous Women and US Servicemen, World War II* (2016), coedited with Judith A. Bennett.

Abenaki language, 302
Aborigines, 4, 195–212; Australian schools for, 196–209, 211; "civilizing mission" for, 199, 200, 202, 206–7; family structure of, 200; naming practices of, 200, 210
Aborigines' Protection Society (UK), 123, 130n55
Achebe, Chinua, 176
Adams, Arthur, 282n1
'Aerepō, Iviiti, 140
'āina (land), 34, 45, 46, 53n13
Algonquian language, 299, 303
ali'i (chiefs), 37, 40–44, 49, 56n27, 57n34
Althaus, Gerhard, 179–80
Amane of Poyes, 64, 66
American Board of Commissioners for Foreign Missions, 40
Anglican Church Missionary Society, 81, 198–202, 206–8, 211, 265
Anglo-Boer War, 252
Angurugu Mission School (Australia), 198–209, 211
Anindilyakwa people, 22–23, 66–67, 195–212, 213n42
anonymous authorship, 257. See also copyright law
Apapa, Bégui, 66
Apégu, Pwädé (Poindet Apengou), 63, 65–66
Aperahama, Pōkino, 153n57
Apess, William, 16–17
Apollinaire, Guillaume, 74
Appi, Tia Houé, 66
Arabic language, 22, 176, 178–83, 189–90
Aratangi, Papa, 146–48, 152n40
Aratangi, Tere'ēvangeria, 132, 140–45, 149n3, 153n57
archives, 15; Cherokee, 31, 56n31; Cook Island, 141; Hawaiian, 31–51, 277; "hidden," 32, 60, 277; Lakota, 31, 56n31; Māori, 31, 265, 272, 277;

"remembering" techniques of, 104; Tahitian, 56n31
'are kōrero (storytellers), 131–34, 140–43, 146–49
ari'i (chiefs), 159, 160
Ari'i-paea-vahine, Tahitian queen, 163, 164, 171n20
ariki (chiefs, mediums), 137, 145–46
Arista, Noelani, 19–20, 84, 277
Arthur, Walter George, 8
Ashton, Jeremy, 239n29
Asma'u, Nana, 178
Atkinson, Alan, 202
A'ua'u 'Enua. See Mangaia
Auguste, Oué, 68
Australia, 5–7, 72–73, 195–212, 248; Aboriginal schools of, 196–97, 211; evangelization of, 10, 202–9; Groote Eyland, 195–98, 206; "History Wars" of, 5; suffrage in, 213
Austral Islands, 22, 132, 154–70
awikhigan (books and letters), 302
awikhigawogan (writing), 303

Baird, Jessie Little Doe, 56n31
Ballantyne, Tony, 75, 80, 83–84, 175, 177
Ballara, Angela, 279, 286n56
Banerjee, Sukanya, 254–56
Bantu languages, 176, 179, 258. See also Swahili
Baptist Mission Society, 178
Barber, Karin, 14–16, 257–58
Barghash b. Sāïd, Sayyid, Sultan of Zanzibar, 179
Barton, David, 81
Bassett, Judith, 83
Bayly, C. A., 90
Bays, Glen, 221–22, 229–34, 237, 240nn58–59, 241n65
Becker, C. L., 104
Bécu, Gaston, 64
Beier, Ulli, 226

Paterson, Lachy, 75, 287n79; Hunter on, 175, 177, 182
pā tīkoru (*tapa* cloth sanctuary), 142, 145–46, 152n48
Peabody Museum, Salem, 156, 157
Pearl Harbor (Puʻuloa), 45, 49
Pequot people, 16–17, 298, 300, 304
Peru, 4, 156, 295–96
Peters, Bertha, 114–16
petroglyphs, 108–10
Philippines, 106, 127n13
philology, 9
pictographs, American Indian, 108–10, 297–98, 303. *See also* wampum
Pietism, 201
pilou (dance ceremonies), 74
piri (riddles), 168
Plaatje, Sol T., 258
Plato, 296
Pobati, Léon, 66
Poetai, Teriimana, 156
Poindi, Daniel, 66
Polo, Mchezo wa, 187
polygamy, 107, 205
Polynesian family manuscripts (*puta tupuna*), 154–70; of Leeward Islands, 158–66; of Rurutu, 155–58
Pomare II, Tahitian king, 163
Ponga, ʻAkaiti, 135, 140
Poomä, Dui Bwékua, 71–72, 74, 76
Pöömô, Dui Novis, 79n56
Popol Vuh, 296
Porapora (Borabora), 22, 158–59, 165, 171n3
potlatches, 110, 113, 124, 126
Powell, Kirsty, 241n73
praise poems, 15, 257, 259, 260
print cultures, 10–25; in Australia, 202–3; in Hawaiʻi, 31–51; in New Caledonia, 80–94; Protestantism and, 12, 201; in Tanzania, 180–83. *See also specific peoples*
Printer, James, 299
prophecy narratives, 106, 114–16
Protestant American Board, 34
Protestant ladders, 119–21
Protestant print culture, 12, 201
pseudonyms, 257. *See also* copyright law
Pūaha, Rāwiri, 273
"publication event," 290, 304
Pukui, Mary Kawena, 35, 53n12, 54n16
pule (prayer), 37
Pumetacom's War (1675–76), 299
puna (districts), 144
Purchas, Samuel, 9
Puritans, 292–93, 298
puta (books), 154, 158
puta tupuna. See Polynesian family manuscripts

Puʻuloa (Pearl Harbor), 45, 49
Pwädé Apégu (Poindet Apengou), 63, 65–66
Pwëloaa, Bwëë Apwá, 65, 71–72

quipu (knotted strings), 295–96
quotation techniques, 18, 257
Quran, in Swahili, 189

Rademaker, Laura, 22–23, 66–67, 104
radio, 217, 230, 232–34, 236–37
Raʻiātea, 22, 158–66, 171n3
Rakahanga. *See* Cook Islands
Rakauruaiti, Ravengenge, 140
Ramanujan, Srinivasa, 187
Rarotonga, 134, 139, 140, 147, 150n9
Rasmussen, Birgit Brander, 16
Reichel, Kealiʻi, 38–39, 55n23
Reilly, Michael P. J., 21–22, 87, 154, 155
Richards, Charles, 229
Richards, William, 56n27, 58n50
Rimatara, 156
Ripahau, Hôhepa (Matahau), 265
Rivierre, Jean-Claude, 79n56
Roanoke people, 305
Robertson, David, 126n2
Robertson, William, 9
Roehl, Karl, 183, 189, 190
Rogers, Everett M., 217, 218, 235, 236
Rolleston, William, 89
Rongo (Mangaian god), 137–38, 151n19
Rotorua, 281
Round, Philip, 299, 312n48, 313n60
Rousseau, Jean-Jacques, 296
Royal Copyright Commission (1878), 247–48
Royal Society Te Apārangi, 268
Rubusana, Mpilo Walter Benson, 23–24, 253–56, 258–60, 262n35
Rurutu, 22, 154–58, 165, 169
Russell, Henry, 85, 91

Salaün, Marie, 77n9
Salem witchcraft crisis, 301
Salesa, Damon I., 4
Salic law, 166
Salish people, 21, 101–26, 127n6, 128n22, 128n26, 129n42, 129n54
Salmon, Ariʻitaimai, 171n20
Sandlin, Jennifer, 238n8
Sanskrit studies, 9
Sassamon, John, 299
Saura, Bruno, 22, 87, 104
Saussure, Ferdinand de, 166
schools. *See* English-language schools
Schweitzer, Ivy, 24–25, 94, 247
Scollon, R., 87

Scollon, S. W., 87
Scott, Duncan Campbell, 117
Scottish Enlightenment, 9
Scribner, Sylvia, 13–14, 87
Selwyn, George Augustus, 264, 265
semasiographic writing, 298
Seneca people, 297, 300
Sequoyah, Cherokee leader, 16, 299, 312n30
Sergeant, John, 292
Sewell, William H., Jr., 13
Sheehan, John, 92
Shortland, W., 283n8
Siikala, Anna-Leena, 154
Siikala, Jukka, 154
SIL. See Summer Institute of Linguistics
Silva, Noenoe K., 17
"skeptic mind," 22, 166–70
Skinner, Kate, 192n2
slaves, slavery, 15, 81, 84, 107, 136–38, 144–45, 253, 301
smílha (spirit dances), 110
Smith, Linda Tuhiwai, 284n27, 286n59
Smith, Marian, 114
Smith, S. Percy, 153n54, 286n56
social Darwinism, 107
Society for the Propagation of the Gospel in Foreign Parts, 290–92
Society Islands, 21, 132, 134, 171n3; family manuscripts of, 154–70
Society of the Divine Word, 227
Sokoto Caliphate, 178
Solomon, Anna, 235, 236, 241n74
Somalia, 175, 178, 189
South Africa, 248–60, 262n33
space-based communication, 105–12, 116, 119, 122–25
Spalding, Eliza, 120
Spalding, Henry, 120
Spitulnik, Debra, 237n5
Stack, J. W., 268, 274
St'a'saluk (Salish visionary), 113–16
Stationers' Hall, 253–54
Stead, Oliver, 288n86
Stevens, Leonie, 8
Stevens, Michael, 18
Stewart, Dugald, 26n27
St. John's College, 264
Stokes, Judith, 208–9
Street, Brian V., 82, 87, 170
Strunk, William, 229
suffrage, 62, 202, 213
Sukuma language, 179
Sultani, W. M. O. Ngurau, 186
Summer Institute of Linguistics (SIL), 221–26, 229–30, 234, 237, 238n10, 238n18
Sumner, Ninito, 171n20

Swahili, 175–91; Arabic influence on, 176, 178–83; Bible in, 180, 183; as lingua franca, 176, 178–80, 191; non-native speakers of, 176

Taft, William Howard, 106
Tahiti, 154–56, 170; Tamatoa-Pomare line of, 165; tomite titles of, 156
Tahitian language, 134, 150n9, 154, 166–67; archives of, 56n31; Bible in, 155
Tahitoe, Ra'iātean king, 160–61, 164–65
tahu'a (priest, oracle), 160–62
Tahuantinsuya people, 295–96
Tamahērangi, Raihania, 91
tamanawas (dances), 110
Tamatoa dynasty, 158, 160–62, 163, 164–65
Tanganyika, 22, 175–83, 186–91
tāngata mōhio (knowledgeable persons), 272
Tanzania, 22, 175–91
taperas (Kanak Christian songs), 79n59
taro, 133, 136, 137, 144
Tasmania, 5–8
Tau, Te Maire, 283n6
Tauranga, 281
Tāwhai, Mohi, 264, 283n8
Taylor, Jim, 200–201, 206
Taylor, Richard, 279–80
Te 'Akatauira people, 141, 145
Te Āti Awa people, 92, 266, 281
Te Aute College, 90
Te Maru-o-Rongo, 21, 134, 136–38, 142–46
Te Nahu, Ārihi, 85, 91–92
ténô (epic poems), 20, 70–76, 79n51
Te Punga Somerville, Alice, 272
Te Rangihaeata, 278, 282n1
Te Rangi Hiroa (Peter Buck), 149, 150n12
Te Rangikaheke, 88
Te Rangitāke, Wiremu Kīngi, 92–93
Te Rauparaha, 24, 85, 263–82, 283nn6–7, 285n48; Burns on, 272–75, 277; Butler on, 274–75, 277; Collins on, 275–77; death of, 266, 269; family of, 270–71; Travers on, 268–69; Wakefield on, 279; White on, 269–72
Te Rauparaha, Tāmihana, 24, 92, 263–82, 283nn6–7, 284n13, 287n79
Te Rēweti Te Hiakai, 91
Terooatea, Daniel, 157, 158, 166
Te Waharoa, Hākopa, 92
Te Whatarauihi Nohorua, 283n9, 287n81
Te Whiwhi, Mātene, 265, 283n11
Thomas, Nicholas, 111
Thompson, David, 108, 112
Thomson, Robert, 163
Thucydides, 167
Thy, Tiatéa, 68
tikanga Māori (Māori custom), 85